Freedom Through Understanding

LAMA YESHE
& LAMA ZOPA RINPOCHE

Freedom Through Understanding

THE BUDDHIST PATH TO HAPPINESS
· AND LIBERATION

Edited by Nicholas Ribush

LAMA YESHE WISDOM ARCHIVE • BOSTON
www.LamaYeshe.com

A non-profit charitable organization for the benefit of all
sentient beings and an affiliate of the Foundation for
the Preservation of the Mahayana Tradition
www.fpmt.org

First published 2009
20,000 copies for free distribution

LAMA YESHE WISDOM ARCHIVE
PO BOX 356, WESTON, MA 02493, USA

Library of Congress Cataloging-in-Publication Data
Thubten Yeshe, 1935-1984.
Freedom through understanding : the Buddhist path to happiness and liberation / Thubten Yeshe & Thubten Zopa, Rinpoche ; edited by Nicholas
Ribush. — 1st ed.
p. cm.
Includes bibliographical references.
Summary: "On their first-ever trip to Europe, two Tibetan lamas offer a
weekend seminar based on their famous one-month Kopan meditation
courses on the lam-rim, the stages of the path to enlightenment, teaching
on the nature of the mind, the perfect human rebirth, the nature of samsara,
compassion and wisdom"—Provided by publisher.
ISBN 978-1-891868-22-1
1. Religious life—Buddhism. 2. Meditation--Buddhism. I. Thubten Zopa,
Rinpoche, 1945- II. Ribush, Nicholas. III. Title.
BQ5410.T59 2009
294.3'44—dc22
2009022783

ISBN 1-891868-22-5

10 9 8 7 6 5 4 3 2 1

Cover photograph by Carol Royce-Wilder • Cover line art by Robert Beer
Interior photographs at Kensington unknown, at Royal Holloway
by Dennis Heslop • Designed by Gopa & Ted2 Inc.

♻ Printed in the USA with environmental mindfulness on 30% PCW
recycled paper. The following resources have been saved: 60 trees,
1,670 lbs. of solid waste, 27,502 gallons of water, 5,710 lbs.
of greenhouse gases and 19 million BTUs of energy.

The teachings in this book are available on DVD

Please contact the LAMA YESHE WISDOM ARCHIVE
for more copies of this and our other free books

···Contents···

Editor's Preface   11

1. What is Meditation?   17
   Lama Yeshe

2. An Introduction to the Path to Enlightenment   35
   Lama Zopa Rinpoche

3. Making the Most of Your Life   51
   Lama Yeshe

4. How to Meditate   69
   Lama Yeshe

5. The Importance of Motivation   81
   Lama Zopa Rinpoche

6. The Lives of Others   93
   Lama Zopa Rinpoche

7. Rinpoche Answers Questions   107
   Lama Zopa Rinpoche

8. The Shortcomings of Attachment   119
   Lama Yeshe

9. Giving and Taking on the Breath   139
   Lama Yeshe

10. Making Life Meaningful   151
    Lama Zopa Rinpoche

11. Lama Answers Questions   167
    Lama Yeshe

Suggested Further Reading   189

The group at Royal Holloway College, 21 September 1975

··· Publisher's Acknowledgments ···

W E ARE EXTREMELY grateful to our friends and supporters who have made it possible for the LAMA YESHE WISDOM ARCHIVE to both exist and function: to Lama Yeshe and Lama Zopa Rinpoche, whose kindness is impossible to repay; to Peter and Nicole Kedge and Venerable Ailsa Cameron for their initial work on the ARCHIVE; to Venerable Roger Kunsang, Kyabje Rinpoche's amazing assistant, for his kindness and consideration; and to our sustaining supporters: Barry and Connie Hershey, Joan Halsall, Tony Steel, Vajrayana Institute, Claire Atkins, Thubten Yeshe, Roger and Claire Ash-Wheeler, Richard Gere, Doren and Mary Harper, Tom and Suzanne Castles, Lily Chang Wu and Hawk Furman.

We are also deeply grateful to all those who have become members of the ARCHIVE over the past few years. Details of our membership program may be found at the back of this book, and if you are not a member, please do consider joining up. Due to the kindness of those who have, we now have several editors working on our vast collection of teachings for the benefit of all. We have posted our list of individual and corporate members on our website, www. LamaYeshe.com.

In particular, we thank our anonymous benefactor for so kindly sponsoring the production of this book and the accompanying

DVDs of this unique teaching occasion.

Furthermore, we would like to express our appreciation for the kindness and compassion of all those other generous benefactors who have contributed funds to our work since we began publishing free books. Thankfully, you are too numerous to mention individually in this book, but we value highly each and every donation made to spreading the Dharma for the sake of the kind mother sentient beings and now pay tribute to you all on our website. Thank you so much.

Finally, I would like to thank the many other kind people who have asked that their donations be kept anonymous; my wife, Wendy Cook, for her constant help and support; our dedicated office staff, Jennifer Barlow and Ven. Ani Tenzin Desal; Ven. Ailsa Cameron for her decades of meticulous editing; Ven. Connie Miller, Gordon McDougall, Michelle Bernard and our other editors; Ven. Kunsang for his tireless work recording Lama Zopa Rinpoche; Ven. Thubten Labdron, Ven. Thubten Munsel and Dr. Su Hung for their help with transcribing; Sandy Smith, Kim Li and our team of volunteer web editors; Ven. Bob Alcorn for his incredible work on our Lama Yeshe DVDs; David Zinn for his digital imaging expertise; Jonathan Steyn for his help with our audio work; Mandala Books and Wisdom Books for their great help with our distribution in Australia and Europe; and everybody else who helps us in so many ways. Thank you all.

If you, dear reader, would like to join this noble group of openhearted altruists by contributing to the production of more books by Lama Yeshe or Lama Zopa Rinpoche or to any other aspect of

the Lama Yeshe Wisdom Archive's work, please contact us to find
out how.

—Dr. Nicholas Ribush

Benefactor's Dedication

This book and the DVD of these teachings are dedicated to Walter I.
Nathan, who passed away on 6 April 2006.

Through the merit of having contributed to the spread of the Buddha's
teachings for the sake of all sentient beings, may our benefactors
and their families and friends have long and healthy lives,
all happiness, and may all their Dharma
wishes be instantly fulfilled.

· · · · ·

Lama Yeshe answers questions at Kensington Town Hall.
The editor assists.

··· Editor's Preface ···

THE TEACHINGS in this book are typical of the incredibly inspiring teachings that Lama Yeshe and Lama Zopa Rinpoche were giving together at the time. They are what inspired many of their students, like me, to drop whatever we were doing and devote ourselves to following the Lamas full time. When Rinpoche said, "Each of us needs to think like this: 'All sentient beings have been extremely kind to me in the past, they're kind to me in the present, and they will continuously be kind to me in the future. They are the field from which I receive all my pleasure—past, present and future; all my perfections come from other sentient beings. Therefore I must attain enlightenment. Seeking everlasting happiness for myself alone, not caring about other sentient beings, giving them up, having no concern for their welfare, is selfish. Therefore, I must attain enlightenment, the most sublime happiness, in order to release all sentient beings from suffering and lead them on the path to enlightenment by myself alone, as this is my responsibility,'" we felt, "Yes, that's what I must do," and devoted our lives to the Dharma.

The Lamas started teaching Buddhism to Westerners in the late 1960's. The first full meditation course was held at Kopan Monastery, Nepal, in 1971. After the sixth Kopan course, March 1974, upon the invitation of their students, the Lamas made their first trip to the

West. They went again the following year and every year after that until Lama Yeshe passed away in 1984. The teachings in this book are the first the Lamas ever gave in Europe—a September 1975 weekend seminar near London that reflected the style of the Kopan courses. As their roadie and teaching assistant on that 1975 voyage, I was fortunate enough to be at this seminar and again observe the profound effect the Lamas' teachings had on people, especially those meeting the Dharma for the first time.

As ever, the Lamas stressed the importance of compassion, in particular its ultimate expression in the highly developed mind of *bodhicitta*. Lama Yeshe said, "This weekend we are very fortunate in that we have the opportunity to cultivate bodhicitta and put the actions of our body, speech and mind into the path to liberation, the path of control. This is so worthwhile."

And Lama Zopa Rinpoche proclaimed, "Bodhicitta is a realization, the intuitive determination to attain enlightenment for the sake of all other sentient beings. The pure thought of bodhicitta is never concerned for oneself but instead is always concerned for other sentient beings, how to free them from suffering and lead them along the path to enlightenment. Bodhicitta is always thinking of how to benefit other sentient beings in the wisest, most extensive way. It is a realization concerned only for other sentient beings, giving up oneself and taking most care of others."

As well as giving profound teachings, the Lamas also led several meditations, which are included here. When reading this book, when you come to the meditations, pause for a few moments and think about what the Lamas are saying, as was their intention. In this way you will get much more out of the book than just reading it through and then moving on to something else.

But wait! There's more! By some miracle, these teachings were videotaped and all the tapes but one have survived to this day. We have digitized the tapes and almost the entire the seminar will be available on DVD not too long after this book is published. This is by far the earliest video we have of the Lamas and it is a great joy to watch them as they were in 1975.

Since this seminar is so short you can get only a brief albeit sweet taste of Dharma by reading this book. In order to help you go deeper we have included a recommended reading list at the back of the book.

Also, since many of our other free books contain a glossary and there's an extensive one on line at www.LamaYeshe.com, we have not included one in this publication.

I hope this book helps you as much as it has helped me.

Lama Yeshe

WHAT IS MEDITATION?

Kensington Town Hall, London
18 September 1975

··· 1 ···

What is Meditation?

MEDITATION IS THE WAY we realize the nature of the mind. Therefore it's something that we absolutely have to do. Since Western education does not explain how the mind functions in everyday life, many Westerners these days are seeking out meditation because they are not satisfied with what they've been taught about the mind.

Buddhism always talks about suffering. This turns some Westerners off: "We're happy; we're not suffering; what's our problem? Why should we listen to teachings on suffering?"

Well, you can think in that way if you like, but in fact, if you check more deeply into how your mind functions in everyday life, you'll realize how dissatisfied you are and how up and down your uncontrolled mind actually is. That up and down itself is suffering, that's all. It's very simple. When Lord Buddha talked about suffering he didn't mean simply physical pain, like toothaches, headaches and so forth. Those kinds of suffering are very temporary; they're nothing. But if you check within yourself, whether you're rich or poor, famous or unknown, you'll always find dissatisfaction, a kind of uncontrollable, ever-changing energy of dislike. That energy too is suffering.

From the beginning of human evolution on this earth up to now, people have constantly sought something worthwhile, pleasure and happiness, in many different ways, but most of their methods have been completely wrong. They've sought happiness here while all the time it's been over there, in exactly the opposite direction. You're educated—check historically what people have believed through the ages and how they've sought fulfillment in different ways. You can see. Most times they've gone in totally the wrong direction.

So now people are finally beginning to realize that happiness is not dependent upon external development or material wealth. These days you don't even need a lama to explain it to you because the manifest world itself demonstrates the up and down nature of mundane reality—socially, economically and in many other ways. That makes it easy to realize that material things aren't everything. As a result, people are now beginning to investigate better ways of achieving a happy and joyful life. Meditation is one of the ways.

Mental attitude

In the West, meditation has recently gained some popularity. Most people have heard of it and many have tried it, but if you check why these people are meditating, the reason they're trying it out, a question arises. Actually, you can ask the same question in relation to why people are practicing religion. In general, people are meditating or following a spiritual path because they want to be happy, but from the Mahayana Buddhist point of view, whether or not you get the desired result from your meditation practice depends mainly on your mental attitude, or motivation. For meditation or any other implemented spiritual philosophy to bring happiness, it has to be done for the right reason.

Many people think that meditation means sitting someplace doing nothing while your mind toys with an object. That's a misconception. Your mind playing with an object, trying to concentrate, is not enough. Of course, I understand that way of thinking. Your mind is tired; you've heard so many things, so many philosophies, so much this, that and the other that all you want is a bit of peace and quiet and you think that single-pointed concentration will give it to you. But that's not enough.

Meditation is a tool. The most important thing is your motivation for using that tool, for practicing meditation; the way you are using it. That's what matters. Otherwise there's a danger that your meditation will simply become some kind of mindless routine, the way some people go to church on Sunday. They don't check their motivation; they just go. And not just in the West; Eastern people do the same thing. They go to the temple just because everybody else is going, because it's the local custom. Meditating or practicing religion for that kind of reason is a total misconception.

Also, practicing meditation just to experience temporal happiness, just to make this life happy, is also mistaken. That's a tiny goal; it's selfish and it's wrong. If all you're trying to do is make this life comfortable, your goal is really not worthwhile.

Ordinary people think that the purpose of meditation is to make the mind calm and peaceful, but that's not enough. Of course, when you create a calm, peaceful environment, you can integrate your mind and make it calm and peaceful, but that's not liberation. Liberation is complete freedom from the uncontrolled, up and down, selfish mind. When you reach beyond that kind of mind you've reached a worthwhile goal.

Meditation isn't just a mental game where you sublimate one mundane state into another. When we meditate, we're not joking, playing with hallucinations. The purpose of meditation is to gain joyful inner freedom and everlasting peace—in Buddhist terminology, nirvana or enlightenment. But the words don't matter that much—what you do have to know is what kind of goal you're aiming to achieve.

So the mental attitude I'm talking about, the best kind of motivation, is what Mahayana Buddhism calls bodhicitta, the enlightenment attitude: total dedication of your body, speech and mind to the benefit of others. If you meditate with that kind of mind, your mind automatically slips into the vehicle that will carry you to your desired destination—enlightenment—without delay. If you don't, if your subconscious motivation is selfish, then even if you think intellectually, "I'm doing this meditation in order to realize enlightenment," you're dreaming. That's not bodhicitta.

Also, some people think that the only kind of meditation is single-pointed concentration and strive for years to attain it, but because they are motivated by self-attachment, even if they do achieve this level of concentration, their mind is still agitated. That can happen because they're meditating with the wrong kind of motivation—selfishness. Bodhicitta is where you totally sacrifice yourself for the benefit of others.

When I say "sacrifice" I don't mean in the Hindu sense of blood sacrifice—human or animal—such as we often see in Nepal. It's not like that. I'm talking about your sacrificing the actions of your own body, speech and mind with knowledge-wisdom, totally dedicating them to the benefit of others.

As long as you have that dedicated enlightenment attitude, the pure, innermost thought of bodhicitta, no matter what your everyday actions, they're automatically beneficial. Similarly, your meditation practice is also successful and free of frustration.

Often you meditate with much superstition, with the expectation of easily attaining the highest goal of enlightenment. That's a misconception; you're psychologically sick from the very beginning. When you begin with a sick mind you can only finish up sick.

Of course, dedicating every day of your life, your entire body, speech and mind, to others, is one of the most difficult things you can do, but if you can do it, your life automatically has purpose. When your life has purpose, you naturally experience satisfaction and enjoyment. True enjoyment comes from within, from your mental attitude, not from without or from single-pointed concentration.

You can't concentrate in the busy confusion of your workplace; you can't sit cross-legged in the supermarket. You have to deal with people. But when you do deal with people, if you have the pure thought dedicated to others, they automatically give you good vibrations—because of the projection of your own mind.

If, however, your mind is clouded with thoughts such as "These people are no good," you automatically have a negative projection of others. That leads you to always blame them for how you feel: "He hurt me; she hurt me." Actually, nobody else hurts you. You hurt yourself because you lack the knowledge-wisdom to understand yourself; you haven't integrated wisdom into your everyday life.

In the terminology of Buddhism, self-cherishing is schizophrenic. I know that Western psychology thinks schizophrenia is something else, interprets it differently, but Buddhism thinks selfish motivation itself is schizophrenic and the cause of mental illness.

Experiment for yourself; I'm not saying you have to accept what I'm telling you just because I said it. When you get up in the morning, instead of thinking how difficult your mundane life is, generate the strong motivation, "Today I'm going to totally devote the energy of my body, speech and mind to others." If you really dedicate yourself in that way, your day will go very smoothly. Try it out.

The human problem is that people have to interact with each other and when problems arise, as they inevitably do, they blame others for them. This is a misconception. So bodhicitta isn't just an idea—it's a psychological method for treating the sick mind.

Also, physical actions aren't necessarily the best way of benefiting others. You need to investigate for yourself what the best way of helping others is. Actually, hunger or physical suffering are not the main human problem. To help others in the most effective way, you have to discover human potential. And not just *human* potential: even every insect has a mind and therefore the potential to be led into everlasting, peaceful enlightenment. You need to see that, instead of suffocating yourself emotionally with thoughts like, "I want to help others; they need help, I can see that they're suffering, but I can't see that I can do anything about it."

When you can see the potential of the human mind, the innate beauty of human beings and humans' infinite possibilities, you begin to see the solution to any problem that might arise. To the Mahayana Buddhist way of thinking, every human problem has a solution. For a start, every human problem has a cause; problems don't arise without cause. And if you eradicate a cause, its effect also disappears, doesn't it? That's scientifically verifiable.

Knowledge is the path to liberation

Buddhism isn't some fanatical religious trip. It's a philosophical way of living life. And also, to study Buddhism you don't need to believe in something extreme. It's a matter of investigating, examining and experimenting on yourself. It's not just belief. Without understanding, belief can be very dangerous. So what Lord Buddha emphasized was that understanding is the path to liberation, knowledge is the path to liberation.

Thus Buddhism emphasizes understanding; understanding is the path: no understanding, no path to liberation. Perhaps you're not sure about that. Ordinarily, people think, "This is religion, this is Buddhism," and paint their own picture of Buddhism and religion. For example, there are more than a hundred of us here—I can almost guarantee that each of us has a different understanding of what constitutes the path to liberation. Check up. Although we all might say, "Liberation is this, this, this," using the same words, at the same time our limited mind will be painting its own unique picture of our personal interpretation of the path to liberation. In fact, in our practice we may not be doing anything positive; our life may have nothing to do with the path to liberation.

So you have to check carefully to see if you're on the right path or the wrong. You should not proceed along your chosen path blindly. It's much more important that you investigate your spiritual path than the goods you buy, for example. When you go to the supermarket you spend much time checking products—"Should I buy this? Maybe this? Maybe that?"—but when it comes to choosing which path to the highest goal of enlightenment is best for you, which path is right, which is wrong, you check nothing. Checking is never a mistake; checking is most important.

Checking is meditation; observing is meditation. As I said, meditation doesn't mean just sitting in some corner doing nothing. You can meditate when you are walking down the street, checking, investigating your mind's view of things. That's meditation. Are you perceiving reality or a hallucination? When you analyze your mind like this, you're meditating.

We often talk about positive and negative actions. Everybody says things like, "Today you're so positive; today you're too negative." It's common. But how do you know which actions are positive and which are negative? You need to know how to check. How do you ensure that your meditation is positive and a vehicle leading to enlightenment? How do you know?

It doesn't depend on the meditation itself—it's your motivation for doing it that directs your mind into the right channel.

So how do you tell if you're on the wrong path? How do you discriminate? You need discriminating knowledge-wisdom. That's the path of meditation, the path to liberation. You have to be able to discriminate right from wrong. If you mix everything together, all you get is soup.

Method and wisdom

I'm not being judgmental, saying you're this or that; I'm just explaining how to go about meditating. We all need happiness; how do we check that the path we're on will bring us to that goal, that it's the most effective way of leading us to happiness? That's what we need to know.

Also, Mahayana Buddhism strongly emphasizes the simultaneous actualization of method and wisdom. Wisdom without method cannot produce enlightened realizations. That's very true: many religious people and meditators have wonderful ideas but lack the method for putting those ideas into action. Then their great ideas become useless.

Similarly, in the West, many people have great intellectual wisdom but not too much method. This is a problem. As Lord Buddha said, intellectual knowledge alone is not enough to gain realizations.

I don't have much more to say right now but I hope you all will actualize the method and wisdom that constitute the path to liberation and find everlasting peace as soon as possible. And now, if you have any questions, please ask anything you like. There's nothing wrong with our discussing all this. Tibetan Buddhism is very open. If you like, you can even tell me everything I've said is wrong. No problem. In that way I learn as well. I'm not enlightened, so discussion is most worthwhile.

Q. Lama, you were forced out of Tibet. How have you made exile work?

Lama. Well, as long as people know how to put their life together, it doesn't matter if they lose their home and country, they can still have a good life. For me, every country on earth is my home. Having to leave Tibet hasn't made me worried or miserable. I'm OK. Here I am meeting English people, eating English food, enjoying it very much. But it's a good question. It's true that when some people are forced to leave their home they are psychologically damaged and get sick as a result. But in general, Tibetan people understand cause and effect—the law of karma—and when they find themselves in a foreign country they're able to accept that their past actions have put them into that situation and thus find it easier to accept. Denying reality can make you want to kill yourself.

Q. You said that we should check within ourselves as to whether what we're doing is right or wrong according to our motivation. But isn't there the danger of over-analyzing everything and getting so tangled up that not only do we gain nothing from it but end up worse than when we started? Or would you say that that's a good state to be in?

Lama. You're right; it can be dangerous if you check too much using the wrong method. But if you check the everyday actions of your body, speech and mind with skillful method and wisdom, there's no danger; the more you check the more conscious and aware you become. Most of the time in our relationships with family and friends we act unconsciously and finish up hurting those closest to us. I agree; if you check your mind in a confused way you won't find anything and it can in fact be dangerous. Therefore I say that if you are seeking everlasting, peaceful inner liberation, you need perfect method and perfect wisdom. So it's not an easy job. Even if you have single-pointed concentration, that's not enough.

Q. Do external factors such as diet, sleep habits and livelihood affect the quality of one's meditation? In particular, is the food you eat important? For example, I'm a vegetarian but many people aren't and meat is considered to make people more aggressive and blood-thirsty. This is not something that can be easily proved, but many people, including me, tend to believe it. What is your view of this point especially?

Lama. We do have some dietary restrictions when doing certain meditations where there are some foods that we should eat and others that we shouldn't, such as meat, eggs, garlic, onion and radish. But when doing certain other kinds of meditation, those foods can be taken. Now, while in general ordinary people shouldn't eat too much meat, eggs or garlic, if you're used to a diet containing them, because of this conditioning, suddenly stopping eating them can shock your body. Also, even if you don't eat such foods, sometimes you might need to do so for health reasons. So it's better to take the middle path and not be too extreme. In Tibet, we would sometimes eat meat but we were forbidden from eating meat of animals that we had killed ourselves or ordered killed or that had been killed especially for us. Those three kinds of meat have tremendous negative vibrations associated with them and can make your meditation foggy rather than clear.

Q. I've heard of Tibetan lamas exorcising demons. What are demons?

Lama. Sometimes it can be possible that superstitious, primitive people believe that they're controlled by a spirit and get sick as a result, so lamas have certain methods of healing such people. But in general, by "demon" we mean the energy of the ego. There's no external demon, lying somewhere in wait for you. The Buddhist connotation is that the demon, devil or whatever you call it is within you.

There are thousands of different kinds of mind, some of them positive, others negative. Some of those negative minds are demonic and when they manifest they completely occupy your mind. At such times you become a kind of demon. When the demon mind takes over, wisdom, or your positive mind, has no room to function. However, by developing your meditation practice, perfecting your motivation and gradually purifying your mind, you can automatically control that negative energy. So that's the reason that meditation is worthwhile.

When Westerners feel psychologically unwell they tend to seek a therapist for help. The Buddhist point of view is all living beings have both positive and negative energy simultaneously existent in their mind. By meditating we can gradually increase the positive, decrease the negative and continuously develop until all the negative energy has been completely eliminated.

Therefore the Tibetan Buddhist approach to training the student is gradual; we guide students along the graduated path to liberation. These days Zen is very popular in the West; some Zen practitioners talk about instant enlightenment, like instant coffee. We think that's impossible. We think the mind has to evolve, or develop, gradually, just as modern science talks about gradual evolution. Accordingly, we have degrees of meditation from the beginning of the path up to the end. Some people have just one favorite meditation that they always do, from when they start meditating up to the end of their lives. The Tibetan tradition says that that's wrong: instead, you should do one meditation; when you reach a certain point, go on to the next, then the next and so forth, in a logical order. This is what we mean by the gradual, or graduated, path to liberation.

Q. When we meditate, do we concentrate on our breath or do we just let our mind go free?

Lama. If you're a beginner, it's better just to focus on your breath rather than let your mind become occupied by mundane thoughts. It's very useful. Actually, Tibetan Buddhism doesn't consider focusing on your breath to be real meditation; we call it preparation for meditation. Why? If your mind is emotionally bothered, totally occupied by strong attachment or strong hatred, it's impossible to meditate. What you can do at such times to create a good foundation for meditation is to manipulate your mind by concentrating on your breath and feeling sensations. If you do that, your mind will automatically calm down: the object with which your hatred is obsessed goes away, the object with which your attachment is obsessed goes away, and you are then free to direct your mind into any meditation that you choose.

Q. When you are doing checking meditation, what do you think about?

Lama. Many things can be the focus of analytical meditation; there are many different topics upon which you can meditate. You can't simply specify this or that. Also, Buddhist meditation depends a lot upon the individual meditator, what each person needs at any given time.

Q. In Western medicine there's a growing interest in the benefits that meditation can bring to people suffering from stress, both
physical and mental. I wonder if in your trips to the West you have
been in contact with doctors who are beginning to take an interest
in this particular practice. Have you been able to talk to them and
point out the deeper meaning of meditation?

Lama. A few months ago I met a group of psychiatrists in Melbourne, Australia, and we had a very interesting discussion about
patients with mental problems.[1] I've also spoken with American
doctors on similar topics. I think they're still seeking and growing, experimenting scientifically, and as a result their theories are
also constantly changing and growing. I think they're doing good
work. Also, Tibetan Buddhism has more in common with science,
logic and philosophy than with what the average person considers
religion.

That's all we have time for tonight. Thank you very much for coming. If I've made any mistakes, please excuse me.

[1] See " A Buddhist Approach to Mental Illness" in Lama Yeshe's *Becoming Your Own
Therapist,* free from the Lama Yeshe Wisdom Archive.

Lama Yeshe & Lama Zopa Rinpoche

WEEKEND SEMINAR

Royal Holloway College, Surrey

19–21 September 1975

An Introduction to the Path
to Enlightenment

B ECAUSE OF MY broken English you might find it difficult to
understand what I'm saying, but it's important to try to focus
not on the language itself but on the meaning of my words; and, if
possible, to feel it.

All human beings and even the tiniest of creatures desire happiness and freedom from suffering. But our biggest problem is that
although we desire happiness, we don't know what actually causes
it; although we don't want suffering, we don't know what causes
that either. That's our biggest problem.

Most living beings, no matter how much they wish for happiness,
spend most of their time destroying the cause of happiness; and no
matter how much they do not want suffering, they constantly rush
to create its cause. All this comes about because sentient beings lack
method and wisdom.

Earth's original human inhabitants did not have minds as negative and cruel as those of today. As a result, the actions of their
speech and body were not as violent and harmful as those of the

people we see around us now, and life was much more peaceful then. But gradually, as their delusions of anger, attachment, pride and jealousy arose more frequently and strongly, their minds became increasingly cruel, negative and harmful, and the actions of their speech and body became more violent and destructive. And no matter how much we have progressed in external development since those times, life has simply become busier and more dangerous; no matter how many material things, such as nuclear weapons have been developed, instead of bringing true peace, all they have brought is more danger.

However, we can't blame external things for all these problems; the actual cause is the internal factor—the unhealthy, dissatisfied mind, attachment, hatred and so forth. Even though people have undertaken external development with the expectation that it will bring happiness, that's a wrong conception. Happiness does not arise principally from external things but from the internal factor, the mind.

For example, people who have all the material things they need and desire—gourmet food, beautiful clothing, a luxurious apartment and so forth—are not necessarily happy. They get unhappy and depressed because they feel dissatisfied and don't know why; and since they also don't understand the meaning of human life, some of them think there's nothing left to enjoy, get completely despondent and kill themselves.

All such problems come from the mind, the internal factor, attachment. Instead of bringing satisfaction and happiness, all these desirable external things bring only more dissatisfaction.

Similarly, with respect to the suffering that arises from problems caused by other people—enemies, family members, countrymen—even if we were to kill all the other human beings on earth, even all other living beings, and remain here alone, still we would not experience happiness or peace. Stopping suffering and receiving happiness does not depend on making all other humans, all other living beings on earth, non-existent. Since doing so would not bring peace or happiness to the mind it shows that this is not the right method, not the way to receive happiness. By being alone with no other people, friends or other living beings around, we would feel lonely and very unhappy. Those problems also arise from within, from the internal factor, attachment.

Even when we get the material objects or close friends we desire, after a while we get bored and lose interest. That also comes from the internal factor, the dissatisfied mind, attachment.

Our physical body dying, becoming non-existent, does not mean that our suffering is over; the mind does not stop when the body does. Even though our body no longer exists, our mind is still in suffering—as long as our mind is under the control of the delusions of ignorance, attachment and anger, it is not free from suffering. The delusions themselves are the worst suffering, the root of every problem people and animals experience; The delusions are like the root of a tree—if there were no root there'd be no branches, leaves or fruit, which produce more seeds. So if there were no root of the delusions—ignorance, attachment and hatred—there wouldn't be any of the problems that we and other living beings experience, such as sickness, old age, death and so forth.

Body and mind are completely different

The first thing we need to understand is that the causes of our present life's mind and our present life's body are different. Our present life's mind came from its own cause, continued from its own cause, our previous life's mind. And our present life's body came from the union of our parents' sperm and egg—our mind did not come from these atoms, these physical things. Also, our mind did not come from our parents' mind.

If the principal cause of our present life's mind were our parents' sperm and egg, then all the problems and sufferings we experience in our life would have been caused by our parents and they would be their root cause. In that way our parents would become our enemy—if they had not given birth to us we would not have had to experience this suffering.

But it is not like this. Our parents are never the source of our problems. No matter what problems we experience—ugly body, deformity, handicap, whatever—it is not our parents' fault; it's our own fault. There's nothing to blame our parents for.

Also, the mind and the body are two completely different things: the mind is a formless phenomenon; the body has form. The body is composed of atoms; the mind is not. Their natures are completely different.

Just as space, whose nature is empty, does not become the nature of earth, form, the nature of earth, form, cannot become the nature of space, emptiness. In that way, the physical body never causes the mind, never becomes mind. The nature of the mind is clarity and it has the ability to see, or perceive, objects.

In addition, as soon as they've been born, baby humans and animals know how to drink milk without having to be taught by their parents; they automatically know how to suckle. And even little puppies know how to engage in sexual intercourse without needing to be shown. All this is because of habits created in previous lives. Because of habitual actions in previous lives, the newborn do such actions spontaneously without being taught.

Also, some children, without being trained or taught, are naturally very compassionate and don't want to harm other people or insects. Even if they see insects fighting or people in trouble, they have a strong, intuitive wish to help relieve that problem; they have intuitive compassion. But other children are automatically very impatient and cruel; whenever they see insects crawling around they immediately want to kill them. They have a very cruel personality.

Why do these children have different personalities? Why are they born with them? It's because in their previous lives, one child's mind was trained in patience and compassion while the other used to be very impatient, angry and cruel, giving much harm to others. So when they were born in this life, those personality traits, compassionate or cruel, carried over.

Another way of saying this is that children born with different personalities or different types of body are experiencing the result of previous lives' actions. So whatever qualities the child is born with—good personality, instinctive knowledge, great intelligence, perfect, beautiful body and senses—they are the result of actions created in previous lives with a virtuous, positive mind. And a child born with a cruel or harmful personality and physical handicaps is experiencing the results of actions done in previous lives with a cruel, negative mind, such as ignorance, attachment and hatred.

Furthermore, even in the West in modern times, many children can remember previous lives. Similarly, in the East, there are many people who also remember previous lives: where they lived, how they lived, their families and other people and places. Likewise, many meditators, as their mind develops through meditation practice and they reach a certain level of realization, can remember past lives and see future ones: where they will be born, in which country, in which family. And, according to their level of realization, they can make preparations before they die and choose where they want to be born and into which family.

In our case, just because we don't remember our past lives and our minds are incapable of seeing our future ones doesn't mean that our past and future lives don't exist. Arguments such as "I don't remember" or "I don't see the future" do not disprove past and future lives' existence. If such reasoning were sufficient we could assert "I was never in my mother's womb" because we don't remember it—the experiences we had, how we lived, how we entered it, how our mind was conceived there. If we search our mind with respect to these points it's completely dark; there's no clarity.

So forget about remembering previous lives or seeing future ones, we don't even remember how we came out of our mother's womb, what happened when we were a small baby, how our mother took care of us. We don't even recall any of that, so there's no way we can say we were never in our mother's womb just because we don't remember. That's no proof.

If the reasoning "I don't know" were valid then we'd have to say we don't exist. Why? Because we don't know what we are. If we check, "Who am I? What am I?" we can't see anything. But just because we don't see who or what we are doesn't prove that we don't exist. "I don't know what I am so I don't exist" is a silly reason and cannot prove that we don't exist.

And besides there being people who remember their own previous lives and see their future ones, there are also people who can see other people's past and future lives, even in the West.

Thus the mind does not cease when the body ceases; the mind continues. Our present mind's life continued from our previous life's mind; that previous life's mind continued from its previous life's mind; that came from its previous life; that again came from its previous life and in this way the continuity of mind has no beginning. Similarly, the continuity of mind has no end.

So even though this present life's physical body disappears, the mind still continues. And as long as the mind is under the control of the delusions—ignorance, attachment and hatred—it is not free from suffering; the mind is in suffering. As long as our mind is not free from suffering, no matter how many different bodies we take, we always encounter problems. Whether we take an animal body or a human one, no matter what kind of rebirth we take, as long as our mind is not free from suffering we can never experience true peace or real happiness.

Why is our present body not free from suffering? It's because our mind is not free from suffering. So just like this, as long as our mind is not free of the delusions, no matter what kind of body we take, whatever rebirth, it is always in suffering, always involved in various problems. Since this is the actual evolution of suffering, nothing external, even thousands of atomic bombs, can stop it because nothing external can destroy the delusions, the root of all suffering.

Putting an end to suffering

What can really cease, completely destroy, the root of suffering, the delusions? That's the practice of Dharma. So that's the purpose of religion, why it exists. Why do we need to follow religion, practice meditation or Dharma, whatever we choose to call it? The actual reason is that there's nothing other than Dharma, or meditation, practice that can destroy the root of suffering, the delusions.

However, the meditation we practice should serve to destroy our delusions, our unsubdued mind. If it does not, it's the wrong meditation; it's useless. In the same way, the purpose of following religion is to completely destroy the root of suffering, the delusions; the unhealthy, unsubdued mind. If the path or religion we're following does not do that, does not serve to decrease our delusions, then the path we're following is imperfect; there's something wrong with it. What we're practicing is wrong.

The purpose of practicing Dharma is also to destroy these delusions. However, practicing Dharma does not mean just doing ritual things; practicing Dharma does not mean just reciting mantras; practicing Dharma does not mean just worshipping, making offerings and so forth. Just doing these things does not mean we're practicing Dharma. Simply wearing robes is not practicing Dharma; nor does reading texts of Lord Buddha's teachings, the Buddhadharma, mean we're practicing Dharma.

There's a story about the great Tibetan yogi Dromtönpa meeting an old man who was trying to practice Dharma. The old man was circumambulating a temple thinking he was practicing Dharma but the great yogi Dromtönpa said to him, "Your going around the temple is good but wouldn't it be better if you practiced Dharma?"

The old man thought by practicing Dharma the yogi must mean reading Dharma texts, so he stopped going around the temple and instead started reading texts. When Dromtönpa saw him next he said, "Reading texts is good but wouldn't it be better if you practiced Dharma?"

So the old man thought if circumambulating and reading texts aren't practicing Dharma, the yogi must mean he should meditate and started doing that. When, after some time, Dromtönpa saw him sitting cross-legged he said, "Meditation is very good but wouldn't it be better if you practiced Dharma?"

At this point the old man was somewhat confused and irritated and exclaimed to Dromtönpa, "Practice Dharma! Practice Dharma! What do you mean, 'practice Dharma'?"

"Renounce this life," the yogi replied.

What did the great yogi Dromtönpa mean by "renounce this life"? He meant we should renounce suffering, which means renouncing the worst of all sufferings, the delusions—ignorance, attachment, anger, pride, jealousy and so forth—all the negative minds that are the root of all suffering. This is what practicing Dharma really means: facing the root of suffering, the delusions.

So no matter what religion people follow—Christianity, Hinduism, Islam, Buddhism or any other—as long as their practice diminishes and destroys the root of suffering, that is the real Dharma, that is the actual path, the real path that brings true happiness, everlasting happiness. So it's extremely important that whatever we do, whatever meditation we practice, whatever religious actions we engage in, we use it to destroy the root of unhappiness, suffering. That's the most important thing to concentrate on.

But releasing only oneself from suffering by practicing Dharma is insufficient. Seeking release from suffering and everlasting happiness for oneself alone is selfish because all the happiness and perfections of our past, present and future lives have been received dependent upon the kindness of other sentient beings. Also, even if we have freed ourself alone from all delusions we still haven't received all the realizations and complete knowledge of a buddha; we still have the subtle obscurations of the dualistic mind to purify.

For example, say there's a family where the parents are starving and their son has found some food and his stomach is full for today but there's no food for tomorrow. So, just being fed today with nothing for tomorrow doesn't mean he's self-sufficient and should not make arrangements not to starve in future. Also, he should help others avoid similar problems too. Similarly, since all our happiness and resources have been received through the kindness of all sentient beings and we still have not received all realizations and have subtle obscurations to purify, we must attain enlightenment for the sake of other sentient beings.

If we attain enlightenment, the highest goal, the most sublime happiness, even each ray of light that emanates from our holy body has the power to release other sentient beings and lead them on the path to enlightenment. As a buddha, we can manifest billions of bodies and show different methods according to sentient beings' level of mind to release them from suffering and lead them to enlightenment.

Also, with his holy speech a buddha can explain the Dharma in different languages according to each sentient being's need and therefore enlighten numberless sentient beings. And with his holy omniscient mind a buddha can see all the numberless sentient beings' different thoughts, different levels of mind, different personalities, different desires; the omniscient mind sees every single thing that exists, all past, present and future, and in this way can enlighten numberless sentient beings by showing different methods.

An enlightened being has that much power and knowledge—all knowledge, complete; there's nothing missing—and no ignorance whatsoever—not a single self-cherishing thought, not a single dualistic mind, not one single defect. The enlightened mind is completely pure.

By attaining enlightenment we can release other sentient beings from suffering and enlighten them very quickly, and this is the highest goal of practicing Dharma, especially the Mahayana: to attain enlightenment for the sake of other sentient beings. The way we attain enlightenment is by following the graduated path, which includes all the teachings of the Buddhadharma.

How can we attain enlightenment through the graduated path? That is because the nature of our mind is not one with the delusions or the dualistic mind, which are the main hindrances to enlightenment, or buddhahood, which has all knowledge and complete purity. The nature of our mind is only temporarily obscured by these hindrances, so when we follow the graduated path the temporal obscurations—the delusions and the dualistic mind—gradually diminish. When they have been finally removed, our mind becomes completely pure. When the mind becomes completely pure, it becomes omniscient.

Why is our present mind not an omniscient, fully knowing mind? That is because of the hindrances, the obscurations, the dualistic mind. When they have been completely purified, our present mind becomes omniscient. When our mind becomes omniscient, we become a buddha, an enlightened being.

Another reason is that the graduated path explains absolute nature, the right view of the nature of the mind, the nature of the self, the nature of all existence. Ignorance, the main obscuration, is ignorant of the right view, the absolute nature; ignorance does not understand absolute nature. That is the worst obscuration, the biggest delusion—ignorance, not knowing the absolute nature of the self or any other existence.

So by following the graduated path we receive the wisdom realizing absolute nature, or *shunyata*. When we realize the wisdom of shunyata, ignorance, the false mind that does not see the absolute nature, dissolves, finishes. That's one basic reason why the graduated path diminishes, or purifies, the obscurations and the dualistic mind.

The path to enlightenment

This graduated path to enlightenment is not something that nobody has experienced, traversed. It's the path that all the past, present and future buddhas have traveled on their way to completing all the realizations of the path to enlightenment. Guru Shakyamuni Buddha himself experienced it and on that basis showed it to his followers, handing the teachings down to Manjushri, the Buddha of Wisdom, and Maitreya, the next buddha to come. And then these buddhas handed it down to their own followers, such as the great philosopher and pundit Nagarjuna, who received enlightenment, Asanga and many other eminent pundits. They attained all the realizations of the graduated path and in turn handed the teachings down to their own followers. In this way the teachings passed down to other fully realized pundits such as Shantideva, Atisha and others who had complete control over their mind, eventually reaching great Tibetan pundits and yogis such as Lama Tsongkhapa and many other followers of the great Atisha. From them, the teachings of the graduated path to enlightenment have been handed down to the high lamas of the present, such as His Holiness the Dalai Lama, his tutors (Kyabje Ling Rinpoche and Kyabje Trijang Dorje Chang) and many other high lamas, and we have received the lineage of these teachings from them.

So the subject matter—the meditation, or the teaching—of this seminar is the graduated path to enlightenment, the lineage of which we have received from the abovementioned present-day great lamas, who themselves received it from the previous Tibetan and Indian pundits, and which originally came from Guru Shakyamuni Buddha.

If you follow and practice this path, it definitely works. Gradually, your mind becomes more and more free of delusions. As your delusions diminish you get closer to enlightenment. When you reach the end of the path you become a buddha.

If you have any questions or doubts, if anything is unclear, you don't have to feel depressed. It's good to have questions and doubts. They help you to develop your knowledge. You should think about them, discuss them with older students or ask your teacher.

Meditation on the continuity of mind

In the next session, meditate on mental continuity. The way to do this is to first cultivate a pure motivation for doing the meditation. The mind that starts the meditation should be as pure as possible and totally uninvolved in ignorance, attachment or anger. So start by generating bodhicitta by thinking, "I am going to do this meditation in order to reach enlightenment for the sake of all sentient beings."

Next meditate on your breath for a few minutes and then move into an analytical meditation on the continuity of life.

Check your mind, starting with your present mind, thinking that this year's mind came from last year's mind, last year's mind came from the previous year's mind and so on, going further and further back until the time you were a baby. From there go back to the time you were in your mother's womb. Then go back from that to the time of your conception and when you reach that point, try to go even further back to see where your mind came from, what kind of previous life. Then think that that previous life's mind came from its own previous life, and that from another and so on, back and back.

This is an analytical meditation that helps you realize reincarnation. Also, it gradually helps you realize the absolute nature of your mind.

Making the Most of Your Life

THIS WEEKEND we are very fortunate in that we have the opportunity to cultivate bodhicitta and put the actions of our body, speech and mind into the path to liberation, the path of control. This is so worthwhile.

Despite having had many previous lives and having lived many years in this one, if we really check, from the time we were born up to now, we'll find that we haven't acted seriously for even one day because most of the time our mind has been completely occupied by uncontrolled thoughts and superstition. So we are very fortunate to have generated the enthusiastic feeling of wanting to help others and ourselves in the highest way possible.

Since we were born we've wasted practically every moment of every day, month and year. Instead of making our time worthwhile and using it to bring happiness, we've engaged in only useless actions and used our precious life for nothing. At the time, we've thought that what we've been doing is useful but if we check we'll see that it really has not been.

Perhaps you'll disagree; you think that what you've done has been worthwhile because you've taken care of your life, preserved yourself and made money. But is that fulfilling your human potential? Is

that all you can do? If that's all you can do you're no better than a cat
or a rabbit. Having profound human potential but using your life
as an animal does is such a waste of time. You have to realize how
incredibly tragic that is.

If you check up deeply to see if, since you were born until now,
you've done anything that was really worthwhile in bringing you
true happiness and a joyful life, do you think you'll find anything?
Check up. Don't look at others; check yourself. It's not complicated:
you have your body, speech and mind; just these three. Which of
their actions have been worthwhile?

I'm going to suggest that most of time your actions of body,
speech and mind have produced only frustration and confusion.
Check up: how many hours are there in one day? During how much
of each of these hours have you been aware? How much of each
hour has been positive? Check that way; it's very simple. The Buddhist way of checking is very scientific. Anybody can do it; we're not
trying to be exclusive. It's realistic. Check for yourself.

Even though you might say that you're following a spiritual
path or leading a meditator's life, you're not serious. It doesn't matter if you sit in meditation, go to church on Sundays, visit the temple regularly or do any other kind of customary religious activity;
that doesn't mean anything. The actions that you need to do are
those that actually lead you to everlasting, peaceful happiness, the
truly joyful state, not those that simply bring up and down transitory pleasure. Actions that bounce you up and down are not true
Dharma, not true meditation, not true religion—here I can make a
definitive statement. Check up: you might think you're doing something spiritual but is your polluted mind simply dreaming?

Relative and absolute

Here I'm talking about what Buddhism calls your relative nature. You might think, "How can you describe my nature just like that? My nature has many different aspects." That might be the Western idea of it but the Buddhist idea is much simpler: we say your nature has two aspects, relative and absolute.

So when I describe how you are, I'm talking about your relative nature. Sometimes we talk about higher ideas, something absolute. Perhaps you've read books that talk about the absolute nature. Forget about the absolute—first you have to know the way your relative body, speech and mind function in everyday life. That's very important. You can't just jump straight into inner freedom.

When Western science talks about evolution it describes a process of gradual development. Even I know that and I'm somewhat stupid and uneducated; I haven't even been to school. Nevertheless, when I hear Western scientists talk about mind control, to me it sounds rather primitive. Of course, I'm sure they would say that I'm the primitive one!

However, ever since you could talk you've been saying, "My mind is this; my mind is that," but actually, you have no idea what your mind is. The nature of the mind is not some Eastern custom. You've had a mind from the moment you were born—you can't say that it's an Eastern custom. Also, Buddhism doesn't talk about customs; customs aren't important. So describing the mind isn't an Eastern custom. Anyway, here I'm talking about your relative nature.

It's your relative mind that functions in your everyday life. For example, whenever things go wrong in your interactions with people—family, friends or society in general—you always blame somebody else. Check your mind—you do. That's a misconception. In fact, all your problems, both physical and mental, come from ignorance—a lack of intensive knowledge-wisdom—and attachment. These two mental factors are the biggest root of *any* problem, social or individual. Check up, but this time check up on your *own* mind.

Think about when you cheat others through lying or when you kill, taking another's life. Check up: why do you do such things? The root is ignorance; the motivation is attachment, involvement in your own pleasure. The energy of ignorance, a lack of intensive knowledge-wisdom, is like a king or queen and attachment is like a director. It's the mind; it's your mind. I'm not talking about something else. And your mind contains the association of these two things: ignorance and attachment.

These two factors are the principal cause of all problems, physical and mental. If you do not realize this you'll never be able to solve your problems because you'll continue thinking that their cause lies outside: "I'm not happy, I'm not going to see him again; I'm not happy, I need a bigger house; I'm not happy, I need a better car." You can never put an end to problems that way. Especially in the West, we always think that money is the solution to all problems. It's not true; that's a complete misconception.

Don't think, "Lama's putting me down...that's not how I think." I'm not talking about intellectual thought; I'm talking about something much more deeply rooted in your mind. Human problems don't originate from intellectual thought. Actually, if you could see what goes on in your mind, you wouldn't believe it. Even though you're not consciously aware of this materialistic way of thinking, deep in your subconscious there are forces leading you in a circle from one trip to another to another to another, constantly changing. This is what we mean by cyclic existence. We go round and round but never reach beyond the circle. Our entire way of living is a joke. We give children toys to play with... we're the same; it's just a different game.

We like to boast, "This modern generation is so well educated, we know so much. We're well versed in social theory, economics, inflation and so forth." But it's not that the current generation is more intelligent and older ones were foolish. Why? Because the external world itself is changing automatically and all you're doing is observing natural occurrence. So don't think that you're so much smarter than previous generations.

However, some of you do see that it's worthwhile to seek something beyond mere material comfort, but if you don't seek with the right attitude you're still going to circle in samsara. Even if you try to meditate, do yoga or follow some other spiritual trip, you're still going to go round and round. So make sure you have the right mental attitude and the right view and that you're on the right path by recognizing how the wrong mental attitude leads you down the wrong path to the wrong goal.

Often Western people say, "Don't be negative; be positive." They like to talk about the positive but not the negative. But negativity exists; why not talk about it? You don't have to talk about it angrily but it's important to demonstrate and know how the negative mind functions. From the Buddhist point of view, that's very important.

That's why I always say that Buddhism isn't a diplomatic religion, always saying nice things. We like to call things as they are, without hesitation. So don't be shocked; you should expect me to say things that are not particularly nice. Don't worry.

Of course, we do have nice qualities, beautiful qualities. Equally, so do all other living beings, even fish and chickens. We all possess good qualities of mind. But at the same time we all possess a negative nature that can bring us down. So we need to be shown and know both the good and the bad within us. Then we can let go of fear. Otherwise, our every move can make us fearful.

As long as you don't have the inner understanding or knowledge-wisdom of what constitutes real happiness and a truly joyful life and just sit around expecting the world to somehow get better, you're dreaming. How can the world possibly get better by itself?

Take inflation, for example. How's that going to improve? Inflation comes from attachment. It does—but I'm sure that political economists don't know that! Month by month, year by year, they go on, "This, this, this, that, that, that," but they don't know that inflation is actually due to attachment. Why is that?

You check up. It's not that the economy is strong and suddenly worsens for no reason. It's due to selfishness and attachment. Some people have too much but worry about not having enough. So they hoard and then the economy inflates. It's not that there are insufficient material goods; there's plenty of food, plenty of goods. It's the selfish mind that causes inflation.

Anyway, check this for yourselves; it's not true just because I say so. Still, if you investigate you'll see how attachment, the self-ish mind, creates problems for both the individual and society and destroys everybody's inner peace and joyful life.

Look at religious wars. There's one going on right now;[2] and not only now—throughout history. Religious wars come from attachment. I'm talking about how attachment functions. Two small children fighting over a piece of candy comes from attachment; two huge countries fighting each other also comes from attachment; and religious people fighting each other comes from attachment, as well.

Actually, those religious people fighting each other all think that religion is wonderful but fighting is not a religious action, is it? For them, religion is just an idea, that's all. Those who fight religious wars are not religious people. Religion is about compassion and universal love. How can killing become a religious action? It's impossible. It comes from attachment.

So you can understand how attachment is the biggest problem in the world. "My religion is good, therefore I'm going to kill you." That's ridiculous. People who think like that are simply destroying themselves.

If I were to do that I'd be turning religion into poison. What I was doing would have nothing to do with religion. But even though my actions were the opposite of religion, I'd be thinking, "My religion is good." Instead of being medicine to solve my psychological problems, because of my distorted mental attitude, my religion would be

[2] Lama may have been referring to the conflict in Lebanon, which had started just a few months earlier.

poison. Even though I'm thinking, "This is my religion," not a minute of my actions would be religious.

For example, I have the idea that my *thangka*[3] is my religion. Then if somebody tries to burn my thangka I get upset because I think he's destroying my religion. That's a misconception. A painting isn't religion. People who think material things are religion misunderstand the meaning of religion. Religion is not external; Dharma is not external. It's only in the mind.

The Bible says the same thing. The New Testament contains wonderful teachings by Jesus but many people don't understand what they mean. For example, he said that people who worship idols are not following him. That's very true; that's a fantastic teaching. We have to understand how to integrate religion with our everyday life, put it into action and solve our problems, not think that material things like church and property are religion. That's ridiculous.

In other words, people who worship idols thinking that the material atoms are their religion and don't realize the nature of their own consciousness or spirit have no idea of what religion really is. Jesus gave perfect teachings explaining this; we just don't realize.

Ego and attachment

Attachment and ignorance produce many misconceptions in our life. How? For example, we often think, "This is good; this makes

---

[3] A *thangka* is a Tibetan religious painted scroll.

me happy," but if we investigate a little further we'll find that such thoughts are misconceptions; that the things we think make us happy actually cause suffering.

Evel Knievel is a good example of this.[4] He believes his death-defying, daredevil stunts to be pleasure. Even when he nearly kills himself, after he recovers, even though he's decided to quit, his ego and attachment tell him, "This is your profession, your job; you have to do it again." So he does and nearly dies once more. Why does he put himself through all this?

Well, we ourselves do the same thing. I mean, in one way what we do is completely different but from another point of view it's exactly the same. Why? Through misconception. We do things that bring us suffering but cling to them as wonderful causes of happiness. Check up on the things you do, physically and mentally— you'll see that what I'm saying is true.

Perhaps it will be clearer if I give an example from our own experience. We're always attached to food, aren't we? As a result, we eat with greed and our stomach is often upset. This comes from attachment; it's common.

Actually, people think that food should preserve body and life, but eating with ignorance turns nourishment into poison and kills us. Everybody knows this; check up. Why do most people die? It's because they eat things that finish up killing them. If you really look

[4] He was in the news around this time. From his website: 31 May 1975: a record crowd of over 90,000 at Wembley Stadium in London, England, watched as Evel crashed upon landing, breaking his pelvis after clearing 13 double-tiered buses. He died 30 November 2007.

into it you'll nearly always find that the person made some mistake or other.

What I'm saying is simple but you have to realize it more deeply; it's not just an idea. If the meditation you do is just an idea, if you're simply on some kind of trip, then it's not worthwhile. Proper meditation scientifically demonstrates the reality of your nature, your relative nature. This is well worth knowing. When you know the nature of your own mind—how your mind torments you, how it brings you suffering—your mind can then cooperate with your life. Most of the time our mind does not cooperate with our life. As a result, we don't know what's going on in our life.

Look at the Western world in particular. We're too involved in objects of sense gravitation attachment[5]; we over-exaggerate the importance of the sense world such that it's constantly exploding in front of us. The way we're brought up, we automatically believe that the external world brings us happiness. It's true; check up. Perhaps we don't assent to this intellectually, but if we look more deeply into our mind we'll see that that's what we believe. That misconception is deeply rooted in our consciousness.

I'm not talking about something intellectual. Forget about the intellectual. Just penetrate more deeply into your own mind and investigate your lifelong beliefs, what you think is best for you and what you think is not. Everybody holds to such beliefs. Don't think, "I'm not like that. I just go with the flow." That's not true. Don't think, "I have no fixed ideas." The nature of attachment is such that

---

[5] Editor: For several years I thought Lama was trying to say "sense *gratification* attachment" and would try to correct him (to no avail) but eventually it became clear to me that he knew exactly what he was saying and meant the irresistible gravitational pull that objects of attachment have upon our mind.

you always have fixed ideas of what is best for you: "This is me, therefore that is best." Check up on your "this is me."

So attachment to "this is best for me" based on ego's conceptualization of "I'm Thubten Yeshe, this is me," the conception of I, my mind's fixed idea of who and what I am, this association of ego and attachment, has nothing whatsoever to do with my reality, relative or absolute.

While I'm saying this you should be meditating, checking up on whether or not what I'm saying is exaggerated or exactly right. Check up on this right now. What I'm talking about is how the ego and attachment are associated, how they relate to each other.

What I'm saying is that the fundamental cause of attachment is the conceptualization of ego, and in reality this ego does not exist within you, either relatively or absolutely. But the ego mind projects and paints "I am this," you get a fixed idea of what you are, and then you start worrying, "I am this, therefore I should have that; I am this, so I need to maintain my reputation; because I'm this, I need that." You check up.

Such fixed ideas of what you are, how you should be, which are completely mental projections, hallucinated, polluted projections, have nothing whatsoever to do with reality, either relative or absolute.

A meditation on how you exist

Why don't you take a couple of minutes right now to check up on what you are, how you exist. When you ask, "What am I?" a concrete, substantial idea of "this is me" will reveal itself.

Your color is not you, your I. Your form is not I. Your nose is not I. Your leg is not I. Your heart is not I. So where is that idea, your conceptual idea of ego? Where is it?

Your imaginary I, your hallucinated ego, was not created by God, Krishna, Buddha or anybody else. It was created only by your own mind, your own misconceptions.

When you realize that your imaginary, conceptualized I is non-existent, suddenly something substantial and concrete disappears from within your heart. Your heart becomes restful rather than restless; your heart's restless energy is released. It's incredible; it's so powerful. As a result, your body becomes less intense and tight.

There is no self-existent, concrete I, ego. All transitory phenomena, your physical body and all that appears is totally non-self-existent. However, you—your superficial mind—have always thought that within your five aggregates,[6] you truly exist. Your mind, your

---

[6] The five *skandhas*, or aggregates, are the five psycho-physical constituents that make

conceptualization of I, ego, always feels that within your body, within your five aggregates, an "I am" really exists. You have always thought, and also felt, that something exists within you. If you check up carefully you will find that this is simply a projection of your hallucinating mind.

From the Hinayana point of view, your self and the entire sense world are non-self-existent; only inner reality is self-existent. But from the point of view of the Madhyamaka, a Mahayana school, even inner reality is also non-self-existent; nothing at all is self-existent, concrete, as the ego perceives. It's impossible for anything to be self-existent.

In other words, to keep it simple, when you feel miserable, it's because of misconception. Misconception produces miserable conditions; misconception holds a misconceived object that has nothing whatsoever to do with the reality of either your inner world or the outer sense world.

That's why Lord Buddha said that all your frustration and confusion results from your own actions and is not created by God. God doesn't create evil actions, does he? The Bible doesn't say that God created evil. Nevertheless, many people have the misconception

_____

up a sentient being: form, feeling, discrimination, compositional factors and consciousness.

that because God created everything, God created evil. Philosophically, that's a dubious position, but philosophy's not important here. You just have to know what the Bible's saying.

Many people think that the Bible is mistaken. The Bible's not mistaken; *you're* mistaken because you interpret the Bible with a lack of knowledge-wisdom.

Negative comes from the mind

So it's really worthwhile if you can discover that all your false conceptions and miserable experiences come from attachment and the polluted I, the conceptualization of ego; if you can realize this you will release the tremendously uptight energy of bondage.

Also, it's not just a matter of your believing something. Through experimentation comes experience; through experience comes realization. We don't call mere intellectual understanding realization; without experience, knowledge is dry. From the day we were born until now, we've all been dry, and if we don't actualize the teachings, don't gain experience, we'll remain dry until the day we die. Dry, like dry wood.

However, as I talk about the relative nature of your own mind, don't think, "Oh, my mind is garbage; I'm the worst person on earth." Instead of thinking in that way, realize that "It's incredible. I'm not the only one with such problems. All other living beings in the universe have them too."

Now I'm sure that there have been times in your life when you've thought, crying emotionally, "I want to make my life worthwhile;

I want to help others." That's ridiculous; it's so emotional. If you really want to help others, the way to think is, "First I need to realize the nature of my own mind and how to stop human problems. Then I'll really know how to help others."

If you don't understand your own problems and know how to help yourself, how can you possibly think you can help others? You're just being emotional: no wisdom, no method; you're just joking.

First realize your own situation: "It's not just me; countless beings on this earth are in the same situation, full of misconceptions, and, as a result, are greatly conflicted both physically and mentally." Our minds are full of conflict and when that mental energy transmutes into the physical level, our bodies also get sick. In that way, all sickness comes from a diseased mind; the sick mind manifests as a sick body.

So the way to expand love and compassion is to first understand yourself; *then* you can relate to all other living beings. That's good. The problem is that much of the time we don't even have compassion for ourselves, we don't comprehend ourselves, so how can we then have love and compassion for others? It's impossible. Even if we say we love others, it's just words, emotion. We say, "I love you," but true love first has to be for *you*. You have to know your own situation, what you are. This leads to sincere love for yourself, and from that, sincere love for others. Without doing it that way, you're joking.

Most of the time what you call love is selfish; it's purely attachment. Also, although sometimes your meditation might not be attachment, most of the time it is also selfish, attachment. Check up; really check up. I'm not joking; I haven't come here to joke. It's true. As long as you grasp at something concrete and cling tightly to your own comfort, it's still selfish, even though you think you're a meditator on a spiritual trip. It's still selfish.

Why am I talking about this, emphasizing this? Because even if you're a meditator, as long as you're seeking something concrete for yourself, it has the psychological effect of making you easily frustrated. Even if you're on a spiritual trip, it's still self-cherishing. In other words, you still have the conceptualization, ego's fixed idea, "I'm this, my realization is that," which has nothing whatsoever to do with true realization.

So it's worthwhile for you to realize your own situation and the way you live. This is not just some philosophical point of view. Check how your life is, how you think, what sort of mistakes you make and how your misconceptions are related to what you experience. Analyze how all that happens and how it's related to attachment. By realizing that, instead of then worrying about your own problems you can see that all universal living beings are in the same situation. Then automatically, intuitively, love and compassion ensue. With such understanding, even your greatest enemy can become a good friend—yesterday you didn't even want to see him but today he appears beautiful to you. It's true, because it's all your projection.

Actually, when you look at other people and think, "She's ugly, she's good; he's ugly, he's bad," it's totally your own mental projection. Who on this earth is absolutely good? Who? Please tell me.

Who, in London, is absolutely beautiful? Who is absolutely ugly? There's nobody you can point to, for sure. You check up on that. It's interesting, isn't it?

I'm talking about scientific fact, not something you have to believe in. If you really believe that there's something in London that's absolutely beautiful, please prove it to me scientifically. You can't. The thing is, we always accept things too easily; we never check. We call that kind of attitude sluggishness; its nature is absence of intensive knowledge-wisdom.

··· 4 ···

How to Meditate

Mantra

MANTRA HAS the power to separate your body, speech and mind from ordinary, mundane thought. The vibration of a mantra can automatically unify the split, scattered mind into single-pointedness. Reciting a mantra can focus your mind into the here and now rather than leaving it to run all over the place as it usually does. So that's very useful and is one of the reasons we recite mantras.

The mantra of Guru Shakyamuni Buddha is TA YA THA OM MUNÉ MUNÉ MAHA MUNAYE SOHA. OM means magnificent knowledge-wisdom and power and MUNÉ MUNÉ MAHA MUNAYE contains three meanings: control, great control, greatest control, or conquest, great conquest, greatest conquest. We all need to control or conquer our uncontrolled mind, don't we? We don't need to conquer other sentient beings; we need to conquer our own uncontrolled mind. The connotation of the mantra is along those lines. So it's very useful.

[Lama and the students recite the mantra three times.]

If all negative actions and unhappy feelings come from false conceptions, then the only way to overcome these actions and feelings is to purify and release our false conceptions by perceiving the right view. Perceiving the right view is not something that can just be done instinctively. It takes time to develop right conceptions and perceive the right view.

Meditation

In order to awaken, or become conscious, we need to practice meditation. We tend to think we're conscious most of the time but actually we're not; we're unconscious. Check up; really check up. But by gradually developing our meditation practice we slowly, slowly integrate our mind with reality.

Also, when we meditate we often encounter obstacles to our practice and experience much trouble and frustration. The fundamental character or absolute nature of our mind is clean clear—we call this nature clear light—but relatively it is obscured by misconceptions and other hindrances that prevent us from seeing reality. It's like the sky obscured by clouds—when a strong gust of wind comes and blows away the clouds, the underlying clear blue sky is revealed. It's the same thing with our mind. Therefore, when we try to meditate, we encounter hindrances and lack of clarity and find it very difficult to concentrate single-pointedly on an object. When this happens, instead of getting disappointed we should employ the methods contained in Tibetan Mahayana Buddhism to purify our mind.

When our meditation is not going smoothly we should not push. The mind is like a baby; babies don't like to be pushed—we have to treat them differently. Instead of pushing them we have to play with them in a psychologically skillful way. Then they're OK.

Similarly, we have to play a little with our mind. When it becomes impossible to meditate, we shouldn't push. Instead, we should just leave our mind where it is and do some purification practice. This will decrease obstacles and make our mind more powerful.

Unfortunately, many people do try to force it. This just makes them aggressive and frustrated and angry with their friends: "I don't like you this morning; I didn't have a good meditation. Instead of making me calm and clear it made me uptight." Such people don't have skillful wisdom; they don't know how to integrate their practice.

Also, every time you meditate, cultivate bodhicitta and totally dedicate your practice to others: "It doesn't matter whether my meditation is good or bad, I'm not doing it for me, I'm doing it solely for the benefit of other sentient beings." If you have that kind of dedicated mind, even if your meditation is not that good, you're not disappointed; you're secure in the knowledge that whatever you did was for the benefit of others. Then, even if you're not successful, you're still relaxed. You know that you tried your best and that your attitude—concern for others rather than the selfish "I'm miserable, I want to be happy, therefore I'm going to meditate"—is the most important thing. If you meditate with self-cherishing and it doesn't work, you get really disappointed.

Therefore, before you meditate or do any action, actually, it's incredibly important to dedicate it to others by cultivating bodhicitta. Take going to work, for instance. Most people in this country work for a boss, so before you go to work you should dedicate, "May my life today be beneficial for others." That's the way to avoid frustration. If your motivation is selfish, concern for only your own pleasure, your work is always troublesome; your mind is sick, not happy. You get uptight with your supervisors.

These are important points. Don't think that only sitting in meditative concentration is important. It is important but it's not everything. All the time, no matter what you're doing—meditating, working, walking down the street, cooking, making soup—always try to have good motivation. If your motivation is pure you can take all those actions into the path to liberation. It's possible.

Otherwise, even if you do meditate, if your motivation is wrong, the action too becomes wrong. Even if you go to church or the temple, if you go with a negative mind, it's a waste of time; it's not even a religious action; it's purely samsaric.

Perhaps you don't know what samsara means. It's a Sanskrit word, but that doesn't matter; don't worry about the word. It refers to worldly, mundane things. In Tibetan, it's *khorwa*, which means circle, or cyclic. However, I don't have time here to explain Buddhist philosophical terms. If you want to learn that sort of thing you'll have to go to university. Since our time together here is so short, I just want to talk on the practical level.

Try this simple experiment for yourself. Next time somebody asks you for a cup of tea or coffee, check to see how you feel within. Often you'll find that at your heart there's a background buzz of irritation, so even though you say, "Yes, OK," you don't mean it; selfish motivation makes you insincere. Since you don't have a mind dedicated to others, even though you bring the person their tea, you're unhappy about having to do it; you do it begrudgingly.

If your mind were dedicated, you'd be happy to serve others. You wouldn't be psychologically bothered. You'd bring the tea or coffee joyfully, seeing even this small act as worthwhile, as a step on the path to liberation. It's not that the tea or coffee is so good; it's your sincere motivation, wanting to help others, that gives you much pleasure to serve them and makes you happy.

This is simple human psychology, not something religious or fabricated. It's the psychological effect of dedication to others.

Actually, we know all this from our own life experiences. Trouble between wife and husband, husband and wife, boyfriend and girlfriend and girlfriend and boyfriend... all these things come from the selfish mind. You know—if you're selfish you have trouble in your relationships.

And it's not a question of intelligence: "Oh, I'm intelligent, I have to get angry." If you check more deeply you'll see it's totally self-cherishing and attachment that are involved.

If the mind is dedicated, a wife is totally dedicated to helping her husband and a husband is totally dedicated to helping his wife. If you have the attitude, "I want to help you" rather than "I want you to help me," you'll have no trouble.

Look at the unconditional loving kindness a mother has for her only son. Even if he does stupid things, she still thinks he's good; she thinks, "He's so cute—look at what he does." Actually, what he does is stupid, but the reason it gives his mother pleasure is because she sees him in such a positive light and has so much love for him that she wants everything he does to be good and projects good onto even the stupid things he does. If somebody else were to do the same things she wouldn't like them at all. It's all to do with her motivation. You check up—I'm sure my example is apt.

You can see how different mental attitudes affect people's behavior and the way they interpret things. If you actualize bodhicitta meditation—train your mind in totally dedicating yourself to other sentient beings—nobody will trouble you. It's true; I'm not joking. Nobody will make trouble for you. And you will see others as beautiful; nothing will appear ugly or make you uptight. The reason you get uptight at the moment is because your schizophrenic, neurotic mind projects negativity onto objects.

You'll see that both Buddhism and Christianity talk about heaven and hell, but the connotations are quite different. Buddhism holds that there is no such heavenly place externally existent, but when an individual's mind has developed and completely released all ordinary conceptualizations of the I, the ego, then whatever that person perceives—the whole earth, all human beings—becomes transcendentally beautiful; for that person, that view is heaven.

You can understand that, can't you? I'm talking in psychological terms. You don't have to necessarily believe that heaven or hell are out there waiting for you, but you can easily understand how the polluted projections of ordinary mundane thought make you miserable and through releasing such conceptualizations you can develop a healthy mind and perceive a perfect view. It's so logical;

I'm talking about this in the logical sense, not in some higher metaphysical way.

It's incredible, really: if you put the things you learn into action, if you put your meditation into practice, everything you perceive in your entire life enhances your wisdom; everything that appears to you increases your understanding. If you don't put what you learn into action, even if Jesus or Lord Buddha were to manifest before you right now and give you teachings, it wouldn't help that much. Just because Jesus and Lord Buddha are high beings doesn't mean your mind would automatically open in their presence. No—you have to develop it yourself. That's why Lord Buddha said that it's your own positive actions that lead you to enlightenment and your own negative actions that bring you down.

Because of their scientific education and understanding of progressive evolution, Westerners often find it difficult to accept that a human being can become an animal. They think such regression to be impossible. Actually, it's possible. As I said before, the sick mind can manifest at the physical level; this is the same thing. It doesn't matter that you look like a human being—your mind can degenerate such that you behave worse than an animal. The mental energy generated in that way can later transform at the physical level and come to occupy an animal body. That's possible.

But don't think that this means your human body somehow changes into an animal body. I'm not saying that. When your consciousness separates from your present human body, since it contains the energy of the animal mind, that mental energy transforms into an animal body.

However, right action and wrong action are determined by right thought and wrong thought: right wisdom leads to right actions; wrong conceptions lead to wrong actions.

If we put the energy of the human body, speech and mind in the right direction, it is so powerful. The problem is that our life has no direction and that's why our energy is fragmented. Check up on how your life is right now—does it have direction? If not, you're wasting all the energy of your body, speech and mind.

Therefore you need the discriminating knowledge-wisdom to distinguish between right and wrong. In order to develop that, you have to understand your mind and know how positive and negative minds arise. Since all actions arise from the mind, without checking your mind, how can you determine the nature of your actions?

Anyway, it is very useful to seek the right view, the ultimate reality of your nature, through meditation. And you also need to understand your relative nature, which is extremely uncontrolled, ignorant of reality, full of wrong conceptions, and the source of all frustration and suffering. Once you do, you should then extend that understanding to all universal living beings, even the insects around you now. Meditate, right now, understanding that all living beings in the universe, not just the beings in your immediate vicinity, are in the same situation as you are—their relative nature intoxicated by attachment—and generate much love and compassion for them all.

Guided meditation

Seeing that you and all other universal living beings are in exactly the same situation, ask yourself, "How can I best help others?"

Check: is giving them bread, candy or chocolate the best way to help? That's ridiculous, isn't it? That's an insufficient way of helping because living beings' problems with their uncontrolled mind do not come from a lack of bread; their problems derive from a lack of knowledge-wisdom—not understanding what they are or how they exist, relatively or absolutely.

It doesn't matter whether one person is wealthy, another is poor, one is beautiful, another ugly or one is dancing, another is not—in fact, all beings are equal in experiencing suffering caused by false conceptions. They're equally the same in this: king, queen and pauper. As long as misconceptions and the polluted conceptualization of I, ego, rule their mind, they're equally the same. Eastern or Western, there's no difference; it doesn't matter. They're all equally the same: they all want happiness and don't want suffering. But because their actions are driven by misconception, even though all they want is happiness, all they get is suffering. So it's misconceptions that are the biggest obstacle to freedom and inner joy.

Also think: these misconceptions are just temporary obstacles—momentary, transient. It's possible for all beings to totally transcend these obstacles and reach the everlasting peaceful inner freedom of liberation.

Now visualize Lord Buddha. Actually, what is Buddha? Buddha is universal compassion and omniscient knowledge-wisdom, which is in the nature of everlasting peace and joy. So visualize that that wisdom mind manifests in front of you as the radiant light body of Lord Buddha. If you can't visualize Lord Buddha you can just see me here in front of you. From the crown of the head of Lord Buddha (or Lama Yeshe), a powerful stream of radiant white light emanates, enters the crown of your head and passes down your central channel like an extremely strong waterfall into your heart. This purifies all the impurities of your body's nervous system.

Then, from Lord Buddha's (or Lama Yeshe's) throat, a powerful beam of radiant red light emanates and enters your throat, purifying all your impurities of speech, such as telling lies and creating disunity between people.

Then, from Lord Buddha's (or Lama Yeshe's) heart, a powerful beam of radiant blue light emanates and enters your heart, filling it with blissful, joyful energy and purifying all your false conceptions. Your entire bodily nervous system and mind are completely filled with blissful radiant light.

Concentrate on feeling the unity of you and these lights that have entered you.

Dedication

Thank you very much. Now dedicate the merit of having done this meditation. What does that mean? Whatever we do, there's some kind of mental energy generated. Even though we don't see this at the physical level, it's there. Merit is the kind of energy generated by positive actions, such as the meditation we just did. So instead of thinking, "Oh, I just meditated; how good I am," and building our ego, we should direct our positive energy to the benefit of others. That is very useful.

We can't be certain of how we're going to be—sometimes we're up, sometimes we're down. And sometimes we get angry and anger destroys our positive energy, our merit. That's like spending time cleaning a room and when you're finished throwing dirt all over it. We meditate, making our mind clean, clean, clean, and then we get angry and foul it all up again.

So dedicating our merit protects it from destruction by anger and in that way we don't waste our energy. Dedication is also useful in that our meditation becomes not for pleasing our ego but for benefiting others and bringing us to enlightenment, or inner freedom. Actually, that should be our only purpose for meditating; we should not be doing it for pride: "I'm that, this, this, this." Being somebody is not important.

[Lama chants the dedication prayer: *Ge-wa di-yi....*[7]]

Actually, it's not necessary to chant a prayer; a prayer is not the words. You have to know that. We use words when we pray but the actual prayer is not the words. In fact, prayer is in the mind.

Dedication is a form of psychological treatment. Many times, after we have done something religious or meditated—or even after some mundane activity—we feel proud: "I did this, I did that." We're so proud of what we did.

---

[7] Due to the merits of these virtuous actions
May I quickly attain the state of a guru-buddha
And lead all living beings without exception
Into that enlightened state.

There's no reason to be proud. Pride is a symptom of the sick mind. Therefore, instead of feeling proud, we should dedicate everything we do to the benefit of other sentient beings, to bring them into everlasting peaceful enlightenment. If we do that, then psychologically, we won't feel proud; there won't be that strong feeling of "*I* did something."

For example, say a husband works and his wife stays home. When he comes home he can feel resentful: "I'm so tired. I worked hard all day; all you did was stay home and do nothing." He puts on a big show that he did this tremendous job but actually, there's no reason for him to show off. Going to work and doing his job is his duty.

It's the same thing when we meditate; there's no reason to show off to others: "Oh, I just did this great thing." Just totally dedicate your actions to others as much as possible. Then there's no sick reaction of pride. Otherwise, we do these things and all we get is more mental illness.

Dedication is something practical we can do for others; it's not just some empty Tibetan custom.

··· 5 ···

The Importance of Motivation

B EFORE LISTENING to this teaching you need to cultivate a
pure motivation, because the action of listening to teachings
has to be different from your usual life activities. If your listening
to teachings—an action that you feel is special compared to what
you usually do—is no different from or higher than your regular
daily activities, such as eating, drinking, sleeping and so forth, then
this particular action, listening to teachings, is actually not special,
higher or holy.

The actual antidote to suffering

As I mentioned briefly before, the practice of religion, spirituality or
Dharma—whatever you call it—has to be a method that completely
destroys all suffering, a method that can bring about the complete
cessation of suffering, and not just temporarily. For example, the
simple, everyday sufferings that people and even animals recognize
as suffering—fever, headaches, other kinds of pain—can be temporarily stopped by even external things, such as medicine, without
the need of Dharma, or religion. So, if that were all we could do,
there'd be no purpose for religion to exist.

However, religious activity should go to completely ceasing the continuity of suffering, and that depends upon completely eradicating the root of all the billions of sufferings that exist—ignorance and all the other delusions that spring from the root of ignorance.

So true peace—everlasting happiness, real freedom—is received whenever we completely cease the root of suffering: ignorance and the other delusions. In other words, cessation of ignorance, attachment and anger is real freedom, true peace—the peace that never changes; the peace that once received can never change, is everlasting.

Why is it impossible for true peace to change, or disappear? Why can we never come down from that? Why is it impossible to fall from true peace back into suffering? That is because once we've attained everlasting happiness there's no longer any cause to make us once again get caught up in the bondage of suffering.

Why is that we're happy one day but sad the next? For instance, one day we receive some good news or find ourselves in a beautiful, desirable place or receive a nice gift or meet a special friend and as a result feel extremely happy—so happy that we almost don't know what to do with ourselves, so happy that we can even do crazy things that endanger our life—but then after a while, a day or two, that happiness we received by meeting certain conditions goes away, doesn't last. When we meet a desirable friend, eat delicious food or put on luxurious clothes, at first we feel happy but that happiness does not last. Why does the initial happiness we experienced by meeting certain conditions not last? What makes it change? Why do we get tired of sense pleasures instead of continually experiencing pleasure, feeling happiness?

That is mainly because our mind is not free from the root of suffering. Why? Since our mind is under the control of ignorance, attachment, anger and the other delusions, the pleasure we receive by meeting certain conditions changes, does not last. However, from the Dharma point of view, the feelings that we identify as pleasure are considered to be merely samsaric pleasure—as certain heavy temporal sufferings decrease, just that decrease itself is labeled pleasure.

For example, if you are carrying a heavy load on your back and after some time get tired, that's a type of suffering. Thinking that the heavy load is causing you to feel tired, you put it down. At that moment you feel light and the suffering you were experiencing diminishes a little; it doesn't completely go away, but it decreases a bit. So, we label that small decrease of suffering "pleasure"; we call that feeling of less suffering that the uncontrolled mind and body experience "pleasure." Also, although that pleasure is felt quite strongly at first, it doesn't last.

Similarly, a person who has been sitting cross-legged for a while starts to get pain in his back and legs and thinks it might be better to stand up. When he stands up, because of that change in the conditions, the pain he felt while sitting diminishes and he thinks, "This is pleasure." But, thinking that standing is pleasure, if he tries to remain standing all day and night, or even for just an hour or two, he gets tired. Again, the pleasure he felt at first does not last;

it changes. At first, sitting became a problem; he stood to relieve it; but then standing became a problem so he thought that he should sit down again to relieve it.

So, these are just a couple of examples, but our life is full of similar ones. We always try to change. "Maybe this is better," so we try something else. But then we get bored with that; another problem arises. Then again we change, "maybe that is better." We change people: "Maybe I'll like him, maybe I'll like her, maybe I should live with him, maybe I should marry her...." We're always changing food, clothing and other objects of the senses.

All this shows clearly that there's something wrong with our body and mind, that our body and mind are the root of our suffering.

So what is the mistake we make? Why is it that no matter how much we enjoy the pleasures of the senses, there's no end? No matter how much we experience sense pleasures, there's nothing to complete, nothing to finish. We experience one thing, it finishes; we try something else, that finishes too; we have another experience, that doesn't last either.... We try and try again and that's what we've been doing from the time we were born until now. And not just in this life—since beginningless time, we've been experiencing one temporal, samsaric pleasure after another, chasing experiences that are not true pleasure and always change and finish, and we're still not satisfied. Furthermore, the effort that we've had to put in to gain these pleasures of the senses, again and again, by trying different methods, this too has not ended since beginningless time; this work is also unfinished.

So what causes these pleasures not to last and for us to have to seek one pleasure after another, continually exerting effort and experiencing the suffering and misery of diminishing pleasures? Why does this happen? The reason we are in this situation of dissatisfaction and suffering is that our mind is under the control of delusion and karma.

What is karma? Karma is action produced by delusion. Because our mind is under the control of delusion and karma, our body is also under the control of delusion and karma; as long as our mind is not free, our body is not free either. Therefore, real freedom is the mind's being completely free of delusion and karma, and when the mind is free from the bondage of delusion and karma, the body, which is the house of the mind, also becomes free from the bondage of delusion and karma. When the body and mind are both free from suffering, the bondage of delusion and karma, at that time, whatever different bodies the mind takes, those bodies don't experience sufferings such as rebirth, illness, pain, aging and death.

For instance, at the moment, whenever we meet an undesirable object of the senses, we suffer: when it's raining or snowing and we don't have enough clothes or a heater, we feel cold and suffer; when it's hot and we don't have air conditioning, again, we suffer. It's like this with our other senses. With respect to our sense of taste, when we encounter food that we don't like, we're unhappy and suffer. Similarly with our sense of hearing: when we hear bad news or some other sound we don't like, again, we're unhappy and suffer. It's the same with our senses of sight and touch: whenever they contact undesirable objects, we suffer. When we sit for a few minutes with crossed legs, they hurt. So all the time, continuously, we're experiencing one problem or another. All the time, as we meet the different sense objects, we experience all kinds of different problems.

Just look at our body: there's not one tiny part—not even the size of a pore or the tip of a needle—that doesn't feel pain, that's not in the nature of suffering. Therefore, when thorns, needles and the like touch our body, even though they're so fine-pointed, so small, we feel great pain. Even though the external conditions are so tiny, virtually nothing, the pain we experience is incredible.

This clearly proves that our mind is not free, that it's living in suffering, and because of that, our body is also living in suffering. Why are our mind and body living in suffering? Because they are bound by delusion and karma, controlled by delusion and karma.

When we attain nirvana—complete freedom, cessation of the bondage of delusion and karma—no sense object can cause us problems or unhappiness. Even if thousands of atomic bombs were to be dropped, they could not bring unhappiness or suffering to any living being whose mind had reached that level, complete freedom from delusion and karma.

The teachings divide the sufferings of beings living under the control of delusion and karma into three: pervasive, or all-embracing, suffering; changeable suffering, which means temporal pleasures, which are not real, true happiness; and suffering of suffering, the heavy, gross sufferings that even animals recognize as suffering.

Why is pervasive suffering called pervasive, or all-embracing? It's because not only are our feeling, discrimination, compositional factors and consciousness under the control of delusion and karma but also there's not one single tiny part of our body that's free of delusion and karma.[8] Since our whole body is under the control of delusion and karma, that type of suffering is called pervasive. Because our whole body is under the control of delusion and karma, we find problems everywhere. As long as our mind and body are living in pervasive suffering, controlled by delusion and karma, all the other different types of suffering arise constantly, continuously, one after the other.

So basically, it's like this: all suffering results from impure, or negative, actions; impure, negative actions are created by the impure, or negative, mind, that is, the delusions. All happiness results from virtuous, or positive, actions; virtuous, positive actions are created by the virtuous, or positive, mind. So the evolution of happiness, where happiness comes from, and the evolution of suffering, where suffering comes from, are completely different. Happiness and suffering arise in completely different ways.

Since we desire happiness and do not desire suffering but are living in suffering, it is extremely important for us to understand this evolution. But mere intellectual understanding is not sufficient. To really stop the continuous experience of suffering—in the present and into the future—and to continuously experience happiness, intellectual understanding is not enough. We have to act; we have to make an effort.

Seeing other people, meditators, with a pure mind creating good actions that result in happiness and believing and expecting that

[8] See note 6, page 62.

through their effort we can also experience happiness is mistaken. Thinking "I don't have to do anything; I can experience happiness, the good result created by other people's positive actions" is wrong. Without making an effort ourselves, without changing our mind, without making our mind virtuous, positive, and on that basis creating actions, there's no way we can experience any kind of happiness—temporary or everlasting. Without individual effort there's no way to experience any kind of happiness. This kind of misconception is like a hungry person expecting to feel full after his friends have eaten.

However, the main point I want to emphasize is that we have to act right now. If we do, if with wisdom we change our mind, make our motivation positive, virtuous, then even though our present action might be being created by the poisonous mind, the delusions, the cause of suffering, right away that present action becomes positive, virtuous. In other words, to use the Sanskrit term, it become good karma, which brings only happiness.

Generating the pure motivation of bodhicitta

But experiencing temporary happiness is not enough. We need to gain everlasting happiness, the complete cessation of all suffering. However, just one person, oneself, attaining everlasting happiness is also insufficient. There's a higher goal than individual liberation, the mere cessation of suffering. That goal, the highest goal, is enlightenment, the most sublime happiness: a state where all delusions have been completely purified, there's not a trace of dualistic mind, and one has gained all knowledge, all realizations, and nothing is missing.

Also, all sentient beings are experiencing continual suffering and have neither the wisdom nor the method to know how to escape from it. They don't know what is the cause of suffering, what is the cause of happiness or what real, everlasting happiness is. They have neither the wisdom to understand these things nor a method to practice; they have no path to follow.

Each of us needs to think like this: "All sentient beings have been extremely kind to me in the past, they're kind to me in the present, and they will continuously be kind to me in the future. They are the field from which I receive all my pleasure—past, present and future; all my perfections come from other sentient beings. Therefore I must attain enlightenment. Seeking everlasting happiness for myself alone, not caring about other sentient beings, giving them up, having no concern for their welfare, is selfish. Therefore, I must attain enlightenment, the most sublime happiness, in order to release all the sentient beings from suffering and lead them on the path to enlightenment by myself alone, as this is my responsibility."

So irrespective of the motivation or thought you had before, at this moment, right now, strongly dedicate your action of listening to these teachings to the benefit of other sentient beings, to their happiness. Feel deeply in your mind, "I am going to listen to the teachings in order to gain the most sublime happiness of enlightenment for the sake of all sentient beings," feeling in your mind that you are the servant of all sentient beings, feeling in your mind that releasing all sentient beings from suffering and leading them on the path to enlightenment is your principal goal, the most important thing you can do. "For that reason, I am going to listen the teachings."

Today's subject is a Mahayana teaching that explains the graduated path to enlightenment, the path that all past, present and future buddhas have traversed on their way to enlightenment; the path that the entire lineage of followers of Guru Shakyamuni Buddha, all those previous, fully-realized Indian and Tibetan pandits, all the high lamas, have also traveled to enlightenment. As all these great masters gained all the realizations of the path to enlightenment completely, this is a teaching that has been handed down with their full experiences and is not just words.

To attain enlightenment for the sake of other sentient beings quickly, to attain this most sublime happiness, this completely pure state, complete knowledge, depends upon receiving the principal cause of enlightenment, bodhicitta. Bodhicitta is a realization, the intuitive determination to attain enlightenment for the sake of all other sentient beings. The pure thought of bodhicitta is never concerned for oneself but instead is always concerned for other sentient beings, how to free them from suffering and lead them along the path to enlightenment. Bodhicitta is always thinking of how to benefit other sentient beings in the wisest, most extensive way. It is a realization concerned only for other sentient beings, giving up oneself and taking most care of others.

The pure thought of bodhicitta is the complete opposite of the self-cherishing thought, which is only concerned of oneself, which always thinks about how to take care of oneself, which doesn't care about other sentient beings, which causes other sentient beings to suffer. Self-cherishing is a thought that doesn't care for other sentient beings but for only oneself; self-cherishing thinks, "Only I am important; I am the most important of all." Bodhicitta is the complete opposite of this.

So what is the most important thing to do in order to receive enlightenment quickly? Try to receive the pure thought of bodhicitta. But receiving the pure thought of bodhicitta depends on receiving preliminary realizations, such as compassion.

Just having partial compassion, compassion for your friends but not other living beings, compassion for desirable objects, living beings that look beautiful to you, but not those who appear ugly or violent is not enough. Anyway, what we normally believe to be compassion is usually not compassion but attachment; it's based on attachment. The compassion we need to receive bodhicitta is impartial compassion, compassion for all sentient beings excluding not even one; equal compassion for all sentient beings, not just the suffering humans and animals we see with our eyes. We have to have compassion for all suffering sentient beings.

At our present level of mind there are many sentient beings that we can see but there are also many different types of sentient being that we can't see. For example, ours is not the only universe; there are huge numbers of universes, many different worlds, that we can't see, and in many of those live other sentient beings. Even today scientists are discovering and describing new galaxies that they didn't believe existed before. In those galaxies are planets upon which live different sentient beings leading different lives that we don't see because of our limited intelligence, limited power of mind. Even on earth there are beings that we don't see, beings that we will see when our mind is ready, when it has the power to see them, in the same way we presently see humans and certain kinds of animal. So there are many different types of sentient being and they live in six different realms. In order to generate compassion for all sentient beings it's necessary to understand the different sufferings that sentient beings experience.

···6···

The Lives of Others

I T'S EASY TO KNOW about the animal realm because we can see many types of animal and their suffering is easy to understand. But in addition to humans and animals there are many other types of living being, such as *pretas*.[9]

Hungry ghosts

Preta is a Sanskrit term and is sometimes translated as *hungry ghost*. Their most common sufferings are those of hunger and thirst, which is a result of their karma, actions they created in previous lives. They can't find even a small drop of water for eons and their lives pass with the constant suffering of thirst. And no matter how much they search, they also can't find even a tiny bit of food and experience great hunger. And they have many other kinds of suffering.

First, even though they see a beautiful lake of water they are prevented from reaching it by fearful, karmically created protectors—mental visions, manifestations of the pretas' previously created

---

[9] See *The Great Treatise* or *Liberation in the Palm of Your Hand* for details of the different kinds of being in samsara.

karma. These protectors have terrifying bodies such as those we might see in a nightmare, which is also karmically created. So even though the pretas think they've finally found some water, they are unable to reach it.

Some pretas don't encounter protectors but when they reach the place where they saw the water from afar it either disappears completely or turns into a filthy pond of pus, blood and excrement that even pretas can't ingest.

Even if this doesn't happen and a preta manages to get a drop of water into its mouth, because of its previous karma, actions created out of delusion, its mouth becomes toxic and the water just disappears. Also because of their karma, many pretas' mouths are very tiny, like the eye of a small needle, so it's even hard to get anything into their mouth let alone their stomach. And even should some food or drink reach a preta's stomach, it bursts into flames, like oil thrown on a fire, and burns it badly. So pretas have much suffering of not finding food or drink or encountering these various obstacles and are always hungry and thirsty as a result. And their bodies look awful—very ugly, shriveled and dry, with very thin arms and legs, tiny necks and a huge, distended stomach.

Many hungry ghosts, such as those who live on smell and others who search for food in various places, live in the human realm. Yogis—advanced meditators who have achieved higher realizations and have certain mental powers—and even ordinary people who have the right karma have told many stories of preta sightings at different locations on this earth.

These days we see pictures of starving children in Africa, for example, where their abdomens are very distended, their limbs very skinny and their skin discolored and dry. Although their suffering is very minor compared to that of the pretas, we can see it as a reflection of what hungry ghosts must endure. Of course, the pretas undergo many other sufferings as well.

Hell beings

Then there are the hell (Skt: *narak*) beings. As a result of negative karma created out of delusion, they have to experience extremes of heat and cold, such as constant and repeated incineration on red-hot iron ground. Hell realm beings don't need parents like we do; they are just born there spontaneously. For example, if a person creates the cause to be reborn in hell in his next life, right after he dies, because the potential to be reborn there is ripe, his mind goes straight to the intermediate state of a hell being and then, without needing parents, spontaneously gets reborn in that realm, in a way similar to that in which we go into a dream after we fall sleep. But unlike the hell described in the Christian bible, this is not a permanent state; nevertheless, the person has to remain in great suffering there for a long time, until the result of his previous actions finishes. When the karmically determined time for suffering in that realm is up, that being's mind takes birth in another realm, according to its previous karma. So it all depends on karma, but it's not as if once you're reborn in hell you have to stay there forever.

The beings in the hot hells have to endure a wide variety of dreadful sufferings. They have to live on red-hot, burning iron ground while fearful-looking, karmically created protectors chop them into pieces, or they spontaneously find themselves trapped in an oven-like red-hot burning house with no doors or windows and have to experience terrible suffering until the karma created by their previous actions is expended. Or they can find themselves in a huge pot of boiling water, cooked like rice. And when these sufferings finish the beings are suddenly born on ground covered with swords such that they cannot step anywhere without cutting their feet and legs.

When we dream of being in a certain country or a beautiful house or a suffering, dirty place, it's not that somebody has created these places for us; it's a karmic vision of our own mind. It's the same with the experiences of the hell beings: the red-hot ground, the windowless houses, the pots of boiling water and so forth are all karmic visions that are the result of actions created out of delusion in previous lives.

So the main hell sufferings are those of hot and cold; in addition to the hot sufferings briefly mentioned above, there are also unbearable sufferings in the cold hells. After life as an animal or a human, a being with the karma to be reborn in a cold hell dies and is suddenly reborn in a completely dark place full of ice mountains with a body that becomes oneness with ice, like meat in a freezer. There is incredible suffering: the body cannot move because it's stuck within ice crevices or underneath the ice mountains, it splits and develops thousands of cracks, turns red and blue and becomes infested with many insects that eat it from the inside, while many other karmically created sentient beings, such as certain type of birds with very long beaks, come to peck and eat the body from the outside. So the suffering is incredible.

However, whatever the suffering place, all these conditions have not been made or arranged by others; they are creations of that being's mind. What kind of mind is it that creates such suffering places in which beings get born there and suffer, then die and again the place changes and becomes another suffering place? That kind of mind is the negative, non-virtuous mind—the mind of ignorance, anger, attachment, pride, jealousy and other delusions; such suffering places are created by the negative mind.

The animal realm

Then there are the animal sufferings. Animals that are kept by people can have slightly better lives, depending on people who take care of them; such animals are generally a little more fortunate than those who live in the wild. Animals who live in oceans and forests experience much suffering, the most common being that of being eaten by others.

Even tiny creatures that are hard to see with the naked eye have other insects that eat them, just as larger animals such as elephants and tigers or those in the ocean, like whales and sharks, are attacked and eaten by others. And in earlier times there were even huger animals that lived on land and in the sea that were attacked and eaten by smaller ones getting into their bodies and eating them from within. So even big animals can be killed by small ones; every animal has its natural enemy that can kill and eat it.

On top of that they are also susceptible to the general sufferings of hunger and thirst and heat and cold. In addition, each animal has its own specific suffering according to the kind of animal it is.

So all those sentient beings—animals, pretas and hell beings— are not free like humans are; human beings have much more freedom than do the sentient beings in the lower realms. The animals that live in forests or in the ocean are always afraid—they don't enjoy human freedoms and don't have the methods to enjoy life as humans can. That's why the lower realms, the realms of the animals, pretas and hell beings, are called evil destinies [Tib: *ngän-song*]; those are the suffering realms.

The upper realms

With respect to the upper realms, there's not only the human realm; there are also the realms of the *suras* and *asuras*, whose enjoyments are much greater than those of humans. Their abodes, food, clothing and everything else are much richer, more pure than those of humans; beyond compare, in fact. However, those beings' minds are so dominated by attachment to sense objects that they don't have a chance of seeing suffering the way humans do.

There are all kinds of human being: we can see some who have much enjoyment, others who have much suffering. Suras don't have the opportunity that we do to develop the wisdom understanding the nature of suffering because they are surrounded by fabulous enjoyments and possessions, have many hundreds of friends and experience very few problems in their lives. So because of their great attachment and inability to see suffering or realize its nature, they have no chance to practice Dharma.

Asuras' lives are in many ways similar to those of the suras in that they enjoy the same riches, but they are more mischievous in nature and their minds are more foolish than those of the suras.

There are also other types of sura, or long-life god, in the formless realm, where again, they don't have a chance to practice Dharma because they're unconscious from birth to death.

So in the three lower realms and in the sura and asura realms the beings have no chance to practice Dharma. It's only the human realm that gives us that chance, where it's relatively easy to practice Dharma, receive the whole path and quickly attain enlightenment.

The perfect human rebirth

However, just being born human isn't enough; one needs a perfect human rebirth, with eight freedoms and ten richnesses, which is extremely difficult to find but once found is highly meaningful. For instance, one needs to encounter the teachings, possess perfect physical senses and follow the path to enlightenment.

Therefore our present human rebirth is highly meaningful, not meaningless, because we have met the Dharma, through which we can completely free ourselves from the bondage of suffering and receive everlasting happiness. With this perfect human rebirth we can also attain enlightenment—in this lifetime or the next, or in a lifetime beyond those, and then release other sentient beings from all their life problems and suffering and also lead them into the most sublime happiness of enlightenment.

Since this present human rebirth is so highly meaningful in these various ways, not to use it to fulfill its purpose and achieve these higher goals is a huge waste, the greatest possible loss. Having met the teachings and a spiritual friend to explain them and then not to practice will make it extremely difficult, virtually impossible, to meet the teachings and a teacher again in future lives. Therefore, while we have this chance, we should try as hard as we can to get closer and closer to enlightenment, day by day, month by month, year by year, by following the teachings.

The main path, the principal method, that brings us closer to enlightenment is cultivating bodhicitta, training our mind in the pure thought of bodhicitta as much as possible. In order to receive the highly beneficial thought of enlightenment, bodhicitta, we need the prerequisite realization of impartial compassion—equal compassion for all sentient beings. That depends on seeing all sentient beings in beauty, and that depends on understanding how extremely kind all sentient beings have been to us.

So what we therefore need to do is to equalize the discriminating thought that differentiates between sentient beings as enemy and friend. When we identify certain beings as "enemy," hatred arises and we create negative karma by fighting with them. And when we identify others as "friend," the delusion of attachment arises and by acting under its control we again create more negative karma.

So to see all sentient beings equally in beauty, just as a mother sees her only child—as so beautiful, as most dear, as her own heart—we need to realize their kindness, and before that we need to equalize the thought that discriminates others as friends and enemies. If we don't, we'll always see others in that way and as a result create negative actions out of attachment and hatred.

The equilibrium meditation

At present, the only beings we see in beauty are our friends. Since we don't see those who harm us in the same way, we don't have love for them. As long as we feel like that, there's no way we can receive bodhicitta and obviously no way we can attain enlightenment. Therefore we must first equalize the thought that sees other sentient beings as friend or enemy, but we don't do that by running ads in the paper or on TV asking, "Please everybody, equalize yourselves as friend and enemy"! Instead, what we do is a very important meditation called the equilibrium meditation.[10]

The equilibrium meditation is especially important at times like this, when there's much violence and unhappiness in the world and people so strongly differentiate between friends and enemies and then act upon these distinctions to get rid of enemies by denouncing, harming and destroying them. This is no way to put an end to enemies. In fact, it only creates more. The more enemies you

---

[10] See Lama Yeshe's *Ego, Attachment and Liberation*, Appendix 1, free from the LYWA, for Lama Zopa Rinpoche's equilibrium meditation. Also on line at www. LamaYeshe.com.

destroy, the more you make. Such methods simply ensure an end-less supply of enemies.

However, what we believe to be friends and enemies are mere conceptions. We just *think* friends are real friends and enemies are real enemies. They are just projections of our own mind. There is no such thing as a real friend or a real enemy out there, existing with-out depending on our mind.

The thing is, the way we believe others to be absolute friends and absolute enemies is completely wrong; our view is totally mistaken. The evolution of such discriminations is as follows.

First of all, I am attached to myself, my own "I," and my body, my possessions and my happiness. Then, when somebody disturbs my happiness or my possessions, I get angry and discriminate that per-son as an enemy. On the other hand, when somebody supports my happiness, attachment arises and I call that person a friend. Further-more, I believe that person to be an absolute, real friend—qualities that exist nowhere.

But that's how friends and enemies arise. When somebody gives me something, benefits me a little or helps my happiness, I see that person as a friend; when somebody harms my pleasure, my anger sees that person as an enemy. I give people different names accord-ing to their actions—friend and enemy do not come from their own side; there's no such thing. First I project a person as a friend or enemy and then I believe it to be real, coming from that person's side.

So the equilibrium meditation, in which we equalize others as friend and enemy, is practiced on the basis of understanding how we discriminate others according to their actions of helping or harming.

Begin by visualizing all sentient beings, as infinite as space, surrounding you. Your mother is to your left, your father to your right; your worst enemy is in front of you, your most cherished friend is behind.

Now look at your enemy in front of you and ask yourself why you dislike that person. See what reasons come up. Perhaps he beat, cheated, criticized or harmed you in some other way. Then look at your friend and think how that person also harmed you in the same way in the past. So, if that person harmed you in the past just as your present enemy did, why do you now consider that person a friend? See what reasons come up—it's because that person helped you in some way. Then think how your enemy also helped you in the same way in the past. So since they have both harmed and helped you in the past, why do you now consider one to be a friend and the other an enemy?

If you think that your enemy has harmed you more than your friend has, if that conception arises, if you see that in this life your enemy has harmed you more than your friend has, then remember that this life is just one in a beginningless continuity for all beings, including your enemy and friend, and that therefore this enemy has helped you numberless times in previous lives and this friend has harmed you numberless times in previous lives—so the reasons to discriminate one as friend and the other as enemy are equal. In other words, the enemy in front of you has harmed and helped you numberless times in previous lives and is therefore equal in having been enemy and friend. And the friend behind you has also helped and harmed you numberless times in previous lives and is therefore also equal in having been friend and enemy.

So the feeling you should get from applying the logic of this evolution to your present enemy and friend when you look at them is one of equanimity, as if you're looking at strangers: no attachment to your friend and no aversion to your enemy. When you see these two as equal, there's a feeling of peace in your mind. No violent thoughts, no uptightness, just a feeling of relaxation.

So after you have equalized enemy and friend, you do the same thing with your father and mother—equalize their being friend and enemy. Then, after you have equalized these four people, equalize all sentient beings as having equally helped and given harm numberless times from beginningless previous lifetimes until now. Therefore all sentient beings are exactly equal in having been friend and enemy. Then, whenever you get the strong feeling of equanimity with respect to all sentient beings, just concentrate on that; when your mind reaches that point, hold it for as long as you can.

There are many different ways to do this meditation but what I've just described is the very basic, simple technique of equalizing all sentient beings as friend and enemy. If you train your mind in this meditation—especially when you receive the realization—whenever somebody harms you or somebody praises you or gives you gifts and so forth, because you have equalized your discriminating thought, you don't discriminate such people as enemy or friend, you have a feeling of equanimity for all, no matter what they do to or for you. If somebody bothers you, disturbs your pleasure or possessions, the delusion of anger does not arise; if somebody praises you, the delusion of attachment does not arise. Your mind is constantly at peace.

No matter where you go, wherever you travel, even if you're with a group of cruel, violent people, your mind doesn't change; your mind is unaffected by the conditions. Therefore you don't create any more negative actions, don't make others unhappy or cause them suffering; you don't create any more negative karma. Therefore you don't have to experience the suffering results that are caused by delusion and negative karma; you avoid all the future life problems that come from such causes.

However, this meditation is extremely helpful in your quickly realizing bodhicitta and attaining enlightenment and is extremely important in helping bring peace to the world and to your family and relationships. Disharmony and fighting come from the discriminating thought that differentiates between enemies and friends: "She helped me; she's my friend. He hurt me; he's my enemy, I'm going to destroy him."

Therefore the practice of this meditation is extremely beneficial and as you practice it, you yourself become a psychiatrist, you yourself become a psychologist—and that's the best way to solve problems: to work within your own mind.

··· 7 ···

Rinpoche answers questions

IF YOU HAVE any questions, please ask.

Q. When we do the purifying breath meditation, do we start by exhaling our negativities and so forth in the form of black smoke or by inhaling the qualities of enlightenment in the form of white light?

Rinpoche. I think it's more comfortable if first you visualize that all your delusions and wrong conceptions leave in the form of smoke or fog as you breathe out. In other words, purifying first seems more comfortable to me. It's similar to when you want to put delicious food into a pot. If the pot is dirty you're not going to feel comfortable putting food into it; it's obviously much better if the pot is clean. So just as you first clean a pot before putting something into it, purify yourself before inhaling the enlightened qualities.

Sometimes when you do breathing meditation you don't have enough time to visualize because your breaths are too shallow. Therefore it might help you to concentrate if you inhale slowly and build up some air inside and then when you breathe out you can exhale more slowly and get a better visualization. This gives you time to make your concentration stronger and longer lasting.

Q. When I'm meditating on one topic my mind sometimes goes to other Dharma topics. Since they are still Dharma, are they considered to be distractions?

Rinpoche. Actually, when you're meditating on one topic and then think of others, you have to stop doing that. If, for example, you're analyzing the nature of the mind and trying to concentrate on that and then think of something else, something that's not the object of your meditation, that's definitely a distraction. When you're concentrating on the nature of the mind and other thoughts arise, you have to stop them.

However, there are certain levels of mind that you reach after realizing emptiness where in meditation you don't have thoughts that differentiate between subject and object as you do now. That doesn't mean you're unconscious; it doesn't mean that you have no thoughts whatsoever arising in your mind. It's not like you're asleep—there are certain stages of meditation in which the thought discriminating between subject and object stops, but in general it depends upon what meditation you practice. Not all meditation techniques are the same; there are different ways of meditating. Basically, all meditation is divided into analytical meditation and single-pointed concentration. In certain practices you use any thought that arises as the actual topic of meditation; whatever picture comes into your mind, instead of becoming a distraction it becomes your object of meditation.

Q. When the mind travels from life to life, what actually goes on and what is left behind? What propensities, such as memories or knowledge and wisdom, go into the next life?

Rinpoche. What actually goes on is the mind carrying the imprints that have been left upon it by actions of the body, speech and mind. Imprints are actions' latent potential; they're like seeds planted in the ground. So actions leave imprints on the mind and they are carried from life to life. That's why we see different children, even those of the same parents, having different levels of intelligence and different interests and abilities and so forth—it's because they have brought different propensities from previous lives.

For example, when people study Dharma, some find certain topics easier to understand than others. This is because they have studied and understood that topic well in previous lives. For instance, because of the imprints left on his or her mind, a person who has trained in the teachings on ultimate reality in previous lives can find it much easier to understand emptiness in this life than somebody who has not undergone such training. Those imprints come out in experience, like seeds planted in the ground sprout when the conditions are right. Some people might even be able to understand difficult teachings simply by reading them and not need a teacher to explain them; the understanding just comes from their mind.

In Tibet there were many high lamas who were reborn with Dharma knowledge in their mind as a result of their previous training. Even as children, they could read or recite prayers without being taught, explain teachings without studying them and so forth, not having lost their knowledge between death and rebirth.

Such people have more control and less pollution of ignorance in their mind than ordinary people, and since they are born with pre-existing knowledge they don't have much need of a teacher. Because they don't have the deep ignorance of ordinary people, they can remember their past life, despite the time interval and passage through their mother's birth canal, which cause ordinary, ignorant people to forget their previous life all together, let alone what they learnt during it. Also, rather than having the instinctual knowledge that incarnate lamas do, what comes naturally to ordinary people without being taught are anger, pride, jealousy, attachment and other delusions, which can manifest even in infancy.

Q. I thought Buddhism teaches that there's no permanent self, but from what you're saying it sounds like there's a permanent self or soul that doesn't stop at death but continues from life to life.

Rinpoche. It's true that since the continuity of mind has no beginning the continuity of the self has no beginning. After the death of our previous life, as the continuity of our mind continued into this life, so did the continuity of our self. The self, or I, does not cease at death; as the mind continues, the I continues—into the intermediate state and then into the next life. If the mind were to cease there'd be no way for the self to exist. But the mind never ceases; it always continues.

Q. So doesn't that mean that the self, or I, is self-existent?

Rinpoche. Oh, I see what you're asking. You're thinking that because, when I described the analytical meditation of checking the mind back into the mother's womb and then back into the previous life, I mentioned the continuity of the self, that it's permanent and even self-existent, and that that's contradictory because Dharma texts usually talk about non-self or no self. Well, the first thing to understand is what the words in the books actually mean. You have to go beyond the words and understand the reasons behind those words being used in the way that they are.

So, when you read no self, it can sound as if the self doesn't exist but that's not what it means; it does not mean that the self does not exist. If the teachings said that the self did not exist, there'd be no reason to practice Dharma or to meditate because if there were no self there'd be no person; no person experiencing suffering; no person in the bondage of suffering; no person to follow the path; no person to gain liberation, complete freedom from suffering; no person to attain enlightenment.

So if the Dharma were saying that there's no self, and therefore no person to meditate, what would be the need for meditation? The Dharma would be saying not to practice Dharma, not to meditate. But it's not like that.

There are many other teachings that talk about no form, no nose, no tongue, no five senses and so forth. However, even though the negative word "no" is used, what it means is that there's no *self-existent* I, no *self-existent* person, no *self-existent* sense or object. Also, when the Dharma teachings talk about non-self-existence, they are not saying that you don't exist while in fact you do. It's not like any of that.

When the Dharma teachings say something does not exist they are referring to something that we think is there but in reality is not;

something that we see, or view, to exist but does not exist as we conceive. We view objects of our senses—the things we see, hear and feel—as self-existent but we are not seeing their actual nature, their real nature.

For example, when we're watching TV, people act in a certain way and we respond emotionally as if those are real situations...as if we believed what we were looking at was true. Or when we're at the movies and there's a landslide on screen and we get scared and move in our seats as if trying to dodge it; as if there were actual danger. Actually, there's no reason to be frightened—it's just a movie, just a picture on the screen—but something in us believes it's real so we try to move out of the way. This is an example of the way we view objects of the senses. The sliding mountain, the huge wave coming toward us in the theater isn't really there...there are no rocks or water on the screen, there's no danger, but we still react is if there were. What appears to us, what we believe, does not exist at all; what we view as self-existent, independent, is completely opposite to the reality of the nature of the object.

Q. How can the study of astrology help us in our Dharma practice?
Rinpoche. It depends on how you study astrology. If you study in a Dharma way, it becomes Dharma; if you don't, it doesn't. If your study helps you subdue or control your delusions rather than strengthen them, it becomes Dharma. So that depends mainly on your motivation; it's your motivation that determines whether your actions become beneficial or not. In other words, it depends on your mind.

Q. What causes bodhicitta to arise?

Rinpoche. Drink as much coffee as possible…I'm joking! One of the most important things you need to have in order to develop bodhicitta is renunciation based on an understanding of the nature of samsara and its shortcomings—impermanence, death and the three levels of suffering, which I was talking about before. If you understand how your own samsara is in the nature of suffering and have renunciation of that, then because of your deep understanding of the evolution of your own samsara, you can easily understand other sentient beings' suffering; how others are trapped in samsara and suffering.

For example, if you've had a really bad toothache, when you see somebody else with a toothache, based on a recognition of your own suffering, you know how the other person feels, how unbearable that pain is; you can feel it. In the same way, when you understand the shortcomings of your own samsara you can easily understand the suffering of others. Then that, coupled with an understanding of how other sentient beings have been extremely kind in the past, present and future, how precious they are, like the parents who took care of us—gave us our body, food, clothing, education, everything—gives rise to great love and compassion, the wish to help them to be happy and free of suffering. And on that basis, bodhicitta arises. So just like a fruit tree grows in dependence upon water and earth, bodhicitta grows by depending on love and compassion, which themselves depend upon an understanding of impermanence, death, the shortcomings of samsara, the sufferings others are experiencing in samsara and their great kindness.

Q. Are statues and ritual necessary to practice Dharma, and if not, why have them?

Rinpoche. Just because some atoms are collected together into a particular shape or somebody is doing a certain chant doesn't make that object or ritual Dharma. Something additional is required. Likewise with certain actions—actions themselves aren't Dharma; the performance of an action is not enough to make it Dharma. Like the example of astrology above, it mainly depends upon the person's mind, upon the motivation with which the action is done.

If the mind of the person meditating, performing a ritual or making offerings is Dharma, one with the Dharma, the action becomes Dharma; it depends upon the person's motivation, the mind that produces the action.

Another way of saying this, of making it clear, is to say that if an action is done with a mind that renounces the three poisonous delusions—ignorance, attachment and hatred—if an action is done with the mind that opposes the delusions, that action becomes Dharma; it's a pure action. Such actions don't have to look religious either. Sweeping the floor, cooking food, doing business or working in a hospital—in fact any kind of action—can become Dharma. Even telling lies or other actions that appear negative can in fact be positive, Dharma actions. As long as such actions are done with the wisdom understanding karma and the knowledge that they will definitely benefit others, bring good results to oneself and others, done with a mind that is one with the Dharma, renouncing attachment to the pleasures of just this life, renouncing the mind that has no concern for the benefit of future lives and is totally focused on just this one, then such actions are Dharma. Even though they look like worldly, everyday actions—like, partying, drinking, watching movies—or even negative—like telling lies and so forth—if they are done with the wisdom that truly knows they are of benefit to oneself and others, the mind renouncing attachment, then they definitely become Dharma, pure and free of danger.

Now, if you want to know if the specific statues that have been arranged here on the altar are necessary for the practice of Dharma, you'll have to ask whoever put them here what his or her motivation was!

Q. If I have, for example, intestinal worms, is it better for me not to kill them and die myself or to take medicine and kill them?

Rinpoche. If the worms aren't that dangerous to your health, it's better to give them as little harm as possible but it really depends on the individual. If they are a threat to your life and you have a very strong mind, great compassion for those sentient beings, wanting them to be free from suffering as quickly as possible, and no self-cherishing thought, thinking, "My happiness is more important then theirs," and it's more beneficial that you continue to live, then perhaps it's better that you take the medicine. However, it's very hard for your mind to be really pure in this way.

Q. Can you please say more about wisdom and motivation?

Rinpoche. Wisdom is the mind that understands the importance of motivation in determining whether an action is positive or negative and knows the results of positive and negative actions; the mind that can clearly tell the difference between negative motivation, the cause of suffering, and positive motivation, the cause of happiness.

There are many hindrances to the attainment of enlightenment but there are two basic things we have to do: purify obscurations and accumulate merit. So by completely purifying all delusions and their imprints and completing the accumulation of all merit, we can attain enlightenment. Without accomplishing both these tasks there's no way to become enlightened because there are still hindrances, or blocks. So all the various practices we do—saying prayers, reciting mantras, listening to Dharma teachings, making offerings, practicing charity, adhering to moral discipline and so forth—are included in these two activities of purification and accumulation of merit.

So even though you have the understanding wisdom that sees that a certain action, or karma, will bring benefit, a good result, happiness, and help one receive realizations and enlightenment, that is not enough. These methods, or forms of Dharma practice, that purify obscurations and accumulate merit have to be done until you attain enlightenment. When you're enlightened, you don't need to meditate any more; your work has finished. You don't have to meditate to purify, create merit and gain realizations any longer; that work has finished.

However, the practice of purification and creation of merit has to be continued until it's finished, all the way up to enlightenment. Until then we have to continuously do prostrations, offer mandalas—where with certain prayers we offer the entire universe, all objects of the senses, including those that cause ignorance, attach-

ment and anger to arise within us, thereby renouncing these delusions—and so forth. So there are various kinds of method that we
need to practice in order to attain enlightenment.

Q. What is the quickest single way of collecting merit and cleansing
negativities?

Rinpoche. Cleansing negativities? Taking a shower could be good
... I'm joking! However, to purify in a short time the billions and billions of negative karmas collected over many previous lifetimes and
to quickly accumulate extensive merit, the best, the essential method
is to meditate on, or train the mind in, bodhicitta. If your concern is
to attain enlightenment as quickly as possible, that depends upon
how quickly you purify negativities and how extensively you accumulate merit, and the best way of accomplishing both these aims is
the practice of bodhicitta. Then any action you do, no matter how
small, like offering just one stick of incense or one flower, if it's done
with bodhicitta, the sincere thought wanting to attain enlightenment for the sole purpose of releasing other sentient beings from
suffering and leading them to enlightenment, creates merit as infinite as space itself. In the short time it takes to perform such small
actions with bodhicitta, you purify incredible amounts of negative
karma and accumulate merit as infinite as space. Such are the benefits of the pure thought of bodhicitta.

Q. Is dedicating our enlightenment to the benefit of all beings the
best meditation we can do?
Rinpoche. Of course, that is a very good thing to do. Even though

you're not enlightened now, dedicating your future enlightenment to other sentient beings is very beneficial. There are many meditations like this, where we dedicate the realizations, happiness and pleasure that we have at the moment and our future realizations, happiness and pleasure to others, without miserliness, without attachment. Such meditations are extremely helpful in loosening attachment and such dedication is a practice of charity—as many sentient beings to whom we dedicate, that much charity we make.

Charity is not simply giving material things to others. There are different kinds of charity. Mainly it's mental, an action of the mind, the mind that dedicates to others. It doesn't imply sharing physical objects with all other sentient beings—we can make charity of even one cup of tea or one piece of candy to all sentient beings. This is the power of bodhicitta. If you dedicate one small cup of tea to all sentient beings and as you drink it think that all their sufferings and delusions are completely purified and they receive all realizations up to enlightenment, it is especially powerful and you gain much merit in this way.

··· 8 ···

The Shortcomings of Attachment

I HOPE YOU UNDERSTAND what I was talking about yesterday: how worthwhile it is to understand the nature of your own self-cherishing and attachment.

Sometimes you might think, "I want inner freedom; I want some kind of magic, higher meditation." If you do, you're dreaming, not facing the reality of what you are right now. Because what you always have to deal with throughout your life, with other people, with your mind, all the time, from birth to death, is attachment. All your problems—mental problems, external problems, internal problems, whatever you consider to be a problem, everything—comes from attachment. Understanding this to be your reality is wisdom and the path to liberation, the vehicle that carries you to everlasting peaceful enlightenment. It's so worthwhile.

Also, it's so logical—you don't have to believe in something that's hard to swallow; you don't have to believe in anything. You can prove logically that attachment is your main problem, the principal cause of all your personal problems and the problems you have with those around you.

These are not merely dry words; they derive from life experiences.

It's very important to know this. That's why Lord Buddha always emphasized understanding as the path to liberation.

These days in the West there are many books that talk about the magic and mystery of Tibet, so when people see that a Tibetan lama is coming to give a meditation course, they think, "Oh, maybe I can learn some magic," and attend with that expectation.

But we don't need to teach you magic—your mind is already magic; the magic of attachment has been within you from the time you were born until now. Magic is not the path to liberation; don't expect me to do something funny. Some people do, you know. They expect lamas to do magic and make them hallucinate. Don't expect that. Instead, simply understand what your life is, how complications arise, what it is that complicates your life, what makes you happy…those are the things you should understand. That makes your attendance at this seminar worthwhile. You're not dreaming; you're down to earth and realistic about the way to develop your mind. And with that attitude, you won't be disappointed; you know clearly what you're going to do, what your trip is—meditation, spiritual practice or whatever.

Otherwise there's a danger of doing things without really knowing what you're doing. Many people are like that. Intellectually they say, "I want liberation, inner freedom, nirvana, enlightenment" —they know all the big words but they don't actually know what to do.

But at least you now know that in reality, all false actions, misery, unhappiness and negative energy come from the self-cherishing thought of attachment, and as long as you know that and prove it through your own experience, that simple understanding is enough for you to really change your actions, to really put a stop to selfish thoughts, and that's what's most worthwhile.

Otherwise what happens is that you learn all about this religion or that philosophy but don't change your attitude or behavior; you can't even stop smoking or drinking. Even though you say it's not good to smoke or drink, because you haven't changed inside, there's no change in your external actions either.

From Tibetan lamas' point of view, if your actions don't change, even though you might think or say, "Attachment is the cause of all my problems," it's not really true for you; you haven't realized it. Mere intellectual comprehension is not realization. It's worthwhile to understand these things.

If we don't identify the psychological root of problems we can never cut them off, never rid ourselves of them. In order to overcome an enemy we have to identify that enemy and know where to find him. Otherwise we're shooting in the dark. Similarly, in order to destroy the root of our miserable energy we have to know exactly where it is; then the antidotes we apply will go to exactly the right spot. Even one atom of antidote will be part of the solution.

But that's not what we normally do. Normally, our problems are here but we apply the antidote there. Like when things go wrong, we usually blame our family, friends or society. That's totally misconceived. If we think that the cause of problems is external, there's no way we'll ever be able to stop them. In fact, that's why, from the time we evolved on this earth we've never been able to put an end to problems. It's impossible to do it that way.

Since we now realize that attachment is the cause of all our problems and acting under its influence causes us to create negative actions, we must determine that for the rest of our life we will not allow the actions of our body, speech and mind to follow after this deluded mind.

We have to change our mental attitude, our self-attachment to our ego, I, and to transfer that energy to others. That means we should concern ourselves more with others' pleasure than always thinking only of I, I, I. We should make the determination, "Right now, for the rest of my life, I'm going to dedicate the energy of my body, speech and mind to others and change my attitude, my self-cherishing thought of attachment—excessive concern for my own pleasure—to greater concern for that of others. From the time I was born until now, all my pleasure is due to others' kindness. Even my very existence is due to the kindness of other sentient beings; without it I would not exist, I would not have reached even the age of five."

That's true. For example, from the time we were born we've been drinking milk. It's not our own milk we've been drinking; it's that of others, it's others' energy. Think: this is scientific reality. And we need clothes; without clothes we'd die of cold. We don't make our own clothes, do we?

Everything that preserves us—food, clothing, everything comes from other sentient beings. So think how others preserve our life and how without them we'd die. Most of us eat meat; without depending on animals, how could we eat meat? Animals are so kind; they give us clothes, meat and milk. Similarly, all the people who work for us one way or another are also kind.

To give you another simple example, think how Lord Buddha and Jesus Christ gave up their worldly lives and pleasures and totally dedicated their actions to the welfare of other sentient beings, released their own attachment and reached the highest goal of enlightenment. We, on the other hand, are always concerned with nothing but I, I, I and end up miserable.

Actually, psychologically, we're suffering because of attachment, I, I, I, I, I…always I. This attitude of attachment itself is the suffocating mind; it suffocates us and makes us uptight. Attachment makes us feel a kind of intensity at our heart, a tightness; no release, no relaxation. All that comes from attachment.

Lord Buddha and Jesus Christ even gave their bodies for others; many times in previous lives they gave their hands, legs and kingdoms for others. With our present attitude of self-cherishing attachment we can't even give somebody a cup of tea with genuine pleasure; we can't give anybody anything without expectation.

You might be thinking, "Lama must be joking, putting us down, when he says we don't do good things. We do plenty of good things."

Well, perhaps you do give things, practice charity, but check with what kind of mind you do so. I'm sure that when you give others presents you have some kind of expectation. If you do give without any expectation, completely for the benefit of others, with no thought of enhancing your reputation, with no ulterior motive, such as "I have to give him a gift because he's my relative" or "If I don't give her a present she'll freak out," then it's OK. But that's not how we usually give; most of our giving has nothing to do with true charity and is simply an ego trip. As long as we give with expectation, that's not true giving; we're not really dedicating. We have the expectation "If I don't give him a present for his birthday he won't give me one for mine."

Giving like this is just a joke. Out of the whole universe, we choose one atom—one girlfriend or one boyfriend—one tiny bit of energy, and say, "I love you." With much attachment we put an enormous amount of energy into this one concrete object and thus from the beginning automatically set ourselves up for conflict.

By building up such tremendously powerful attachment we create within ourselves a psychological atomic bomb. Our internal energy is so dependent upon this external object—this girl, this boy, whatever it is—that when it moves we shake. Our mind shakes; our life shakes. But this external object is impermanent; by nature, it's constantly changing, changing, changing. But the character of attachment is that it doesn't want things to change; it wants things to stay as they are. So when they do change, great worry and paranoia arise within us.

And when the time comes to separate from our object of attachment through death or any other reason, we feel, "My life is over." Of course, that's not true; you can see how attachment exaggerates: "Now I have no life." Before, you have life; now suddenly you don't? Can you believe it? But that shows you what a totally overestimating, exaggerating mind the basic conception of attachment actually is.

So you can see how miserable feelings come from our building up certain conceptual philosophies on the basic conception of attachment, and that's the way we end up suffering. There's no way your pleasure can depend upon another atom; that's impossible, the materialistic way of thinking. The whole thing's completely wrong.

Of course, you can make a reasonable judgment: "My friend is transitory, changeable; I understand that. When change comes, it comes; when it goes, it goes. Even I have to die; my friend has to die." That's OK; you can make a reasonable judgment. But attachment doesn't do that. Attachment makes this tremendous overestimation of things and that's how we end up incredibly miserable.

You can just see in the world today how people worry about losing others. People worry, "My wife is going to die…my boyfriend is going to run out on me…my girlfriend is going to disappear." All this worry comes from attachment, excessive concern for one's own pleasure. Ironically, even though we call it pleasure, it's not actual pleasure.

Philosophy

Attachment considers relationships to be happiness but if you check with knowledge-wisdom you'll find that they're actually suffering. Why? Because they result in suffering. We think that worldly pleasure is happiness, that we're using our body and mind for enjoyment, but in fact our body and mind are in the nature of suffering. Why? Because they cause us to suffer. That's why Buddhist literature, especially that of the Hinayana school, emphasizes that everything changeable and transitory is suffering in nature.

If you understand that philosophy and ask yourself, "Why does it say that?" when you reflect on your everyday life and how the subject—your mind—interprets the object—the sense world—and how you relate to it, you'll see that such Buddhist philosophical assertions are very true.

We should have some understanding of philosophy. Many Westerners approaching Dharma think, "Enough with philosophy; I don't like philosophy All I want to do is practice." They're dreaming. Attachment *itself* is philosophy—you were born with it. You didn't learn your attachment at school or from other people; you were born a philosopher. Don't think philosophy comes from books, like you read something and go, "Now I know something; I'm a philosopher."

People need philosophy. The ancient Christian and Western worlds had fantastic philosophy. But then people had difficulty because religion and philosophy often contradicted each other—so some gave up religion, others gave up philosophy.

Nowadays, therefore, we find religion is mostly separate from philosophy because many people think religious teachings are wrong because they're contradicted by science. Actually, Christianity contains wonderfully relevant philosophy that is really worthwhile taking into our lives, but people just don't understand.

As I said, many people say they just want to meditate and don't want anything to do with philosophy but they're wrong; we all need philosophy. Philosophy gives us the whole picture and within that context we can discriminate how our energy is going. If we don't have some kind of overarching philosophy and have the attitude, "Whatever comes, comes; whatever goes, goes," that kind of hippie thinking is wrong. We have to have some kind of understanding, otherwise we'll get lost.

This earth is home to so much superstition, so much garbage philosophy, that if you don't have a correct philosophy, right understanding, you'll led by the nose first in one direction, then another, by whatever you hear. Somebody says "This," and you say, "Yes, yes, yes, yes, yes," and run after that; somebody else says "That," and again you say, "Yes, yes, yes, yes, yes," and run off following that. You have no direction, no precise understanding. But you need direction and understanding, otherwise it's very dangerous. If you don't have a philosophy that can help you judge between right and wrong—what is the right attitude, what is the wrong attitude—if you don't have the discriminating knowledge-wisdom to distinguish between positive and negative, you don't know where you'll end up. That's why I say it's very dangerous.

I recently saw a film set in India—you might have seen it yourselves—where a man seeking realizations goes to a yogi for guidance and is given instead the misconception that if he kills a thousand people he'll receive inner realizations and liberation. Believing this wrong advice, he goes out and kills many people, cutting a finger off each person, making a finger rosary and wearing it around his neck. Thus he was called Angulimala [Tib: Sermo Threngwa].[11] So this is not a Tibetan story; it comes from India at the time of the Buddha.

The Buddha saw with his clairvoyance that Angulimala had killed 999 people and was looking for his thousandth victim, so he went to where Angulimala was and appeared on the road in front of him. Seeing what he thought was his final victim, Angulimala ran towards him, but even though the Buddha manifested walking

---

[11] Skt: anguli, finger; mala, rosary; Tib: sermo, finger; threngwa, rosary. See the entry for Angulimala in Wikipedia.

extremely slowly, no matter how fast Angulimala ran he could not catch him. Somehow, this made him reflect on what he'd been doing and he gradually realized how wrong he'd been. He vowed never again to do such actions, became a Buddhist monk and eventually attained arhatship.

Therefore, it's very dangerous if you don't have a well-founded guiding philosophy and just accept whatever people say at face value. You have to be careful. Tibetan followers of Mahayana Buddhism are very concerned about this kind of thing. You have to check up for yourself. In the West there are so many trips that you can get caught up in; there are thousands of things going on. Of course, there are some good ones among them, worthwhile things, but there's also a lot of garbage, and that's what's dangerous. So be careful.

That's why we always say to take the middle way and avoid the extremes of overestimation and underestimation. We have to take the middle path. To do that we have to understand the wrong paths—how our mind overestimates and underestimates things. We always have to check up, and to do that we need to develop the discriminating knowledge-wisdom that knows how our mind is functioning.

Losing your mind

For example, people considered crazy by society lack the ability to discriminate between normal behavior and extremes. Whenever they encounter great problems, that energy hits their heart or brain or mind—whatever you want to call it—and they become completely unconscious, in that they don't know what they're doing or afterwards remember what they did. I'm sure you know what I mean; I don't need to describe the actions of crazy people. If such people could understand the direction in which their energy and mental conceptions were headed and had control over their actions, they'd be able to pull themselves back from going there and appearing crazy.

It's true; what I'm saying is clear. If you possess discriminating knowledge-wisdom, the ability to check up in the right way, you'll never go crazy because you'll be able to tell when your mind is tending toward extremes and bring it back. By knowing when your mind is becoming extreme, you can prevent it from going there. Otherwise, you think you're OK—"I'm all right, my life is going well, I hang out with my friends, I have enough to eat, I can take care of myself"—but along comes one piece of bad news that taps into the tremendous energy of your attachment and you become unconscious, lose control and become, in other words, crazy.

How does this happen? It's because the potential energy for us to become crazy exists within us right now. Don't think, "There's no way I can become crazy." You can. As long as you have the up and down mind of attachment it can break down any time. It's possible. Therefore it's worthwhile to continuously develop the knowledge-wisdom with which you can cut through that kind of situation and protect your mind by keeping it in a peaceful environment. You must develop knowledge-wisdom, otherwise it's in there and you can go crazy at any time. Don't think I'm exaggerating; check up.

At the moment you have perfect conditions and the intelligence to discriminate between right and wrong; you have tremendously powerful positive energy potential and to use it well is really wonderful. That's how you distinguish yourself from animals. Otherwise, as I said before, what's the difference between humans and birds? Birds also lead everyday lives: they eat food, fill their stomach, go to sleep, get up the next morning…how is that different from most human beings? We're a lot like that. We go to the supermarket, buy things, talk about this and that and go to sleep. Don't think that these are the limits of human ability; even animals can do all that.

Therefore, dears, it's worthwhile to determine to do something really meaningful with this life, and that is to dedicate your life's energy to the benefit of others. As long as you sincerely dedicate yourself to others with the understanding that attachment is the cause of all problems, you will automatically be happy. If you realize this you will naturally enter the path to happiness and joy and will have nothing to worry about.

What I'm saying is that it's necessary to reach a conclusion at the end of each analytical meditation. If you do an analytical meditation, understand something, but then just leave it at that—"Oh, OK, now I understand something"—your meditation has no power; there's no conclusion. You don't have the strength or energy to put what you've understood into action in your everyday life.

However, in general, the conclusion you need to come to is the great determination that "for the rest of my life, as much as I possibly can, I will avoid the mental attitudes of attachment and self-cherishing and to the best of my ability dedicate myself to and concern myself with the welfare of other sentient beings. In particular, since other sentient beings' main problems are not material but attachment and ignorance, a lack of knowledge-wisdom, the best way in which I can help them is to give them the light of knowledge-wisdom, to put the energy of their body, speech and mind in the right direction. In order to do that, I first have to correct my own actions and slowly, slowly gain knowledge-wisdom and realizations myself. In that way I can automatically give others good vibrations and knowledge-wisdom." To dedicate in that way is extremely worthwhile.

Giving

Also, Tibetan lamas have a special mind training technique for releasing attachment and the self-cherishing thought where we transform our body into thousands, millions and billions of bodies and give them to all sentient beings. Actually, we should do this meditation right now.

When we did the equilibrium meditation before, we saw ourselves surrounded by all living beings in the universe; it's the same thing here. We transform our body into beautiful things—not horrible ugly things that we don't want—and give them to all sentient beings. We do this because at the moment we cling to our body with tremendously powerful attachment energy; giving it away to others begins to break that down.

Not only do you give your body to others—now meditate on giving them all your possessions. Your house transforms into thousands of houses, the food in your refrigerator multiplies thousands of times, and so forth with all your other enjoyments. Send all this out to all sentient beings with much compassion, realizing that all beings are equal in wanting happiness and not desiring suffering, but always act out of ignorance and therefore have to constantly experience suffering, confusion and dissatisfaction.

This kind of meditation is not a joke or something funny. It's very useful. Prior to practicing it your attachment might make you feel unhappy when giving somebody even one cent or a cup of tea, but through training your mind you can slowly, slowly reach the point where you give things away with much joy and pleasure. This is experience—I'm not saying it's my experience but there are many people whose it is, in both the East and the West. So it's something we too need to gain—the ability to happily give away our body and all our material possessions.

There's a true story about a Tibetan lama who was incredibly miserly; he couldn't give away even one cent let alone any of his other possessions to others. He asked his teacher what he could do about his incredible miserliness. His teacher said he should start by giving something from one hand to the other, thinking, "Now I'm giving this," visualizing that he was actually giving to other sentient beings. That was how his teacher taught him to start learning to give to others with pleasure, and that's the kind of charity that we have to develop by training our mind—giving without attachment.

When they hear the word "charity," many people probably think it has something to do with religion. From the Buddhist point of view, charity is the antidote to attachment. Also, people think that we can only make charity by giving material things but that's not what charity actually means. True charity is giving sincerely without expectation. That mind is charity. Giving others material things is not necessarily charity.

For example, if, with attachment to having a good reputation, you think, "I'm a very religious person and want others to know it, so I'm going to donate a million dollars to charity," that's just an ego trip. Instead of becoming an antidote to attachment and helping you develop knowledge-wisdom, that way of giving merely strengthens your ego.

Often, what you think to be a spiritual practice is simply an ego trip, attachment. You need to check up on that. That's why, despite your practice, you still haven't found a solution to your problems. You're hypocritical, because you have no understanding of what spirituality really is; your actions aren't serious Dharma actions. If you're going to act, don't do so out of some pretentious, high-sounding intellectual philosophy but act simply, sincerely. Start off small; practice what makes sense for the level you're at. If you begin your Dharma practice that way, you'll really solve your problems.

If you get lost in the intellectual and don't act appropriately, what's the point? You're still wallowing in garbage.

Although actions are very important, don't overreach. Don't attempt advanced practices before you're ready; start off slowly, small. Don't think that you can start at the end. Do a little bit every day and gradually, gradually you'll progress and see yourself develop.

Even Lord Buddha said, "Don't accept what I say just because I said it. That's the wrong approach." He said, "Check what I teach, and if you think it suits your level of mind, with clear understanding, adopt it." It's like shoes…you should wear only comfortable ones that fit your feet. In other words, before you start meditating or doing any spiritual practice, make sure that you're one hundred percent certain of what you're doing. In that way, your practice will be very comfortable and through your own actions you'll be able to see how you're developing.

Often, the problem with the Western way of thinking is that you want too much of everything. You have too much samsara, too much sense gravitation attachment…everything is exaggerated for the sake of sense pleasure. And then, when you get into meditation or some other spiritual trip, you bring that energy with you; you bring that materialistic attitude into your Dharma practice. That's a big misconception. Be down to earth; that's the more realistic way to develop spiritually. It's so worthwhile, very worthwhile.

Also, human potential is so powerful. Normally we think that rockets and atomic energy are very powerful but the power of rockets and nuclear energy comes from human beings, from the power of human intelligence, which understands how to manipulate material things to make them powerful. Look around at all the large, fantastic buildings on earth—where do you think they came from? They were designed and made by human beings, not by God.

Cause and effect

So, as a human being, you should always remember how powerful you are and not devalue yourself, thinking, "I'm nothing; I can't do anything." That's ridiculous. You are really worthwhile, incredibly intelligent and endowed with powerful energy. Of course, you can use your powerful energy in a positive or a negative way. Therefore human beings can also be dangerous. Why is the world today dangerous? It's because of the human mind, which has created weapons, war and environmental problems.

We often hear people lament, "The world is so miserable; there are so many wars." Instead of worrying about war, what you first need to worry about is integrating yourself, making yourself clean clear. Then your pure vibration will automatically contribute to world peace and benefit others. Otherwise, if out of confusion and a lack of understanding you say, emotionally, "This miserable world is just too much for me now," that's useless. It's just emotion; it's not compassion. No wisdom; no method.

Certain problems can be solved but there are others that, at the moment, are beyond solution. For example, Buddhism always talks about karma, but the karma we talk about is not something fixed. Karma means cause and effect. When a cause is already in our mind, there, right now—such as the cause to become crazy—if we apply the right method we can get rid of it before it ripens. But once that cause has brought its result and we've become crazy, it's too late. That problem is pretty much beyond solution. So the time to implement a solution is before a karmic result has ripened. Once a problem has manifested it's much more difficult to solve.

Both Hindu and Buddhist philosophy use the Sanskrit word karma but the connotation is different. Hinduism believes that karma is completely unchangeable, predetermined...something like that. Buddhism asserts that as an impermanent phenomenon, karma is changeable. Karma is your mental attitude putting your energy in a certain direction, producing a chain reaction, and you can break that chain before the result ripens.

Also, karma is the energy of your body, speech and mind. Don't think it's something else. Why do we call it karma? Because the energy of the cause relates to another energy and that produces a reaction in yet another energy. That's all. It's scientific; I'm not talking about some religious thing. Scientists themselves have discovered that the energy of the four elements—earth, water, fire, wind—doesn't arise without cause; there's always a cause: one energy relates to another and produces a third, and so it goes on. If you don't know that, please visit a scientific laboratory! I'm joking—I haven't been into a scientific laboratory in my life! Anyway, it's true—you check up. Maybe I'm joking, maybe I'm not... I'm not sure!

Everything you see, hear, smell, taste or touch produces a reaction, either positive or negative. This is karma. That's why I say Buddhism is scientific: you can experience this for yourself today, right now. It's true; it's so simple. That's why we say that meditation develops higher conscious awareness; and when you develop it, you can see how each movement you make produces a different reaction.

Take *Time* magazine, for example. The publishers there are expert psychologists; at some level they understand karma. They put something special on the cover that they know will attract people's attention—often the face of a man or woman. People see the cover, react to it, buy the magazine and *Time* gets the money, that's all! Actually, that's karma.

It's the same with other advertisers in the West. I think they're fantastic. If you investigate why they do what they do, you get a glimpse of Buddhist psychology. I myself learn from that; it helps me understand how the Western mind works. It's incredible, really, the way the human mind thinks: "If we do this, people will react like that...." Marketers know; that too is karma.

When you walk down a London street you see, hear and smell things, but mostly you're unconscious of them all; whatever you perceive automatically reacts in your mind, but you're completely unaware of it. When we practice meditation, we gradually become more conscious; if we don't practice meditation, our unconscious mind gets stronger and instead of developing, our mind degenerates and we become more and more unconscious. You can see how that's possible, can't you?

If you understand true human psychology, the nature of the human mind, you'll be able to integrate your mind and life; they'll work together harmoniously. If your mind is split, your life is split; it has no direction and you're unhappy and lost—even if you know precisely where in the world you are.

· · · 9 · · ·

Giving and Taking on the Breath

E ARLIER WE DID a meditation for training our mind in detachment by giving away all our possessions, including our body,
to other sentient beings. This time we're going to do the same thing,
sending all sentient beings all our goodness—our knowledge-wisdom, good qualities and positive energy.

Technically, the way we do this is to mentally transform all this
goodness into white light and, as we exhale through our right nostril, send this light into others' left nostril. As they breathe in it enters
their heart and they experience an extremely joyful feeling.

Then, when you breathe in, inhale all others' sickness and problems in the form of smoky black energy—it leaves their right nostril, enters your left nostril and goes into your heart. This is the kind
of negative energy and suffering that your association of ego and
attachment completely dislikes. For countless lives, and even in this
one from the time you were born up to now, you have been trying to avoid such problems as much possible, always obsessed with
goodness for yourself, I. So this time, bring all that negativity into
your heart; it completely mashes your ego and attachment. They
freak out—let them freak out.

Totally changing the attitude of your ego-attachment's attitude is very useful because the personality of attachment is limitless want: "I want every pleasure the universe has to offer." And at all costs, attachment wants to avoid any unpleasant feelings whatsoever. So this time we act in completely the opposite way. Without the slightest hesitation, we send all our goodness, wisdom and joyful life energy—all our positive physical, mental and verbal energy—to others. We exhale through our right nostril and send joyful, blissful white light energy into all other beings' left nostril without discrimination—not just our dear friend; all living beings in the universe.

Then bring their biggest problems, those that you don't even like to see, let alone experience, in through your left nostril into your heart, where they smash into your ego and attachment, which completely vanish as a result; your ego completely freaks out.

Normally your ego's attitude is such that if somebody who is not a friend barges uninvited into your house, you freak out: "How dare you come in without knocking?" Compared to your *heart*, this is nothing! So visualize bringing all sentient beings' problems and sickness through your left nostril into your heart.

We call this kind of meditation *tong-len*. *Tong* means giving; *len* means taking. And we also say *lung wai gyö par cha*. *Lung* means breath: to give and take together with breathing.

In summary, send all your goodness, the positive energy of your body, speech and mind, your mental control, whatever, out on your breath through your right nostril. It enters others' left nostril and goes down to their heart, which completely fills with joyous energy. Rejoice. Then bring others' worst diseases and psychological problems—everything your ego dislikes—in the form of black smoke, in on your breath through your left nostril into your heart.

Perhaps you find it difficult to bring sickness and so forth into your heart. However, visualize old people in the West, many of whom are like vegetables, suffering greatly in nursing homes; they don't know what's going on. Send them positive energy. Think of all the people dying of hunger and thirst—such things do exist in the West, even though there might be supermarkets full of food nearby; because of their individual situation, many people still go hungry. Think about wars: thousands of people killing, thousands of others dying. Send your positive vibrations to all people suffering like this. Visualize that your positive energy enters dead people's bodies and they come back to life; take all their bad karma and its results in the form of black light in through your left nostril into your heart.

Even with your dearest friend, the situation can arise where you have to make the choice, "There's no way out, either my friend has to suffer or I do." When it comes to that point, even though intellectually you say, "I will take any suffering for your happiness," when the actual situation arises your self-cherishing is going to make the decision for you. Check up; be honest: you're going to choose happiness for yourself and let your friend suffer.

Normally we consider ourselves clever and intelligent because we know how to avoid disease and things like that. We feel so superior. Actually, it's just attachment—obsession with pleasure and aversion to the unpleasant. This is not a good attitude. Of course, avoiding disease and so forth in order to remain healthy and use your life for the benefit of others is OK but doing so with self-cherishing is not.

So this time, bring others' sickness into your heart. Let your ego freak out; let your attachment freak out. And when you do this meditation, from the psychological point of view it's especially important to watch how your ego reacts to your bringing others' sickness into your heart. Transform others' TB, cancer and so forth into black light and bring it through your left nostril into your heart and check how your ego likes it. You'll find there's a tremendous ego reaction when you do this.

Again, consider old people in the West. They're incredibly miserable. They don't have any mind training to help them understand themselves; they have no meditation with which they can keep their mind together. I've seen this myself; this is my scientific experience. When people in the West get old they become incredibly miserable, much more so than old people in the East. This is going to happen to all of us as long as we don't die. At the moment we don't even want to see old people's faces but every day we ourselves are getting closer to having that kind of face.

Think about it: if all of a sudden your face became that of a one-hundred-year-old person, do you think your ego would freak out? Check up now; it's possible, not a dream. The potential is there. Every day you're getting closer to having an old person's face.

However, if we train our mind in releasing attachment and developing detachment, even if we get old we'll have no problem; we'll be able to deal with the situation and comprehend our own mind. Even though physically we may be one hundred years old, our mind will remain young, like that of a child. It's possible. This is the power of the human mind...and we can progress the human mind into everlasting peaceful, joyful realization, whatever you call it: nirvana, enlightenment, salvation—it doesn't matter; they're just words. What matters is that you can gain insight into ultimate reality. That's so worthwhile. Therefore, mind training is extremely important. Those who have trained their mind can deal with any bad situation that arises, transform it into joyful energy and in that way always have a joyful life. Irrespective of whether the world is up or down, they always remain joyful.

So really bring what you normally don't like to even hear about into your heart and check how your ego reacts; examine how you feel.

Tibetan lamas do twenty-one repetitions of this meditation, sending out their good qualities to others on their breath through their right nostril and bringing in others' bad qualities, sickness and any other problems in the form of black light through their left nostril into their heart, and check how their ego reacts.

At the same time they make the following determination: "For countless lives, and even from when I was born up to now, I have always grasped at temporal pleasure. With a grasping attitude and the self-cherishing thought I've wanted the best happiness for myself and tried to avoid all suffering. I now recognize this as the main psychological problem behind all my mistaken actions. As long as I don't change, as long as I don't do something about this, I'll continually experience unhappiness and miserable reactions. Real everlasting joy and true happiness are beyond the attachment of the self-cherishing thought, so for the rest of my life, as much as I possibly can, I'm going to put all my energy into releasing attachment and the self-cherishing thought. This is my main path to real liberation, inner freedom and enlightenment."

Feeling equilibrium with all universal living beings is really powerful, as is the experience of sending all your goodness to others and bringing into yourself all their sickness and problems. The result you get is incredible joy; your mind is really balanced and you enter the middle path. Attachment and hatred are exaggerated extremes, so if you can stay on the middle way between them and deal with people from there, it's really worthwhile and most beneficial, because most of our problems arise from dealing with other human beings.

More shortcomings of attachment

Check up: Lord Buddha said that we should not be attached to even the realizations of nirvana or enlightenment. He also said that it's wrong for his followers to be dogmatically attached to his doctrine, that that's another type of psychological sickness or disease.

That's incredible, isn't it? Most of the time we think, "My idea's good," but if somebody says, "Your idea is bad," we freak out. That's attachment. Lord Buddha said, "I don't want any of my disciples to be attached to concepts, such as the highest goal of enlightenment or any of my other philosophies or doctrines." Also, in Tibetan Buddhist tantric yoga there are vows forbidding us to criticize the doctrine of any other religion. Can you imagine? Lord Buddha has us take vows against that; it's incredible. This is a fantastically skillful method and shows how wonderfully well he understood human psychology. Unbelievable, isn't it?

I mean, worldly people are going to say, "My idea is best," and if you contradict them they freak out. That's because of their attachment; they're not realistic. Lord Buddha says that instead of freaking out, don't have attachment in the first place, because as long as you're attached to your religious ideas and philosophies you're setting yourself up for inner conflict, and that will destroy your inner peace and joy.

Therefore we should take the middle path and avoid extreme views as much as we can. That's the *real* path, the *true* path to liberation, enlightenment or whatever you call it; the words don't matter. If you reach beyond attachment and self-cherishing I can guarantee that your life will be free of physical and mental problems and there's no way that you'll engage in mistaken actions—the door to suffering will forever be closed. But whenever you open the door of attachment and self-cherishing you also open the door to all problems.

The greatest human problems are actually rebirth, aging and death, but if you are free of attachment you can even die with much pleasure; dying is like going home. If you die with attachment to your material possessions, friends and reputation, your death will be miserable; if you don't have attachment you'll have an incredible death; your experience of dying will be blissful, joyful.

Really, Buddhism teaches us how to die. Buddhist education starts at the beginning of life and continues all the way through to its end; it's a total experience. Actually, it's not that difficult; it's easy. If you have the skillful method and wisdom to release attachment and self-cherishing your life will always be happy. You don't need to pretend; it will be natural. Happiness will be natural; control will be natural—you won't have to pretend.

If you plant a seed it's natural that it will grow. Similarly, if you plant the seeds of the knowledge-wisdom solution to releasing attachment, it will automatically develop. That's why I always say that the human mind is very powerful—positively powerful and negatively powerful. You can direct it either way; it's flexible. The energy of the human mind is not fixed.

You can see how the energy of attachment and selfishness is like a needle in your heart; when you release it you feel incredible joy. You lose that uptight tendency in your heart and you're physically relaxed.

The benefits of meditation

Through meditation we can really reach a state of everlasting joy, so if we don't do something to get there we're really foolish, aren't we? And we can reach that joyful state without having to spend any money. But we forget that and instead get overly concerned with material things and, exaggerating their value, run after sense objects of attachment. We're totally unrealistic.

Do a comparative check: which offers you more, material things or knowledge-wisdom? Of course, material things do give you some level of comfort, but if you spend all your life working only for them, when you die you end up with nothing. On the other hand, if you spend your time developing knowledge-wisdom and releasing attachment and self-cherishing, it's incredibly powerful—your whole life becomes content. Even if the earth goes up into the sky and the sun and moon crash down to earth, no matter how much the external world changes, control and wisdom are always with you. Material things always cheat you—sometimes they're there, sometimes they're not. Many rich people die hungry. It's never certain; money is no insurance or guarantee against hunger. I think you know that, but it's important. Really check up, seriously.

So for at least a short time every day, compare the benefits of chasing materials with those of developing your mind. You have plenty of time to do so. You just need to meditate and train your mind for ten minutes, twenty minutes, half an hour every day in the meditation techniques we've been teaching you here. These practices are incredibly powerful. In just a short time you can produce such joyful energy in your heart. That's much more worthwhile than running after transitory samsaric pleasures, which simply bring one miserable, useless result after another.

The potential for pleasure and joy is already within your mind; you don't need money to buy it. Anyway, you can't buy that kind of joy; it's already there within you. If you use that energy skillfully it will *always* be with you. Whether you go up into the sky or down into the ground, it will always come with you. Material possessions are the exact opposite.

Meditating is also much easier than going to the supermarket. You probably think I'm exaggerating, but think about it. Going to the supermarket is not necessarily that easy. First, you can't walk; you have to go by car. Then, maybe your car doesn't work. Anyway, you know; I don't have to go into details. There can be all kinds of difficulty in getting to and from the supermarket. Check up. In contrast, a short meditation can immediately relax you and keep you consciously aware all day. That's really worthwhile. It can bring you everlasting joy. Physically you may be old but mentally you can be experiencing an incredibly joyful awakened state of mind. It's so worthwhile. We're all going to get old but we can make sure that when we do, our life will still be joyful. It's possible and therefore so worthwhile that we abandon collecting garbage with attachment, which is so unreasonable.

However, I'd like you to check up for yourselves; I'm not trying to push my ideas onto you. You're intelligent, so check up for yourselves. Actually, Western people aren't that easy. You have much learning but you've also picked up a lot of garbage. But now you can look into that garbage and learn from it; you have much experience to check on. It's much more difficult to teach primitive people the things we're talking about here; they find it much harder to understand subjects that Westerners find easy.

· · · 10 · · ·
Making Life Meaningful

IN ORDER TO MAKE the action of listening to teachings the cause of everlasting happiness, complete freedom, it is necessary to make that action Dharma. Furthermore, in order to make the action of listening to teachings the cause of enlightenment for the sake of all sentient beings, it's necessary to cultivate pure motivation, the pure thought of bodhicitta.

So it's necessary to feel, or at least think, as follows: "Releasing myself alone from all samsaric suffering is not sufficient. There are numberless other sentient beings who have been extremely kind to me, and those sentient beings are in continual suffering, not having the wisdom or method to escape from suffering and receive everlasting happiness. As it's my responsibility to release all sentient beings from suffering and lead them to the most sublime happiness of enlightenment, I must first receive enlightenment myself. For that reason I'm going to listen to these profound teachings."

The subject that you're going to listen to is a Mahayana teaching that contains the graduated path to enlightenment that all past, present and future buddhas have traveled on their way to complete awakening and is a path that has also been experienced by the disciplic succession of the lineage.

The perfect human rebirth

This present human rebirth is extremely meaningful with respect to attaining both temporal and ultimate goals and highly meaningful every hour, minute and second. How is this perfect human rebirth so precious and useful in attaining even temporal goals? For example, if we want to receive a perfect human rebirth again in future so that we can continue practicing Dharma and following the graduated path to enlightenment by once more meeting a spiritual friend, we can create the cause for this result in this life by living in pure moral conduct, practicing charity and making stainless prayers. This present perfect human rebirth offers us the capability of doing this.

This perfect human rebirth also gives us the opportunity of creating the cause to be reborn as the king of a country, a wealthy person, or as a god in the sura or asura realms—where lives are long and enjoyments transcendent—by practicing charity, living in moral discipline and making prayers to achieve such temporal goals.

This perfect human rebirth is also highly meaningful in that it allows us to achieve the ultimate goals of either the everlasting happiness of complete freedom from samsara or the most sublime happiness of enlightenment.

And this perfect human rebirth even offers us the opportunity of attaining enlightenment in this life or within a few lives rather than taking many eons. How is that possible? The graduated path to enlightenment has two divisions: the sutra graduated path, or Paramitayana, and the tantric graduated path, or Vajrayana. Since all the teachings of both divisions exist at this time, this perfect human rebirth gives us the chance to practice them: by following the Paramitayana path we can reach enlightenment after many eons but by following the Vajrayana path, the shortcut path to enlightenment, we can reach it much more quickly, without taking that much time.

Furthermore, this perfect human rebirth is extremely useful every second, every minute, every hour. This is especially so these days, when the Mahayana teachings still exist, have not degenerated, and we have had the great fortune of meeting these teachings and can practice their essence, bodhicitta. Since we are able to generate the pure thought of bodhicitta, in even a minute we can purify the obscurations and negative karma collected over eons, in our countless beginningless previous lives in samsara. With this perfect human rebirth, by generating the pure thought of bodhicitta we are able to purify negative karma collected over billions of eons and create infinite merit as vast as space, in the shortest period of time.

Therefore this perfect human rebirth that we have received this time is extremely useful. It is so precious; much more precious than a universe filled with jewels. Even if we had a universe full of jewels they could not bring us what the perfect human rebirth can. They could not even bring us a future perfect human rebirth let alone supreme enlightenment. The value of the perfect human rebirth we now enjoy is beyond compare with a universe full of jewels.

Also, as meaningful as this perfect human rebirth is, that much difficult it is for other rebirths, such as those of the animals, pretas, suras and asuras, to be as meaningful in achieving those goals.

Those other rebirths are nowhere near as meaningful or precious as this present perfect human rebirth.

However, even though we have received this perfect human rebirth, from the time we were born until now we have not recognized it as meaningful or precious. Not only have we not recognized it as precious, we have actually thought that it's meaningless, that being born human has no meaning. In other words, all we've done is make ourselves more ignorant. Instead of encouraging ourselves we've put ourselves down, which has served only to make our life not meaningful.

The way we've been using our perfect human rebirth is like a child who has an extremely precious jewel in its hand but doesn't recognize its value so throws it down the toilet. We waste our perfect human rebirth in exactly the same way. We have this extremely precious thing in our hand but, not recognizing its worth, completely waste it.

Even though this perfect human rebirth is highly meaningful, if we don't use it to attain goals that other sentient beings find extremely difficult to attain—such as the highest goal of enlightenment, everlasting happiness or temporal goals such as a human rebirth—and instead use it simply to pursue the happiness of just this life, the happiness of today, our actions are no higher than those of animals, whose sole concern is temporal pleasure and whose aims are always directed toward that end.

As this perfect human rebirth has meaning, if we don't use it accordingly, if we live our lives the way animals lead theirs, always striving for temporal pleasure, then it's as if we weren't born human but as one of those lower realm beings. Why? Because our actions are no higher than theirs; what we do is not more special than what they do. From tiny creatures too small to see with the naked eye all the way up to the largest of animals, all their daily activities, all the things they do with their body, speech and mind, are done with attachment to the transient pleasures of just this life.

So now check up within yourself: "Since the day I was born, have I created any meaningful actions with my perfect human rebirth, any actions worthy of this human rebirth, any actions higher than those of animals, any meaningful actions done without attachment to temporal pleasure, actions that lead to the higher goals of better future lives and the ultimate goals of liberation and enlightenment?" Check how many meaningful, worthwhile actions—if you can find any—you have done with this perfect human rebirth from the time you were born until now; check to see if any of the actions you've ever done have been higher than those of animals.

Also check like this: "All the daily activities of the twittering birds flying from tree to tree and the insects crawling around on the ground are done with attachment to temporal pleasure. Are any of my daily activities—eating, drinking, walking, talking and sleeping—any different? Do I do anything without attachment to temporal pleasure or are all my actions the same as those of birds and insects, who do everything with attachment to temporal pleasure?" Check this.

Check everything you do from morning to night, your usual daily activities.

Check one day's activities to see if there's even one action that's higher than an animal's, done without attachment to temporal pleasure.

When you check like this you can clearly see whether you're living the life of a human being or that of an animal; checking the actions of your daily life in detail makes it obvious.

However, when we investigate in this way we can hardly find one single action that is pure—higher than the actions of dumb animals. The way our minds think is the same; the way we lead our life is the same. We can't find anything higher. The only difference is that our body has a different shape and we live in a house; there's no difference in the way we think. Basically, we're no different from the dog that lives outside. If we check properly, this is what we find; it's very upsetting.

The difficulty of receiving a perfect human rebirth

Now, if we could receive this perfect human rebirth again and again and again and again, easily, one after the other, again and again and again, then perhaps we wouldn't have to worry. If perfect human rebirths came as easily as rice grows—you plant rice seedlings, they grow, produce more seeds, you plant those and get more rice—if when we died we automatically received another perfect human rebirth, we wouldn't have to concern ourselves that much with making this life meaningful. It wouldn't be so dangerous to waste it But it's not like this; it's not like this.

It will be very difficult to receive such a perfect human rebirth again; very difficult. Why will it be so difficult? Why is it extremely difficult to find another perfect human rebirth? That's because we have not received this present perfect human rebirth without reason; this perfect human rebirth is not without cause. Why in this lifetime have we received a perfect human rebirth, met the teachings and had the chance to meditate, to control our mind? It's because in many of our previous lives we observed the law of karma, lived in moral discipline, created much charity and made many prayers to receive this present human rebirth. Many of our previous lives worked very hard, expended much effort, to create the cause of this precious human rebirth.

So this human rebirth is not something that has been received without cause, kind of independent, self-existent. It's not like this. Therefore, receiving a perfect human rebirth in future depends upon whether we, in this life, create the cause of a future perfect human rebirth; it's in the hands of our present human rebirth. If in this life we don't create the cause for a perfect human rebirth, we won't receive one in future; if in this life we do create the cause of a perfect human rebirth, we will receive one in a future life. It all depends upon our present life.

Why, then, is it extremely difficult to receive a perfect human rebirth? It's because the cause is extremely difficult to create. For instance, let's check like this, from the point of view of moral conduct. If we check in this way we'll be able to figure out whether or not we'll receive a perfect human rebirth again. Think, "From the time I was born until now, have I observed any moral conduct such as not killing, not stealing, not engaging in sexual misconduct. In this life, have I observed such moral discipline or not?"

Also check, "Have I not told lies, not gossiped, not spoken harshly, not slandered others? Have I observed any of these moral disciplines in my life or not?"

As well, check, "Have I not generated ill will, covetousness or the heresy of believing there's no ultimate reality, no Buddha, Dharma and Sangha and no past and future lives? Have I observed any of these moral disciplines in my life or not?"

Now think, "Have I observed any of these moral disciplines for even a day?"

If you find that you have observed such disciplines, then that's something to feel happy about, rejoice over.

So now, after checking, think, "If I were to die now, could I receive a perfect human rebirth again?" Question yourself.

So that's checking to see whether or not we've observed any moral discipline in our life. We don't need to investigate that carefully to see whether or not, with negative mind, we've done the opposite: the three immoral actions of body—killing, stealing and sexual misconduct—the four immoral actions of speech—telling lies, speaking harshly, slandering and gossiping—or the three immoral actions of mind—generating ill will, covetousness or heresy. If we check how many such actions we've created from the time of our rebirth until now we don't need to worry we won't find any. It's easy to see that we have; we don't have to spend much time looking.

Anyway, what I mean is this: it's not sure that we'll receive another human rebirth let alone a perfect human rebirth in our future lives. Therefore, now that we have received a perfect human rebirth we absolutely must extract its essence. What is the essence of the perfect human rebirth? It's the three temporal and ultimate goals I mentioned before, the highest of which is enlightenment. So while we hold the jewel of the perfect human rebirth in our hand, we have to ensure that we create the cause for enlightenment, because it's most uncertain that in future we'll have this chance again.

We can see that it's most uncertain because it's so easy for us to find how many negative actions we have done in our life, the various action of our body and speech done with negative mind, with ignorance, attachment, anger and the other delusions. Since we have created these negative actions so many times, the ten immoral actions that I just described, it's inevitable that we will experience their result.

What makes actions such as killing, stealing and lying negative is that they are done out of delusion. If we do the same actions without delusion or self-cherishing, with bodhicitta, they are not immoral.

Buddhadharma explains that what makes an action immoral is not the action itself but the mind that creates it.

The results of negative karma

So, there are four karmic results of immoral actions. Take, for example, the immoral action of killing, causing the death of other living beings. One of the four results is called the ripening result: rebirth in one of the three lower realms, the hell, hungry ghost or animal realms. The second result for the person who has killed others is, even if—after a long time, as the result of some previously created good karma—he is born in the human realm, his life is short; he gets killed by another person. This is called the result similar to the cause in experience. What you do to another eventually comes back upon you.

The third result of the immoral action of killing, killing with a negative mind, is even if—after some time, as the result of good karma—the person is reborn human, he again kills other beings. This is called the result similar to the cause in action, or habit. The previous action of killing created the tendency to kill again. For instance, in this life we sometimes find it difficult to control certain violent actions—those habitual impulses come from similar previous actions.

The fourth result of the immoral action of killing has to do with the place in which one finds oneself; this is called the possessed, or environmental, result. Even if, after some time, the person who has killed is reborn human, he loses the essence of his enjoyments; the enjoyments where he lives have no essence. Also, the environment is very dangerous, with much fighting and life danger.

It's also like this with the other immoral actions of body, speech and mind. For example, every day on television or in the newspapers we hear about problems all over the world. Some places are very wet, muddy and prone to flooding; others are always rife with factional fighting and disharmony.

Even on the family level we always see examples of fighting between parents or children. Some men can never get on with their wife, no matter how many they have; their relationships always fail, there's constant disharmony. And some women are the same; no matter how many husbands they have, their marriages never last, they always fight, they're never happy. Some people are always getting abused or criticized by others; no matter where they go other people always speak badly of them, causing them much suffering. These kinds of disunity or disharmony, not getting along in relationships, are especially the result of the immoral action of slandering others, causing disharmony between others.

Then there are other people who—no matter how much they try to accumulate material possessions, no matter how much money they receive through making business—always lose what they have, can never hang onto it. No matter where they go, their possessions always get stolen. Even if they stay in one place they get robbed again and again, or if they don't lose their possessions, they don't have enough time to enjoy them. Problems such as these result from the immoral action of stealing in previous lives.

Other people, even though they have a good house or excellent material possessions and so forth, their things don't last; they wear out quickly or easily get broken. And there are others who can never get good enjoyments; whatever they get is always of poor quality. No matter how hard they try they can never get anything good. Others can't find work or always get fired from their job. Many things like this happen.

There are people who have to live in areas where it's hard to find food or water. Others have to live in very ugly places full of thorns, or on very high, steep mountains that are difficult to move around on, or in dry, barren deserts. Even though life in such places is very difficult, somehow, without choice, they have to spend their lives there.

There are many other examples that could be given, however, all such experiences are the result of immoral actions that have to be experienced in the human realm, not to mention the other results of even greater suffering that come from rebirth in the lower realms.[12]

And opposite to the ten immoralities is observing the ten moralities. Because in the past we did that, at the present time we find ourselves in the upper realms receiving many enjoyments. Whatever we try to get, we receive. If we want food, we get it; if we want clothes, we get them; if we want to be in a beautiful place, we can go there. Things come easily to us; our life is easy. Other things like having intact sense organs, a beautiful looking body, a good personality, patience and the respect of other people and having control over

---

[12] See the *Sutra of Causes and Effects of Actions* on the LYWA website, www.Lama Yeshe.com.

others, where they do what we tell them—all these are the results of previously created good karma, adhering to moral discipline.

The root of suffering

Now let's do a short meditation.

All the suffering in the six samsaric realms—the hell, hungry ghost, animal, human, asura and sura realms—comes from ignorance, which is the creator of samsara. Ignorance creates samsara, the world of pain.

What is that ignorance that is the creator of samsara? That is the ignorance that does not realize the true nature of the self, the absolute nature of the self.

Therefore, to not experience all the sufferings of samsara and be completely free from their cause, ignorance, we must completely destroy ignorance, the cause of all samsaric suffering. To do that, we must realize the true nature of the self.

Realizing the true nature of the self depends upon recognizing ignorance, the mind that is unclear as to the nature of the self.

It's like this: if your body is dirty and you want to clean it, you first have to identify the dirt. In the same way, in order to realize the true nature of the self, what the self is, you first have to recognize ignorance, the mind that makes us view the I in completely the wrong way, a way that is opposite to the reality of the self. The way we view the self is the way ignorance conceives of the self.

So first concentrate on the thought, whatever you're thinking now. Just watch that thought and as your mind gradually becomes relaxed, calm, then check up how you see the self, how you conceive the self, or how the I appears to you. First concentrate on thought; as your mind gets calm, relaxed, check carefully how the I, the self, appears to you, or how you conceive it.

If you find something, if you find the truly existing I, the truly existing self, search for where it is. When you find the truly existing I, the real I, check whether it's the body or the mind and whether it's within your body-mind or outside of it. Check in this way. If you can't find it, if you see the emptiness of the self, then just concentrate on that.

If you do find a real self, then check whether it's the body, the mind or the mind-body combination. You have to look for this truly existing self from head to foot, searching in every part of your body to try to find exactly where it is. If you don't find it and then come to the conclusion that the self does not exist at all, then that's a wrong conception; you've fallen into the extreme of nihilism. That conclusion does not make you free of suffering.

But if the feeling of the emptiness of the self comes to you more or less effortlessly, rather than running away from that you should practice concentrating on it, just for the auspiciousness of meditating on emptiness, seeking the true nature of the self.

That's all I have to say this time. If, as a result of having come to this seminar, you now see that your human life has great meaning and that there are many good things you can do with your life that you were not aware of before, things that benefit all sentient beings, then that gives meaning to your having come here. If you now know that you can again receive a perfect human rebirth, completely release yourself from your delusions and attain enlightenment for the sake of all sentient beings and you wish to attain those goals, and you wish to study continuously and meditate in order to escape from suffering and receive enlightenment for the sake of others, then it's most worthwhile that you attended. That's extremely important for your own peace of mind and that of others.

However, the most important thing is to try to keep your mind away from giving harm to others as much as possible; to try to control your mind as much as you can. Keep your mind away from the harmful mind—that is the essence of Dharma, the most important thing. Whether you meditate or not, the essence of meditation is to stop the harmful mind from arising as much as possible. That keeps you and those around you in peace.

I'm happy to have made a Dharma connection with you all and to have had the chance to help you a little with the Dharma but it's important that you maintain a continuous wish to meditate and study the Buddhadharma more deeply. Then, if you have time, perhaps you will have the chance to practice the meditations more and more deeply.

··· 11 ···

Lama Answers Questions

The best answers come through meditation

WHENEVER HUMAN PROBLEMS ARISE, instead of getting nervous and worried, you're better off meditating and checking up. Meditation is like a computer—whenever regular people have a problem, they turn to their computer for answers; similarly, whenever meditators have a problem, they meditate. And through meditation they get answers. The answers are there; the calm, clear mind gives knowledge-wisdom the space to come up with answers. The foggy mind is an obstacle; it makes the answers invisible. So meditation really is the best way to check up and find solutions to your problems.

We usually think we get answers by asking questions and that's true up to a point; certain things can be answered that way. But if you're unaware, even if the lama gives you a good answer, it doesn't really register; it goes right over your head. That's because the way you're asking is not serious. If you want to question something deeply and really, seriously meditate on it, when the answer comes it's so powerful. You *become* the answer, you *become* that knowledge; it doesn't just remain as some kind of superficial fact.

Often when you ask somebody a question and the person says, "This, this, this," you might receive a little wisdom but we don't consider that to be true knowledge.

So meditation is really worthwhile; it gives you the answers you want. Meditation is the real personal computer. Answers you discover for yourself through meditation are much more meaningful, much deeper, than those you get from somebody else's replies to your questions. You ask, "Please could you tell me blah, blah, blah"; the other person replies, "Blah, blah, blah"; you think "OK, that's good." But then another problem comes to occupy your mind because you don't have the penetrative concentration to cut through the fog of your confusion. That's why I always say that human beings are so powerful. Potentially, we have fantastic energy; we just have to use it in the most professional way.

Every human being has a beautiful quality. If we only look at people's superficial external appearance we will never find true beauty but if we look at their deeper human qualities—what people can do, the positive actions they can create and the power of the human mind—we will see everybody as beautiful. In fact, all universal living beings have *some* beautiful qualities.

If everything that existed in the world were to appear as beautiful, there'd be no way for the miserable mind to arise. The view of the miserable mind is foggy—the subject, the mind, relies, or depends, on the object it perceives. Transforming the external world into beauty prevents the ugly mind from arising by giving it no space.

So it's really worthwhile that you people, having realized that happiness can never be found in the superficial sense world alone, are seeking a joyful life through internal happiness, fully convinced—not "maybe, maybe"—that this is the way. You *have* to make that decision. If your mind still harbors the doubt, "Maybe the supermarket really does contain everything I need," your meditation will be no good and you won't get any realizations.

Also, you shouldn't spend your life on useless pursuits. For example, there's so much garbage on television; when you watch it your unconscious mind automatically absorbs that garbage reflection. So you have to exercise the discriminating wisdom that assesses whether what you're doing is worthwhile or not.

I'm not saying that television itself is bad. I'm saying that, according to your mind, you have to check up whether what you're watching is useful or not. Does it lead to wisdom or to the completely concrete attachment that causes conflict in your mind? Check up. This is really worthwhile.

Actually, you're much better off watching the internal television of your mind. Regular TV is so boring; the same old programs on the same old topics over and over again. You don't really want to watch. But when you watch your mind, it's incredible; it's much more interesting. There's always something new; if you think about it, every experience is new.

This is really true. I'm not exaggerating. Every moment of mind is interesting. If you check your mind in meditation for ten or twenty minutes a day, it's so worthwhile.

In Tibet, after listening to lam-rim teachings and receiving a clean clear intellectual understanding, people would often go into retreat to put the teachings into action; they'd experiment to see if what the lama said really worked or not. They would seriously check up. Of course, Western life is so busy that you don't have the time to do long retreats, but if every now and then you could spend a two- or three-day weekend in strict meditation it would be very powerful and most worthwhile.

And with respect to this seminar, we've been talking so much that you haven't had much time to meditate; but if we'd allowed more time for meditation you wouldn't have received the teachings you need, so we've just had to try the best we can.

Now I can try to answer any questions you might have, bearing in mind that the real answers are those you get through meditation. As I said before, those answers become incredibly powerful and meaningful. Verbal answers often aren't as meaningful. However, if you have serious questions, please ask.

Q. Lama, last year in Nepal you said that fully ordained nuns have over one hundred more vows than fully ordained monks do. Also, we see far fewer pictures of Tara than we do of male manifestations of Buddha. So I was wondering if you could say something about women. Sorry!

Lama. Lord Buddha gave fully ordained monks, *gelongs,* 253 vows and fully ordained nuns, *gelongmas,* 364. The reason for the difference is that women have incredible wisdom and very quick minds. Men are normally a little bit slow but women can put things together and come to immediate conclusions much more rapidly. Also, the way women's bodies are constituted makes them more susceptible to vibrations of the sun, moon and earth, and they undergo monthly internal changes as well. All this has a psychological effect. So women's minds change much more quickly than do men's. Women are very intelligent; they have the wisdom to quickly put things together.

In addition, women's desire does not arise frequently but when it does it can be very strong and last a long time; it can feel very uncomfortable, like being poked by a needle. Men also have desire but while it's often present it's not as strong.

Q. So the greater number of precepts is because women are less able to control desire?

Lama. Yes, that's right. That's why I'm talking about this.

Q. So it's bad karma to be born female?

Lama. No, not necessarily. You asked a general question so I'm generalizing in my reply. Certain individual women have great control. There are female buddhas. So actually, you can't generalize. However, Lord Buddha considered that men and women have equal potential to gain liberation in this life. Also, Lord Buddha didn't just say the words—he showed the method, the path to liberation. So women's liberation—inner liberation—is very good. Anyway, women have qualities and abilities that men don't and vice versa. Both have their own individual characteristics.

Also, when we ordain women, Lord Buddha said that first we should give five precepts—precepts being the way we start training the mind—for say a month; then perhaps eight; then maybe more. Proceed slowly and wait, sometimes for a year, then check up to see whether she can manage or not. Traditionally it was very strict; the purpose was to make sure. Of course, generally it's the same thing with men. They too have uncontrolled desire. But men also have their own specific characteristics, psychologically and physically.

But there's no way you can say that men can attain liberation or enlightenment and women cannot. That's impossible. In Tibet, some- times even senior monks would take teachings from higher nuns.

Q. If one has overcome strong attachment or aversion in this life, would one be placed in contact with the same people or places in the next life?

Lama. It's possible, yes. It's also logical. If in this life you train your mind such that your attachment gets less and less, at the time of death your powerful determination and the force of your karmic mental energy can lead you into perfect contact with familiar people or places so that you have the opportunity to help them again.

Q. You said last night that a man couldn't be religious if he points a gun and shoots another man who is religious. What bothers me is that you hear of Thai monks blessing guns that are then used in Vietnam, Vietnamese monks burning themselves to death in Saigon, and Tibetan monks disrobing and fighting the Chinese. Can you explain all this, please?

Lama. Thank you, it's good to ask about such things. I think monks who bless guns do so out of misconception, no matter who they are. Psychologically, that will come back to bother them. As for the monk who burnt himself in Saigon, there could be two things. If he has incredible compassion for the Vietnamese people suffering in the war and burns himself in order to demonstrate their suffering, I don't think that's foolish; but if he doesn't have compassion and is just doing it out of anger, that's foolish.

Q. Is it true that Tibetan monks have disrobed, fought the Chinese and therefore killed some?

Lama. Yes, some Tibetan monks have done that. There are different kinds of Tibetan monk. When the Chinese came, some monks did return their vows to senior monks who didn't go to war. You can't stop that kind of individual anger. Actually, they were wrong to do that. If they'd asked the senior monk if they should go, he would have said, "That's foolish; a misconception. You want to fight but you're already the best kind of soldier. You want to give up being a member of the best army, the Sangha, to join a junk army." That monk is already a soldier; he's fighting the internal enemy of the delusions, which is what really brings him down. That's a great question; you're right to ask.

There are many religions in the world, Buddhism among them. When their followers act in mistaken ways it's not the religion that's wrong; it's the people who have the misconceptions. And it's not only misconception—uncontrolled attachment is so powerful: "Oh, my nation, my country … I'm going to lose the place where I eat and sleep." So acting out of uncontrolled attachment, these Tibetan monks abandon their ordination and rush off to fight. They're foolish; I agree. That's exactly what I was talking about before. I don't even consider those people to be Buddhist. They're so emotional; their wisdom is so limited.

Q. What do we do if we recognize our negative mind? Do we just face it or do we react to it? Sometimes it seems the reaction could be to not want to face it.

Lama. What kind of situation do you mean? Be specific.

Q. For example, when we're meditating and see, "Oh, now I'm proud" or "Now I'm angry," do we just recognize this and say to ourself, "OK, I'm angry," or do we say, "I'm angry and this is not good"? What do we with the negative mind? When we find the negative mind, what do we do?

Lama. When you find that your negative mind has arisen, instead of just letting it go, apply the appropriate antidote. Even better, as soon as you find your negative mind starting to arise, stop it right there; don't let it go any further. Many Western psychologists say that when you're angry, let it out, don't suppress it; they tell you to get more angry. They mean well, but according to Lord Buddha's psychology, they're wrong. Every moment of anger creates a karmic imprint; every moment of unchecked anger builds up the energy of anger within you.

What's better is to recognize the anger within you and as soon as you feel it start to arise, instead of letting it come and recognizing and expressing it, try to digest it. That's the best way. Western psychology says, "No, no, no...don't keep your tremendous anger energy in, let it out; express your anger." So that allows the person to be overtly angry. That's foolish. It's not good because your anger energy builds up. Actually, any action you do over and over—positive or negative—builds up the corresponding kind of energy.

Let me give you an example. How do you control anger if you're a person who has great difficulty doing so? When you get up in the morning, bring to mind the characteristic nature of anger. First of all, anger comes from the root of ignorance, and the cooperative cause for its arising is a huge build-up of superstition. Its function is to destroy all your pleasure. Even your face becomes the picture of misery. Check the faces of people who are always angry: they're always kind of tense, tight. Check up; they're different.

Anyway, first thing in the morning, because you're not angry at that time, examine the shortcomings of anger and see clean clear what the nature of anger is. After that, generate much compassion for yourself: "If I keep behaving in this way I'll ruin my life. But it's not only me. All universal living beings also destroy their beautiful, enjoyable lives by getting angry. A moment's anger can destroy the lives of a couple that has been together for years. They do this to themselves. It's incredibly foolish. The nature of anger is pure foolishness; today I'm not going to get angry at all. I dedicate my life today to the opposite of anger: patience. From now until I go to bed tonight, I'm going to control my anger, with much compassion for all universal living beings."

When you make that determination in the morning, the whole day goes like that. In the evening you check up: "What a surprise. Normally I'm always angry but today I didn't get angry at all. I'm so glad, so appreciative, so happy." Then dedicate your positive energy to others and, rejoicing, go to sleep.

The next day you almost won't need to generate strong energy to maintain your control; it will be easy. Then the day after that it will be easier still…and the next and the next, until you've managed to control your anger for a week. If you can control it for one week, the second week will definitely be easier. Then you'll have been able to control it for a month. So two months will be easy. Then you'll have controlled it for a year. Once you've done that you'll practically never get angry again. Finally you'll finish up saying to people, "I find it impossible to get angry. Please would you teach me how?" You might have to go to anger school to learn how to do it! It's possible. That's true. You can reach a point where there's no way anybody can make you angry.

So that was a good, practical question. Just stopping the problem of anger is most worthwhile; that's incredible. The nature of anger is misery and the angry mind is uptight. Angry people suffer greatly; their faces are different and they totally destroy their enjoyment of life. So at least controlling your anger is most worthwhile. If there's no anger between a married couple there's no way their life will be miserable; it's impossible. They will always have a good relationship, a good home and good vibrations.

Many times Westerners are too intellectual, always looking for some kind of higher meditation. They're not realistic. If you just practice not getting angry it's so worthwhile. That itself is liberation, inner freedom; that's more realistic and so worthwhile—in everyday life you're dealing with people, so you don't get angry with your wife, husband, friends or anybody. You always have a good time.

Q. Please could you say more about the dedication of merit?

Lama. We have an analogy for why we dedicate the energy of merit. Say you're riding a big, powerful horse. If you have no bridle the horse will run wild and you won't end up where you want to go. Although the horse's energy is perfectly strong and it can run really well, without control you'll finish up falling off and hurting yourself badly. Similarly, if you have the powerful energy of merit and don't dedicate it, if somebody suddenly says something to you that makes you angry, your merit immediately disappears.

Creating merit and then destroying it is like first cleaning a floor, then, when you've finished, putting *ka-ka* all over it, dirtying it up again. This is a good example of what we normally do. Therefore, you should dedicate whatever positive energy you have to benefit others, instead of letting it go without direction, like a powerful horse without a bridle.

Also, whenever you dedicate your positive energy to others, the energy you dedicate is like a drop of water put into the ocean—as long as the ocean remains, that drop of water is never exhausted. Similarly, when you deposit your positive energy into the bank of enlightenment for the benefit of others, it becomes exhaustless.

Not only that. When you do something positive you might automatically feel proud: "Oh, I did such a good meditation." Pride is a psychological problem; dedication is the solution. Therefore, it's very important to dedicate your merit. Otherwise we often generate pride, boasting, "I did this; I did that." You make a big show of your virtue. Dedicating merit is like putting money in a bank. You bank your money to protect it; dedicating merit protects it in your internal bank.

Q. When you do something good and you know what it's for, is that dedication?

Lama. No, that's not dedication. Dedication is the mind that thinks, "I have not done this positive action for my own salvation or pleasure but totally for the benefit of others."

Q. So you let go of it?

Lama. Yes, you let go; put your energy in one direction. Don't let it go like an uncontrolled, powerful horse. If I were to talk about merit in detail it would take much time, but briefly, it's not that easy to dedicate merit properly; you have to bring to mind the emptiness of three things: yourself, the person dedicating the merit; the merit itself; and the way you dedicate. Dedicating with understanding of the empty nature of these three things is the best way to dedicate, absolutely worthwhile. Dedicating with pure knowledge-wisdom releases all the misconceptions of self-attachment to these three things. This is the *prajnaparamita*—perfection of wisdom—way of dedicating. It's difficult, but, if you can manage, you should do it that way. Otherwise our dedication is mixed with attachment. In Tibetan we call this *ngo-wai kor-sum*–dedicating in the circle of the three.

Q. How does one use the rosary (Skt: *mala*)?

Lama. One thing that a mala is used for is to count mantras. Sometimes we have a certain number of mantras we have to count on a daily basis or in retreat and we use it for that. In some retreats you have to recite one, two, five or even ten million mantras; each day we bless our mala and use it to count the number of mantras we recite. We also use it to treat certain illnesses. For example, some people are made sick by spirit possession and can be healed by a mala placed on their head, but the person doing this needs long experience and to have received the power of the mantra.

Q. Can we go beyond time, like reincarnate in the past?
Lama. No, that's not possible. Each rebirth is the result of previous karma and takes place in a different environment, so they're never the same. For example, say from the time you were born until now you've lived with the same family in the same London house— you feel as if you and the things around you are the same. But if you check up carefully, from the time you were born, every minute your environment and your experience have been changing; everything is totally different. If we just look at things superficially we have the attitude, "Oh, every morning I drink coffee, I have the same lunch, I have this family, this house…it's all the same." But they're not the same; thinking that they are is a misconception born of superficiality.

If you check your life experiences scientifically you'll see that each one is different. Even from the beginning of this seminar up until now, everything's different: your experiences, your perceptions, your view and your consciousness. Of course, you can say something like, "Last year I was a black woman; perhaps in my next life I'll be a black woman again." Is that sort of superficial thing what you're asking? That can happen but there's no way you can be exactly the same as you were in a previous life. Is that clear? Perhaps you'd better ask me your question again.

Q. Are you saying that karma goes forward all the time?
Lama. That's right, yes. It's impossible for karma to go backwards. If it were then it would be possible for me to become a five-year-old child in this life.

Q. A lot of people do become children when they get older.
Lama. Come on, dear; that's just street language. We need to talk about this scientifically. When we talk generally we say things like, "Your mind is like a baby's." That doesn't mean the person has become baby. We're talking about a one-hundred-year-old person's becoming a five-year-old. That's impossible. Can you prove scientifically that it can happen? You can say somebody's *like* a child; that doesn't mean the person's a child.

Q. But things seem to go in a circle.
Lama. Yes, things circle, but the experiences themselves are different. You can't say they're always the same thing. If you check scientifically you'll see that they're different.

Q. Can you say specifically what meditations we should be doing when we first wake up in the morning and right before we go to sleep at night?
Lama. The best meditation to do in the morning is the development of single-pointed concentration; at night you should do

purification. Before you go to sleep, check back on your day: "Since I awoke this morning I've done many things and gone many places." So you check up: "What kind of mind did I have here? What kind of mind did I have there?" Check how many positive minds you had and how many negative. The conclusion you'll probably come to is, "Most of my actions were negative; not so many were positive." So before you go to sleep, do a purification meditation and then go to sleep with a happy, joyful, clean clear mind. That's very useful.

Actually, it's best not to go to sleep with a foggy, uncomfortable mind. If you go to sleep in an agitated condition, you keep generating that energy all night. For example, if you go to sleep angry, anger energy builds up in your mind all night. Therefore, it's much better to make your mind calm and clear before you go to sleep. And if you can actually go to sleep in meditation, your entire sleep energy becomes the everlastingly peaceful path to liberation. So meditating prior to going to sleep is very, very useful. And we also have special methods of meditating while you're asleep called dream yoga that are in the further reaches of the graduated path to liberation, so you can study those later.

That's a wonderfully practical question. When you get up in the morning, instead of thinking in a conflicted, mundane way, "What am I going to do today?" and rushing into the kitchen as your mind immediately goes into your refrigerator, get up slowly and meditate. Relax, make your mind calm and clear, and dedicate yourself to making this day's life meaningful in the highest way instead of living like an animal. That way you're not up and down all day because the powerful determination you generate in the morning keeps you on track. Even if somebody suddenly hits you, you remain in control. That's possible, through the will power of the mind.

Your mind is incredibly powerful, I tell you. You have to know how. We think external things are so powerful but they're all manmade. Real power actually lies within us. We created all these things; our internal power manifests the external world. If we direct this power inward we can create the inner realization of enlightenment. That's why generating proper motivation in the morning is very important.

Thank you for your questions. Now, one of the students has made small Manjushri lapel buttons, which is very auspicious. Manjushri is the manifestation of knowledge-wisdom, so now I'm going to bless these buttons and offer them to you. I'll also give you the transmission of the Manjushri mantra to facilitate the growth of knowledge-wisdom within you.

[Lama Yeshe and Lama Zopa Rinpoche do puja to bless the Manjushri buttons.]

Mantra transmission

Now, if you can, instead of visualizing me, Thubten Yeshe, sitting here with this body of meat and bone, immediately transform it into the radiant red-yellow light body of Manjushri. At my heart is the Divine Wisdom Manjushri mantra. From this mantra a duplicate transcendent mantra manifests and comes from my heart through my mouth like a rosary. This electric rosary energy goes into your mouth and down to your heart three times: the first time, it comes to your heart; the second time, it sinks into the first mantra; the third time, it again sinks into your heart mantra, making it indestructibly powerful, magnetically powerful to attract enlightened realizations through your developing knowledge-wisdom.

While visualizing all this, repeat the mantra:

OM AH RA PA TSA NA DHIH; OM AH RA PA TSA NA DHIH; OM AH RA PA TSA NA DHIH.

Now let's recite it together:

OM AH RA PA TSA NA DHIH DHIH DHIH DHIH DHIH.... (X3)[13]

From your heart, blissful red-yellow radiates all throughout your entire body, energizing great joy.

[Lama Yeshe and Lama Zopa Rinpoche chant.]

By receiving the transmission of this mantra you're not making a commitment to recite it daily but you can if you like; doing so would be most worthwhile. It's a specific method for gaining knowledge-wisdom.

---

[13] DHIH is the seed syllable of Manjushri. It is often recited repeatedly, either alone or after a repetition of the mantra OM AH RA PA TSA NA, in order to benefit the speech in the ways Lama mentions below.

For example, in Tibet, if a monk was a bit slow in understanding things he would practice Manjushri in order to gain quick knowledge-wisdom. Also, this mantra is incredible for people who can't talk properly because of trouble with their tongue. After just a month they can talk properly. I'm not joking; this is people's experience. If you recite this mantra before talking or giving a speech the power of your words can be greatly increased. So it is a very good to recite this transcendental mantra. Manjushri is nothing external; Manjushri is all enlightened beings' supreme transcendental knowledge-wisdom transformed into such a red-yellow light body. That's what we call Manjushri—the embodiment of knowledge-wisdom.

Conclusion

And now we've come to the end of this very short seminar. I've enjoyed it very much and have been very happy to meet you beautiful people. I pray that next time we meet we can spend more time together; that would be better. It's been a little rushed this time, so please forgive us for that. However, if you have any questions arise you can write us. These days, the world is very small. Also, if you have questions, you can talk to Chime Rinpoche or Akong Rinpoche, who both live in the UK.

We're also going to offer a protection cord blessed by Lama Zopa Rinpoche to anybody who wants; you can wear it around your neck if you like. It offers psychological protection. It's not that we think there are demons from which you need to be protected.

Also, the Manjushri buttons are worth keeping. They can be very useful in reminding you of the knowledge-wisdom you have gained instead of allowing your mind to be always occupied by mundane thoughts. This kind of image is not merely a material object but a reminder of knowledge-wisdom. It gives you teachings without words. When you look at an image of the Buddha sitting in the meditation posture you feel something, don't you? It automatically gives you some control. That's why we have this kind of art, not because we somehow believe that this is really God or Buddha. It gives off a positive vibration.

Also, when you get back home, check up on how you have decorated the place you live. This can give you a clue as to your psychology, what interests your mind, what kind of mind you have. Anyway, what's best is to keep the inside of your house very clean, clear and simple instead of cluttering it with all kinds of garbage. When everything in your house is clean, clear and orderly, your mind becomes simple, clean and clear. Don't keep all kinds of mixed up things, many pictures, crazy stuff around. Look at the art of people who are psychologically disturbed. Everything they draw is so complicated and disordered. So don't make your environment like that; your mind is conditioned—you haven't yet reached beyond conditions.

Art can sometimes be useful. Religious art explains things beyond words. Even shopkeepers understand this kind of psychology, as you can see from their window displays.

I think that's all I can say. Thank you so much for everything. Now we're going to dedicate the merit we've created during this seminar to the benefit of all sentient beings, to lead them into enlightenment, the everlastingly joyful state of consciousness.

Ge wa di yi nyur du dag
Lama sang gyä drub gyur nä
Dro wa chig kyang ma lü pa
De yi sa la gö par shog

Thank you again. Perhaps I'll say one more thing. Sometimes young people take teachings from a lama then go back home and push their ideas onto their parents and friends, agitating them. You shouldn't do that.

The things you've learned here are for your own liberation, not to push onto other people. We don't believe in pushing our ideas onto people, trying to convert them to Buddhism. That's not right. Don't push your parents or friends; just live naturally. Just put what you've learned into action as much as you can. Don't push your ideas onto others.

If you live the teachings, those close to you will get a good vibration from you, through your actions. Some young people get all excited, "Oh, now I've found something really special," and lay their trip onto others. Don't push that way. Also, don't accost strangers in the street and say, "Come with me, I'll show you the path to liberation." That doesn't work either. Be realistic; be natural. Of course, if somebody approaches you with questions, at that time you can answer to the best of your ability. But if people don't ask, don't push—that's not the characteristic nature of Buddhism. Act as much as possible; that's the way to gain realizations.

So thank you again for everything and we'll see you again soon— in the sky!

SUGGESTED FURTHER READING

See page 2 for the list of books previously published by the Lama Yeshe Wisdom Archive. All of these will enhance your understanding of the teachings in this book. Also, thousands of pages of Lama Zopa Rinpoche's lam-rim teachings and many teachings by Lama Yeshe may be found on line at www.LamaYeshe.com.

GENERAL

Rabten, Geshe. *The Essential Nectar: Meditations on the Buddhist Path.* Editing and verse translation by Martin Willson. Boston: Wisdom Publications, 1984, 1992.

Yangsi Rinpoche. *Practicing the Path: A commentary on the* Lam-rim Chenmo. Edited by Miranda Adams. Boston: Wisdom Publications, 2003.

Yeshe, Lama, and Zopa Rinpoche, Lama. *Wisdom Energy: Basic Buddhist Teachings.* Edited by Jonathan Landaw and Alexander Berzin. Boston: Wisdom Publications, 1976, 2000.

DEEPER

Pabongka Rinpoche. *Liberation in the Palm of Your Hand: A Concise Discourse on the Path to Enlightenment.* Edited by Trijang Rinpoche. Translated by Michael Richards. Boston: Wisdom Publications, 1991, 2006.

Sopa, Geshe Lhundub, with David Patt. *Steps on the Path to Enlightenment: A Commentary on Tsongkhapa's* Lamrim Chenmo: *Volumes 1–5.* Boston: Wisdom Publications, 2004, 2005, 2008 (Vols. 4 & 5 to come).

Tsong-kha-pa. *The Great Treatise on the Stages of the Path to Enlightenment: Volumes One, Two & Three.* Translated by the Lamrim Chenmo Translation Committee. Ithaca, New York: Snow Lion Publications, 2000, 2002, 2004.

Yeshe, Lama. *Introduction to Tantra: The Transformation of Desire.* Edited by Jonathan Landaw. Boston: Wisdom Publications, 1987, 2001.

Zopa Rinpoche, Lama. *The Heart of the Path: Seeing the Guru as Buddha.* Boston: Lama Yeshe Wisdom Archive, 2009.

LAMA YESHE WISDOM ARCHIVE

The LAMA YESHE WISDOM ARCHIVE (LYWA) is the collected works of Lama Thubten Yeshe and Lama Thubten Zopa Rinpoche. Lama Zopa Rinpoche, its spiritual director, founded the ARCHIVE in 1996.

Lama Yeshe and Lama Zopa Rinpoche began teaching at Kopan Monastery, Nepal, in 1970. Since then, their teachings have been recorded and transcribed. At present we have well over 10,000 hours of digital audio and some 70,000 pages of raw transcript. Many recordings, mostly teachings by Lama Zopa Rinpoche, remain to be transcribed, and as Rinpoche continues to teach, the number of recordings in the ARCHIVE increases accordingly. Most of our transcripts have been neither checked nor edited.

Here at the LYWA we are making every effort to organize the transcription of that which has not yet been transcribed, edit that which has not yet been edited, and generally do the many other tasks detailed below.

The work of the LAMA YESHE WISDOM ARCHIVE falls into two categories: archiving and dissemination.

Archiving requires managing the recordings of teachings by Lama Yeshe and Lama Zopa Rinpoche that have already been collected, collecting recordings of teachings given but not yet sent to the ARCHIVE, and collecting recordings of Lama Zopa's on-going teachings, talks, advice and so forth as he travels the world for the benefit of all. Incoming media are then catalogued and stored safely while being kept accessible for further work.

We organize the transcription of audio, add the transcripts to the already existent database of teachings, manage this database, have transcripts checked, and make transcripts available to editors or others doing research on or practicing these teachings.

Other archiving activities include working with video and photographs of the Lamas and digitizing ARCHIVE materials.

Dissemination involves making the Lamas' teachings available through various avenues including books for free distribution and sale, lightly edited transcripts, a monthly e-letter (see below), DVDs, articles in *Mandala* and other magazines and on our website. Irrespective of the medium we choose, the teachings require a significant amount of work to prepare them for distribution.

This is just a summary of what we do. The ARCHIVE was established with virtually no seed funding and has developed solely through the kindness of many people, some of whom we have mentioned at the front of this book and most of the others on our website. We sincerely thank them all.

Our further development similarly depends upon the generosity of those who see the benefit and necessity of this work, and we would be extremely grateful for your help. Thus we hereby appeal to you for your kind support. If you would like to make a contribution to help us with any of the above tasks or to sponsor books for free distribution, please contact us:

LAMA YESHE WISDOM ARCHIVE
PO Box 356, Weston, MA 02493, USA
Telephone (781) 259-4466; Fax (678) 868-4806
info@LamaYeshe.com
www.LamaYeshe.com

The LAMA YESHE WISDOM ARCHIVE is a 501(c)(3) tax-deductible, non-profit corporation dedicated to the welfare of all sentient beings and totally dependent upon your donations for its continued existence. Thank you so much for your support. You may contribute by mailing a check, bank draft or money order to our Weston address; by making a donation on our secure website; by mailing us your credit card number or phoning it in; or by transferring funds directly to our bank—ask us for details.

LAMA YESHE WISDOM ARCHIVE MEMBERSHIP

In order to raise the money we need to employ editors to make available the thousands of hours of teachings mentioned above, we have established a membership plan. Membership costs US$1,000 and its main benefit is that you will be helping make the Lamas' incredible teachings available to a worldwide audience. More direct and tangible benefits to you personally include free Lama Yeshe and Lama Zopa Rinpoche books from the AR-CHIVE and Wisdom Publications, a year's subscription to *Mandala*, a year of monthly pujas by the monks and nuns at Kopan Monastery with your personal dedication, and access to an exclusive members-only section of our website containing special, unpublished teachings currently unavailable to others. Please see www.LamaYeshe.com for more information.

MONTHLY E-LETTER

Each month we send out a free e-letter containing our latest news and a previously unpublished teaching by Lama Yeshe or Lama Zopa Rinpoche. To see more than seventy back-issues or to subscribe with your email address, please go to our website.

The Foundation for the Preservation of the Mahayana Tradition

The Foundation for the Preservation of the Mahayana Tradition (FPMT) is an international organization of Buddhist meditation study and retreat centers, both urban and rural, monasteries, publishing houses, healing centers and other related activities founded in 1975 by Lama Thubten Yeshe and Lama Thubten Zopa Rinpoche. At present, there are more than 150 FPMT activities in over thirty countries worldwide.

The FPMT has been established to facilitate the study and practice of Mahayana Buddhism in general and the Tibetan Gelug tradition, founded in the fifteenth century by the great scholar, yogi and saint, Lama Je Tsongkhapa, in particular.

Every quarter, the Foundation publishes a wonderful news journal, *Mandala*, from its International Office in the USA. To subscribe or view back issues, please go to the *Mandala* website, www.mandalamagazine.org, or contact:

FPMT
1632 SE 11th Avenue, Portland, OR 97214
Telephone (503) 808-1588; Fax (503) 808-1589
info@fpmt.org
www.fpmt.org

The FPMT website also offers teachings by His Holiness the Dalai Lama, Lama Yeshe, Lama Zopa Rinpoche and many other highly respected teachers in the tradition, details about the FPMT's educational programs, audio through FPMT radio, a link to the excellent FPMT Store, a complete listing of FPMT centers all over the world and in your area, and links to FPMT centers on the web, where you will find details of their programs, and to other interesting Buddhist and Tibetan home pages.

DISCOVERING BUDDHISM AT HOME
Awakening the limitless potential of your mind,
achieving all peace and happiness

Over 2500 years ago, Shakyamuni Buddha gained direct insight into the nature of reality, perfected the qualities of wisdom, compassion, and power, and revealed the path to his disciples. In the 11th Century, Atisha brought these teachings to Tibet in the form of the lam-rim—the stages on the path to enlightenment. The lam-rim tradition found its pinnacle in the teachings of the great Tibetan saint Je Tsongkhapa in the 14th Century, and these teachings continued to pass from teacher to student up to this present day.

When Lama Thubten Yeshe and Lama Zopa Rinpoche transmitted these teachings to their disciples, they imparted a deeply experiential tradition of study and practice, leading thousands of seekers to discover the truth of what the Buddha taught. This tradition is the core of *Discovering Buddhism*— a two-year, fourteen-module series that provides a solid foundation in the teachings and practice of Tibetan Mahayana Buddhism.

HOW IT WORKS: Each *Discovering Buddhism* module consists of teachings, meditations and practices, readings, assessment questions, and a short retreat. Students who complete all the components of each course receive a completion card. When all fourteen modules have been completed, students receive a certificate of completion, a symbol of commitment to spiritual awakening.

This program is offered in FPMT centers around the world, as a home study program and, beginning in 2009, as an interactive online program.

HOME STUDY PROGRAM: Each *Discovering Buddhism at Home* module contains audio recordings of teachings and meditations given by qualified Western teachers, and a text CD containing the course materials and transcripts of the audio teachings, and an online discussion board overseen by senior FPMT teachers. FAQ pages help the student navigate the program and provide the best of the discussion board's questions and answers. Upon completion of a module, students may have their assessment questions evaluated by senior FPMT teachers and receive personal feedback.

Discovering Buddhism at Home is available from the FPMT Foundation Store, www.fpmt.org/shop. For more information on *Discovering Buddhism* and the other educational programs and services of the FPMT, please visit us at www.fpmt.org/education.

OTHER TEACHINGS OF LAMA YESHE AND LAMA ZOPA RINPOCHE CURRENTLY AVAILABLE

BOOKS PUBLISHED BY WISDOM PUBLICATIONS
Wisdom Energy, by Lama Yeshe and Lama Zopa Rinpoche
Introduction to Tantra, by Lama Yeshe
Transforming Problems, by Lama Zopa Rinpoche
The Door to Satisfaction, by Lama Zopa Rinpoche
Becoming Vajrasattva: The Tantric Path of Purification, by Lama Yeshe
The Bliss of Inner Fire, by Lama Yeshe
Becoming the Compassion Buddha, by Lama Yeshe
Ultimate Healing, by Lama Zopa Rinpoche
Dear Lama Zopa, by Lama Zopa Rinpoche
How to Be Happy, by Lama Zopa Rinpoche

About Lama Yeshe:
Reincarnation: The Boy Lama, by Vicki Mackenzie

About Lama Zopa Rinpoche:
The Lawudo Lama, by Jamyang Wangmo

You can get more information about and order the above titles at www.wisdompubs.org or call toll free in the USA on 1-800-272-4050.

TRANSCRIPTS, PRACTICES AND OTHER MATERIALS
See the LYWA and FPMT websites for transcripts of teachings by Lama Yeshe and Lama Zopa Rinpoche and other practices written or compiled by Lama Zopa Rinpoche.

DVDs OF LAMA YESHE
We are in the process of converting our VHS videos of Lama Yeshe's teachings to DVD. *The Three Principal Aspects of the Path, Introduction to Tantra, Offering Tsok to Heruka Vajrasattva, Anxiety in the Nuclear Age, Bringing Dharma to the West* and *Lama Yeshe at Disneyland* are currently available. More coming all the time—see our website for details.

DVDs OF LAMA ZOPA RINPOCHE
There are many available: see the Store on the FPMT website for more information.

What to do with Dharma teachings

The Buddhadharma is the true source of happiness for all sentient beings. Books like this show you how to put the teachings into practice and integrate them into your life, whereby you get the happiness you seek. Therefore, anything containing Dharma teachings, the names of your teachers or holy images is more precious than other material objects and should be treated with respect. To avoid creating the karma of not meeting the Dharma again in future lives, please do not put books (or other holy objects) on the floor or underneath other stuff, step over or sit upon them, or use them for mundane purposes such as propping up wobbly tables. They should be kept in a clean, high place, separate from worldly writings, and wrapped in cloth when being carried around. These are but a few considerations.

Should you need to get rid of Dharma materials, they should not be thrown in the rubbish but burned in a special way. Briefly: do not incinerate such materials with other trash, but alone, and as they burn, recite the mantra OM AH HUM. As the smoke rises, visualize that it pervades all of space, carrying the essence of the Dharma to all sentient beings in the six samsaric realms, purifying their minds, alleviating their suffering, and bringing them all happiness, up to and including enlightenment. Some people might find this practice a bit unusual, but it is given according to tradition. Thank you very much.

Dedication

Through the merit created by preparing, reading, thinking about and sharing this book with others, may all teachers of the Dharma live long and healthy lives, may the Dharma spread throughout the infinite reaches of space, and may all sentient beings quickly attain enlightenment.

In whichever realm, country, area or place this book may be, may there be no war, drought, famine, disease, injury, disharmony or unhappiness, may there be only great prosperity, may everything needed be easily obtained, and may all be guided by only perfectly qualified Dharma teachers, enjoy the happiness of Dharma, have love and compassion for all sentient beings, and only benefit and never harm each other.

LAMA THUBTEN YESHE was born in Tibet in 1935. At the age of six, he entered the great Sera Monastic University, Lhasa, where he studied until 1959, when the Chinese invasion of Tibet forced him into exile in India. Lama Yeshe continued to study and meditate in India until 1967, when, with his chief disciple, Lama Thubten Zopa Rinpoche, he went to Nepal. Two years later he established Kopan Monastery, near Kathmandu, in order to teach Buddhism to Westerners. In 1974, the Lamas began making annual teaching tours to the West, and as a result of these travels a worldwide network of Buddhist teaching and meditation centers—the Foundation for the Preservation of the Mahayana Tradition (FPMT)—began to develop. In 1984, after an intense decade of imparting a wide variety of incredible teachings and establishing one FPMT activity after another, at the age of forty-nine, Lama Yeshe passed away. He was reborn as Ösel Hita Torres in Spain in 1985 and recognized as the incarnation of Lama Yeshe by His Holiness the Dalai Lama in 1986. Lama's remarkable story is told in Vicki Mackenzie's book, *Reincarnation: The Boy Lama* (Wisdom Publications, 1996) and Adele Hulse's official biography, *Big Love*, (forthcoming from LYWA).

LAMA THUBTEN ZOPA RINPOCHE was born in Thami, Nepal, in 1945. At the age of three he was recognized as the reincarnation of the Lawudo Lama, who had lived nearby at Lawudo, within sight of Rinpoche's Thami home. Rinpoche's own description of his early years may be found in his book, *The Door to Satisfaction*. At the age of ten, Rinpoche went to Tibet and studied and meditated at Domo Geshe Rinpoche's monastery near Pagri, until the Chinese occupation of Tibet in 1959 forced him to forsake Tibet for the safety of Bhutan. Rinpoche then went to the Tibetan refugee camp at Buxa Duar, West Bengal, India, where he met Lama Yeshe, who became his closest teacher. The Lamas went to Nepal in 1967, and over the next few years built Kopan and Lawudo Monasteries. In 1971 Lama Zopa Rinpoche gave the first of his famous annual lam-rim retreat courses, which continue at Kopan to this day. In 1974, with Lama Yeshe, Rinpoche began traveling the world to teach and establish centers of Dharma. When Lama Yeshe passed away in 1984, Rinpoche took over as spiritual head of the FPMT, which has continued to flourish under his peerless leadership. More details of Rinpoche's life and work may be found in *The Lawudo Lama* and on the LYWA and FPMT websites. In addition to many LYWA and FPMT books, Rinpoche's other published teachings include *Wisdom Energy* (with Lama Yeshe), *Transforming Problems, Ultimate Healing, Dear Lama Zopa, How to Be Happy* and many transcripts and practice booklets.

DR. NICHOLAS RIBUSH, MB, BS, is a graduate of Melbourne University Medical School (1964) who first encountered Buddhism at Kopan Monastery, Nepal, in 1972. Since then he has been a student of Lama Yeshe and Lama Zopa Rinpoche and a full time worker for their international organization, the Foundation for the Preservation of the Mahayana Tradition (FPMT). He was a monk from 1974 to 1986. He established FPMT archiving and publishing activities at Kopan in 1973 and with Lama Yeshe founded Wisdom Publications in 1975. Between 1981 and 1996 he served variously as Wisdom's director, editorial director and director of development. Over the years he has edited and published many teachings by His Holiness the Dalai Lama, Lama Yeshe, Lama Zopa Rinpoche and many other teachers and established and/or directed several other FPMT activities, including the International Mahayana Institute, Tushita Mahayana Meditation Centre, the Enlightened Experience Celebration, Mahayana Publications, and now Kurukulla Center for Tibetan Buddhist Studies and the LAMA YESHE WISDOM ARCHIVE. He was a member of the FPMT board of directors from its inception in 1983 until 2002.

The B

Betty Neels's [...]
of readers ar[...]
special 2-in-1 collection offers a unique
opportunity to relive the magic of some of her
most popular stories.

We are proud to present these classic romances
by the woman who could weave an irresistible
tale of love like no other.

So sit back in your comfiest chair with your
favorite cup of tea and enjoy these best of
Betty Neels stories!

Romance readers around the world were sad to note the passing of **Betty Neels** in June 2001. Her career spanned thirty years, and she continued to write into her ninetieth year. To her millions of fans, Betty epitomized the romance writer, and yet she began writing almost by accident. She had retired from nursing, but her inquiring mind still sought stimulation. Her new career was born when she heard a lady in her local library bemoaning the lack of good romance novels. Betty's first book, *Sister Peters in Amsterdam*, was published in 1969, and she eventually completed 134 books. Her novels offer a reassuring warmth that was very much a part of her own personality, and her spirit and genuine talent live on in all her stories.

Betty Neels

HEAVEN AROUND THE CORNER

and

CAROLINE'S WATERLOO

HARLEQUIN® THE BETTY NEELS COLLECTION

ISBN-13: 978-0-373-60110-3

Heaven Around the Corner and Caroline's Waterloo

Copyright © 2015 by Harlequin Books S.A.

The publisher acknowledges the copyright holder of the individual works as follows:

Heaven Around the Corner
Copyright © 1981 by Betty Neels

Caroline's Waterloo
Copyright © 1980 by Betty Neels

This edition published by arrangement with Harlequin Books S.A.

For questions and comments about the quality of this book, please contact us at CustomerService@Harlequin.com.

Printed in U.S.A.

CONTENTS

HEAVEN AROUND THE CORNER   7

CAROLINE'S WATERLOO   191

HEAVEN AROUND
THE CORNER

CHAPTER ONE

THE SEPTEMBER SUN, shining from an early morning sky, cast its impartial light on the narrow crowded streets, the smoke-grimed houses, several quite beautiful churches and the ugly bulk of the Royal Southern Hospital, giving a glow to its red bricks and a sparkle to its many narrow windows. It was a splendid example of mid-Victorian architecture, crowned with cupolas and a highly ornamental balustrade and rendered even more hideous by reason of the iron fire escapes protruding from each wing. And inside it was even uglier, for here the sun was unable to reach all its staircases and passages, so that the dark brown paintwork and distempered walls tended to cast a damper on anyone passing through them.

But the girl going down the stairs two at a time noticed none of these things. Her neat head with its crown of light brown hair was full of excited thoughts. She had passed her State finals; she was a fully trained nurse at last—the world was her oyster. She was determined on that, despite the Principal Nursing Officer's gracious speech as she was handed the fateful envelope. There

was a place for her at the Royal Southern, that lady told
her; Night Staff Nurse on the surgical wing and the
prospect of a Sister's post very shortly, and there was
no need for Nurse Evans to decide at once...

But Louisa Evans had already decided instantly; she
was going to leave, not only the hospital, but if possible, England too, although she prudently forbore from
saying so at the time. At the end of the day, when she
went off duty, she was going to write her resignation
and hand it in and then she would go home for her
two days off and tell her stepmother. She checked her
headlong flight for a second, dreading that, but it was
something which had to be done, and she had made up
her mind to that weeks ago when she sat her exams.

She went along a narrow corridor, up another flight
of stairs, across a wide landing and through the swing
doors leading to Women's Surgical. Just for the moment the future wasn't important, only the delicious
prospect of telling Sister and the nurses on the ward
that she was an SRN.

And she had no need to tell anyone. Sister, coming out of her office, took one look at Louisa's happy
face and said: 'You've passed—congratulations, but
of course I knew that you would.' And after that the
news spread like wildfire, with the patients, only too
glad to have something to talk about, telling each other,
nodding their heads and saying, with hindsight, that of
course Nurse Evans had been bound to pass, she was
such a good nurse. And as for Louisa, she floated up
and down the ward, doing her work with her usual ef-

ficiency while a tiny bit of her mind pondered the problems of what she should do and where she should go.

A problem solved sooner than she had expected: She had been to her midday dinner—a noisy meal she shared with friends who had reached her exalted position too—and she was back on the ward, changing Mrs Griffin's dressing, when that lady asked her what she intended doing.

Louisa, aware of how news, false as well as true, travelled with the speed of light round the hospital, said cautiously that she hadn't quite made up her mind, and rolling the lady carefully back into a sitting position, rearranged her pillows, smoothed the counterpane and prepared to depart with her dressing tray.

'Well, don't go for a minute, Nurse,' begged Mrs Griffin. 'Listen to this: "Trained nurse urgently required for lady patient travelling to Norway in a month's time for an indefinite stay. Good salary and expenses paid." What do you think of that?' She folded the *Telegraph* and handed it to Louisa, who read it carefully, and having an excellent memory, noted the telephone number. 'It sounds fun,' she observed cheerfully. 'Someone'll be lucky.' She drew back the curtains and with a parting nod raced off down the ward to clear the tray and get on with the next dressing. But before she did that, she jotted down the telephone number on to the hem of her apron.

She went off duty at five o'clock, composed her letter of resignation and handed it in for delivery to the office and then went to telephone from the box in the entrance hall. There was no one about; she could see the porter on duty, sitting with his feet up, sipping tea during his brief break. All her friends were already in the Nurses' Home, getting dressed for the party they were all going to later on that evening. She dialled the number.

The voice at the other end asked her to wait a moment and after a few seconds another voice spoke. Louisa had had all the afternoon to rehearse what she was going to say and she was listened to without interruption. When she had finished, the voice, a woman's, high and somehow breathless, said: 'I have interviewed several nurses already, but none of them suit me. Come and see me tomorrow morning about eleven o'clock.'

'I'm on duty until the early afternoon...'

'Oh, well, the afternoon then, about three o'clock. I'm at the Connaught Hotel, and ask for Miss Savage.'

Louisa put the receiver down slowly. Miss Savage had sounded petulant; she wondered what complaint the lady suffered from, but the only way was to go and see her and find out. Even if she were offered the job, she need not accept it.

She started to stroll along the passage to the small door which opened into the Nurses' Home. On the other hand, if she were offered the job it would be like the answer to a prayer—she had been longing to leave the hospital for some months now, not because she was unhappy there—on the contrary, she had enjoyed every minute of the three years she had spent within its walls—but because her stepmother, living not too far away, had been able to keep tabs on her for that time, knowing that she had set her heart on training as a nurse and wasn't likely to leave the Royal Southern and was therefore unlikely to escape. But now she could do just that… She quickened her steps, intent on not being late for the party.

They had all decided to dress rather grandly for the occasion. Louisa, burrowing around in her cupboard, wasted a good deal of time deciding whether the pale blue crepe would look better than the sage green silk jersey. On second thoughts she didn't like either of them, she had had them too long although she hadn't worn them all that much. She chose the green and rushed off to find an empty bathroom.

Half an hour later she was dressed and ready—a rather small girl and a little too thin, with a face which wasn't quite pretty although her eyes, large and hazel and fringed with long curling lashes, redeemed it from plainness. Her hair, long and fine and silky, she had fastened back with a silver clasp because there hadn't been time to do anything more elaborate. Presently her friends trooped in and they all went into the hospital to the residents' room where the housemen and some of the students had laid on a buffet supper. The room was packed already, with everyone talking at once and quite a few dancing to a barely heard tape recorder. Louisa, popular with everyone because she was ready to lend an ear to anyone who wanted it, was quickly absorbed into a group of young housemen, all of whom looked upon her as a sisterly type to whom they could confide their troubled but fleeting love affairs, for she never told them how silly they were but listened to their outpourings, giving sympathy but never advice. For a girl of twenty-two she had a wise head on her shoulders, albeit a rather shy one. Her stepmother had taken care that she had had very little chance of making friends while she was at school and when she left, until she had succeeded at last in her ambition to train as a nurse; she had been kept too busy to do more than meet the people Mrs Evans approved of, most of them elderly or at least middle-aged, so that she still retained the feeling of not quite belonging among the young people at the hospital, certainly she had shied away from any of the young men of her acquaintance who had hinted at anything more serious than a kiss, and they, once they had laughed about her among themselves, but kindly, had taken to treating her like a sister.

She joined the dancers presently and except for short pauses for food and drink, didn't lack for partners for the rest of the evening. The party broke up around midnight and they all went their several ways, yawning their heads off and grumbling at the prospect of getting up at half past six the next morning. All the same, they made a pot of tea and crowded into Louisa's room to drink it and discuss the party, so that it was an hour later before she went finally to bed, too tired to give a thought about the next day.

She dressed carefully for the interview in a thin wool suit with a slim skirt and a short loose jacket, it was a pretty grey and she wore a silk shirt in navy to go with it; a suitable outfit, she considered, making her look older than her years, which she considered might be a good thing.

The hotel looked grand and she went inside feeling

a great deal less calm than she looked, but the reception clerk was pleasant and friendly and she was led to the lift and taken several floors up and along a thickly carpeted corridor until the porter tapped on a door and opened it for her.

Louisa had expected to be interviewed in one of the reception rooms of the hotel; presumably her patient was confined to her room. And a very handsome room it was too, splendidly furnished with wide french windows and a balcony beyond—and quite empty. She walked into the centre of the room and waited, and presently a door opened and a chambermaid beckoned her. It was an equally luxurious room, this time a bedroom, and sitting up in the wide bed was, she presumed, Miss Savage.

Miss Savage wasn't at all what Louisa had expected her to be. She had entertained the vague idea that the lady would be elderly and frail: the woman in the bed was still young—in her thirties and pretty with it. She had golden hair cut in a fringe and hanging in a gentle curve on either side of her face, her make-up was exquisite and she was wrapped in soft pink, all frills and lace.

She stared at Louisa for what seemed a long time and then said surprisingly: 'Well, at least you're young.' She nodded to a chair. 'Sit down—you realise that we may be in Norway for some time if you come?'

Louisa said, 'Yes,' and added: 'Will you tell me something of your illness? I couldn't possibly decide until I know more about that—and you must want to know a good deal more about me.'

Miss Savage smiled slowly. 'Actually I think you'll

do very well. You're young, aren't you, and haven't been trained long.'

'I'm twenty-two and I became a State Registered Nurse yesterday. I've not travelled at all...'

'Nor met many people? From the country, are you?'

'My home is in Kent.'

'You won't mind leaving it?'

'No, Miss Savage.'

The woman picked up a mirror and idly examined her face. 'I've got a liver complaint,' she observed. 'My doctor tells me that I have a blocked duct, whatever that is, I'm not bedridden but I get off days and he insists that if I go to Norway I should have a nurse with me.' She shot a glance at Louisa. 'My brother works there—he builds bridges—somewhere in the north, but I've arranged to take a flat in Bergen for a month or so.'

'You have treatment, Miss Savage?'

'Doctor Miles looks after me, he'll recommend a doctor to treat me.'

'Yes, of course. But if you can get about, will you require a full-time nurse?'

Miss Savage frowned. 'Certainly I shall!' She sounded petulant. 'I often have bad nights—I suffer from insomnia; you'll have more than enough to do.' She put the mirror down and began to buff her nails. 'I intend to go in a little over three weeks—you'll be free then?' She glanced up for a moment. 'You'll be paid whatever is the correct rate.'

Louisa sat quietly. It seemed a strange kind of interview, no talk of references or duties. She had the impression that Miss Savage wasn't in the least interested in her as a person. The job was just what she had hoped for, but there was something about this girl that she didn't like. That she was spoilt and liked her own way didn't worry Louisa overmuch, but there was something else that she couldn't quite put her finger on. On the other hand, if she didn't take what seemed like a heaven-sent chance, she might have to stay in England.

'I accept the job, Miss Savage,' she said at length. 'You will want references, of course, and I should like a letter from you confirming it. Perhaps you'll let me know details of the journey and my duties later on? Will you be travelling alone or will your brother be with you?'

Miss Savage gave an angry laugh. 'He's far too busy, wrapped up in his bridges...'

Why did she want to go? thought Louisa silently. Surely Norway, unless one went there for winter sports, would be rather an unsuitable place in which to convalesce? And she had the impression that the brother wasn't all that popular with his sister, but that was no concern of hers.

All the way back to the Royal Southern she wondered if she had done the right thing, and knew that when she got back there she had, for there was a letter from her stepmother, telling her that she was expected home on her next days off and threatening to telephone the Principal Nursing Officer if Louisa didn't go. There were guests coming, said the letter, and they expected to meet her, and why hadn't Louisa telephoned for a week? She was an ungrateful girl...

Louisa skimmed through the rest of the letter; it

was merely a repetition of all the other letters from her
stepmother. She would go home because if she didn't
there would be a lot of unpleasantness, but she wasn't
going to say a word about the new job. Perhaps once
she was out of the country and out of reach of her stepmother, she would be left to lead her own life. She
wrote a brief reply, scrambled into her uniform and
went back on duty.

She told Sister before she went off duty that evening,
and later on, after supper, those of her friends who had
crowded into her room for a final pot of tea before bed,
and her news was received with some astonishment.
Louisa had always been considered a rather quiet girl,
well liked and ready to join in any fun but unlikely to
do anything out of the ordinary. There was a spate of
excited talk and any amount of unsolicited advice before they finally went to their own beds.

There were two days to go before her days off. She
used them to good advantage, arranging to get a pass-
port and recklessly drawing out quite a big slice of her
savings to buy new clothes. Common sense made her
pause though before doing that. Supposing Miss Savage changed her mind, she might need the money...

But Miss Savage didn't disappoint her; there was a
letter confirming the job and a promise to advise her as
to travel arrangements in due course. Louisa counted
her money and promised herself one or two shopping
excursions. But first she had to go home.

She caught an early morning train to Sevenoaks;
she could have gone the evening before, but that would
have meant another night to be spent at home, but now

she would be there well before noon and if there were people coming to lunch, her stepmother wouldn't have much time to talk to her. She got into the Ightham bus and settled down for the four-mile journey, looking with pleasure at the country they were going through. The trees were beginning to turn already and little spirals of blue smoke rose in the cottage gardens where the bonfires had been started. And the village looked lovely, too, with its square ringed by old houses. Linda paused to pass the time of day with some of the people who knew her and then walked up the narrow lane leading to her home.

The house was old and timbered and stood sideways on to the lane, surrounded by trees and large gardens. Louisa opened the little gate set in a corner of the hedge, well away from the drive, then walked across the grass and in through a side door leading to a low-ceilinged room furnished with rather old-fashioned chairs and small tables. There were bookshelves on either side of the open hearth and a rather shabby Turkey carpet on the floor. She was halfway across it when the door opened and Mrs Evans came in.

'There you are!' Her voice was sharp and held no welcome. 'You should have come last night—Frank was here. And why on earth did you come in this way? You know this room isn't used.' She looked around her with a dissatisfied air. 'So shabby and old-fashioned.'

Louisa put down her overnight bag. 'It was Mother's sitting room,' she said flatly, 'and Father loved it.'

Mrs Evans shrugged thin, elegant shoulders. 'Did you pass your exams?' and when Louisa nodded:

'Thank heaven for that, now perhaps you'll see some sense and settle down. I must say Frank's been patient.'

'I've no intention of marrying Frank, and I'm rather tired of saying so.'

'Then you're a fool. He's got everything—money, that splendid house in the village, that gorgeous car and a villa in Spain. What more could a girl want? Especially when she's not pretty. You're not likely to get another chance like that.' She gave Louisa a quick look. 'You've not fallen in love with one of those young doctors, I hope?'

'No. Why are you so anxious for me to marry Frank Little?'

Her stepmother's answer was a little too careless. 'He's devoted to you and he'll be generous.'

Louisa studied her stepmother; still quite young, pretty and very elegant; extravagant, too. She had been left everything in the will, but Louisa suspected that she had spent most of it during the last three years and had deliberately cultivated Frank Little, hoping for an amenable son-in-law who would pay her bills—and an equally amenable stepdaughter who would marry him.

Well, I won't, thought Louisa. If only her stepmother had been fifteen or ten years younger she could have married him herself. The fact of her father's marriage to a woman so much younger than himself still hurt Louisa. It wouldn't have been so bad if she had loved him. She still wondered at his marrying her; this scheming, clever woman who had twisted him round her little finger and had never forgiven Louisa for not allowing herself to be twisted too. She could think of nothing to say and picked up her bag.

'There are several people coming to lunch,' said Mrs Evans. 'You'd better go and tidy yourself.' She turned and went out of the room ahead of Louisa and crossed the hall to the drawing room, and Louisa went upstairs to her room. While she did her face and tidied her hair she thought about leaving England; she would miss her home, but that was all. She would have to come once more before she went because her stepmother would demand it and if she refused she might wonder why. The temptation to tell her was very great, but Mrs Evans was clever enough to prevent her going. She knew so many people, influential people who could perhaps put a spoke in Louisa's wheel. A car coming up the drive and rather noisy voices greeting each other interrupted her thoughts. She gave her unremarkable person a final inspection in the pier glass, and went downstairs.

The drawing room seemed to have a lot of people in it, but only because they were all talking at once a shade too loudly. Louisa shook hands all round, took the sherry she was offered and made small talk. She knew the five people who had arrived, but only slightly; they were friends of her stepmother's who had never come to the house while her father was alive, but now they were regular visitors. There was one more to come, of course—Frank Little.

He came in presently, a man in his late thirties, rather short and plump, with an air of self-importance which sat ill on his round face with its weak chin. He stood in the doorway for a moment, giving everyone there a chance to greet him, and then went straight to Louisa.

'Your dear mother assured me that you would be here,' he stated without a greeting. 'I know how difficult it is for you to get away.' He took her hand and pressed it. 'I can only hope it's because you knew that I would be here that you came.'

Louisa took her hand away. It was a pity he was so pompous; otherwise she might have felt sorry for him. 'I didn't have to make any special effort to come home,' she told him politely, 'and I didn't know you'd be here.'

Which wasn't quite true; he was always there when she went home. She moved a little way from him. 'What will you drink?'

He sat next to her at lunch, monopolising the conversation in his over-hearty voice, making no secret of the fact that he considered her to be his property.

And he was at dinner too, ill-tempered now because she had escaped that afternoon and gone for a walk— her favourite walk, to Ivy Hatch where the manor house of Ightham Moat stood. She had got back too late for tea and her stepmother had been coldly angry.

And the next day was as bad, worse in fact, for Frank had waylaid her on her way back from the village and rather blusteringly asked her to marry him, and that for the fourth time in a year.

She refused gently because although she didn't like him she didn't want to hurt his feelings. Only when he added angrily: 'Your mother considers me to be the perfect husband for you,' did she turn on her heel and start walking away from him. As she went she said over her shoulder: 'She is not my mother, Frank, and I intend to choose my own husband when I want to and not before.'

He caught up with her. 'I'm coming up to see you this evening—I'm invited for dinner and there'll be no one else there.'

So after tea she went to her room, packed her bag, told her stepmother that she was leaving on the next bus and went out of the house. Mrs Evans had been too surprised to do or say anything. Louisa, leaping into the bus as it was about to leave, waved cheerfully to Frank, about to cross the village square.

She arrived back at the Royal Southern quite un-repentant, prudently asked one of her friends to say that she wasn't in the home if the telephone went and it was her stepmother, and retired to soak in a hot bath until bedtime.

The ward was busy and she spent almost all her free time shopping, so that she was too tired by the end of the day to have second thoughts about her new job. And at the end of the week she received a letter from Miss Savage confirming it, asking her to call once more so that final details might be sorted out and giving her the day and time of their flight.

And this time when Louisa got to the hotel, it was to find her future patient reclining on a chaise-longue and rather more chatty than previously. 'Uniform,' she observed, after a brief greeting. 'You don't need to travel in one, of course, but you'd better have some with you. Dark blue, I think, and a cap, of course. Go to Harrods and charge it to my account.'

'Will you want me to wear them all the time?'

'Heavens, no—you'll get your free time like any-one else. Besides, I shall be going out quite a bit and I shan't want you around.'

Louisa blinked. 'I think I should like to see your doctor before we go.'

Miss Savage shrugged. 'If you must. He's a busy man—you'd better telephone him. I'll give you his number.' She yawned. 'Take a taxi and come here for me—a friend will drive us to Heathrow. Be here by ten o'clock.' She frowned. 'I can't think of anything else. I shall call you by your christian name—what is it? You did tell me, but I've forgotten.'

'Louisa, Miss Savage.'

'Old-fashioned, but so are you. OK, that's settled, then. I'll see you here in ten days' time.'

Louisa got to her feet. She had been going to ask about clothes; after all, Norway would be colder than London, or so she supposed, but somehow Miss Savage didn't seem to be the right person to ask. Louisa said goodbye in her composed manner and went back on duty. After her patients on the ward, with their di-agnoses clearly written down and an exact treatment besides, she found Miss Savage baffling. Her doctor would remedy that, however.

But here she was disappointed. Miss Savage's treat-ment was to be negligible—rest, fresh air, early nights, good food. 'Miss Savage is on Vitamin B, of course, and I shall supply her with nicotinic acid as well. I've already referred her case to a Norwegian colleague who will give you any information you may wish to know. You, of course, realise that she suffers from dyspepsia and a variety of symptoms which will be treated as they arise.'

Louisa listened to the impersonal voice and when it had finished, asked: 'Exercise, sir?'

'Let our patient decide that, Nurse. I'm sure you understand that she'll have days when she's full of energy—just make sure that she doesn't tax her strength.'

'And notes of the case?' persisted Louisa.

'They'll be sent to her doctor in Bergen.'

She put down the receiver. Miss Savage was a private patient, which might account for the rather guarded statements she had just listened to. Certainly, from her somewhat limited experience of similar cases on the wards, the treatment was very much the same, and unlike the patients in hospital, the patient would probably have more say in the matter of exercise and food. As far as Louisa could see, she was going along to keep an eye on Miss Savage, and not much else. But at least it would get her away from Frank.

The thought was so delightful that she embarked on a shopping spree which left her considerably poorer but possessed of several outfits which, while not absolutely in the forefront of fashion, did a great deal for her ego. She went home once more and because it was the last time for a long while, endured her stepmother's ill-humour and Frank's overbearing manner. There was less than a week to go now and she was getting excited. It was a good thing that the ward was busy so that she had little time to think about anything much except her work, and her off duty was spent in careful packing and a great number of parties given as farewell gestures by her friends.

She wrote to her stepmother the evening before she left and posted it just before she got into the taxi, with such of her friends as could be missed from their wards crowding round wishing her luck. Once the hospital was out of sight she sat back, momentarily utterly appalled at what she was doing, but only for a brief minute or so. She was already savouring the heady taste of freedom.

She was punctual to the minute, but Miss Savage wasn't. Louisa, gathering together the bottles and lotions and stowing them tidily in an elegant beauty box, hoped they wouldn't miss the plane. But a telephone call from reception galvanised her patient into sudden energy and within minutes there was a knock on the door and three people came in—a young woman, as elegant as Miss Savage, and two men. They rushed to embrace Miss Savage, talking loudly and laughing a great deal, ignoring Louisa and then sweeping the entire party, complete with bellboys, luggage and an enormous bouquet of flowers, downstairs. Louisa felt that she had lost touch, at least for the moment. Once they were on the plane she would get Miss Savage to rest—a light meal perhaps and a nap…

No one spoke to her and they all piled into an enormous Cadillac and roared off towards Heathrow. She sat in the back of the car, with the young woman beside her and one of the men. Miss Savage sat beside the driver, and for someone with a liver complaint who was supposed to take life easy, behaved in a wild and excitable manner, but Louisa realised that it would be useless to remonstrate with her. She was bubbling over with energy, and the man who was driving was encouraging her.

At Heathrow they got out, and to Louisa's horror, they all booked in for the flight. One of the men must have noticed the look on her face, because he patted her on the shoulder. 'Not to worry, Nurse—we're only taking Claudia to Bergen. Once she's there, she's all yours.'

And a good thing too, thought Louisa, watching the gin and tonics Miss Savage was downing once they were in flight. They were travelling first class and the plane was barely half full, which was perhaps a good thing considering the noise she and her friends were making. They had gone quietly enough through Customs. They had arrived with only a few minutes to spare and there had been no time for chat, but once on board they had relaxed. They might have been in their own homes, so little did they notice their surroundings. To Louisa, tired and apprehensive, the flight seemed endless. She heaved a sigh of relief when the plane began its descent and through a gap in the clouds she saw the wooded islands and the sea below, and then a glimpse of distant snow-capped mountains. Just for a moment she forgot her patient and her problems, and thrilled with excitement. Here was a new world, and only time would reveal all its possibilities.

CHAPTER TWO

BERGEN AIRPORT WAS small compared with Heathrow. It took only minutes for them to clear Customs, summon two taxis and start the drive to Bergen. Louisa, sitting in the second car with the elder of the two men, hardly noticed him, there was such a lot to see. The country was wooded and very beautiful and the road wound between trees already glowing with autumn colour. She had been surprised to see on a signpost that Bergen was twelve miles away to the north; somehow she had expected to plunge straight into the town's suburbs. Presently they came to a village and then another, and then after twenty minutes or so, the outskirts of Bergen. Louisa was a little disappointed, for the busy road they were now on seemed very like any other busy road anywhere in England, but only for a moment. Suddenly they were in the centre of the town, skirting a small square park surrounded by busy streets. Her companion waved a vague hand at the window. 'Nice little tea room there,' he volunteered, 'very handy for the shops—Claudia's got a flat near the theatre.'

Which, while interesting, meant nothing to Louisa.

They turned off a shopping street presently and came upon another small park set in the centre of a square of tall houses, and at its head, the theatre. The taxis stopped half way along one side and they all got out. Miss Savage's flat was on the first floor of a solid house in the middle of a terrace of similar houses, a handsome apartment, well furnished in the modern Scandinavian style, with its own front door in the lobby on the ground floor. A pleasant-looking young woman had opened the door to them and shown them up the short flight of stairs and disappeared down a passage, to reappear presently with a tea tray. Louisa, bidden to pour tea for everyone, did so, and then at Miss Savage's casual: 'Have a cup yourself, Louisa, then perhaps you'd unpack? There's a maid somewhere, see if you can find her,' went to do as she was bid.

The flat was larger than she had supposed. She had opened doors on to three bedrooms, a bathroom and a cupboard before she came to the kitchen. There was another girl here, young and pretty and, thank heaven, speaking English.

'Eva,' she said as they shook hands. 'I come each day from eight o'clock until seven o'clock in the evening. In the afternoon I go for two hours to my home.' She smiled widely. 'You would like coffee?'

Louisa hadn't enjoyed the tea very much. 'I'd love a cup, but I was going to unpack.'

'Then first I show you your rooms and then the coffee. You are the nurse, I think?'

'That's right.' Louisa followed her back down the passage; first her own room, light and airy, well furnished too, with a shower room leading from it, and then her patient's, much larger, with a bathroom attached and a balcony looking out over the square. Louisa, fortified by the coffee and five minutes' chat with Eva, went back there presently and started to unpack. It took quite a time, for Miss Savage had brought a large wardrobe with her; for an invalid she appeared to expect a good deal of social life. Louisa arranged the last scent bottle on the dressing table, arranged the quilted dressing gown invitingly on the bed, and went in search of her patient.

The tea party was still in full swing, only now a tray of drinks had taken the place of the tea and Miss Savage's pale face was flushed. Before Louisa could say anything, one of the men called out: 'All right, nurse, we're just off—got a plane to catch. Look after our Claudia, won't you?' He winked broadly: 'Keep her on the straight and narrow!'

Their goodbyes took another five minutes and when they had gone the room was quiet again. Quiet until Miss Savage burst into tears, storming up and down the room, muttering to herself, even waving her arms around. All the same, she managed to look as pretty as ever, like a little girl who couldn't get her own way. Louisa's kind heart melted at the sight of her; with a little difficulty she urged her patient to sit down and then sat beside her. 'You're tired,' she said in her quiet, sensible voice. 'It's been a long day, and it's not over yet. Suppose you have a nap for an hour and Eva and I will get a meal ready for you. You haven't eaten much, have you?'

'I want to go home,' mumbled Miss Savage, and buried her head against Louisa's shoulder.

'Then why don't you? We can pack up in no time at all and after you've had a good night's rest we can get a flight back...'

'Fool!' declared Miss Savage. 'Do you really suppose I wanted to come? To leave my friends and all the fun...'

Louisa, who hadn't taken offence at being called a fool, quite understanding that her companion was suffering strong feelings about something or other, had asked merely: 'Then why did you come, Miss Savage?'

'He made me, of course. I have to live, don't I, and if he stops my allowance what am I to do?'

'Who's he?' enquired Louisa gently. 'You don't have to tell me, only it might make it easier if you did—perhaps we can think of something.'

'My beastly brother. I detest him—he's mean and high-handed and he made me come here so that he can make sure that I don't spend too much money—and don't have my friends.'

'Very unreasonable,' commented Louisa. 'And what about me? I cost money, don't I?'

'Oh, he pays for you—it was one of the conditions...' Miss Savage paused and rearranged her words. 'The doctor said I had to have someone to look after me...'

'I should think so indeed!' declared Louisa indignantly. She still didn't like Miss Savage overmuch, but probably her way of life was the result of having a despot of a brother who bullied her. 'Does your brother know you came here today?'

Miss Savage nodded. 'Yes—but you needn't worry, he won't come here. He's miles away—the last I heard of him he was north of Tromso, that's on the way to the North Pole—well, it's a long way beyond the Arctic Circle.'

Louisa produced a handkerchief and wiped Miss Savage's face for her. 'I can't quite see why you had to come to Norway. If your brother wanted you to lead a quieter life, couldn't you have gone to live for a time in the country in England? It would have been much cheaper.'

She couldn't see her patient's face so she didn't see the cunning look upon it. Miss Savage sounded quite convincing when she said: 'But my friends would still come and see me!'

'You'll make friends here,' declared Louisa. 'I thought the town looked delightful, didn't you? In a few days, when you've rested, we'll explore. There are bound to be English people living here.'

Miss Savage sat up. She said: 'You're much nicer than I thought you were. I daresay we'll have quite a good time here. You will help me, won't you? I mean, if I make friends and go out sometimes?'

Louisa answered her cautiously: 'Yes, of course, but you have to rest, you know, but I don't see why we shouldn't work out some sort of a routine so that you can enjoy yourself. No late nights, at least until the doctor says so, and take your pills without fail and eat properly and rest—that's important.'

'It all sounds utterly dreary,' Miss Savage smiled charmingly at her, 'but I'll be good, really I will.'

Suiting the action to the word, she went to her room, took off her dress and allowed Louisa to tuck her up under the duvet.

Louisa unpacked, consulted with Eva about their evening meal and then, for lack of anything else to do for the moment, went to sit by the sitting room window. There were people in the street below, hurrying home from work, she supposed, taking a short cut across the little park and disappearing round the corner of the theatre at the far end. The sky was clear, but there was a brisk little wind blowing the leaves around and she wondered what it would be like when autumn gave way to winter. From what she had seen of the town she was sure she was going to like it. She hoped she had brought enough warm clothing with her: Miss Savage's luggage had contained thick woollies and a couple of anoraks and fur-lined boots, and there was a mink coat which one of the men had carried for her... Her thoughts were interrupted by the telephone and she went to answer it quickly before it disturbed her patient. A man's voice, slow and deep, asking something or other.

'I'm sorry, I don't understand you...'

'You are the nurse?'

'I'm Miss Savage's nurse, yes.'

'I should like to speak to her. Her brother.'

'She's resting—we only arrived an hour or so ago. Perhaps you'll ring tomorrow.' Louisa's voice was cool, but not nearly as cold as the man on the other end of the line.

'I shall ring when it is convenient to me,' he said, and hung up on her, leaving her annoyed and quite sure

that he was just about the nastiest type she had ever encountered. Why, even Frank seemed better!

She told Miss Savage later, when that lady, remarkably revived by her nap, joined her in the sitting room.

'And that's the last I'll hear from him—obviously
he's no intention of coming to see me.' She sounded
delighted. 'If he rings again, Louisa, you're to say that
I'm shopping or asleep or something. I'm hungry, have
you arranged something or shall I go out?'

'Eva has cooked a meal for us; it's all ready being
kept hot. Eva goes in a few minutes.'

'What a bore! Oh, well, you'll have to do the chores.'

It hardly seemed the time to point out that she was
a nurse, not a maid; Louisa prudently held her tongue
and went to tell Eva that she could dish up.

Miss Savage's vivacity lasted for the whole of the
meal, although her appetite, after a few mouthfuls of the
excellently cooked cod, disappeared entirely—indeed,
presently she got up from the table, leaving Louisa,
who was famished, to hurry through her meal, which
seemed a shame, for the pudding was good, too, and
the coffee following it excellent. At least Miss Savage
accepted coffee, lying back on the big sofa facing the
window, looking suddenly as though she'd been on her
feet for days and hadn't slept a wink.

'Bed,' said Louisa firmly, 'a warm bath first—do
you take sleeping pills? The doctor didn't mention
them...'

'There are some in my bag, but I don't think I'll need
them tonight.' Miss Savage yawned widely, showing

beautiful teeth. 'I'll have breakfast in bed—coffee and toast, and don't disturb me until ten o'clock.'

Later, with her patient in bed and presumably sleeping, Louisa cleared away their supper things, tidied the kitchen ready for Eva in the morning and went back to the window. It was very dark outside, but the streets were well lighted and there were plenty of people about and a good deal of traffic. The pleasant thought struck her that if Miss Savage wasn't to be disturbed until ten o'clock each morning, she would have time to take a quick look round after her own breakfast. She could be up and dressed by eight o'clock and Eva would be in the flat then, so that if Miss Savage wanted anything there would be someone there. She didn't know much about private nursing, but it seemed to her that this case wasn't quite as usual; only the vaguest references had been made to off duty, for instance, and what about her free days? She should have made quite sure of those, but she had been so eager to get the job, and although it might not turn out to be exactly what she had expected at least she was out of England, beyond her stepmother's reach, and moreover, in a country which, at first sight, looked delightful.

She went to bed and slept dreamlessly all night.

She was up and ready for Eva when she arrived, and since Miss Savage hadn't said anything more about uniform, she had put on a pleated skirt and a thin sweater.

Eva was surprised to see her already dressed, but she wasted no time in making coffee and unwrapping the still warm rolls she had brought with her. She shared Louisa's coffee too, sitting at the kitchen table while

she told Louisa where the shops were and how to go
to them. It wasn't nine o'clock when Louisa, a quilted
jacket over the sweater and a woolly cap and gloves,
left the flat; there would be time to explore and perhaps
she could persuade Miss Savage to go for a short walk
once she was up. She crossed the little park as Eva had
instructed her and turned into Ole Bull Pass and then
into the main shopping street, Torgalmenning, where
the shops were already open, although there weren't
many people about.

Louisa walked briskly down its length, intent on
reaching the harbour Eva said she simply had to see,
promising herself that the next time she would stop
and look in all the shop windows. It didn't take her
long; there was the harbour, bustling with life, ferries chugging to and fro, freighters tied up in the distance. It was overlooked on two sides by rows of ancient
houses, many of them wooden and all of them beautifully cared for and most of them converted into shops.
She walked a little way beside the water, looking across
to the mountains in the distance and then nearer to the
neat colourful houses clinging to the skirts of the mountains behind the town. There was a fish market too, but
she didn't dare to stop to inspect it for more than a minute or two; quite a different matter from the fish shops
at home, and she had never seen such a variety. She
paused for another minute to stare across the water at
a castle—she would have to find out about that, too…
She had no more time; she retraced her steps, aware
that there must be another way back to the flat, probably shorter—tomorrow she would discover it.

She had time to change into her uniform when she got back; there was more chance of Miss Savage doing as she was asked if she was reminded that Louisa was a nurse.

At exactly ten o'clock, Louisa tapped on the door and went in, put the tea tray down by the bed and drew the curtains. Miss Savage wakened slowly, looking very pretty but just as listless as the previous evening. She sat up slowly without answering Louisa's cheerful good morning, merely: 'What a hideous uniform—it doesn't do anything for you at all, but I suppose you'd better wear it—that doctor's coming this morning.'

'Then you'd better stay in bed when you've had your breakfast,' said Louisa cheerfully, ignoring the bit about the uniform. 'He'll want to examine you, I expect.'

Miss Savage yawned. 'I don't want any breakfast.'

'Coffee? Rolls and butter and black cherry jam?' invited Louisa. 'I'll bring it anyway.'

'Not for ten minutes.'

It was amazing what those ten minutes did for her patient. Miss Savage was leaning back against her pillows, looking quite different, positively sparkling. What was more, she drank her coffee, ate a bit of roll and then went to have her bath without any fuss at all. Louisa made the bed and tidied the room and had Miss Savage back in it seconds before the door bell rang.

Doctor Hopland was elderly, portly and instantly likeable. His English was almost accentless and he appeared to be in no hurry. He listened to Louisa's rather scant information about her patient, nodded his head in a thoughtful way and observed that beyond keeping an eye on Miss Savage he thought there was little he could do. 'I have had notes of the case,' he told Louisa. 'Unhappily there are many such these days and you will understand that there is not a great deal to be done. Miss Savage is co-operative?'

It was hard to give an answer to that. Louisa said slowly: 'On the whole, yes, but she does like her own way...'

'I understand. Well, nurse, all you can do is to persuade her to eat good wholesome food and rest whenever she is tired, and as well as that get her into the fresh air. She is in bed, I take it?'

'I thought you might like to examine her, doctor.'

'Certainly. Shall we do that now?'

Miss Savage submitted very nicely to Doctor Hopland's services, in fact she was so meek that Louisa was astonished, but not nearly as astonished as she was an hour later, when Miss Savage, whom she had left reading a book in bed, came into the sitting room and declared that she was going out to see something of Bergen.

So they spent an hour or two looking at the shops and Miss Savage bought several expensive trifles and an armful of books which Louisa was given to carry. 'And how about a bottle of sherry in case anyone calls?' asked Miss Savage gaily. 'And don't frown like that, Louisa, I know I mustn't drink it. I wonder where we buy it?'

They couldn't see a drink shop and, on reflection, Louisa couldn't remember having passed one, so she went into the bookshop they had just left and asked one of the assistants.

'The nearest one is on the other side of Torget, quite a walk away, and there are quite a lot of restrictions—you can only buy drinks at certain hours.' She glanced at her watch. 'They're closed now and don't open until this evening.'

Miss Savage's voice was high and peevish. 'I never heard such nonsense—you must get it then, I suppose.'

'Is it so urgent?' asked Louisa. 'I mean, do you know anyone here who's likely to come to see you?'

They were walking back to the flat. 'That's beside the point and no business of yours,' said Miss Savage nastily. The charming mood of the morning had quite gone, as Louisa expected, and she had a difficult afternoon and an even worse evening, with her patient lolling on the sofa, refusing meals and playing the tape recorder far too loudly. It was a relief when she was told to go and buy the sherry.

She didn't hurry. It was good to get away from the flat; besides, she was hungry, for she hadn't been given the time to eat her own meal at midday and when tea came, Miss Savage had demanded this and that so that by the time it had been poured out, it was tepid. So now Louisa whipped into a snack bar, had a coffee and a large satisfying bun, and feeling much better, walked on down to the harbour, along Torget, with its mediaeval houses lining the pavement, and then turned up the side street whose name she had carefully written down, and found the off-licence.

It seemed a great fuss for one bottle of sherry, she

decided as she walked briskly back again. It was cold now, but the shops, although closed, were still lighted and there was still a lot of traffic. She went indoors reluctantly; Eva would be gone by now and if Miss Savage was still so peevish she saw little hope of enjoying a pleasant supper.

Miss Savage was sitting at the window, watching TV and so amiable that Louisa almost dropped the bottle in surprise. What was more, her patient made no difficulties about supper. She sat down to the table and even though she ate almost nothing of it, pushed the beautifully cooked cod round the plate, chatting with the utmost good nature while Louisa thankfully ate. She went to bed presently, leaving Louisa to clear the table and then sit writing letters until she went to bed herself.

On the whole, not a bad day, thought Louisa as she laid her head on the pillow and in no time at all, slept dreamlessly.

And that first day seemed to set the pattern of all their days for the next week. Miss Savage was unpredictable, of course, but Louisa had got used to that by now; she could cope with the near-hysterical condition her patient would work herself into within minutes. She even got her to eat at least a little of each meal and, for a time each day, go for a walk. It was a pity that Miss Savage had no interest in museums and no desire to take the funicular to the top of the mountain behind the town and walk around and admire the view which Eva assured them was spectacular. Louisa promised herself that when she had some free time to herself, she would do just that. There was a restaurant there too, so that she might even possibly have her lunch there. And though the tourist trips had ceased, there were regular small steamers going to Stavanger and Haugesund and several of the fjords not too far distant. Presumably they ran all through the winter. Coming back one evening from posting letters, Louisa decided that with her first pay packet she would invest in a thicker quilted jacket; a sheepskin one would have been nice, but she didn't think she would have enough money for that. She was certainly going to buy a couple of thick knitted sweaters with their matching caps and gloves; she had already bought wool and needles and embarked on a long scarf, and judging by the cold crisp air, she would be glad of it soon enough.

It surprised her rather that Doctor Hopland hadn't called to see his patient again. True, he had told her to telephone if she was worried at all, and she supposed that there was little that he could do. She carefully checked her patient's temperature and pulse each day, saw that she took her pills and did her best to see that she led a quiet pleasant life, but she felt uneasily that she wasn't earning her salary. On the other hand, if Miss Savage should take a turn for the worse, at least she would be there to nip it in the bud and get the doctor at once.

She found such a possibility absurd when she got back to the flat. Miss Savage was sitting in the big chair by the window, playing Patience with such an air of contentment that it was hard to imagine she had anything wrong with her at all. She was charming for the rest of the evening too and astonished Louisa by saying that she should have most of the next day to herself. 'Go out about eleven o'clock, once I'm up,' she suggested, 'and don't come back until it begins to get dark—about four o'clock. I shall be fine—I feel so much better, and Eva can get my lunch before she goes, and you know I like to take a nap in the afternoon.'

Louisa looked doubtful. 'Suppose someone calls or telephones during the afternoon—there'll be no one there except you.'

Miss Savage shrugged her shoulders. 'I shan't bother to answer—they can call again, can't they?'

Louisa went to bed quite prepared to find that in the morning her patient would have changed her mind. But she hadn't. Indeed, she got up earlier than usual after her breakfast and urged Louisa to go out as soon as they had had their coffee. 'And mind you don't come back until four o'clock,' she called gaily.

Louisa, walking smartly through the town towards the cable railway, reviewed the various instructions she had given Eva, worried for a few minutes about Miss Savage being by herself and then forgot it all in the sheer joy of being out and free to go where she liked for hours on end.

The funicular first, she had decided, and a walk once she reached the mountain top, then lunch and an afternoon browsing among the shops. There was a large department store she longed to inspect, but Miss Savage hadn't considered it worth a visit. And she would have tea at Reimers Tea Rooms, which Eva had told her was the fashionable place for afternoon tea or morning coffee. There was a great deal more to see, of course, she would have to leave Bergenhus Castle until the next time, as well as the Aquarium and Grieg's house by the Nordasvann lake, not to mention the museums. She hurried up the short hill which took her to the foot of the funicular, bought her ticket and settled herself in the car with a sigh of pure pleasure.

It was wonderful. She had never experienced anything like it—she had a good head for heights and craned her neck in all directions as the car crawled up the face of the mountain, and at the top she was rewarded by a view of the fjords and mountains to take her breath and when she had got it back again she walked. There were paths everywhere, and everywhere mountains and lakes and scenery to make her eyes widen with delight, and when at last she was tired, she lunched in the restaurant—soup and an omelette and coffee—and then went back down the mountain in the cable car.

It was early afternoon by now, but the flat wasn't more than ten minutes' walk away from Torgalmenning. Louisa walked slowly, looking in shop windows at the silver jewellery, porcelain and beautifully carved wood, took another longer look at the winter clothes set out so attractively in the boutiques and came finally to Sundt, the department store, where she spent half an hour browsing from counter to counter, working out prices rather laboriously, deciding what she would buy later. It was almost time to go back to the flat; she would have time for a cup of tea first, though. She found the tea room without trouble and sat down at one of the little tables. It was already crowded with smartly dressed women, and Louisa, once she had overcome the few small difficulties in ordering a tray of tea and one of the enormous cream cakes on display, settled down to enjoy herself. She even had an English newspaper, although as she read it England seemed very far away.

She got up to go reluctantly, but content with her day; even the thought that Miss Savage might be in one of her bad moods didn't spoil her feeling of wellbeing. In fact she was quite looking forward to telling her about her outing. This happy state of mind lasted until she opened the door of the flat and started up the stairs. There were voices, loud angry voices, and then Miss Savage's all too familiar sobbing. Louisa took the rest of the stairs two at a time, opened the inner door quietly and made for the half open sitting room door. Miss Savage was lying on the sofa, making a great deal of noise. She had been crying for some time if her puffy pink eyelids were anything to go by and from time to time she let out a small gasping shriek. She saw Louisa at once and cried in a voice thick with tears: 'Louisa— thank God you've come!'

Louisa took stock of the man standing by the sofa. He was tall and spare, with dark hair and an aquiline cast of feature. Moreover, he looked furiously angry, in a towering rage in fact, so that she took a deep breath before she spoke.

'I don't know who you are, but you will be good enough to go at once. Miss Savage has been ill and whoever you are, you haven't any right to upset her in this way.' She held the door open and lifted her chin at him and met dark eyes glittering with rage.

'The nurse?' His voice was crisp. 'I'm Miss Savage's brother, and since this is strictly a family argument, I will ask you to mind your own business.'

'Well, I won't,' said Louisa stoutly. 'You may think you can bully her, but you can't bully me.' She opened the door a little wider. 'Will you go?'

For answer he took the door away from her and shut it. 'Tell me, what is my sister suffering from, Nurse? Did the doctor tell you? Did she explain when you were engaged? And the doctor here? Has he said anything to you?'

Louisa opened her mouth to speak, but Miss Savage forestalled her by uttering a series of piercing cries and then dissolving into fresh sobs. Louisa brushed past the man, wiped Miss Savage's face for her, sat her up against the cushions and only then turned her attention to him.

'Your sister has a blocked bile duct, she also has dyspepsia. That's a kind of severe indigestion,' she added in case he didn't know, 'I believe you wanted her to come to Norway, presumably to convalesce. We had made some progress during the last week, but I doubt if your visit has helped matters at all. Quite the contrary.'

It was annoying to see him brush her words aside as though they didn't mean a thing. 'You're young. Recently trained, perhaps?'

She supposed she would have to answer him—after all, it was probably he who was paying her fees. 'About six weeks ago.'

His laugh wasn't nice and she flushed angrily. 'Probably you're a good nurse,' he observed in a voice which gave the lie to the statement, 'but you're inexperienced—just what Claudia was looking for.'

'I don't know what you mean.'

'No? I suggest that you put Claudia to bed—she must be exhausted after such a display of emotion. Tell Eva to give her some tea and then come back here. I want to talk to you.'

'I don't think there's much point in that.'

His voice was soft. 'Probably not, but I must point out that I employ you, even if it was my sister who engaged you.' He went to the door and opened it and stood waiting. He had his temper under control by now, and he looked dangerous. Louisa helped Miss Savage on to her feet and walked her out of the room. She said in a voice which shook only very slightly: 'You're despicable, Mr Savage.'

He gave a short laugh. 'Shall we say half an hour, Nurse?'

She didn't answer.

CHAPTER THREE

HALF AN HOUR wasn't nearly long enough in which to regain her cool, thought Louisa, and walked, outwardly composed and inwardly quaking, into the sitting room. Mr Savage was standing at the window, looking out and jingling the loose change in his pockets, and she brightened a little. Perhaps he had recovered from his nasty temper—but when he turned round she saw with regret that she was mistaken; his mood was as black as ever although at the moment he had it under control. She didn't much care for the iciness of his voice when he spoke, though.

'Ah, Nurse, I was beginning to wonder if your courage had deserted you.'

Louisa was, for the most part, a mild-tempered girl, prepared to give rather more than she took, but only up to a point. 'I can't quite see,' she observed in a reasonable voice, 'what I have to be courageous about. True, I dislike being bullied, but a loud voice and a nasty temper don't count for much, when all's said and done.'

She crossed the room and sat down on a small hard chair because it was easier to be dignified like that.

Her companion's eyes narrowed. 'Clever, are you?' he wanted to know. 'I've a few questions to ask, and I want truthful answers.'

She stared back at him. 'I can lie with the best of them,' she assured him, 'but never about patients.'

He laughed unpleasantly. 'I'll have to take your word for that. Tell me, why did my sister engage you?'

Her eyes widened. 'Well, she wanted a nurse to accompany her here.'

'There were other applicants?'

'Oh, yes—she told me, but they were all older and she wanted someone younger.'

'Ah, and inexperienced.'

She let that pass. 'Why?'

'I'm asking the questions, Nurse. What's your name?'

'Evans—Louisa Evans.'

'Well, Nurse Evans, presumably you saw my sister's doctor?'

'Naturally, and he gave me my instructions and informed me as to the nature of Miss Savage's illness.'

He gave her a sharp look, eyebrows lifted in faint surprise. 'So you know all there is to know about her?'

She surveyed him coolly. So he thought her incapable of doing her job just because she was young and not greatly experienced, did he? She drew a breath and recited the details of her patient's condition, adding kindly, 'If you don't understand the medical terms I'll explain…'

He turned a fulminating look upon her. 'It would be

unwise of you to be frivolous, Nurse Evans. I shouldn't try if I were you.'

'I'm not. You're not a doctor, are you?'

'I'm a civil engineer, I build bridges. The reason I asked you that question may not be apparent to you at the moment.'

'It's not.' She got to her feet. 'At least, I daresay you think I'm not old or wise enough to look after your sister. I hope you feel better about it now. She's making a little progress, or was… I don't know why you had to upset her, Mr Savage, and I don't want to be impertinent, but your visit hasn't helped much, has it?' Her tongue tripped on, speaking the thoughts she had no intention of uttering. 'I can't for the life of me think why she had to come to Norway. She must have a home somewhere in England; I don't believe she lives in a London hotel; she told me that she came because you made her…but there's no reason for that, surely? You work miles away, don't you?'

He had come to stand close to her, his face expressionless, but all the same Louisa had an urge to retreat behind the nearest chair, sternly suppressed. She had the extraordinary feeling that he was on the point of telling her something and at the last minute changed his mind. When he did speak it was to say: 'I wanted her to be nearer to me so that I could visit her easily. I should perhaps explain that we're not the best of friends, Nurse Evans. Claudia is my stepsister, she's only a little younger than I, and we met for the first time when my father married her mother, who had been a widow for some years. We are, in fact, not related—

all the same, as we bear the same name I feel some responsibility towards her.' He looked down at her and actually smiled—a thin smile. 'She's been seen by a doctor since you arrived here? I did arrange...'

Louisa said impatiently: 'Yes, the doctor came. I have his phone number and he'll call again in a week's time.'

'He gave you no further instructions?' Mr Savage's deep voice sounded curt.

'No, none at all. He told me to carry on as before and to call him if I was worried about anything.'

He moved away from her at last and went to stand at the window again, half turned away from her. 'There seems little point in staying,' he said at length, and turned to look at her, frowning. 'I'm not sure if I'm doing the right thing...'

'Well, you are,' said Louisa firmly. 'You upset Miss Savage and I can't think why you came if you don't get on together—you could have telephoned.'

'My dear good girl, we're talking at cross purposes.' He started for the door. 'I shall telephone from time to time and I shall expect a report from you.' He paused, took a notebook from his pocket, scribbled a number in it and tore out the page. 'You can reach me at this number if you should need to.' He saw her face and gave a crack of laughter. 'Something you don't intend to do; you think I'm a tyrant and a bully...'

'As a matter of fact, I do,' said Louisa in a matter-of-fact voice. All the same, the room seemed empty and rather lonely when he had gone.

A small sound made her turn her head; Miss Savage was standing in the doorway. 'He's gone?' She gave a sly smile. 'I'm not really like that, you know, Louisa—making such a fuss—I wanted him to go away, you see.' She twisted her hands together and added in a wheedling voice: 'You're not cross, are you? Was he very rude to you?'

For some reason Louisa found herself saying no when she should really have said yes. She said mildly: 'I think your brother only came to see if you were settled in—I'm sure he has your interest at heart; he wanted to know just how you were...'

Miss Savage gave a giggle. 'I bet he did! Did he ask about my friends? The ones who came over with us?'

'No.' Louisa wasn't sure if she liked Miss Savage in this mood.

'Oh, good. I didn't tell him and I didn't have time to ask you not to mention them. He doesn't like them.'

Understandably so, thought Louisa; she didn't like them herself.

'Well, he won't be coming again for ages,' said Miss Savage in a satisfied voice. 'They've just started another bridge somewhere at the back of beyond and once the snow comes travelling around isn't all that easy.'

Louisa thought otherwise. There were domestic flights all over the country; she had collected handfuls of leaflets from a travel agency because she had an inquisitive mind that liked to know about such things. Besides, the friendly woman at the newspaper kiosk had told her that there was a daily steamer that sailed the entire length of the country, right to the Russian border, and back again, calling at dozens of isolated villages.

Louisa didn't think that the snow made much difference to the Norwegians—after all, they'd lived there for hundreds of years and by now would know how to deal with their weather. It did put her in mind of something else, though. 'Will we be staying here all winter?'

'Fed up already?' demanded Miss Savage apprehensively. 'I'll make him pay you more… Don't go, Louisa.'

Louisa smiled at her patient. 'I don't intend to, and I'm not in the least fed up. I think it's marvellous here. The reason I asked was because I'll have to buy some thicker clothes; it's almost November and I thought I'd get one of those quilted coats and some lined boots.'

'Oh, is that all?' Miss Savage had picked up a copy of *Harpers* and was turning the pages. 'Why don't you get a fur coat? You'll get your wages in just a couple of weeks—Simon said something about it, but I wasn't listening. I expect you know when it's due to be paid? You have to go to the Bergen Bank and ask for Mr… He wrote the name down somewhere.' She turned the magazine over: 'Here it is, written on the back—Helgesen.' She added mockingly. 'Simon seemed to think you needed someone to keep an eye on your money, I suppose. The tight-fisted so-and-so!' Her voice became full of self-pity. 'He's got more money than is good for him and he gives me barely enough to live on.'

Probably he was mean, thought Louisa; he certainly was unpleasant enough to add meanness to his faults, but after all, Miss Savage lived in great comfort and if a mink coat and hand-made Italian shoes were anything to go by, not to mention the luxurious flat in which they lived at present, then her ideas of meanness and Miss Savage's weren't on the same plane.

'My room's in rather a mess.' Miss Savage looked up briefly from her magazine. 'Be a good girl and tidy it for me, will you? I'm exhausted.'

Louisa went. Miss Savage was bone idle, but she had been ill. Louisa knew from experience that getting over an illness was as bad in some ways as actually being in the throes of one. The room looked as though it had endured an earthquake. Miss Savage had wreaked her rage on the soft furnishings to an alarming degree; the bed had its pillows flung in all directions as well as the duvet; there wasn't a cushion in its rightful place and not only had a bottle of perfume been smashed to bits but a jar of one of the expensive creams Miss Savage used had been flung on to the carpet, making a very nasty mess.

Louisa set the room to rights and spent a long time clearing up bits of glass and lumps of face cream. By the time she got back to the sitting room, Miss Savage was asleep, the magazine fallen to the ground. Louisa stood looking at her and thought how very pretty she was, even with her mouth open. She frowned a little, because the prettiness seemed somehow blurred round the edges and was beginning to sag a little, but that was probably because Miss Savage had cried so long and so hard. She would let her sleep for another hour while she went to see what Eva had got for their supper, and presently when she wakened her patient, she was relieved to find that she seemed to have recovered completely from the afternoon's upset. Indeed, Miss Savage spent

most of the meal planning their next few days. Rather
to Louisa's surprise she suggested that they might visit
the Museum of Arts and Crafts—already several of
the museums had closed for the winter—and if they
enjoyed it, they could visit the rest during the weeks
ahead. 'Because there's nothing much else,' she declared. 'Piano recitals, if you like such things, and the
cinema—I'll need some new clothes too.' She yawned.
'It's going to be deadly here,' and at Louisa's enquiring
look: 'Oh, I can't go back to London, Simon will stop
my allowance if I do.' Her voice became plaintive. 'I
depend on it utterly.'

'Well, once you're quite well again,' began Louisa, feeling her way, 'could you get a job? You know
all about clothes and some of those boutiques must be
super to work in.'

She was rewarded with a look of horror which was
quite genuine. 'Me? Work? My dear Louisa, you must
be out of your tiny mind! I couldn't possibly—I mean,
it's all right for someone like yourself, presumably you
expected to have to earn your living; even after you get
married your sort usually do a job, don't you? I should
die!' And just in case Louisa didn't see her point, she
added pettishly: 'I'm still far from well.'

There was no point in arguing. Louisa went away
to warm the soup Eva had left and inspect the contents
of the casserole in the oven. She still didn't like Miss
Savage, but she was sorry for her too; she was missing
such a lot of fun. Who would want London anyway? As
far as Louisa was concerned anyone could have it, just
so long as they left her Bergen to explore. And there

was plenty to do: the theatre, cinemas, some wonderful shops and cafés, and, she hoped, the chance to ski; she had asked about that and been told that there were ski slopes not far away where she could be taught... once she could get Miss Savage to agree to her having a free day at least once a week. She set supper on the table and made soothing conversation with her patient and presently helped her to bed, since she had become lachrymose again.

But by the morning she was once more her normal self, eating little, it was true, and disinclined to get up, but once she was dressed, Louisa persuaded her to put on her mink coat and its matching cap and go into the town with her. It was a bright day but cold, and they went first to Riemers for their coffee before spending an hour wandering about the shops. The visit to the museum had been forgotten, of course, but Louisa was glad that Miss Savage was at least out of doors, taking an interest in things, and just for once not grumbling; indeed, over lunch she insisted that Louisa should have the afternoon off. 'Because it's getting cold and you'd better get that coat you were talking about. I hope you have enough money, because I've got none,' she finished carelessly.

So after settling her on the sofa with a pile of paperbacks and a light rug, Louisa went off on her own. She knew what she was going to buy. She had seen just what she wanted in Sundt's department store and she went straight there; a quilted jacket with a fleecy lining and a hood. She chose a green one with a brown lining and teamed it up with thick brown slacks and leather boots, then added a thick wool sweater to wear with it and matching mitts and cap. They all added up to a quite formidable sum, but she hadn't spent more than a handful of kroner since they had arrived and pay day wasn't far off. Feeling pleased with herself, she walked the short distance to Riemers and had tea, then started for the flat. It was almost dark by now and the sky had darkened; there had been snow for some weeks in the north of the country, a friendly waitress had told her, and any day now it would snow in Bergen. Louisa sped through the brightly lighted streets, dreaming of skiing and wishing she could get away for long enough to visit some of the nearby islands by the local steamers.

As she neared the flat she saw that its windows blazed with lights and a slight unease jellied into horrible certainty as she opened the door. Miss Savage had visitors; Louisa could hear their loud voices and louder laughter as she went up the stairs. She didn't need to open the door to know who they were.

The three of them turned to look at her as she went in across a room hazy with cigarette smoke. They all held glasses in their hands too, although Miss Savage, sitting on the arm of a chair, had nothing in hers.

Louisa was greeted with shouts of welcome and when they died down Miss Savage called: 'Aren't I good, Louisa? No drinks, but you see how useful that bottle of sherry is being.' She giggled and they all laughed with her except Louisa, who, aware that she was being stuffy, nonetheless was unable to laugh. It was curious that the first thought that entered her head had been concerning Mr Savage; he would be furious if he knew that these rather wild friends of his stepsister's had arrived; without even asking she knew that he would never approve of them. When the hubbub had died down a little she said hullo in a pleasant cool little voice, refused a glass of sherry and waited to see what would happen next.

It was the woman who spoke—Connie someone or other. She had a strident voice in which she was doing her best to make conciliatory talk. 'How marvellous our Claudia looks, nurse—you're to be congratulated. We just had to see how she was getting on—we're staying a couple of nights at the Norge. You'll let her come out to dinner this evening, won't you? We'll take great care of her.'

It was obvious to Louisa that it wouldn't matter what she said. Miss Savage would go if she had a mind to. She said briskly: 'Of course I don't mind, only don't be too late back, please.' She saw them exchange glances and knew exactly what they were thinking: that she was a bossy young woman who liked ordering people about. If she had said that on a hospital ward they would have accepted it without a murmur. 'And don't wait up,' said Miss Savage. 'Be an angel and run a bath for me, will you? I simply must change.'

Eva brought everyone coffee while they were waiting and presently Louisa excused herself on the plea of consulting with Eva about the next day's meals, and from the kitchen she was called to help Miss Savage fasten her dress, a curiously quiet Miss Savage, hardly speaking and then in a hesitant fashion.

'Do you feel all right?' asked Louisa in a casual

voice. 'If you'd rather not go, I'm sure Eva and I can get a meal for you all here.'

Miss Savage was busy pinning a brooch in place. 'Of course I'm all right—don't fuss, for God's sake.' She caught up the mink coat. 'I get little enough fun.'

The flat was gloriously peaceful when they had gone, and presently, when Eva had left for the day, Louisa went along to the kitchen and got her supper, then carried it through to the sitting room and ate it in front of the TV, not really watching it, but it was company. Not that she was lonely; she had plenty to occupy her thoughts, and at the back of her mind a nasty nagging worry that there was something wrong about Miss Savage. Looking back over the days, Louisa realised that her behaviour wasn't consistent; as bright as a button for an hour or so and then listless; bursting into tears for no reason at all and at other times so irritable. She worried round the puzzle like a dog with a bone and came no nearer the answer.

It was almost ten o'clock when the phone rang and she hurried to answer it. Miss Savage in the throes of dyspepsia, or suffering a violent headache. She lifted the receiver and the very last voice she wanted to hear spoke.

'Nurse Evans? I should like to speak to my sister.'

Louisa readjusted her thoughts. 'Good evening, Mr Savage. I'm afraid Miss Savage isn't here—she's out with friends.'

His voice was sharp. 'You know these friends, Nurse?'

She said thankfully: 'Oh, yes—they're from England,' and then wished she hadn't spoken. Miss Savage hadn't wanted him to know about their trip over with her, probably she wouldn't want him to know that they had come again, but it was too late now. The voice, no longer sharp but definitely unpleasant, went on: 'When did they arrive?'

'While I was out this afternoon.' She could have cut through the heavy silence with her scissors.

'You say you know these friends?' It was like being cross-examined.

'I met them in London at Miss Savage's hotel.'

His voice had become silky. 'Ah, yes, just so. Connie, Willy and Steve—I'm right?'

Louisa gave a great sigh of relief. 'Oh, good, you know them, so that's all right.'

'I know them, Nurse Evans, and it is not all right. These friends are one of the reasons why I wanted Claudia to come to Norway—you must have seen how unsuitable they are for someone in her…' he hesitated, 'state of convalescence, and why did you not go with her?' He was coldly condemning.

'Because I wasn't asked,' snapped Louisa. 'I'm not your sister's keeper, you know.'

He said, 'I beg your pardon,' with cool insincerity. 'You don't know how long they're staying in Bergen?'

'They mentioned two nights at the Norge—that's a hotel…'

'I'm well aware of that, Nurse. You will endeavour to stay with her as much as possible until they leave. I'm unable to get away from here at the moment, so I must rely on you.' His tone implied that he was expecting the impossible.

She said stiffly: 'I'll do what I can, Mr Savage,' and was rewarded by a disbelieving grunt and the click of the receiver.

Louisa marvelled at his rudeness. 'Almost as bad as Frank in quite a different way,' she observed out loud, and sat down to wait for Miss Savage to come home.

It was almost midnight when she did and even then her friends seemed to think that they should come in for a last drink, but Louisa, standing at the door, wished them a firm goodnight and shut it equally firmly. Miss Savage had had a splendid evening, she told Louisa, the food had been delicious and she had drunk only one glass of white wine. 'You see how good I am,' she observed as Louisa helped her to bed. 'I'm going to have lunch there tomorrow and drive out to Troldhaugen to see Grieg's house. You won't want to come, of course?'

'I should like to come very much,' said Louisa quickly, aware as she said it that it was the last thing Miss Savage wanted. 'It's kind of you to ask me.'

Out of the corner of her eye she could see Miss Savage's face screwed up with temper.

There was, Louisa decided at the end of the next day, nothing worse than being an unwanted guest. The expressions on the faces of Miss Savage's friends when they called for her in the morning were bad enough, but Miss Savage's ill temper was even worse. Louisa, mindful of Mr Savage's orders, resolutely ignored the cold shoulders, the snide remarks and the sidelong glances—indeed, being a sensible girl, she ate her lunch with pleasure: lobster soup, cod cooked in a delicious sauce with crisp little potatoes and a sea of vegetables, followed by ice cream heaped with honey, fudge and lashings of whipped cream were things to be enjoyed in any circumstances. And afterwards she sat in the back of the hired car, squashed into a window and totally ignored, until they reached Grieg's cottage home on the shore. The house was shut now that it was winter, but it was quite beautiful by the fjord. Miss Savage, her arm in Connie's, wandered off with the two men behind them, calling to Louisa over her shoulder: 'There's a grave somewhere, if you're interested, Louisa, and a stave church in those woods—it's only a few minutes' walk, so I'm told,' she added mockingly. 'Don't worry, we won't go without you.'

So Louisa went off on her own, walking fast because even in the new quilted jacket it was cold. She found the composer's grave, and his wife's beside it, and then followed the path to the church. Its strange pointed roof reminded her of an Eastern temple without the trimmings and she would have liked to see the inside too, but there again the season was over; it would stay quiet and solitary until May when the tourists would come again. She was glad she had seen it in winter, though. If she had the chance, she would come again, preferably when the snow had fallen. And that wouldn't be long now, judging by the thick grey sky, already darkening into an early evening.

Louisa was surprised when Miss Savage refused to spend the evening with her friends. She was, she declared, tired and intended to go to bed early—and indeed, when they had gone she asked, quite nicely too, if Louisa would bring her some tea, and settled on the sofa where she presently fell asleep, leaving Louisa to drink her tea sitting by the window, watching the first of the snow falling. And when she woke up an hour later, she was still pleasant. 'I think I'll go to bed before supper,' she declared, and yawned prettily. 'It's been quite a day—but fun. They're going back tomorrow. Louisa, I want you to go to that wine shop and get another bottle of sherry—I know we don't get many visitors, but there's none in the place now and probably the doctor will have a glass next time he comes.' She got up and stretched her arms above her head. 'I'll have a bath now.' She strolled to the door. 'Was my brother angry when he phoned yesterday?' Her voice was very casual.

Louisa considered. Mr Savage always sounded angry, in her opinion. 'Surprised,' she essayed, 'anxious that you wouldn't get tired or spoil your good progress—no, I don't think he was particularly angry. I'm sorry I mentioned your friends. He asked me where you were, you see, and I had to answer.'

Miss Savage darted a sidelong glance at her. 'Of course,' she smiled. 'You don't have to worry about it—you did tell him they were leaving tomorrow, didn't you?'

'Yes.' Louisa had got to her feet too. 'I'll get your bath going, shall I? Is there anything special you'd like Eva to cook for your supper?'

'I'm not hungry—we had an enormous lunch, lots of coffee and an omelette.'

Butter wouldn't have melted in Miss Savage's mouth

for the rest of that evening, and it was the same next morning, which she spent lying in bed reading. It was after an early lunch which she took in her bed that she urged Louisa to go and get the sherry. 'It'll be dark soon,' she pointed out, 'and it's going to snow again—you'd better go while you can.'

So Louisa buttoned herself into her thick jacket, pulled her woolly cap well down over her ears and set out happily enough. It was nice to be out in the clear icy air after the centrally heated flat, and the snow, crisp and white, made the whole town sparkle under leaden skies. There would be more snow and Louisa looked forward to it. The shop was on the other side of the harbour and she walked briskly through the main streets, their shops already lighted, pausing here and there to take a look in the windows. Miss Savage had told her not to hurry back, had even urged her to go and have a cup of coffee on her way back, and there was time enough before tea. Louisa was glad that Miss Savage had elected to stay in bed after the excitement of her friends' visit. They hadn't stayed long enough to do any harm, but on the other hand they hadn't been all that good for her—besides, Mr Savage didn't approve of them. Probably he didn't approve of anything much, only bridges.

The shop was only open for a short time each day. She bought the sherry and started back again, stopping on the way to buy an English newspaper and post some letters. It was still only mid-afternoon and already almost dark, but the streets were alive with people and there was plenty of traffic. She turned down past the

Hotel Norge and crossed the little garden in the centre
of the square and went into Riemers. It was full and
cheerful. Louisa ordered a tray of tea instead of the coffee she usually had, and chose a large cream cake to go
with it, eating it slowly while she scanned the headlines
of the paper. It was quite dark by the time she went into
the streets again and she hurried her steps for the short
walk to the flat. Miss Savage's light was on, she saw
with relief as she opened the door; probably she was
still having her afternoon nap. She went in quietly and
peered round the half open door.

Miss Savage was fast asleep, breathing rather thickly,
her face flushed. Louisa went close to the bed and bent
down to look at her closely and was greeted by a heavy
waft of some cloying perfume she didn't like. Discon-
certingly, Miss Savage opened her eyes.

'Snooping?' she asked sharply. 'Did my dear stepbrother put you on to that?'

Louisa straightened up. 'Certainly not! He suggested
no such thing. You were sleeping so heavily and you
looked flushed, I thought you might have a feverish
cold.'

Miss Savage replaced the scowl on her face by a sug-
ary smile. 'You really do look after me well, Louisa.
I'm just tired and I suppose I've lain in bed too long.
I'll get up.'

She was amiability itself for the rest of the evening,
praising their meal although she ate almost none of it,
and full of more plans for the days ahead, and afterwards as they sat, Louisa with her knitting and she leafing through a magazine, she said something suddenly.

'I forgot something today—you'll have to go to the bank tomorrow morning and get some money for me. You won't need a cheque—they've got instructions to pay the miserable pittance Simon allows me.' She nodded carelessly. 'And isn't it time you had some wages?'

'Next week,' said Louisa, frowning over a difficult bit of pattern.

Presently Miss Savage tossed her magazine down. 'How fast you knit.'

'It's not difficult and very soothing. Would you like to try—or do some of that gorgeous embroidery everyone seems to do here?'

'Lord no—I'd be bored in minutes.' Miss Savage yawned. 'I'm going to bed. You know, the thought of a whole winter here sends me round the bend. I could kill Simon!' She floated away, saying over her shoulder: 'Don't come near me until ten o'clock tomorrow, that's time enough for my coffee.' She didn't say good-night, but then she wasn't one for the small courtesies of life.

She was bright-eyed and in a splendid mood when Louisa took her coffee in the morning. 'I feel marvellous,' she declared. 'Go and put on your things and go to the bank, will you? I must pay Eva and there are a lot of food bills…'

It had been snowing again and it wasn't really light yet, but Louisa found it exciting crunching through the snow in her new boots and despite the winter weather the town looked bright and bustling. The Bergen Bank was an imposing building even from the outside. She climbed the wide steps to its enormous doors and went in, to find it even more so on the inside. It was vast with a lofty ceiling, a great many bright lights, and heavy furnishings. She approached the friendliest-looking clerk at the counter and handed him Miss Savage's note, and was rewarded by an instant smile.

'You need to see Mr Helgesen,' he told her, and pinged a bell beside him, and she was led away down a wide corridor to another lofty room, much smaller this time and furnished with a large desk with a young-ish man sitting behind it. He got up as she was ushered in and shook hands, which gave her a chance to study him. A nice face, rugged and good-natured, with blue eyes and close cropped hair. He was stoutly built and a little above middle height, and she took to him at once, and even more so at his friendly voice.

'Miss Evans? Simon Savage told me of you.' He glanced at the note the porter had given him. 'You need money for Miss Savage?'

'Please, she wants to pay her household bills.'

There was a little pause before he said: 'Of course. I'll arrange for you to collect the money she requires. Now sit down for a minute and tell me what you think of Bergen.'

He was the easiest man to talk to. Louisa hadn't realised how much she had missed being able to talk to someone—one couldn't count Miss Savage, who never wanted to talk about anything but clothes and her own discontent… She had been talking for several minutes before she stopped herself with an apologetic: 'I'm sorry, I'm wasting your time and Miss Savage will wonder where I've got to.'

They walked to the door together and shook hands,

and she felt a small thrill of pleasure when he observed: 'I've enjoyed meeting you, Miss Evans. I hope we shall meet again soon. If you need help of any sort please don't hesitate to call upon me.'

She beamed back at him. 'You're very kind. I'll remember that.'

The money safely in her purse, she went out into the cold again, not noticing it because she was wrapped in a warm glow of pleasure. To stay in Bergen for the entire winter was suddenly inviting.

She was crossing the street in front of Sundt's store, the pavement crowded with shoppers, when she thought she glimpsed the young woman Connie ahead of her, but the traffic lights changed and by the time she was on the opposite side of the pavement there was no sign of her. It couldn't possibly be her, anyway; she and the two men with her had gone back to England several days ago. Louisa, walking happily through the snow back to the flat, didn't think any more about her.

CHAPTER FOUR

LOUISA REMEMBERED HER mistaken view of Connie later that day. Miss Savage had been remarkably quiet, even drowsy all the afternoon, and over their cups of tea Louisa tried to rouse her interest with undemanding conversation. She was completely taken aback by Miss Savage's reaction to her casual remark that she had imagined that she had seen her friend that morning. Miss Savage's eyes had glittered with rage and she had put her tea cup down so suddenly that most of the tea spilled into the saucer. 'What utter rubbish!' she exclaimed. 'How could you have possibly seen Connie? They're all back home—why can't you mind your own business instead of imagining things which aren't any of your business anyway? Just because you don't like my friends...'

Louisa, soothing her companion as best she could, found her remarks quite uncalled-for and wondered why she had made them; perhaps she was homesick for London and its life and mentioning Connie had triggered it off. Presently Miss Savage had begun to talk, rather feverishly and about nothing in particular, and Louisa had followed her lead.

The next day or two were passed in a peace and quiet Louisa found surprising and unexpected. Miss Savage was amenable to any conversation made to her and even, when urged, made an effort to eat her meals. The only thing she steadfastly refused to do was to go out. She argued that the snow upset her, that it was far too cold, and that she had no reason to go out anyway. But she insisted that Louisa should go out each day, usually directly after she had taken in her patient's breakfast, 'Because,' as Miss Savage observed, 'it's the one time of day when I don't need anyone—I never get up before eleven o'clock and I like to lie and doze or read.' So Louisa formed the habit of spending the mornings in the town, getting back to the flat round about noon when Miss Savage was usually up and on the point of exchanging her bed for the sofa in the sitting room.

Winter or no, there was a great deal to do, and Louisa happily explored the town in all directions, delighted to find another, not quite as fashionable shopping centre on the farther side of the harbour.

It was a pity that most of the museums were only open in the early afternoons during the winter, but the Bryggens Museum was open for a few hours each day; she went twice to examine the remains of some of the oldest buildings in Bergen. She went to the Historical Museum at Sydneshaugen too, which meant a bus ride to the other side of the town, but she was beginning to feel so at home now that she planned several longer excursions if the weather allowed and Miss Savage would agree to her having a day off. She had broached the subject once or twice and met with evasive answers, and since she had little to do except act as a companion and see that her patient took her pills, ate a sufficient amount and led a quiet life, she felt that she could hardly complain.

The snow had stopped on the morning she went to the Bergen Bank to collect her salary. Rather to her surprise Miss Savage had asked her to get some more money at the same time. It had seemed a great deal when Louisa had handed it over such a short time ago; apparently housekeeping was an expensive business in Norway. She went to the same clerk again and was ushered into Mr Helgesen's office.

And this time he wasn't alone. Mr Savage was there, sitting in one of the leather chairs. Both men got up as she went in, but only Mr Helgesen crossed the floor to shake hands; Mr Savage contented himself with a curt nod, his severe expression not altering one jot. And two can play at that game, thought Louisa as she turned a shoulder to him and addressed Mr Helgesen. 'I think perhaps the clerk made a mistake. I've only come to collect my salary.'

'No mistake, Miss Evans.' Mr Helgesen looked delighted to see her again. 'Mr Savage wished to see you; he has come specially for that purpose.' He added gallantly: 'Of course I wished to see you, too.'

She smiled at him rather shyly. 'Thank you. Oh— I'm sorry, I almost forgot, I have another note from Miss Savage. She asked me to get her allowance while I was here.'

The two men exchanged glances. 'Did you not collect it when you were last here?'

'Yes.' Louisa frowned a little. 'She said there
wouldn't be any difficulty, that I was just to ask…'

'Yes, yes, of course,' said Mr Helgesen soothingly.
'It shall be attended to—if I might have her note?' He
went to the door. 'I'll arrange matters with the clerk.'

Louisa didn't much fancy being alone with Mr Savage. 'Couldn't I get it when I get my money?' she enquired, and made for the door, too.

'Miss Evans,' said Mr Savage. His voice was quiet
but not to be ignored. 'I wish to speak to you.'

She faced him reluctantly and saw his smile. It
wasn't a friendly smile; she sat down without a word
and waited.

'How is my sister?'

It was a difficult question to answer truthfully, and
she hesitated. 'I think she's making slow progress, but
she's unpredictable. I mean, her moods vary all the
time. But she sleeps well—too much, perhaps—and for
the most part she seems content, although she doesn't
like living here. She hardly ever goes out, but one can
hardly blame her in this weather…'

'You go out?'

'But I like it, I think it's lovely, all the snow and the
streets lighted…'

'Spare me your raptures, Miss Evans. Claudia's
friends haven't returned?'

She stared at him in surprise. 'But they went back
to England—Miss Savage was very upset.'

'You are sure of that?'

She hesitated. 'Yes—I should have seen them otherwise. I did think I saw Connie—I don't know her last name—a few days ago, but the pavement was crowded and I lost sight of her. It must have been a mistake.'

'You didn't enquire at the Norge if she was there?'

Louisa said patiently: 'I've just told you—I don't know her name.'

He stared at her with hard eyes and picked up the phone on the desk—a piece of impertinence, she decided, in someone else's office, too. Who did he think he was?

Of course she didn't understand a word he said, but when he put the receiver down his face was as black as thunder. 'The three of them left yesterday evening.'

She said, 'Oh, dear,' and his lip curled. 'I shall accompany you back to the flat,' he told her. 'Does my sister expect you back immediately?'

'As a matter of fact she told me to have two hours off because she intended to stay in bed until lunchtime.'

'Just so,' said Mr Savage; she wouldn't have been surprised to have seen him grind his teeth and sighed quite audibly with relief as Mr Helgesen came back into the room. He glanced first at Mr Savage and then smiled at her. 'I have told the clerk to let you have Miss Savage's allowance. Mr Savage has opened an account for you here; he thought it wiser, since you were in a foreign country and might not realise…it is, I think, rather more expensive here than in England. You can draw any amount you wish, of course,' he laughed a little, 'provided there is still some money there.'

'That's very kind of you, Mr Helgesen.' Louisa

turned round to face Mr Savage getting himself into a sheepskin jacket. 'And I expect you meant to be kind, too, Mr Savage, but I am capable of managing my own affairs, thank you. I promise you that I shan't run up bills all over the town.'

'And I'm too far away to keep you to that promise. Nurse, shall we go?'

He said something to Mr Helgesen and moved to the door, leaving them together. 'Remember that I will do anything to help you, Miss Evans.' Mr Helgesen engulfed her hand in his. 'Are you ever free in the evening? There is to be a recital of Grieg music at the end of the week, I should very much like to take you.'

'And I'd love to come. But I'd have to ask Miss Savage first—you see, I'd have to leave her alone...'

'Perhaps we can think of something. I'll telephone you—if I may?'

'Oh, yes, please.' He really was a dear; what a pity that he and Mr Savage couldn't be in each other's shoes. She shook hands again and walked beside the silent Mr Savage to the desk, where she very defiantly drew out much more money than she needed, and received a bundle of notes for Miss Savage. She quite expected that her companion would make some snide remark, but he remained silent as they went out into the street, and, just as silent, strode beside her on the way back to the flat. Once or twice she was on the verge of some harmless comment, but then she remembered that he had begged her to spare him her raptures...

The flat was quiet as she opened the door; usually Eva was bustling round cleaning. Perhaps she was al-

ready in the kitchen… Louisa went along the passage
and pushed open the half open door. Eva wasn't there,
but Miss Savage was, sitting at the kitchen table, her
bright head on her arms, snoring her head off. On the
table was a glass, not quite empty, and beside it a half
full vodka bottle. Louisa stood and stared, not quite
taking it all in. It wasn't until Mr Savage spoke very
quietly over her shoulder that she turned her head to
take a look at him.

'You may be a splendid nurse, Miss Evans, highly
qualified and skilled and taught everything there is
to know about your profession, but one thing no one
taught you, and that was to recognise an alcoholic when
you saw one.'

'No,' said Louisa, and then: 'Why wasn't I told? The
doctors—you…'

'I believed that either one or other of the doctors
would have briefed you; I had no reason to think otherwise. Indeed, I suggested to Claudia when I arranged
for her to come here that she should engage an older
woman and that she should be told what exactly was
wrong with her patient. Instead, I find a chit of a girl
who hasn't a clue. There seemed no point in telling you
at first, but when I heard that her three boon companions had been here again, I came down to see you and
explain. As you see, I have no need to do so. The matter speaks for itself.'

Louisa gave him a thoughtful look. 'You have no
pity, have you?' she observed quietly. 'I think you're
the most disagreeable man I've ever met. And now will

you carry her through to the bedroom and I'll get her into bed. And then I think you owe me an explanation.'

He didn't answer her, only stooped to lift the still snoring Miss Savage into his arms and carry her down the passage. Louisa, ahead of him, straightened the bed-clothes and then tucked her patient up. 'If you'll wait in the sitting room,' she suggested, 'there are one or two things I have to do. If you want coffee there'll be some in the kitchen.'

She didn't wait to see if he would do as she asked but got busy with Miss Savage, bathing her face gently, soothing her, smoothing her hair, wrapping her snugly, and then tidying the room which as usual looked as though it had been ransacked. Presently, when every-thing was tidy again and she was sure that her patient was still deeply sleeping, she went along to the sit-ting room. It surprised her that Mr Savage had carried through a tray from the kitchen with the coffee pot and two mugs on it. He poured for them both, gestured her to a chair and asked brusquely: 'Well, what do you want to know?'

Louisa took a sip of coffee. 'All the things that I should have been told in the first place, Mr Savage.'

He sat back in his chair, drinking his coffee with the air of a man who had nothing on his mind. He said care-lessly: 'Claudia has been an alcoholic for the last eight years. Everything has been tried—and I mean every-thing. Once or twice it seemed that she had been cured, but she lapsed… These so-called friends of hers—she asks them to get her whisky or vodka or anything else she fancies, and they do. It seems certain that that's why they came to see her again. Surely you would have noticed something?'

'If I'd been warned beforehand, yes. As it was, I believed the doctor's diagnosis.' She added honestly: 'Of course, the diagnosis was correct and I daresay the doctor thought I knew about Miss Savage—it's quite possible, you see, to have all her symptoms for other liver complaints. But now that I know—yes, there were a number of signs I should have been suspicious about.'

'I brought her to Norway because I hoped that away from her friends and the life she led, she stood a better chance of fighting her addiction. It seems I was wrong.'

Louisa put down her cup and met the dark eyes staring at her so coldly. 'Then wouldn't it be a good idea to let her go back to England? She's not happy here; she didn't want to come—she told me that...' She paused, seeking a nice way of putting it.

'She had to, otherwise I should have stopped her allowance. Quite correct.' He got to his feet. 'No, I don't intend to let her go back to England. On the contrary, as soon as she is fit enough, she shall travel up to Tromso, and you will accompany her.'

Louisa choked back an instant denial. 'Isn't that a town in the north?'

'Yes. My work is some fifteen miles away from there—a ribbon bridge is being built between two islands. There's a small community there with a few hundred people.' He passed his cup for more coffee. 'You ski?'

'Of course I don't!' She spoke sharply. 'You don't intend that Miss Savage should live there?'

'Indeed I do—she will be under my eye, and so for that matter will you.'

Louisa said with great dignity: 'I believe I can manage my own life without your help.' She added boldly: 'Perhaps your sister would have had a better chance without your interference.'

'You believe in plain speaking, Nurse, but I'm afraid your opinion holds no weight with me, so let's keep strictly to the matter in hand.'

'I'll take a look at Miss Savage first,' said Louisa. But that lady was still deep in a snoring slumber.

'You have sufficient warm clothing?' enquired Simon Savage as she sat down again. She told him briefly what she possessed and he said at once: 'You'll need more than that—get a pencil and paper, will you?' And when she had, 'I imagine Claudia has almost nothing suitable; you'll outfit her as well.'

Louisa wrote obediently and then lifted her head to look at him. 'You're not really going to send her all that way? She'll be so lonely, and she doesn't like snow or mountains…'

'What a persistent young woman you are! Can you not see that she's almost at her last chance? Perhaps such a drastic step as this will provide that chance. And now be good enough not to argue with me; my mind is made up.'

'Oh, pooh to that,' declared Louisa, and trembled at his icy stare. 'Just supposing she's ill—is there a doctor there?'

'She could be taken to Tromso by motor launch in a very short time. There is a road, of course, but it will

be closed until late April—even May.' He smiled thinly
at Louisa's look of horror. 'You don't care for the idea?'
His voice was silky. 'Perhaps you wish to give up the
case, especially as you've been so misled.'

He wanted to be rid of her; any doubts she had been
harbouring were instantly squashed. 'Certainly not,
Mr Savage! I came to look after your sister, and that's
what I intend to do. As you said, such a drastic change
in her life might be her salvation, and if there's anything I can do to help her, I shall do it.'

His laugh was quite genuine and she went red with
embarrassment and rage. 'I daresay you'll want to be
getting back,' she told him stonily, 'and there are several things I want to do before Miss Savage wakes up.'

'Plenty of time for that, she won't stir until this evening or even tomorrow morning.' He walked to the
door, picking up his jacket as he went. 'And I'm staying in Bergen until Sunday. I shall be round tomorrow
to see Claudia, and by the way, if you want to go out
with Helgesen on Saturday evening, I shall be here—
my stepsister and I have a good deal to discuss, and I
daresay we shall do that better without your well-mean-
ing interference.'

Which remark left her speechless. Eva came back
with the shopping presently and Louisa, always a girl
to get things settled in her mind, went along to the
kitchen, and while lunch was being prepared, got Eva
to tell her all she knew about Tromso.

Eva had looked at her in a puzzled fashion. 'But that
is a very long way away from here,' she pointed out.
'Why do you wish to know?'

Louisa explained, very carefully, letting it appear that Miss Savage's brother was taking her with him for the benefit of her health.

Eva nodded. 'That is a good idea. It will be beautiful—cold, you understand, but most healthy, and they will have each other, that will be nice.'

'I'm not sure if I was supposed to tell you,' said Louisa doubtfully. 'What happens to your job here?'

'Not to worry, Miss Evans, this flat is rented for six months by Mr Savage and I am to be paid for that time, whether I am needed or not. That was the arrangement.'

'Oh, good.' Louisa got up. 'I'm going to see if Miss Savage is quite comfortable—she doesn't want any lunch, so I'll have mine here with you if I may and you can tell me some more about Tromso.'

Mr Savage returned the following day in the morning. He had been quite right; his stepsister hadn't roused until very late in the evening and then she had been difficult to manage. She had a headache for a start, she felt terrible and she had no wish to do any of the things Louisa suggested. But towards midnight she had quietened down and Louisa had been able to wash her face and hands, change her nightie and re-make her bed. She had gone to sleep almost immediately, which was a good thing, for with one thing and another Louisa was tired out. Disliking someone, she decided as she put her thankful head on her pillow, was more tiring than anything else she knew of. And it wasn't her patient she was thinking of.

It was Eva who answered the door, took his coat and assured him that she would bring coffee in only a moment. She seemed to like him and Louisa, coming out of Miss Savage's bedroom, couldn't think why. His 'good morning' to her was accompanied by a mocking smile and the polite hope that his stepsister was feeling more herself.

'Well, she is,' said Louisa, who had just had a slipper thrown at her by that lady, 'much—but she's also very irritable. Please don't upset her.'

'Oh, I won't. I know what a hangover's like, Nurse. And don't look like that; I also know when to stop.' He sat down by the window. 'The weather's changing. We shall have more snow.'

'Indeed?' queried Louisa coldly. 'You can't see Miss Savage yet, you know.'

'Don't be bossy, Miss Evans. When I've had my coffee I shall see my stepsister—I have a great deal to say to her.'

'She has the most appalling headache...'

'Of course she has.' He got up and took the tray from Eva as she came in and smiled so nicely at her that Louisa blinked; she had no idea that he could look like that—quite human. 'Three spoonfuls,' he told her. 'I have a sweet tooth.'

Louisa was glad of her coffee. She had been up early, ministering to Miss Savage, persuading her to drink black coffee, dealing with her headache, ignoring the screams and abuse and ill-temper. Never having been more than slightly tipsy herself, she could only guess how ghastly her patient must be feeling and do her best to get her rational again. She had succeeded to an extent, though. Miss Savage had stopped crying and carrying on and had drunk more coffee and now she was dozing fitfully. 'I won't have her upset,' said Louisa out loud.

'So you have already said,' remarked her companion dryly. 'I suggest that you drink your coffee and go out for a brisk walk, there's nothing like fresh air for clearing the head.' And when Louisa would have protested: 'Have you sufficient money?'

'Plenty, thank you.'

'Very good. We'll discuss clothes and travelling and so on when you return.'

She was dismissed and it would be undignified to protest again. She peeped in at Miss Savage, lying back in her bed with pads on her eyes and the blinds drawn, and then went to her own room and got ready to go out. She was at the door when the telephone rang and when she went to answer it Mr Savage was lying back in his chair, his eyes closed. He looked formidable even like that. Louisa picked up the receiver and found herself smiling because it was Mr Helgesen, wanting to know if she were free on Saturday evening. 'Because if you are, we could have a meal first and then go on to the concert. Could I call for you just after six o'clock?'

'Oh, I'd love that,' said Louisa happily, 'only I quite forgot to ask…' She hesitated and glanced at the figure in the chair. 'Miss Savage isn't feeling very well and I hardly like to…'

'Women never listen,' observed Simon Savage nastily. 'I remember very clearly telling you that I would be here on Saturday evening. I daresay you're due quite a lot of off duty.'

'Thank you very much,' said Louisa into the phone, ignoring Mr Savage, 'I'll be ready just after six o'clock.' They wished each other goodbye and she rang off. She said rather snappily to the somnolent Simon Savage: 'Of course I listened, but how was I to know you meant it?'

'I always mean what I say—you'll know that in future.'

She flounced out of the room and by a great effort of will, didn't bang the door.

She had a list of shopping to do for Eva and she went first to the fish market, not only to buy fish but to admire the flowers. It amazed her that they were still to be bought in such bitter weather, although at a price she was unable to afford, but just looking at them, spaced out in such an unlikely fashion among the stalls of fish, was a pleasure. She chose her cod with a careful eye, bought a bag of cranberries, went to the little kiosk by the market and bought a *Telegraph*, then started walking away from the harbour towards the shops, stopping on the way to spend ten minutes in one of the many bookshops. There were as many English paperbacks as there were Norwegian—but then she had come to the conclusion that everyone in Norway must speak English as well as their native tongue. She did a little window-shopping after that; obviously she would have to buy quite a few more clothes and it would be as well to price them first. She wondered how long it would be before Miss Savage would feel like shopping, and when they would be going and how. By air, she supposed; there was an excellent domestic service in the country and surely at this time of year it was the easiest way to travel.

It might be the easiest way, but it wasn't going to be their way. She discovered that when she got back to the flat, to find Miss Savage, looking like something just put through the mangle, sitting back against her pillows listening to her stepbrother, who was sitting on the side of the bed, talking to her in a quiet no-nonsense voice. Without turning his head, he said: 'There you are—just in time to hear the arrangements which have been made. Take off your things and come in here.'

No please or thank you, grumbled Louisa to herself, and took her time about tidying her hair and putting more powder on her nose. She was rewarded by an impatient frown as she went into the bedroom and sat down meekly on the dressing table stool. 'Before we start, Miss Savage, is there anything you'd like?' she asked.

Her patient shook her head and then winced at the pain. 'Who cares what I like?' she moaned, 'Simon least of all.'

Mr Savage didn't appear to hear this; he said at once: 'The sooner you come the better, and since you refuse to fly, I'll arrange for you to travel on the coastal steamer. It will probably be rather rough at this time of year, but the journey only takes five days to Tromso and you'll see some remarkable scenery. In—let me see, today is Wednesday…a week's time you'll be met at Tromso, and as it will be afternoon when you get there, you'd better spend the night there and you can finish the trip by launch.'

'No ice?' asked Louisa a little faintly.

'The Gulf Stream,' said Simon Savage impatiently. 'Inland there's plenty of snow, of course.'

'And are you inland?'

He shook his head. 'An arm of Tromso Sound; a little rural perhaps. We're building a bridge between two islands where it joins the sea, they each have a town and a good scattering of houses but only one road on the larger island.'

It sounded bleak, thought Louisa, and peeped at Miss Savage's face. It looked bleak too. 'It does sound a very interesting journey,' she said bracingly. 'Is there anything to do on board?'

Simon Savage's firm mouth remained unsmiling. 'Nothing at all,' he said blandly.

Miss Savage burst into tears and he got to his feet. 'Perhaps tomorrow we should shop for your clothes,' he observed. 'As you're making this unexpected journey, Miss Evans, and you are employed by me, anything you may need will be charged to my account.'

Miss Savage stopped crying long enough to ask: 'And what about me?'

He turned to look at her from the door. 'When have I ever failed to pay your bills, Claudia?' he asked and, not waiting for an answer, shut the door.

The doctor came shortly after that, pronounced Miss Savage fit to get up if she felt like it, made out a prescription for the headache and before leaving, followed Louisa into the sitting room and closed the door.

'Miss Savage should be all right,' he told her. 'We

must try again, but with discretion. Allow her a drink with her lunch and dinner, Nurse. One glass of whatever she wishes, that is necessary, otherwise the withdrawal symptoms will be too severe. Later, perhaps, we can cut it down to one glass a day, and eventually to none. It is a pity that she has no incentive—if she were married…' He shook his head and sighed, because there was really nothing much that he could do.

'It needs a miracle,' said Louisa again.

She coaxed Miss Savage to eat a little of the light lunch Eva had cooked for her presently and gave her the whisky she asked for, and then to distract her attention from her craving, made a great business of making a list of the clothes they were to buy. Miss Savage even got out of bed towards evening, and though she shivered and shook alarmingly, she spent an hour discussing her wardrobe. No expense was to be spared, Louisa noted, but if Simon Savage was prepared to foot the bills, it was no concern of hers. She tucked her patient up presently, gave her supper and another ration of whisky and then, after her own supper, sat up until midnight until she was quite sure that Miss Savage was soundly asleep.

It was after lunch before Simon Savage came, which was a good thing, because his stepsister had wakened in a bad humour, declaring that she couldn't live unless she had a drink at that very minute and throwing her breakfast tray at Louisa. But somehow, now that she knew what was wrong, Louisa didn't mind too much. True, there was an awful lot of mopping up to be done, but she was beginning to feel sorry for Miss Savage now and even to like her a little. After a good deal of coaxing, Miss Savage consented to get dressed and by the time Mr Savage rang the bell, she was at least approachable.

Mr Savage had taken the precaution of hiring a taxi for the afternoon. It took them from shop to shop and the driver waited patiently outside each one. It certainly made shopping easy, and since Louisa didn't have to worry too much about prices, she began to enjoy herself in a modest way. True, she didn't insist on a fur-lined jacket, a fur cap and suede slacks, but she was quite content with her woollen slacks and the waterproof poplin outfit which, Simon Savage assured her, she would find very useful even if she didn't ski. He ordered her to buy several woollen sweaters, too and a dark green woollen skirt with a quilted jacket to go with it. 'And you'd better have a blouse as well,' he suggested carelessly. 'Probably we shall go to Tromsö and you'll need them for the hotel.'

Which remark sent his stepsister off into another small orgy of buying.

On the whole, the afternoon went off smoothly, and since by the time they got back to the flat Miss Savage was tired out, Louisa saw her into bed, took her tea and then tucked her up for a nap. All this took a little time, of course, but Simon was still there, in the sitting room, doing nothing. She felt bound to offer him tea too, which he accepted with the air of one who had hoped for something better but would make do with what he could get. And when she thanked him stiffly for the things she had bought, he told her peremptorily to say no more about it in such a bored voice that she drank her tea in silence and was quite relieved when he went.

Possibly building bridges was conducive to ill humour and an inability to tolerate the shortcomings of those one met outside of this tricky profession. 'I wonder how they can make an arch without the middle falling into the water,' Louisa asked the empty room. 'One day when he's in a good mood, I'll ask him. Only he never is in a good mood.'

CHAPTER FIVE

MISS SAVAGE WAS at her most difficult for the rest of that day, alternately begging for a drink and abusing Louisa when she didn't get one, and in between that poking sly fun at her. 'You never guessed, did you?' she crowed. 'You thought I was being so considerate, sending you out each morning—and there we were sitting cosily here—they brought the drinks with them, of course. You gave me a fright when you thought you'd seen Connie—I thought it was all up then, only you never suspected, did you? I'm clever, you know. I told the doctor in London that you knew all about me so there was no need to say anything to you, and I told the one here just the same.' She went off into a peal of laughter. 'I wish I'd seen your face when you and Simon found me! I had a drop too much—I didn't mean to fall asleep. But now you know…what are you going to do about it?' She added pathetically with a complete change of manner: 'You won't leave me, will you, Louisa?'

'No,' said Louisa, 'I won't, and I don't know what to do about it anyway—only do as the doctor tells me. And now if you'd put on that dress that's too long, I'll pin it up and get it sewn.' She went on carelessly: 'Do you think it might be a good idea to go to that nice bookshop we found and get half a dozen paperbacks—just to keep us going until we've discovered our way around Tromso?'

'Tromso's miles away from Simon's work,' said Miss Savage sulkily.

'Not so far, and there's this launch... I don't see why we shouldn't go there from time to time, do you?'

'You don't know Simon—he hates anyone to be happy.'

And presently, stitching up the hem of the dress, Louisa began to wonder why Simon Savage should take such a bleak view of life, or was it perhaps that his stepsister made it appear so? But upon reflection, she couldn't recall his smiling, only just that once to Eva. She bit off the thread with small white teeth, but on the whole, she decided, he was better than Frank.

He came the next morning with the tickets for their journey and to tell Louisa that he had arranged for them to be taken by taxi down to the ship. 'She sails at seven o'clock and there'll be dinner on board,' he told her, 'no dressing up or anything like that. If Claudia is feeling off colour I'm afraid you'll have to look after her yourself—there are stewardesses to clean the cabins and so on, but I doubt if their English is very good. How is she?'

'Getting dressed.'

He nodded. 'May I stay for coffee?'

Louisa blinked her long lashes. 'Why, of course—it's your flat, isn't it? I'll ask Eva to hurry up a little.'

He didn't stay long, his visit had been one of duty; he made casual conversation with them both and went with an air of relief. He did pause as he went to remind Louisa that she was going out with Lars Helgesen on the following evening, and would she be good enough to tell Eva that he would be there for dinner with his stepsister.

Lars Helgesen and Simon Savage arrived together, and Louisa, in one of the new dresses, a fine wool jersey in several shades of blue, got up from her chair to greet them. Miss Savage, sulking again because she had to spend a few hours with her stepbrother, was lying on the sofa, wearing a soft woollen rose-coloured housecoat and looking really very pretty despite the deep shadows under her eyes and the downward curve of her mouth.

'Lars Helgesen,' said Mr Savage, 'my sister Claudia.'

Mr Helgesen advanced to the sofa and shook hands, looking bemused, and Louisa, watching him, had to admit that Miss Savage did look glamorous even if she was addicted to the bottle, and certainly was worth a second look. If only she could cure her... She frowned in thought and changed it to a smile as Mr Helgesen suggested that they should go.

Mr Savage hadn't said a word to her, nor did he as they went out of the room. She had been going to tell him that Eva had promised to stay on for a little longer that evening and serve supper, but if he couldn't be civil enough to wish her good evening, he could find out for himself.

'Call me Lars,' said Mr Helgesen. 'I thought we'd

walk, it's not far.' He took her arm and took her down a side street which led to the market, where they crossed Torget into Bryggen and stopped outside one of the old houses there. 'Here we are,' he declared. 'It is a well known restaurant in the town, and you shall eat some of their delicious fish.'

It was warm inside, old-fashioned, and the tables were well filled. Louisa took off her coat and sat down at the table they were led to. She felt happy; Lars was a pleasant companion, even on their brief walk she had discovered that. She looked forward to a delightful evening in his company.

They had sampled the hors d'oeuvres and were well into the fish when Lars abandoned his light chat and asked in a carefully casual voice: 'Miss Savage—Claudia—is she very delicate?' And before Louisa could answer: 'She is so very pretty and so charming, I—I was much struck…'

'She's recovering from a complaint which left her rather low,' said Louisa carefully. 'She has her ups and downs though.'

Lars offered her the sauce. 'Yes? She is still so young.'

Just as carefully Louisa agreed.

'Of course Simon has told me something about her—that was necessary so that I might check her account from time to time—it is understandable that so very pretty a lady should wish to spend money.' Louisa murmured something or other and he went on: 'Simon tells me that you are to go to the village where he works.

He thinks it will be better for her. I shall miss you—both of you.'

Louisa smiled at his earnest face. 'It does sound a long way off, but I'm sure we shall be all right once we're there,' she assured him. 'Have you been there?'

They talked about a great many things after that, finishing their dinner and walking back to the concert hall, and then sat in companionable silence listening to the pianist playing Grieg's music, and when it was over, walking the short distance back to the flat.

'You'll come in for coffee?' asked Louisa, and felt a little thrill of pleasure at his eager 'Yes, please!' It was such a pity that they would have no chance to see each other again, at least until Simon Savage decided to send them back to Bergen, and he might not do that, they might go straight back to England. It depended on his stepsister, didn't it?

They went up the stairs into the quiet flat and found Simon Savage standing by the window looking out into the dark night. His long lean back had the look of a man impatient to be gone. Miss Savage was still lying on the sofa, which surprised Louisa; she had thought that her patient would have had more than enough of her stepbrother's company by now. She turned her head as they went into the room and smiled, her gaze resting for a bare moment upon Louisa before lingering upon Mr Helgesen's face. He crossed the room to her at once. 'I was afraid you would be in bed,' he told her, and took her hand, smiling down at her. Louisa, watching them, allowed the faint, vague idea that Lars had been getting a little interested in herself to slide into oblivion.

Well, it had been silly of her to imagine any such thing in the first place. She looked away and found Simon Savage's dark eyes bent upon her, and it was only too obvious from the look on his face that he had read her thoughts. She flushed angrily. 'I'll get the coffee,' she muttered, and escaped to the kitchen.

He followed her. 'A pleasant evening, Nurse?' he enquired blandly.

'Yes, thank you.' She went on putting cups and saucers on a tray, not looking at him.

'A nice chap, Helgesen.' He watched her through half closed lids. 'Do you have a boyfriend at home, Louisa?'

If she had been expecting that question she would have been ready with a bright answer; as it was all she could think of to say was 'No.'

'I don't say I'm surprised.' He didn't qualify this remark and she didn't answer it, recognising it as bait to make her lose her temper.

'Will you stay for coffee?' she asked sweetly.

He took the tray from her. 'But of course.'

Before the two men went it had been arranged that Lars should take them in his car to the ship—moreover, Louisa heard him arranging to take Miss Savage out to lunch on the following day. She was sure that Mr Savage had heard it as well, but he didn't say anything, not until he was actually on the point of leaving. He said softly: 'You can safely leave it to me, Nurse.'

It surprised her very much when she returned to the sitting room to hear Miss Savage asking her quite humbly if she would mind her going to lunch with Lars Helgesen. 'And I know what you're thinking, but I promise you I'll not drink anything, only tonic water.' She went on dreamily: 'He's sweet, isn't he?'

Louisa, clearing away the coffee cups, wondered if this was the miracle she had hoped for. If it was, she was going to help it along with all her might. 'He's very nice,' she agreed, 'and now what about bed? You want to look your best in the morning.'

There were only three days before they left, and it seemed to Louisa that Lars Helgesen was either at the flat or taking Claudia Savage out to one meal or another. Louisa had awaited her return from their first date in some trepidation, but she need not have worried. Her patient seemed a changed young woman. True, she still needed a drink twice a day, but her temper was no longer something to be reckoned with and she had stopped throwing things about. Moreover, she had asked Louisa to call her Claudia, which was a great step forward and made for friendlier relations all round.

Of Simon Savage there had been neither sight nor sound. He had returned to his work, she knew, but he had made no attempt to telephone or write, nor had he come to say goodbye. She wondered several times what he had said to Lars about his stepsister; whatever it was had made no difference to his feelings towards that lady. Louisa packed, did last-minute shopping and laid in a small stock of books against Claudia's boredom during their journey. She foresaw difficult days ahead, for Claudia wasn't going to take lightly to not seeing Lars. It seemed a pity that they couldn't have stayed in Bergen now that there was an incentive for her to give up drinking, and it was even more of a pity that there was no way of getting hold of Mr Savage to tell him so. She could of course telephone him, but she had the feeling that if she did he would listen to her in silence and refuse to change his plans. Perhaps he was bent on punishing his stepsister, perhaps he really did believe that a stay in the north would be the means of curing her. Louisa didn't feel inclined to give him the benefit of the doubt.

Their last day came and with it Lars Helgesen to take them both out to lunch—the Norge Hotel this time, and although he was equally attentive to both of them, Louisa found herself wishing that she wasn't there. The other two had so much to say to each other, although he was careful to keep their talk light and amusing, and Claudia replied in kind, sipping her one glass of white wine as though she had little interest in it. Over coffee Louisa had the bright idea of remembering that she still needed some wool to finish her knitting, and left them together with a promise to meet later at the flat where they would have tea before driving to the dock.

They weren't back when she got in, so she got the tea tray ready and sat down to wait. And when they did arrive, what with saying goodbye to Eva, last-minute packing and messages, there was barely time for them to drink their rather late tea before they had to leave.

On board, Lars went with them down the curved stairs to their cabin, a quite roomy one with a table and chairs as well as two narrow beds. There was a tiny shower room too and a good sized cupboard. Its large window looked out on to the deck alongside and Louisa found it quite perfect, although from the mutinous look on Claudia's face she guessed that her views were not shared. Certainly there was a tremendous difference between the cabin and the comfort of the flat, but there was all they could need. She murmured something about finding out mealtimes, said goodbye to Lars and left them together. She encountered nobody as she made her way back to the main hall. There was the ticket office there and here people were queuing to get their tickets to whichever of the stops they wanted. The ship would call at a number of places, some quite large towns, some fishing villages, some a mere cluster of houses. Louisa could imagine how welcome the sight of it must be, especially during the long winter, bringing supplies and mail and discharging passengers and taking others on.

She edged past a family group, complete with pram, small baby and a large dog, and went up another winding stair. The dining room was quite large with small tables and an air of cosiness, and a door from it led to the stern of the ship where, she discovered, the passengers who were travelling only part of the way could sit. There was a cafeteria there and a small bar where she was delighted to see that no spirits were sold, only wines, sherry and port. There were already a few people sitting about, and she went back the way she had come, out of the door again and into a lounge, running across the fore part of the ship, from side to side, with large windows on all sides. There was no one there either, so she went up another small flight of stairs and found another lounge, exactly like the one below but used, she guessed, for observing the scenery. She stood for a few minutes, watching the ship preparing to sail, craning her neck to see Bergen alongside and behind her, lights shining from the houses perched high on the skirts of the mountains behind the town. And in front of her the fjord leading to the open sea. It was a dark evening and she could see very little; probably it would be both cold and rough. She went below presently, studied the meals timetable, made her way through the increasing number of passengers back to the cabin and tapped on the door. Someone had just shouted something over the tannoy which she guessed was an order for people to go ashore, for she could feel the engines somewhere under her feet. They would be sailing at any moment now, and surely Lars would be gone.

He had, and Claudia was sitting slumped in one of the chairs, crying. The moment she caught sight of Louisa she shouted: 'I won't go, I won't! I want to stay with Lars—it's cruel of Simon to make me just when I'm h-happy…'

Louisa privately agreed with her. It was cruel of Mr Savage, but then from what she had seen of him he possessed very little of the milk of human kindness. She went and sat down on the edge of one of the beds close to Claudia and took one of her hands in hers. 'Look, it's not as bad as you think. Listen to me—you're much better. You've been trying hard, haven't you, and each day will be easier. This place, wherever we're going, is quiet and very peaceful. You'll sleep well without pills and start eating properly and you'll feel so well that you won't be bored or tired of doing nothing. And the quicker you do that, the quicker you'll come back to Bergen. Don't you see, if you improve as much as that, your brother can't refuse to let you return? And Lars will be here, won't he, waiting for you?'

Claudia pulled her hand away pettishly. 'Oh, what do you know about it? You've never been in love, you've no idea what it's like. When you meet someone and you know at once…'

'It must be wonderful. I've never been in love, as you say, and perhaps I never shall be, but it's happened to you, hasn't it? And you've got to hang on to it. You're one of the lucky ones.'

Claudia turned round slowly to look at her. 'We haven't much in common,' she said, and laughed a little, 'but for a nurse you're not a bad sort.'

Her face crumpled again. 'Do you really think we'll come back soon? And that Lars likes me as much as he says he does?'

'Yes to both questions.'

Claudia was looking at her face in the little jewelled mirror she carried in her handbag. She said defiantly: 'I told him—I told him I was an alcoholic and he just smiled and said that I didn't need to be any more because he was there. Do you suppose I could be cured, Louisa?'

Louisa paused in her unpacking of an overnight bag. 'Yes, I'm quite sure you can. You see, you've got a good reason now, haven't you, and before you never had that, did you?'

Claudia flung the mirror down on the bed. 'All the same, I shall go mad in this beastly little place we're going to, and if I do it'll be Simon's fault.'

'Do you suppose Lars will come and see you?' asked Louisa, and was rewarded by a return of good humour.

'He promised, but he doesn't know when.' Claudia got up and peered out into the dark outside. 'Have we started?'

'Yes, a few minutes ago. Dinner is at eight o'clock. Would you like a glass of wine before then?'

'Whisky.'

'No, wine. You can't buy spirits on board ship, anyway, it's against the law.'

'Oh, well, wine, I suppose.' Claudia looked round her disdainfully. 'I've never been in such a poky little place in my life before, and I've got to share it with you. I can't bear the idea…'

Louisa choked back what she would like to have said. 'It's only for four days—and we shall only sleep here, after all.' She felt the ship dipping its nose into the beginnings of the North Sea, heaving alarmingly. 'And if it's rough you may be glad to have someone here.'

There were barely a dozen passengers in the dining room and the steward led them to a window table where two people were already sitting, and when Louisa said, 'Good evening,' because Claudia was looking annoyed at having to share, she was answered to her relief, in the same language—they were an elderly pair and now that she had time to look at them, American.

They leaned over the table to shake hands. 'Mr and Mrs Foster Kuntz,' they said, beaming, 'and I do believe we're the only English speaking passengers.'

Louisa shook hands and Claudia did the same, ungraciously, and since she had nothing to say, Louisa said: 'Miss Savage is visiting her brother near Tromso. She hasn't been well, and I'm travelling with her.'

'Tromso?' queried Mrs Kuntz. 'That's right in the north. We're going to Trondheim to see our daughter—she's married.'

'To a Norwegian?' asked Louisa hastily, because Claudia was ignoring everyone.

Mrs Kuntz laughed in a jolly way. 'No, he's from the USA, same as us. Got a good job too. We're from Texas—San Antonio, cattle and petroleum; Foster here has done very well from them. We thought we'd have a nice long vacation in Europe and visit Cissie before we go home.'

Louisa said, 'What fun for you both,' and picked up her spoon to start on the soup the steward had set before her. 'Have you enjoyed your trip?'

Mrs Kuntz's answer kept the conversation going in a rather one-sided fashion through the cod steaks and the pudding, so that it wasn't too noticeable that Claudia didn't speak at all. They left the dining room together and Mrs Kuntz whispered: 'Your poor friend—I reckon she must have been good and sick—she hasn't said a word.'

Louisa seized her chance. 'Yes, she has been ill and she's still convalescing. You mustn't mind if she doesn't enter into conversation, she finds it exhausting, and I hope you won't mind if we have our coffee quietly in a corner, because I think she's pretty well exhausted. We'll have an early night; there's nothing much to see anyway, is there?'

Mrs Kuntz laid a kind hand on her arm. 'Sure, my dear, we understand. We'll see you at breakfast.'

Claudia had gone to sit at the opposite end of the saloon, as far away from everyone else as she could manage. As Louisa sat down beside her, she muttered: 'I won't go—it's ghastly, those dreadful people—I'm going to get off at the first stop.' And then: 'I'll kill Simon!'

'Rather pointless,' Louisa said calmly. 'We'd be stuck high and dry miles from anywhere and not nearly enough money to get home.'

'I'll telephone Lars.'

Louisa poured their coffee. 'I think Lars loves you very much, and I thought you loved him—I thought you were doing this for him.'

'You mind your own business!' snapped Claudia.

'Well, I do usually,' agreed Louisa matter-of-factly, 'but it seems a shame that you should give in so easily. And Lars wouldn't believe it of you.'

'You know a lot about him, don't you?' Claudia turned a furious suspicious face towards her.

'No, but I think he's a very honest and kind man who wouldn't give his friendship or his affection lightly.'

'My God, you sound pompous!' declared Claudia.

'Yes, I know, but you did ask me, didn't you? And I do want to help you to get…well again.'

Claudia gave a small sneering laugh. 'Then you'll be out of a job.'

Louisa said soberly, 'Yes, so I shall.' She hadn't thought about that: somehow the hospital, her stepmother and Frank had all faded gently into the past and she couldn't imagine going back to it.

Despite a disturbed night because Claudia was unable to sleep, Louisa was up early. It was still dark when she wakened Claudia and then put on her thick jacket and went outside on deck. It was cold, but the sky was clear and she could see lights ahead—Maloy, a fishing centre, its harbour crowded with boats, its modern wooden houses already dimly seen under the bright lights of the dock. As they drew nearer she could see too that their bright red roofs were powdered with snow, as were the fishing boats. The ship docked and she watched, oblivious of the cold, while the mail was slung in its great net on to the dock, and was loaded with more mail. They were taking passengers aboard too, quite a number, bound for farther up the coast. She would have stayed watching the busy scene until they sailed, but the breakfast gong sent her back to the cabin to see how Claudia was faring.

She was dressed and almost ready, and in a foul temper. She barely spoke to Louisa, nodded to the Kuntzes at the table and sat crumbling toast and drinking coffee while Louisa had her porridge, egg, cranberry jam and toast, carrying on a friendly conversation with their companions at the same time.

'I absolutely refuse to go on deck,' declared Claudia when they were back in their cabin. 'I'm worn out and bored, and what am I supposed to do all day on this ghastly ship?'

Louisa produced a couple of paperbacks, a pack of cards and the latest copy of *Vogue* which she had hidden away in the luggage. 'We'll go to the saloon on the top deck,' she declared, 'and of course you don't have to go out if you don't want to—there'll be plenty to look at through the windows.'

'Mountains and sea. I hope to God there's a comfortable chair…'

Claudia refused to face a window; Louisa settled her in a large, well upholstered easy chair in a corner, laid the books on a table beside her and went to take a look from the long window overlooking the bows.

Maloy was already behind them, but she caught sight of a narrow ribbon bridge behind the village. 'Did Mr Savage build any of the bridges along this coast?' she asked.

Claudia shrugged, already deep in *Vogue*. 'Oh, he had something to do with several of them, I believe. I've never been interested.'

The ship was sailing between the coast and protecting skerries, but presently it was the open sea—the Norwegian Sea—and the ship, incredibly sturdy despite its smallness, pitched and rolled its way round the headland of Stad, past the Runde birdrock, just visible to the west, and presently into the calm of Alesund.

'We're stopping here for a couple of hours,' observed Louisa cunningly. 'Shall we go ashore and get some coffee and take a quick look at the shops? Lunch isn't till one o'clock—there's more than an hour…'

Claudia was looking pale, although she hadn't complained at the rough trip. She said now: 'Louisa, I must have a drink.'

'OK. You won't be able to get whisky, but there'll be sherry or wine. I'll get our coats.'

The few passengers were already crossing the quayside and making for the town, a stone's throw away. It had been snowing and the wind was icy, but both girls were warmly clad, and once in the narrow busy streets, it was warmer. Louisa found an hotel within minutes and sat Claudia down at a window table in the bar, sipping her coffee while her companion drank her sherry, and then ordering more coffee for them both. Claudia was better after that and Louisa walked her briskly up the main street, looking in its shops, buying an English newspaper and one or two more books before going back to the ship. And there once more she was delighted to see that Claudia looked decidedly better and even made an effort to eat some lunch. What was more, she answered, briefly, it was true, when the Kuntzes spoke to her. The ship sailed while they were drinking their coffee and Louisa watched the little town slide away into the distance. There was a mountain behind the houses; one could drive up to its top by taxi and get a splendid view—something she would have loved to do...

It was dark when they reached Kristinasund, and even darker when they docked briefly at Molde, although the sight of the twinkling lights which seemed to cover the mountains behind the town was worth a few cold minutes on deck.

Claudia slept better that night, although it was still rough, and she got up with fairly good grace in plenty of time for breakfast. They were sailing up the fjord to

Trondheim where there was going to be a three-hour
stop, and this time they were among the first to go
ashore. There were taxis on the quayside. Louisa ushered Claudia into one of them, said hopefully: 'The
shops, please,' and got in too.

It was a short drive, but Claudia hated walking, although she was happy enough to linger from one shop
to the next, while Louisa, longing to visit the Nida-
ros Cathedral, which Eva had told her on no account
to miss, wandered along beside her. Clothes could be
bought anywhere in the world, she thought irritably, so
why couldn't Claudia be interested in anything else?
They had coffee presently, spent some time in a bookshop and then found another taxi to take them back.
A successful morning, decided Louisa, and only two
more days to go.

She tucked Claudia up in her bed after lunch and
waited until she was asleep before putting on her jacket
and going on deck again. The weather was still clear,
but there was a grey film on the horizon which she
guessed was bad weather of some sort. And it was getting dark again, although there was still a little daylight
left as they entered the Stokksund Channel. The captain
had told her at lunch to look out for that—a twisting
narrow stretch of water where the ships had to sound
their sirens before each turn. Only the thought of a cup
of tea sent her back to the cabin to rouse Claudia and
go up to the dining room for the simple generous meal.

There were fewer passengers now. The Kuntzes had
gone and several others had disembarked at Trondheim
and those who had got on in their place were Nor-

wegians. They were in the open sea again and it was rough. Claudia lay down on one of the settees in the saloon and promptly went to sleep, and Louisa got out her knitting. She was enjoying it and she felt reasonably happy about Claudia; with luck she would be able to hand her over to her brother in a much better state of health. Beyond that she didn't intend to worry about anything.

The weather worsened as they worked their way steadily up the coast. By morning there was only the dim outlines of mountains and rugged coast to be seen. It had been too dark on the previous evening to catch a glimpse of the land around, and too dark in the early morning to see the iron globe on top of the rock marking the Arctic Circle, although the ship had sounded her siren as she passed, but the clouds lifted briefly after breakfast, just long enough for her to see the Svartisen Glacier, far away in the distance, remote and terrifyingly high.

They stopped at Bodo during the morning and this time Louisa persuaded Claudia to go with her to see the Cathedral, modern and not very large, but beautiful in its way, and then as a sop to Claudia's impatient company, took her to a hotel where she could have her glass of sherry and then coffee. There were some interesting shops too; Claudia bought herself some silver jewellery—dangling earrings and a thick bracelet, and went back, reasonably good-tempered, to the ship.

There was more open sea in the afternoon and just before the light faded completely Louisa, on deck once more, was rewarded with the sight of the Lofoten Wall on the horizon. It looked a mass of barren rock where no one could possibly live, and yet, two hours later, they had docked by a small quay, and tucked into the formidable mountains towering above them was an equally small village, ablaze with lights, boasting a hotel and several shops. Louisa was enchanted and longed to talk to someone about it. It was incredible to her that people could live out their lives amidst such bleakness and, moreover, make such homelike surroundings for themselves.

She managed to convey something of her feelings to the captain when he came into the dining room and he nodded his great bearded head.

'We do not mind the loneliness,' he told her, 'and we are happy to live simply. We have electricity, warm homes, plenty of books and all the sport you could wish for.' He twinkled at her. 'It is a long way from London, Miss Evans.'

'Thank heaven for that,' said Louisa decidedly. 'I could live here, I think—it's possible.'

They reached Tromso the next day, stopping at Harstad and Finnsnes during the morning. They could have gone ashore at Harstad, but Claudia was morose and disinclined to do anything, so that Louisa packed for them both, contenting herself with a quick peep at both places as they docked. As they steamed through the narrow waters leading to the city, she noticed that the country had changed. There were mountains crowding in on all sides, but the country had got friendly and there were farms here and there, surrounded by birch trees, and everything powdered with snow. There was nothing to be seen of Tromso yet, there were too many bends in the waterway, but there were houses scattered along the shores of the islands on either side of them. Holiday homes, she guessed, and wondered how one got to them—by boat, presumably, although presently she could see a road close to the fjord's edge running between the houses, but on the other side, although there were houses, some built high into the sides of the mountains, there was no road at all. And presently Tromso came in sight, built on an island in the middle of the fjord. Louisa could see the bridge now, linking it with the mainland, larger and longer than the slender pillar bridge linking Finnsnes and its neighbouring island, but just as impressive. It was a pity that she disliked Simon Savage so heartily, otherwise she could have found out a great deal more about them.

She went below reluctantly. Claudia was sleeping again; she woke her gently, listened calmly to her mounting grumbles, coaxed her into her outdoor clothes and observed: 'You'll be able to telephone Lars this evening.'

It acted like magic. Claudia's scowl turned to self-satisfied smiles and Louisa was able to go and find a steward to deal with their luggage and then go back for Claudia. Mr Savage had said that they would be met at Tromso, but that was all. Louisa debated the choice of staying in one of the saloons until they were found, or going ashore and waiting on the quay—there was bound to be a waiting room there. On the whole, she thought it best for them to go to the saloon and wait. The reception area by the office was full of passengers waiting to disembark. Most of them had boarded the ship at Bodo and Harstad. The quay was thronged with people, presumably waiting for friends or relations or travelling still farther north, and there was a steady hum of voices and a good deal of toing and froing. It was difficult to imagine that they were surrounded by bare mountains and glaciers, snowbound roads and vast forests. Louisa felt excited and happy, and wished that Claudia could feel the same. She took her arm and pushed her gently into a corner and said: 'Once most of these people have gone, we'll go up to the saloon, it'll be quiet there.'

But there was no need. Someone tapped her on the shoulder and she turned round to find Simon Savage, looking somehow much younger and cheerful. An illusion, of course, for all he did was nod at her in a casual fashion before asking his stepsister if she was ready to leave the ship. If he uttered one word of welcome, Louisa didn't hear it. She said clearly, 'Our luggage is by the office. We had a very good journey, thank you, but your sister is tired.' She glanced at Claudia, who hadn't uttered a word. 'She should rest as soon as possible.'

Just for a moment he looked at her with narrowed eyes and then surprisingly he laughed. 'Bring Claudia, I'll get the luggage,' he said, and turned away.

Horrible man! thought Louisa, watching him shoulder his way through the crowd. He was wearing a sheepskin coat and knitted cap in bright colours. Probably it was that which made him look different, or perhaps

she had hoped he would be… She put an arm round
Claudia's shoulders.

'Come on,' she said cheerfully, 'let's find some tea.'

CHAPTER SIX

THERE WAS HARD-PACKED snow on the quayside, and Louisa felt Claudia flinch as they stepped off the gangway behind Simon Savage and a short, dark, burly man carrying two of their suitcases, but they didn't have far to go. There was a Range Rover parked close to the ship and they were bidden to get in while their luggage was piled in beside them. Louisa barely had time to look around her and take a last look at the ship before they had left the quay behind, driving down a road which curved under a bridge and turned sharply through warehouses, to turn again and enter the town over a wide bridge. The long evening had started, although it was not yet four o'clock, and the shops were brilliantly lighted in what was obviously one of the main streets, its broad pavements lined with bare trees. It ended in an open square surrounded by shops and along one of its sides, a large, solid-looking hotel. Mr Savage parked the car, said over his shoulder: 'This is where you will spend the night,' and got out.

It was more than she had expected, thought Louisa as she joined him on the pavement and waited while he held a hand out to his stepsister, in fact it looked delight-ful. The thought of a comfortable bedroom, a hot bath and a good dinner brought a sparkle to her eye. Even Simon's growling, 'And you'd better make the most of it,' couldn't spoil her pleasure.

It was just as splendid inside: warm, the foyer close-carpeted and furnished with comfortable chairs and lit-tle tables and a pleasant, smiling clerk who welcomed them with friendly warmth. He seemed to know Mr Savage already, for they were whisked away to their rooms with no delay at all; cosy rooms next to each other and with a communicating door and each with its own bathroom. Claudia, who had barely spoken since they had been met, looked around her with a critical eye. 'You wouldn't think they'd be able to manage any-thing like this in such a godforsaken place,' she ob-served bitterly. 'You don't suppose people actually stay here, do you? I mean for holidays…'

'I believe it's popular in the summer, loads of Nor-wegians come up here from the south—there's a road all the way, you know.'

'No, I didn't know, and I don't want to.'

'I'll unpack your overnight bag. Mr Savage said something about tea. You'd like some, wouldn't you? Or shall I ask for it to be sent up?'

Claudia had regained some of her old languid man-ner. 'My dear Louisa, after weeks of nothing but you and my own company, I wouldn't miss a chance to have a look at whatever bright lights there are.'

She turned away to the dressing table and Louisa went back to her own room, where she tidied up her hair, did her face and unpacked her own bag. She got out the green wool skirt and the quilted jacket too and shook out a cream silk blouse to go with them. Presumably they would dine later with or without Simon Savage. She wasn't sure if she wanted him to be there or not.

They went down presently and found him sitting at one of the small tables, the tea tray before him. He got up as they reached him, hoped that they had found their rooms comfortable in a colourless voice and begged someone to pour tea.

'Oh, you do it, Louisa,' said Claudia, 'I'm too exhausted. That fearful voyage! I absolutely refuse to go back by ship.'

Her stepbrother looked up briefly from the *Times* he was reading. 'There are plenty of flights—or the road—when the time comes.'

Claudia drew a hissing breath, but before she could speak, Louisa prudently handed her a cup of tea. She did the same for Simon, then poured her own and sat sipping it until he put his paper down and passed the plate of cakes. He caught her eye as he did so and gave a short laugh.

'You remind me forcibly of my old nanny,' he observed, 'urging me to remember my manners.'

'I haven't said a word, Mr Savage.'

'No, but your eyes did. I can recommend the little round ones with the chocolate icing.'

'And now we're here, perhaps you'll tell us what happens next.' Claudia's voice was sharp.

'We leave tomorrow morning. You can have an hour if you need to do any shopping.'

'I should like to stay here, in this hotel.'

He didn't answer this but observed, 'You're looking better, Claudia, better than you've looked for several weeks. The sea journey did you good—you're half way there, you know. Why not finish it properly this time?'

'I hate you!'

He remained unperturbed. 'Yes, I know, but that's got nothing to do with it.' He glanced at his watch. 'Lars will still be in his office if you want to telephone him.' He waved a hand towards the telephone booth by the reception desk. 'Have you the number?'

She got up without answering and hurried across the foyer, and he handed his cup to Louisa for more tea. 'I must admit you have achieved a good deal in this last week or so, Nurse. Is Claudia drinking at all?'

'Wine or sherry, mid-morning, and a glass with her dinner in the evening.'

He nodded. 'She's in love with Lars Helgesen, isn't she?'

'Yes.'

Simon passed her the cakes and then helped himself. 'Splendid, we must keep that alive at all costs, it might prove the incentive she has never had.'

Louisa eyed him uncertainly. 'Yes, but supposing he doesn't…would he marry her?'

His look mocked her. 'My dear Louisa, if a man loves a woman—really loves her—he'll marry her. Even a termagant like my dear stepsister.'

He really was beastly; perhaps he was a misogynist.

Claudia came back then, looking considerably happier, but presently she said to no one in particular: 'I don't want to come down to dinner—I'll have something in my room.' She gave her stepbrother a quick look, defying him to argue with her, but all he said was: 'A good idea—I'll get a menu sent up presently.' He looked across at Louisa. 'You will dine with me, Louisa? Shall we say half past seven?'

Claudia had got up and she got up too. 'Thank you, Mr Savage.' She gave him a cool nod and followed Claudia to the stairs.

An hour later she was dressing. Claudia, tucked up in bed, with magazines, books and the most recent papers strewn around her, had chosen her meal and was painting her nails, a long and meticulous business. Louisa, bathed and with her hair newly washed, put on the long skirt, the blouse and the little quilted jacket. They made a nice change after days of wearing slacks and woollies and probably she wouldn't have the chance to wear them again for weeks. She did her face carefully, wishing she was strikingly beautiful, witty and self-assured enough to take the shine out of Mr Savage. If she had had more time she might have given herself an elaborate hairdo, but she doubted very much if he would notice anyway, and what did it matter? They both disliked each other so heartily; she had been surprised that he had suggested dinner together. She went to take a last look at Claudia and found a waiter arranging a prawn cocktail, lamb cutlets and a variety of vegetables, and a delicious-looking pudding on the bedtable. There was a glass of wine there too. Louisa, going downstairs, reminded herself to warn Simon Savage...

He was waiting for her in the foyer, very elegant in a dark suit, looking longer and leaner than usual. He also looked ill-tempered, and she sighed. She was hungry for her dinner, but it would be spoilt if he was going to sit in stony silence.

It seemed that he was on his best behaviour, for he offered a drink in a quite friendly voice, and when she ventured to mention the possibility of Claudia ordering something to drink without their knowledge, actually thanked her for saying so. 'Though you have no need to worry,' he assured her carelessly, 'I've taken the necessary precautions.'

And she had to be content with that. She sipped her sherry and looked around her. There were quite a number of people now, all well dressed, which somehow seemed strange when she remembered the miles of barren snowy mountains and the cold, stormy sea they had travelled through. She said: 'I didn't expect this—I mean, all this luxury so far away...'

'There's an excellent air service, the coastal express calls every day except Christmas Day, and there's a first class highway running from Oslo to Nord Kapp.'

'No trains?'

He raised amused eyebrows. 'Through or over the mountains, Louisa?' and when he saw her flush, he added more kindly: 'The nearest railway is from Narvik into Sweden, the main line comes as far north as Bodo.'

At least they had found something to talk about.

'I saw any number of bridges—pillar bridges, as we came.'

'Beautiful, aren't they? Quite a number of islands are no longer isolated, although there are still ferries running in all directions and several local airlines.' He actually smiled at her. 'If you've finished your drink shall we have dinner?'

They had a table by the long window, overlooking the street and the square beyond. There was plenty of traffic still and any number of people. And because the street lights were so bright and numerous, the snow-covered pavements had a charming Christmassy look. Which reminded Louisa to ask: 'Shall we be here for Christmas?'

Simon glanced up from the menu he was studying. 'It depends on several things. Be sure I'll give you plenty of warning. Are you anxious to be in England for Christmas?'

She said: 'Oh, no!' in such a tone of alarm that he asked: 'You like Norway? Have you no family?'

'I like Norway very much,' she told him, and added: 'I'd like soup, please, and then the cod.'

'Trailing a red herring, Louisa, or should I say cod?' and when she didn't answer: 'You have a family?'

He gave their order to the waiter and sat back waiting for her to answer, his dark face faintly bored.

'A stepmother, no one else. Well, aunts and uncles, but they live a good way away...'

'Where?'

'Wiltshire and Cumbria.'

Their soup came and she picked up her spoon, glad

of something to do. She didn't think she liked this ur-
bane manner any more than his usual curt behaviour,
and she wasn't going to answer any more questions.

'You don't care for your stepmother?'

She looked at him across the elegant little table with
its lighted candles. 'No.' She supped the last of her soup.
'I'm not going to answer any more questions.'

He raised quizzical eyebrows. 'My dear girl, I'm
making polite conversation.'

'You're cross-examining me. Is your bridge almost
finished?'

'Yes, the main work was done before the winter set
in; there's not much left to do now, and that mostly
under cover.'

'May we see it?' asked Louisa.

'By all means, but I doubt if Claudia will want to do
that.' He spoke sourly and gave her such a disagreeable
look that she rushed on to the next question.

'Are you going to build any more?'

'Now who's being cross-examined? Yes, I have a
contract for three more bridges, one farther north, the
other two in the Lofotens.'

'We stopped there at a very small village—it began
with an S...'

'Stamsund. You liked it?'

'It was dark, but I would like to have gone ashore...
Lots of bright lights and—and cosy, if you know what
I mean.'

The waiter came with their cod and when he had
gone again: 'You surprise me, Louisa, or are you putting on an act for my benefit?'

She paused, fork half way to her mouth. 'An act? Why ever should I bother to do that with you?'

His bellow of laughter sent heads turning in their direction. 'Aren't I worth it?'

'No,' said Louisa roundly, and applied herself to her dinner. She was a little surprised to find that although she disliked him still she wasn't…scared wasn't the word—intimidated any more.

The cod was beautifully cooked with a delicious sauce and lots of vegetables. She ate it all up with a healthy appetite and followed it by a soufflé, light as air, while Simon ate biscuits and cheese. They had drunk a white wine with their meal, which was perhaps why she found herself telling her companion about Frank. She hadn't meant to, but somehow his questions had led back to her life in England again—the hospitals where she worked, the villages where she lived and quite naturally from there, Frank. It was only when she glanced at him and caught his dark eyes fixed on her so intently that she pulled herself up short.

'I'd better go and see if Claudia is all right,' she said.

'We'll have coffee first.'

She went back to the lounge with him and drank her coffee and talked about the weather, disliking him very much because she suspected that he was laughing at her. She escaped as soon as she could, thanked him for her dinner and asked what time they were to be ready in the morning.

'Eleven o'clock—and I mean eleven o'clock. Unless Claudia particularly wants to do any shopping, I suggest that she has breakfast in bed. We'll breakfast at half past eight precisely.' He looked down his nose at her. 'You're not one of those silly women who don't eat breakfast, I hope?'

Louisa said pertly: 'Perhaps I should have it in my room, then you won't have the bother of talking to me, Mr Savage.'

'I seldom talk at breakfast, Louisa. It will give me the opportunity of giving you any last-minute instructions should it be necessary.'

She gave him a steely glance, wishing she could think of something dignified and really squashing, but she couldn't—though her 'good-night' was icy.

Claudia was lying against her pillows, a box of chocolates open beside her, books scattered in all directions. She looked up as Louisa went in and said: 'Oh, hullo—there you are. Has Simon let you off the hook? I've had a lovely evening,' and she stretched her arms. 'Such lovely comfort, and the nicest chambermaid—I got her to fetch me some more books and some sweets. I suppose you're going to tell me to go to sleep now.'

Louisa smiled. 'No, I won't. We're leaving at eleven o'clock in the morning. Would you like breakfast in bed so that you'll have plenty of time to dress? And do you want to go to the shops?'

'No, but you can go for me—I want some more of that hand cream and I'm almost out of nail varnish. I suppose Simon will allow us to come here to shop as often as we want to?'

'I expect so,' said Louisa, thinking it most unlikely. 'I'll be up fairly early, I'll get anything you want and be back in time to do your packing.'

Claudia nodded dismissal. 'OK. See you in the morning.'

Louisa, back in slacks, boots and thick sweater after a night's sleep, and wishful to keep Simon Savage's mood as sweet as possible, presented herself in the dining room exactly on time. Claudia was still asleep and she took the precaution of asking the reception girl to get a menu sent up to her room within the next ten minutes. Claudia couldn't be hurried and Simon had said eleven o'clock and meant it.

He was there now waiting for her, dressed for the cold, she noticed, and she wondered just how remote and bleak their future home was to be. He wished her a perfunctory good morning and waved her to the table along one wall, set out with a vast assortment of food: bread, toast, butter, jam, dishes of fish in various sauces and a great bowl of porridge.

She wandered slowly round and presently joined him at their table, a bowl of porridge in one hand and a plate laden with toast, egg, jam and cheese in the other. He got up and took them from her and asked: 'Tea or coffee?'

'Coffee, please.' And after that she didn't speak, but applied herself to her meal, quite undaunted by the open newspaper Simon Savage held in front of his cross face. It was a pity, she thought, that he always had to look so very disagreeable; life couldn't be all that bad. Perhaps he had been crossed in love? She giggled at the very idea—no woman would dare—and choked on it as the paper was lowered.

'You were saying?' Simon Savage enquired coldly.

'Nothing.' She gave him a sweet smile. 'I don't talk at breakfast either.'

He folded his paper deliberately and very neatly. 'Take care, Louisa, I'm not the mildest of men.'

She poured herself another cup of coffee. 'We don't agree about much, Mr Savage—about that, though, we do! Will I be able to get all I want from that big shop across the square?'

'Sundt? I imagine so, provided it's nothing out of the way.' He glanced at his watch. 'Don't let me keep you.'

Claudia was having breakfast when she went back upstairs. Louisa warned her to get up as soon as she had finished, got into her jacket and woolly cap, and went out of the hotel. The shops were open, although it was still not light, and inside Sundt was warm and brightly lighted. Louisa bought everything on her list and spent ten minutes going from counter to counter. She would have to send her stepmother a Christmas present, she supposed, and cards to her friends at the hospital, as well as the aunts and uncles she so seldom saw. She had written once to her home, and told her stepmother that she was in Norway with a patient, but she had given no address and her friends to whom she had written were sworn to secrecy. She had never felt so free, nor, strangely, so happy.

She would have liked to have lingered in the shop, but a glance at her watch told her that there was little more than an hour before they were to leave. And it was as well that she went back when she did, for Claudia was still lying in bed, doing absolutely nothing. Louisa, by now well versed in the right tactics, persuaded her out of her bed, under the shower and dressed with half an hour to spare, and that would be barely enough time for the elaborate make-up without which Claudia refused to face the outside world. Louisa packed neatly and with speed, rang for their cases to be taken down and left in the foyer, so that Simon Savage's impatience would be tempered, and applied herself to getting Claudia downstairs on time. As it was they were only five minutes late, a fact which Simon silently registered by a speaking glance at the clock.

It was going to be a lovely day, the blue sky turning the snow even whiter than it already was, and as the Land Rover left the city's centre, the mountains came into view once more, their grey bulk almost covered with snow, making a magnificent background to the tree-covered slopes that skirted them. Simon Savage turned off at the bridge at the end of the main street and took a road running alongside the fjord, and presently stopped.

There were fishing boats and motor launches moored here, and Louisa saw the same man who had met the boat with him on the previous day coming to meet them. She half expected Claudia to make a fuss as they got out, but beyond a furious look at the two men she did nothing at all, and they were ushered on board a motor launch without further ado. It was a roomy enough vessel with a fair sized cabin, comfortably warm and well fitted out. Claudia, huddled in her thick clothes, curled up at once on one of the cushioned benches and demanded coffee, and Simon without turning his head told Louisa to pour coffee for them all. 'There's a galley,' he told her curtly. 'You'll find everything there.'

It was a small place, more like a cupboard, but it did hold an astonishing number of things, and the coffee was already bubbling in the percolator on top of the spirit stove. She found mugs, set them on a tray, found milk and sugar too, and went back into the cabin. They were all there; the man introduced as Sven smiled at her as he took his mug, but Simon gave her austere thanks without looking at her, and as for Claudia, she turned her head away.

But when the men had gone, she sat up, accepted the coffee for a second time and looked around her. 'What a dump!' she declared, looking about.

Louisa, who knew next to nothing about boats, thought it to be the height of comfort, but she knew better than to argue with Claudia; there was a mood coming on, unless she could forestall it…

She fetched rugs from a shelf, persuaded Claudia to take off her fur coat and her cap and gloves, and tucked her up cosily. 'You're tired,' she observed. 'Close your eyes and have a nap. I daresay we'll be there by the time you wake up.'

Just for once Claudia forgot to be arrogant. 'It's going to be sheer hell,' she whispered. 'It'll kill me!'

'It'll cure you—think how happy that will make Lars.'

Claudia closed her eyes. 'Do you think it's very silly of me to make plans? Wedding plans, I mean. Do you think he'll risk marrying me? I'm an alcoholic…'

'Not any more,' declared Louisa stoutly. 'Now close your eyes and make plans.'

Which Claudia did, and presently slept.

The launch was doing a good turn of speed, although the water was choppy. Louisa peered out of the windows and discovered that she couldn't see much for spray, so she put on her jacket again, pulled her woolly cap down over her ears and went outside. Simon Savage was at the wheel, well wrapped against the cold, but when he saw her he said something to Sven, who took it from him and crossed the few feet to the cabin door. He didn't say anything, only pulled her hood up and over her cap and tied the strings under her chin, then kissed her gently.

'You look like a nice rosy apple,' he told her by way of explanation.

She was too surprised to say anything, which was perhaps just as well, for he went on in a matter-of-fact voice: 'If you look behind you'll see Tromsdaltinden. The snow came early this year, so it will be a long winter. Any number of people go there on a Sunday to ski. There's Finmark to the east, and in a few minutes you'll be able to get a glimpse of the Lyngen mountains—these are islands on the port side, look ahead of you and you'll see the fjord divides—we take the left arm, it runs between two islands, and it's there that we're building a bridge.'

Louisa, oblivious of the icy wind, took the glasses he handed her and then looked her fill. 'People live along here—I can see houses.'

'Settlements—fishing folk mostly—they're not far

from Tromso, and there are Hansnes and Karlsoy to
the north; small villages, but there's a road to Tromso
from Hansnes. Once the bridge is open it will shorten
the journey to Tromso.' He gave her a long considering look. 'You like it here, don't you?'

'Yes. It must be lovely in the summer.'

'It is. That's when we do most of our work.'

'Do you ever go home between bridges?' The moment she had spoken she was sorry. He turned away
from her and said shortly: 'You'd better go inside
and see if Claudia is awake; we shall be landing very
shortly.'

Louisa went at once. Just for a few minutes she had
thought that they were beginning to lose their dislike
of each other, and she had to admit that for her part she
was on the verge of liking him, ill-temper and all, but it
was obvious that he didn't share her feelings. Oh, well,
once they were ashore, he'd be working, she supposed,
and they wouldn't have to see much of him. It struck
her then that life might be a little difficult for the next
few weeks, with Claudia to keep amused. She would
have to think of something to occupy them during the
short days. She remembered vaguely that Claudia had
told her that she had learned to ski as a child and there
would surely be a suitable slope not too far away.

She looked out of the window; there were plenty of
mountains, but they all looked quite precipitous. Craning her neck, she could just see the bridge ahead of
them; some way off still, graceful and narrow, standing tall on its pillars. She would have liked to have gone
back outside and taken a good look, but she suspected

that Simon had got fed up with her company and sent her inside unnecessarily soon. A pity, because there was a lot to see now—houses, their painted wood bright against the snow, scattered along the fjord's edge, the mountains at their back doors, and as far as she could see, no road. Racks of cod, minute coves sheltering a fishing boat or two, a solitary church, its short pointed spire covered by snow…

She put the coffee pot on the stove to warm up and wakened Claudia. She managed to keep the excitement out of her voice as she said: 'We're almost there,' because she knew that Claudia didn't share that feeling; indeed she groaned and declared that nothing would make her set foot on such a solitary snowbound spot.

'Well, if you don't go ashore here, Lars won't know where to find you,' observed Louisa matter-of-factly, 'and I'm sure it's not nearly as bad as you think. I've some coffee for you, drink it up and get wrapped up again.'

'You're nothing but a bully,' complained Claudia, 'every bit as bad as Simon. I'm hungry.'

'We'll get lunch as soon as we land,' declared Louisa, and hoped that they would: it wouldn't take much to send Claudia off into one of her moods. They were very close to the land now; through the windows she could see a cluster of houses beyond a small quay, more cod drying on wooden racks and a larger building with 'Hotel' in large letters on its bright yellow painted wall. The houses were brightly painted too, blue and red and pink; they made cheerful spots of colour against the snow and the grey granite mountains all around them.

The cabin door opened and Simon poked his head inside. 'We're here', he told them. 'Come along—Sven will bring the luggage along.'

There was no one on the quay, just a few wooden sheds and a stack of boxes. The road ran left and right and they turned to the left between two rows of small houses. There was a shop and then the hotel, but they went on past it to the last half dozen houses or so. Simon turned off the road here and clumped through the snow to one of these; square, like all the rest, and like its neighbours, standing on its own, facing the fjord, the mountains nudging its small plot of ground. He opened the door and went in shouting something as he did so and turned to hold it wide for them to go in too. The hall was very small with a door on either side, and from one of these an elderly woman came hurrying out.

Simon performed introductions in a perfunctory fashion and added: 'Elsa speaks a fair amount of English; she comes each day and cleans the house and cooks for me.' He opened the other door and ushered them into a small square room, warm from the wood-burning stove against one wall and furnished with simple comfort. 'Get your things off,' he suggested, 'Elsa is bringing coffee, then you can see your rooms before lunch. I'll be out this afternoon, but you'll have enough to do, unpacking and finding your way around.'

The coffee came, hot and delicious, and Sven came in with the bags and sat down to drink his, too; and presently Elsa led them upstairs to two small rooms, simply furnished and warm, with bright rugs and curtains. There was a bathroom too, and Louisa, who had expected a lack of modern amenities, was impressed. Claudia wasn't—she went and sat on the edge of her bed, making up her face. 'What a dump!' she declared. 'It's ghastly—we can't all use that poky little bathroom.'

'Don't see why not,' said Louisa cheerfully. 'We don't all want it at the same time, I don't suppose. Let's get tidy and go down to lunch.'

Something Claudia refused to do. 'I'm tired to death,' she moaned, 'I'll have something on a tray and go to bed with a book.'

And nothing Louisa said would change her mind. She left her sitting there and went downstairs and found the table laid and Simon at one end of it, bent over a large map and a bundle of papers. He looked up briefly as she went in. 'Where's Claudia?' And when she explained: 'She can come down for her meals or starve, I don't care which. Tell her that.'

Louisa eyed him with disfavour. 'No, you tell her,' she said quietly, and then: 'You're too hard on her, you know.'

Simon gave her a baleful stare. 'Don't preach to me, Nurse.' But he went past her and up the stairs and presently came down again, looking grim, with a seething Claudia behind him. Louisa made an uneasy third at table, sitting between the two of them, eating her cod and potatoes in a heavy silence.

With a muttered excuse Simon went away the moment he had finished eating, and Claudia burst into tears. Louisa gave her another cup of coffee, allowed her to cry her fill and then suggested that they should go upstairs.

'I'll unpack,' she said with a cheerfulness she didn't feel, 'and you can have a nap or read, and we can have tea here, by the stove.' She urged a reluctant Claudia upstairs, bathed her face for her, settled her under the duvet, found a pile of books and started to put away clothes. By the time she had finished, Claudia was asleep and she was able to go to her own little room and do her own unpacking. That done, she went to look out of the window. It was almost dark, but there were lights in all the houses, making the snow sparkle. To-morrow she would persuade Claudia to explore a bit—a shop, even a small general store, would be somewhere to go, and perhaps they could get coffee at the hotel. And she was longing to get a closer look at the bridge. She sighed and pulled the curtains, then went down-stairs to look for Elsa and ask about tea.

Claudia had calmed down by tea time and when Louisa, who had been prowling round the little house, mentioned casually that there was a telephone in the hall tucked away in a dark corner under the stairs, she declared that she would ring up Lars at once, but before she could get there, there was a call from him. Louisa, roasting herself by the stove and watching the television programme she couldn't understand, heard Claudia's excited voice and heaved a sigh of relief. The call lasted ten minutes or more, during which time Simon came back, said hullo, in a perfunctory manner, and declared his intention of going across the hall to the small room he used as his office. At the door he paused. 'Any idea how you're going to fill in the time here?' he asked.

'I've brought embroidery and knitting and books for

both of us. We'll go out each day—Claudia told me she could ski, but I can't.'

'You can learn—there's an easy slope close by. We'll make up a party on Saturday. The shop has books and the papers come with the postman by launch every third day.'

'And perhaps we could go to Tromso once in a while,' asked Louisa, encouraged by these suggestions.

'Perhaps.' He was non-committal about it. 'Claudia will probably give you the hell of a time.'

'Yes, I expect that, but I expect her to get better too.' She spoke defiantly and he laughed.

'I hope you're right.' His eyes narrowed. 'And understand this; any hint of backsliding and I want to know at once. Is that understood?'

'Oh, I understand you very well,' said Louisa, her voice a little high with suppressed feelings. 'What a very disagreeable man you are, Mr Savage, with your orders and arrogance. I should very much dislike having you as a patient.'

His dark eyes snapped at her. 'You surprise me, Louisa. I should have thought it would have been the very thing, because I would be entirely at your mercy and you could wreak revenge to your heart's content.' His silky voice had a nasty edge to it. He opened the door. 'Perhaps we'd better keep out of each other's way?' he wanted to know.

She agreed stiffly and when she was alone again, wondered why the prospect left her with the feeling that life would be rather dull.

CHAPTER SEVEN

CLAUDIA WAS STILL asleep when Louisa went down to breakfast the next morning, to find Simon already at the table, spooning up porridge as though he had a train to catch. He got up as she went in, however, wished her good morning and asked her if she preferred coffee to tea. 'And where's Claudia?' he asked indifferently.

'In bed, asleep. I shall take her breakfast up later.'

She met his cold eyes. 'I see no reason why she should be pampered. I brought her here in the hope that the simple life led here would effect a cure.' He sounded impatient.

'Probably you did,' she said equably, 'but there's no reason to rush things, is there? Why put her back up when there's no need? I shall take her breakfast up.' She began on her porridge and dropped the spoon at his sudden roar.

'Are you defying me, Nurse Evans?'

She sugared her porridge. 'Well, yes, I believe I am,' she told him placidly. 'I don't interfere with your bridges, Mr Savage, I don't think that you should interfere with my nursing.'

'Claudia doesn't need a nurse any more.'

She raised her eyes to his. 'You'd like me to go, Mr Savage? You have only to say so. After all, it's you who pays my wages.'

She watched him getting control of his temper while he helped himself to cranberry jam and took some toast. He said evenly: 'Nurse Evans, you may have *carte blanche* with my stepsister, but I advise you to be very careful. I'm not a man to be crossed lightly.'

'Oh, I can see that,' said Louisa airily, 'but if you'll give me a free hand with Claudia, then I promise I won't interfere with your bridges.'

An unwilling laugh escaped him. 'I've never met anyone quite like you, Louisa.' He started gathering up the papers by his plate. 'And you seemed so quiet, almost timid... I shan't be in to lunch.'

She finished her breakfast in deep thought. Obviously he didn't intend to organise any activities for them, that was something she would have to do for herself. She cleared the table and went into the kitchen and under Elsa's kindly eye, prepared a tray for Claudia.

It was still dark outside; she prudently left the curtains drawn, switched on the bedside light and only then wakened Claudia, whose temper, never very sunny in the morning, improved a little at the sight of her breakfast tray.

'However did you manage it?' she asked, and yawned hugely. 'I'm sure Simon said something about eight o'clock...'

'Yes, he did, but we agreed that you should have breakfast in bed.'

'Every day?'

Louisa nodded. 'Why not? I've little enough to do, you know. I thought we might go out presently and take a look at that shop and perhaps have coffee at the hotel…'

'And then what?' demanded Claudia pettishly.

'I'm going to find out about skiing, I'm dying to learn—do you suppose you could teach me?'

Claudia was buttering toast. 'I suppose I could. God knows where I'll get the energy from—it sounds a fearful bore.'

'Perhaps we could try once or twice, and if I'm quite hopeless I'll give it up.'

Claudia had picked up a magazine and was leafing through the pages. 'OK,' she said without much interest, 'I suppose it'll be something to do.'

Louisa was at the door. 'I suppose Lars Helgesen skis beautifully.' She closed the door gently behind her.

There weren't many people about as they crunched through the snow towards the shop, but there was a fair amount of activity on the quay: a fork lifter stacking large cardboard boxes, parcels and bundles of all shapes and sizes being sorted; there were lights everywhere, of course, for it was still not light, although the sky was clear. Several men went past them on snow scooters, going out of sight where the last of the houses clustered on a bend of the fjord. The bridge lay in that direction; Louisa dearly wanted to see it, but she doubted whether Claudia would walk so far. They turned into the shop and were agreeably surprised to find that it housed al-

most anything they might need. What was more, the
post had arrived and among the letters was one from
Lars. Claudia tucked it into a pocket, her pale face pink
so that she looked lovelier than ever, and Louisa vowed
that nothing was going to stop her from making every
effort to cure her of her addiction—'nothing', of course,
was Simon Savage being tiresome. They spent quite a
time in the shop, delighted to find that there was a small
stock of English paperbacks as well as a two-day-old
copy of *The Times*. They bought chocolate, too and
Louisa, finding that they could speak English, asked
the young woman behind the counter about skiing. Her
questions were met with instant offers of skis, boots,
a guide to show them the way and someone to instruct
her. Louisa explained about Claudia teaching her, but
accepted the rest of the offer for the next morning and
when she offered to pay met with such a vigorous re-
fusal to take a single krone that she didn't say another
word. 'You are family of Mr Savage,' she was told. 'He
is our friend and we treat you also as friends—friends
do not pay.'

They went to the hotel next and were surprised
again. It was a small wooden building, not much bigger
than the houses round it, but inside it had a small cosy
bar, an even smaller dining room and a much larger
room where there was a billiard table, dartboard and a
number of small tables and chairs. Louisa guessed that
it was used for a great many things during the winter,
for there was a small screen hung against one wall and a
projector beside it, and in one corner there was a piano.
There was no one else there. They ordered coffee and

the proprietor brought it himself and then sat down with them, proving to be a fount of information, imparted in English, which while not fluent, was easily understandable. The post came twice a week, they were told, books and magazines could be ordered at the shop and came at the same time. It was possible to go to Tromso whenever they wished provided the weather wasn't bad. There was a film show every Saturday evening in that very room and dancing afterwards. And when Louisa observed that there weren't all that number of people to come to it, he laughed cheerfully and told her that the people who lived along the shores of the fjord came in for the evening.

'We are very happy here,' he told her. 'We have the mountains and the fjord and in the summer visitors come and camp along the shore and we are very busy. Besides, there is the bridge. The men who work on it sleep and eat here and go home at the weekends. My hotel is full.'

'Won't it be rather quiet when they go?' asked Louisa.

He looked surprised. 'Oh, no—it will be Christmas.'

They parted, the best of friends, presently, and walked back to the house to find that Elsa had their lunch waiting—soup and bread and a number of little dishes filled with varieties of fish and cheese and pickles. Claudia declared that she was tired, although she had soup and coffee before making herself comfortable on the outsize couch before the stove. Louisa waited for her to ask for a drink, but she didn't, and by the time Louisa had cleared the table she was asleep.

Elsa would be in the house until the evening and was perfectly willing to keep an eye on Claudia. Louisa put on her outdoor things again and went back through the snow, past the last of the houses to where the rough road ended, but there was some sort of path once she had reached the curve of the fjord and she followed it carefully in the twilight which she realised was all there was in place of the daylight. The water looked cold and dark, whipped up into waves by a cutting wind, and she faltered for a moment. Suppose night descended and she couldn't see the path to go back by? And then she told herself that she was silly; the snow scooters had gone that way; it was well used and surely they would be returning soon? She pressed on to the next curve and was rewarded by a sight of the bridge, brilliantly lighted at each end, and she could see and hear men working. She was in two minds whether to go on, but a few flakes of snow sent her sharply back the way she had come, very aware of the looming mountains and the gathering darkness. She had reached the first house when a snow scooter skidded to a halt beside her and Simon Savage got off. He greeted her coldly; 'I shouldn't advise you to go off on your own until you're sure of the way. Only a fool would do that at this time of the year. It's easy enough to get lost.'

'I wanted to see the bridge, and I wasn't being reckless, Mr Savage. I saw some men go this way before lunchtime, and I guessed there would be a path.'

He grunted. 'And Claudia?' It was snowing quite fast now; he looked enormously tall and bulky.

'We had a very pleasant morning. There was a letter

from Lars Helgesen. We went to the shop and then to the hotel for coffee.' She added defiantly: 'And I asked about skiing.'

'Admirable Louisa! I'm sure you'll deal with skis as competently as you do with everything and everyone else. You have someone to teach you?'

'Claudia.'

He gave a great shout of laughter. 'Of course!'

'And there's no need to laugh like that, it will be something to occupy her. Besides, that nice girl in the shop says her brother will go with us. She arranged it all so quickly…'

Simon stood still and looked down at her. 'Of course she did,' he said blandly. 'I'd already told her that you might enquire. Her brother is wholly to be trusted, he may even give you a few tips when Claudia gets bored with teaching you.'

They had reached the house and he parked the scooter in the lean-to and opened the door for her. Louisa took off her things and hung them in the hall, got out of her boots and went upstairs in her stockinged feet, not sure if she was pleased or vexed that he should have bothered to arrange everything for them.

Surprisingly tea was a pleasant little meal, and afterwards Louisa got out a pack of cards and taught Claudia how to play Racing Demon while her stepbrother crossed the hall and shut the door firmly behind him. They met again at supper—lamb chops this time followed by cranberry tart and a great pot of coffee—and Simon was so obviously making an effort to entertain them with light conversation that Louisa took pity on him and helped him out as much as she could. Claudia did no such thing, however, either ignoring him or uttering gibes. Louisa could see him holding back his temper with a restraint which did him credit and prayed earnestly that he might not explode with rage before the meal was over. He didn't: as soon as he could decently do so, he wished them goodnight and went back to his work.

When she went down to breakfast the next morning he wished her good morning with his usual austerity, but added at once: 'You were quite right; breakfast with Claudia at the table would be disaster. It's a pity that we dislike each other so heartily. Perhaps you were right and I shouldn't have brought her here.' He gave her a grim little smile. 'Aren't you going to say I told you so?'

Louisa sat down composedly, helped herself to porridge and sprinkled sugar with a lavish hand. 'No, I'm not, because I'm sure you were right to do so. It's kill or cure, isn't it?' She frowned. 'I wish I knew more about it—alcoholism, I mean, but she is trying, you know. Is Lars coming to visit her?'

'Yes, but I don't know when. Probably next weekend—he'll fly up to Tromso. I haven't told her.'

She nodded. 'That's three days away. Perhaps we could go skiing today?'

'Why not? It's clear weather. I'll tell them to have everything ready for you at the shop, and arrange for Arne to go with you both.' He got up. 'You'll excuse me?' He was gone.

The morning was a huge success. Claudia, once her skis were strapped on, became quite animated, and she

and Arne got Louisa between them bullying and encouraging her in turn, while she tripped up, fell over,
crossed her skis and did everything wrong, but at the
end of an hour or more she found herself actually in
some sort of control of the things and began to enjoy
herself. They went back to lunch, glowing with exercise. Claudia very pleased with herself because Arne
had complimented her on her grace and speed, and
Louisa even more pleased because she had almost got
the hang of balancing, and best of all, Claudia had actually enjoyed herself; not once had she complained of
boredom or evinced a desire to lie down with a book.
She ate her meal with a better appetite and although
she declared after it that nothing would make her stir
out of doors again that day, she did so in a goodnatured
fashion, merely requesting Louisa to make her comfortable on the couch, fetch her a book and a rug, and
then go away and leave her in peace.

Fortunately for her own comfort, Louisa had no wish
to stay indoors. She wrapped herself up once more and
started to walk towards the other end of the road. Not
very far, because there were only a handful of houses
beyond the one they lived in, but once past these, she
found herself walking along the edge of the fjord, going
rather gingerly towards the spot where the shore thrust a
thin finger into the fjord's water. There was a hut there
and she went to peer inside it. Bare now but probably
used in the summer, she supposed, and decided to re-
trace her footsteps to the quay which was after all the
heart and soul of the little place. She was standing at
its far end, peering down into one of the fishing boats

when Simon Savage came to stand beside her. 'You enjoyed your skiing?' he asked, not bothering to greet her.

It surprised her very much that she was glad to see him. 'Very much indeed, and so did Claudia. We thought we'd go again tomorrow.'

'Why not?' He wasn't looking at her, was not indeed the least bit interested. She said rather tartly: 'It's getting cold, I'm going back to the house.'

She hadn't expected him to go with her; they left the quay, went past the shop and when they reached the hotel, a few yards farther on, he stopped. 'Coffee,' he said, and took her arm. 'I know it's tea time, but a cup won't hurt you.'

There were several men in the hotel, sitting at tables, drinking coffee and reading their papers, and Louisa suffered a pang of chagrin as he pulled out a chair at one of these, nodded to her to sit down, said something to the two men already sitting there, and then sat down himself. 'Herre Amundsen, Herre Knudsen,' he introduced them, and then in English: 'Miss Louisa Evans, my stepsister's nurse.'

They were youngish men and probably glad to see a new face, because they talked eagerly about their work at the bridge, their homes in Tromso and their wives and families. They would be moving on soon, they told her, another week or so and the bridge would be opened. And how did she like Norway? they wanted to know. Louisa told them, delighted to find such friendliness. She drank her coffee, and when Simon ordered her another cup she drank that too, hardly noticing, listening to tales of winter storms, avalanches, the midnight

sun, reindeer, the Laplanders…all the things she had
wanted to know about. If Simon Savage had been more
forthcoming she would have asked him days ago; but
he had never encouraged her to ask questions, let alone
talk… He sat back now, content to listen, it seemed, replying only briefly when addressed. Presently he said:
'We'd better go. Wait here while I book a table for Saturday evening.'

'Does it really get so crowded?' asked Louisa, watching him talking to the landlord.

'Very busy—many people come to eat and watch the
film and afterwards they dance. A splendid evening.'

Louisa thought that it might not be all that splendid.
Lars and Claudia would want to talk to each other, she
and her stepbrother would probably not be on speaking
terms, and she would be forced to drop inane remarks
over the high wall of Simon Savage's indifference—
but there would be a film afterwards and she hoped de-
voutly that the men would outnumber the girls so that
she would get a chance to dance. Simon was a write-
off as far as dancing was concerned.

She thanked him for the coffee as they walked the
short distance back and he muttered something to her in
reply, and beyond a few necessary words during tea and
later at their supper, he had nothing further to say to her.

The next few days passed surprisingly smoothly.
They skied every morning, and now that she had got
over her first fright, Louisa was loving it. Claudia was
more or less docile, even grudgingly admitting that she
wasn't as bored as she had expected to be; certainly she
was looking better and years younger and since there

wasn't a great deal of daylight, she had less time to spend in front of the mirror in the mornings and after lunch she was too healthily tired to do more than read by the stove. True, there had been one sticky moment when she had demanded to go to Tromso that weekend, and since Simon hadn't told her that Lars was coming, merely telling her curtly that it wasn't possible, he provoked a burst of temper and tears which took Louisa an hour or more to calm. Indeed, she had intervened and told him severely to go away. He had stared at her for a long moment before he turned on his heel, and she had the quite ridiculous feeling that he was silently laughing.

Lars arrived on Saturday morning while Louisa was cautiously skiing down a gentle slope at the foot of the mountains. Claudia had remained at the top with Arne and it was she who saw Lars first, coming down the slope in fine style to meet him. Louisa, not wishing to be an unwelcome third party, began her patient sideways plodding up the slope again and was halfway there when Simon Savage, coming apparently from nowhere, joined her.

'Keep your skis together and then move your right foot up,' he advised her. She paused to look at him. He did look rather handsome, she had to admit, and not as forbidding as usual. 'Where did you come from?' she wanted to know.

'I fetched Lars from the airport. While he was changing I came across the mountains…' He waved a vague arm at the forbidding heights all around them, and she said: 'But there's nowhere to go.'

'Yes, there is, if you know the way. I'll show you one day.'

They had reached the top and Simon said something to Arne, who grinned and sped away back to the shop far below.

'Now,' said Simon, 'let me see what you can do.'

An opportunity to show her prowess; the slope was white and inviting and not quite so frightening any more. Claudia and Lars had disappeared: she would show her companion just how good she was. She launched herself with what she hoped was effortless grace.

Her skis crossed almost at once and she ended up upside down in the snow, quite unable to get up. Simon pulled her to her feet, dusted her down and turned her the right way. 'Now, start again, and forget about impressing me.'

She shot him a very peevish glance and then, surprising herself, burst out laughing. 'Serves me right, doesn't it?' she asked, and launched herself cautiously. And this time she managed very well and even managed to stop at the bottom without falling over again to turn round in time to see Simon Savage sailing down after all with a careless expertise which swamped her with envy.

She had no chance to tell him how good he was. 'Do it again,' he commanded, 'and this time keep your feet together and don't be so stiff—you can bend in the middle, I hope?'

Louisa had a great desire to burst into tears; she had done quite well and he hadn't even bothered to tell her so, only snapped at her about her feet. She muttered crossly: 'Oh, we're not all as perfect as you are.'

'No,' he sounded quite matter-of-fact, 'but there's no reason why you shouldn't be in time, provided you work at it. Now, are you going to try again?'

She was cross-eyed with weariness by the time he had finished with her, but she had to admit that she had learnt to control her feet and had lost her pokerlike stance. They skied down the slope for the last time and she stood quietly while Simon undid her skis for her and then tossed them over his shoulder with his own. They found Claudia and Lars at the house, very pleased with themselves, and when Claudia said rather pointedly that they were going to spend the afternoon round the stove, Louisa declared that she had letters to write in her room and to her surprise, Simon observed that since they were going out that evening he had some work to do after lunch.

Louisa didn't write letters. The room was warm and comfortable enough but she was lonely. She got on to the bed presently, wrapped in the duvet and slept until Elsa came tapping on the door to tell her that tea was on the table.

But she was sorry that she had gone down, for Simon Savage had a cup in his workroom and the other two, although pleasant enough, quite obviously didn't want her company. She was trying to think of some good reason for taking her cup upstairs with her when the door opened and Simon came in intent on a second cup. On his way back to the door he suggested that she should join him, adding, presumably for the benefit of the others, 'You're interested in bridges—I've just got the plans for the next one to be built. Bring your tea with you.'

It seemed the lesser of two evils. She followed him out of the room and when he stood aside went into the room on the other side of the hall. She hadn't been in it before; it was smaller than the sitting room, with a small wood stove, a square table, loaded with rolls of paper, notebooks and, she presumed, the paraphernalia of bridge building, and two or three chairs. He waved her to one of them, and sat down again at the table, where he became totally immersed in a plan he unrolled, she sat sipping her tea, studying the back of his neck; she rather liked the way his dark hair grew. After a couple of minutes' complete silence she suggested: 'Since I'm interested in bridges shouldn't I see the plans?'

Simon lifted his head to look at her and she thought it such a pity that he looked so remote. 'My dear girl, I said that to get you out of the room. I'd not the least intention of showing you anything.'

She felt so hurt that it was like a physical pain inside her. She put down her cup and saucer on the table and got to her feet. 'That was kind of you,' she told him quietly. 'I won't trespass on your—hospitality any longer.'

She had whisked out of the room, giving him no chance to reply. Not that she had expected him to.

She had a nice cry after that, although she wasn't sure why she was crying, and then had a shower and dressed slowly, ready for the evening. Claudia had told her that she was going to wear a long dress, a lovely woollen affair with a matching stole, so Louisa felt quite justified in putting on the long skirt and the quilted waistcoat. She put on more make-up than usual too and did her hair in a complicated style which she prayed would stay up for the rest of the evening.

Lars, who was staying at the hotel, had already gone there. It only remained for Simon Savage, very stylish in pin-stripes and a silk shirt under his sheepskin jacket, to escort them the very short distance to the hotel.

The dining room was almost full and they went straight to their table, and Louisa, who had been worrying about the drinks, was relieved to find that the men made no effort to go to the bar and drank the tonic and lemon Simon had ordered for them all without a muscle of their faces moving.

The dinner was delicious—thick home-made soup, fish beautifully cooked, and fruit salad, followed by a great pot of coffee. They lingered over it, while Lars, bearing the lion's share of the talk, kept them all laughing, until the film was due to start.

The room was crowded and their entry caused a small stir among the audience, calling friendly greetings, offering them seats. In the end they settled in the middle of a row of chairs half way back from the screen, Claudia and Louisa in the middle, the men on either side of them. The film was *The Sound of Music*, which Louisa had seen more times than she could remember, not that that made any difference to her enjoyment. She sat, misty-eyed, her gentle mouth very slightly open, oblivious of Claudia and Lars holding hands beside her and Simon Savage, sitting well back and watching her face, with no expression on his own features at all. Anyone looking at him might have concluded that he had seen the film too and had gone into a trance until it was over.

When the film was finished the dancing began. The men had surged to the bar, but at the first sound of Abba on the tape, they were back, swinging their partners on to the floor. Louisa, who had watched Lars and Claudia join the cheerful dancing throng, felt a wave of relief when a young giant of a man she had seen several times on the quay advanced upon her with a friendly: 'Yes?' and danced her off too. Only then did she admit to her fear of being left high and dry and Simon Savage coming to find her without a partner. He would have danced with her, of course, with the frigid politeness of someone doing his duty...

The tape came to an end and she was still exchanging small talk with her partner when the music started again, and this time it was Simon Savage who danced her off. A neat dancer, she conceded, and self-assured. After a few minutes she relaxed and began to enjoy herself.

'You are enjoying yourself?' enquired Simon, way up above her head.

'Very much, thank you.'

'It compares not unfavourably with the more sophisticated night spots of London?'

She glanced up briefly. 'I wouldn't know—I've never been to one.'

He didn't answer and she spent several fruitless moments trying to think of something light and amusing to say, but she couldn't—and anyway, Simon was hardly eager for conversation. They danced in silence, and presently, when the tape was changed, they went on dancing, and except for a short spell with Lars and ten minutes of disco dancing with another young man who owned a fishing boat and who had passed the time of day with her on occasion, Simon continued to dance with her for the rest of the evening. He was, she felt, exceeding his duty by doing so, especially as there were several pretty girls there, but it seemed that his duty didn't include talking. Probably he was working out a new bridge.

The evening came to an end. Everyone put on layers of warm clothing and went out into the cold, calling good-nights as they went. Louisa was glad that the distance was short to the house. The idea of facing a trip on the fjord before one got home was rather more than one would wish for at that time of night. She went indoors thankfully and went at once to her room, leaving the others downstairs. It was to be hoped that Simon would have the sense to go to his room too and give the other two a chance to say goodnight before Lars went back to the hotel. She was undressed and in bed, almost asleep, when there was a gentle knock on her door and it was opened.

'You're awake?' It was more a statement than a question, uttered in Simon's voice, surprisingly quiet. He came in, shutting the door behind him, and Louisa sat up in bed and switched on the bedside light.

'Claudia—I heard her come up to bed…'

'Where she is now. There's been an accident—a gust

of wind overturned one of the launches—three men on board, all saved but in poor shape. They are bringing them in now. Will you come down to the hotel as soon as you can?'

'Give me five minutes.' She barely waited for him to be gone before she was out of bed, tearing off her sensible long-sleeved nightie, bundling into woollies, a sweater, slacks, her jacket, her woolly cap crammed down on to her flowing hair. She crept downstairs in her wool socks and wondered briefly if it was all right to leave Claudia on her own, but there was nothing much she could do about that. She closed the outer door quietly and felt the shock of the bitter wind and cold night as she hurried to the hotel.

The door was shut, but there were lights on downstairs. She opened it and went inside and found that the first of the men was already there, lying on one of the larger tables, covered with a blanket. Two men were bending over him, but they straightened up as she went to look and stood back a little. The man was young and suffering, she judged, from his immersion in the fjord, but his colour wasn't too bad and his pulse was fairly strong. She got the men to help her turn him on to his side, made sure that he had a free air passage, and began to strip off his outer clothes. Someone, she was glad to see, had already taken off his boots and there were plenty of dry blankets piled near. She set the men to rub his arms and legs once his clothes were off, took his pulse again and turned round as the second man was brought in—an older man this time, and not a good colour. The four men carrying him laid him on another blanket-covered table and while she took a quick look at him, began to take off his clothes and boots too. Louisa removed false teeth, took a faint pulse and requested towels, and when they came to set to rub the man's legs and arms, presently handing over to her helpers while she went back to look at the first man. He was decidedly better and would be better still for a warm bed and a good sleep once he was conscious. She judged him to be safe enough to leave and went back to the other man.

No one had said very much, doing as she asked them without query, and now the landlord appeared, his wife behind him, carrying a tray loaded with mugs and coffee pots and the potent spirit Aqua Vitae, and hard on their heels came the third patient, carried carefully by another four men, Simon Savage being one of them. He looked across the room as they laid the man, little more than a boy, on a table and said briefly: 'I think he has a broken leg.'

As indeed he had, a nasty compound fracture of the tibia and probably more than that. Louisa set about covering the ugly jagged wound, thankful that he was unconscious still, and then with Simon Savage's help gently straightened the leg and splinted it. There might not be a doctor in the small community, but at least they had an excellent first aid equipment. The boy had had a blow on the head as well, there was a discoloration over one eye, but his pulse was good and his pupils were re-acting. She finished her work with calm unhurry and said: 'They'll need to go into hospital. The first one is not too bad, but he'll have to have a check-up.'

'Lars and some of the men are getting a launch ready now,' Simon told her. 'We'll take them up to Tromso. You'll come with us.'

Orders, orders! thought Louisa. He could have said please, it would have made a trying situation a little less trying. She said, 'Very well,' and then, 'Claudia is alone.'

'Lars is going up there for the rest of the night. Are we ready to go?'

'Who are "we"?' She was taking pulses again, doing a careful last-minute check.

'You, me, Arne and Knut, the boy you were dancing with.'

Louisa took the coffee the landlord was offering her and took a heartening sip. She wasn't sure, but she thought that he had put Aqua Vitae into it, a good idea if they were to face the cold again. Simon Savage was gulping his down too and then Arne and Knut came in, swallowed their drinks, listened to Simon's instructions, and went away again. One by one the three men were carried down to the quay, into the launch and made comfortable. Louisa was barely aboard when Simon shouted for a man to cast off, and took the wheel. There was a hard wind blowing within a very few minutes, and Louisa quite understood how the boat the three men had been in had overturned; she only hoped the launch was made of sterner stuff. They lurched and slithered, and if she had had the time she would have indulged in seasickness, but what with keeping the three men on the benches, taking pulses, and when the first man regained consciousness, reassuring him, she had not a moment to spare.

The journey seemed unending and she wondered how the men on deck were faring. Now and then she heard them shouting to each other above the wind, but their voices were cheerful. The boy with the broken leg came to for a moment and she had a job to quieten him before he drowsed off again. His cries brought Simon Savage into the cabin, together with a blast of icy air. 'All right?' he wanted to know. 'We're coming in now. There should be an ambulance waiting—I phoned ahead.'

It took a little while to manoeuvre the three men off the launch and on to the quay, where two ambulances were parked. Louisa, told by Simon to get into the second one, did so, looking round anxiously to see what everyone else was doing—surely they weren't going to leave her here?

'Don't worry,' said Simon laconically. 'Arne and Knut will wait here in the launch for us.' He shut the doors on her and a moment later they moved off.

She was very tired by now and cold to her bones. The hospital, when they reached it, was a blur of bright lights and briskly moving figures. Modern, she thought, escorting the boy into the casualty department, and well equipped. If she hadn't been so worn out she would have been glad to have looked around her. As it was she was told kindly to sit down and waved to one of the benches and someone brought her a cup of coffee. Everyone had disappeared by now. She closed her eyes and dozed, to be roused presently by Simon Savage. 'We're going back,' he told her. 'One of the ambulances will give us a lift to the launch.'

She nodded. 'The men—will they be all right?'

'Yes. You did a good job, Louisa—thanks.'

He bundled her into the ambulance, beside the driver, and got in beside her, then hauled her out again and helped her on to the launch. 'Inside,' he said, and she sat down thankfully on one of the benches and would have gone to sleep again if Knut hadn't come in with more coffee, laced with Aqua Vitae, and stood over her while she drank it. She went to sleep within minutes, which was a good thing, as they were heading into a gale force wind which sent the launch heaving and shuddering and would have terrified her if she had been awake. As it was she had to be shaken when they finally got back.

'Are we there already?' she asked querulously, and tried to go to sleep again, and when she got another shake, 'I must have gone to sleep.'

'You're swimming in spirits,' said Simon. 'We came back in a gale and it seemed best to knock you out.' He hoisted her to her feet. 'Can you manage to walk?'

The cold air revived her and she managed very well, with his arm around her, and at the door she asked: 'What's the time? I seem to have lost track...'

He opened the door and pushed her gently inside. 'It's almost five o'clock. Are you hungry?'

She discovered that she was and nodded.

'Go upstairs and get ready for bed and then come down to the kitchen.'

Louisa nodded again and stumbled upstairs and into

her room. The sight of her bed almost sent her into it, still dressed as she was, but she had no doubt at all that if she didn't present herself downstairs within a reasonable time, Simon would be wanting to know why not. She undressed and went back to the kitchen, wrapped in the thick dressing gown she had bought for warmth rather than glamour. Certainly there wasn't a vestige of glamour about her. White-faced, her hair in rats' tails, her eyes heavy with sleep, she wandered into the warm little room and found the table laid with plates and mugs and knives and forks. Simon, that most unlikely of cooks, had fried eggs in a pan, made a pot of tea, and cut slices off a brown loaf.

They sat opposite each other hardly speaking, and when they had finished they cleared the table, left everything tidy and went out into the little hall. 'Where will you sleep?' asked Louisa, suddenly remembering that Lars was there.

'It won't be the first time I've slept in a chair.' Indeed, now that she looked closely at him, he looked tired to death.

She said in a motherly voice: 'Oh, poor you! I'll get some blankets and a pillow...'

Simon shook his head. 'Go to bed.' He smiled down at her, a wide, tender smile that made her blink, and then bent his head to kiss her—quick and hard and not at all like the other kiss he had given her. If she hadn't been three parts asleep she would have been filled with astonishment. As it was, she fell into bed aware of a complete contentment, although about what, she had no idea.

CHAPTER EIGHT

It was Elsa who wakened Louisa later in the morning with a cup of tea and the news that Mr Savage had gone to Tromso to see how the three men were faring, and Miss Savage and Herre Helgesen had gone skiing.

Louisa showered and dressed and went downstairs, had a cup of coffee and a slice of toast in the kitchen and set about laying the table for lunch. Everyone would be back soon; it was almost one o'clock. But one o'clock came and passed and she went into the kitchen to confer with Elsa, who shook her head and said that she really didn't know. Miss Savage had taken a packet of sandwiches with her, but she had said nothing about not coming back at the usual time, and as for Mr Savage, he had said nothing at all, merely walked out of the house—it was Herre Helgesen who had told her where he had gone. Luckily it was a meal which would come to no harm. She looked enquiringly at Louisa because she always went home after she had seen to the midday meal and it was already over her normal time.

Louisa assured her that she could cope quite easily

with the dishing up when the others came home and begged her to take extra time off as she had been so inconvenienced, so Elsa got into her outdoor things, wished her a pleasant Sunday afternoon, and hurried off, leaving Louisa to potter in the kitchen for a while and then go back to sit by the stove, but by now it was almost two o'clock and she was famished, so she went into the kitchen again, helped herself to a plate of Elsa's delicious casserole and ate it at the kitchen table and then, because she was still hungry, she cut a hunk of cheese and ate that before washing her plate and setting the tea tray. Somebody must come back soon, the light was already fading fast into black night. She set the kettle to boil on the wood stove in the sitting room and sat down again to read, but presently she let the book fall and allowed her thoughts to roam.

It seemed likely that she would be going back to England soon. Claudia didn't really need her now; Lars had been the miracle that was needed, if Claudia loved him enough she wouldn't drink again as long as she lived—they would marry and live happily ever after in Bergen. And Simon? Presumably he would go on building bridges wherever they were needed in the world. He was entirely self-sufficient and content with his lot. Presumably he had a home somewhere in England. He might even marry one day; he would make a terrible husband, she considered, although just once or twice she had glimpsed a quite different man behind that dark austere face. He had been kind to her, too. She remembered his smile and smiled herself, thinking about it.

Undoubtedly there was another Simon Savage tucked away somewhere...

It was warm in the room and she dozed off, thinking about him still, and awakened to hear Claudia's voice and Lars's deeper tones.

They stopped in surprise when they saw her. 'Have you been here all day?' asked Claudia, and started flinging her jacket and cap and scarf on to chairs and kicking off her boots. 'We thought you'd go with Simon.'

Louisa tried to remember if he'd said anything about taking her out and couldn't—how awful if he had, and she'd gone on sleeping when she should have been up and dressed and ready. 'I didn't wake up,' she said uncertainly.

Claudia shrugged. 'Oh, well, probably he didn't want you, anyway—only he said he was going to the hospital at Tromso, and that's your meat and drink, isn't it?'

Louisa didn't answer but picked up the dropped clothes and asked if they'd like tea. 'There's dinner in the oven,' she explained, 'but it'll keep until you want it.'

They decided to have tea and Lars went into the kitchen to get the tray while Louisa whipped upstairs with Claudia's things. Claudia looked fantastically happy, but she looked tired too.

'Where did you go?' Louisa asked when she got downstairs again.

'Oh, miles and miles—it was heaven,' Claudia answered her carelessly. 'Lars, must you really go back to Bergen?' She smiled at him beguilingly. 'One more day?'

He shook his head. 'No, my dear, I have to go, but I'll come again, as often as I can.'

'Why can't I come with you?' Claudia's voice was dangerously high.

'Because another week or two here is what you need; I want a healthy beautiful girl for a wife and I'm prepared to wait for her.'

Louisa poured tea, feeling de trop, and after her first cup she escaped to the kitchen with a muttered excuse which no one listened to, made herself another pot of tea and sat at the table drinking it. She felt incredibly lonely.

When she went back to the sitting room an hour later, the two of them were so absorbed in their talk that she had to ask twice when they wanted their supper.

'We're going over to the hotel,' said Claudia. 'I daresay Simon will be back, and you can eat together.'

'He'll be able to tell you about the men in hospital,' suggested Lars kindly. 'They're all talking about you, you know, saying how splendid you were.'

'Oh, are they? I didn't do anything.' She smiled at them both and went back to the kitchen and stayed there until they left, calling cheerfully that they wouldn't be late back.

'I've got a key,' said Claudia from the door. 'Go to bed if you want to.'

Louisa went back to the sitting room, cleared away the tea things, plumped up the cushions, made up the stove and sat down. If Simon didn't turn up by seven o'clock she was going to have her supper; the casserole was more than ready and she was hungry.

All the same, it was half an hour after that time when she finally had her supper. She ate it on her lap, wondering if the launch had turned turtle on the way back from Tromso. It was more than likely that Simon had gone to a hotel there and had a slap-up meal—probably with some lovely Norwegian lady, she thought gloomily, and then told herself sharply that it didn't matter to her in the least with whom he went out.

By ten o'clock she had had enough. She washed the dishes, tidied the kitchen and went up to bed. It wasn't long after that that she heard Claudia and Lars come in and after a murmur of voices, Claudia came upstairs. What seemed like hours later, she heard Simon Savage's deliberate footsteps coming into the house. She listened to him making up the stove, going into the kitchen, retracing his steps to his workroom and finally the clink of a glass—whisky; perhaps he was chilled to the marrow, hungry, soaking wet… By a great effort she stayed in bed, although every instinct was willing her to go down and warm up the rest of the casserole. It was an hour or more before he came upstairs and it wasn't until then that she allowed herself to go to sleep.

The next day was a bad one. Claudia, without Lars to keep her happy, was at her very worst. She refused to get out of bed, she threw her breakfast tray at Louisa, declared her intention of leaving for Bergen that very morning, swore that she would kill anyone who tried to stop her, and then dissolved into a flood of hysterical tears. Louisa, picking up broken china, was just in time to meet Simon Savage, coming up the stairs like the wrath of God, and order him down again.

'Don't you dare!' she admonished him. 'She's only upset because Lars isn't here—it'll be all right presently...' She shooed him step by step until they were back to the hall. 'Go on,' she told him firmly, 'go and build your bridge! You don't understand women, even if you do know how to make a bridge stay up.'

His face, black with temper, suddenly broke into a smile. 'I think you may be right there, Louisa. How fierce you are!' He kissed the end of her nose and turned her round. 'Up you go!'

He was wise enough not to come back until well after tea time, and by then Claudia was at least trying for self-control. A phone call from Lars had helped, of course, and Louisa's patient, uncomplaining company. Halfway through a good wallow in self-pity Claudia paused long enough to observe: 'I don't know how you can put up with me—I'd be gone like a bat out of hell if I'd been you.' But before Louisa could answer that she was in floods of tears again.

Simon behaved beautifully when he did come back home. Bearing an armful of magazines and the newest papers, he put them down beside his stepsister, wished the room at large a good evening, and went into his workroom, where he stayed until Louisa summoned him to supper. And during that meal he talked with unusual placidity about Bergen, Lars's house, his work, his interest in sport, and from there he passed to the various churches in the city, remarking that Lars always went to St Jorgen Church. 'It might be a good place in which to marry,' he suggested mildly, 'because they hold English church services there as well.'

Claudia looked up from the food she was pushing round her plate.

'You don't mind if I marry Lars? You've always disagreed with everything I've wanted to do—hated my friends...'

Louisa watched his saturnine features, ready for an outburst. None came. He said mildly: 'Won't you in all fairness agree that I had good reason to dislike them? Do you really want them as friends?' He shrugged. 'Not that it's any business of mine any more, but I'm not sure if Lars will care for them.'

'Oh, I know that—you don't have to preach at me, but I won't want friends now, will I, I've got him.' She got up from the table. 'I'm not hungry. I'm going to bed. Louisa, you can bring me up some coffee and a sandwich later.'

'If it were not for the fact that you would scold me severely, I would have made Claudia apologise for talking to you like that,' remarked Simon evenly.

'She doesn't mean it—she's unhappy...' Louisa gave him the briefest of glances, wishing to appear matter-of-fact after their meeting that morning.

'And you? Are you happy?'

'Yes. You see, Claudia is almost cured, isn't she? Oh, I know she's had relapses before, but this time there's Lars. I think he loves her so much that he's prepared to put up with a good deal.'

'And would you like to be loved like that, Louisa?'

'Yes, of course I should, but it doesn't happen to everyone, does it?'

He didn't reply, but presently said: 'I had planned to

take you both to Tromso for a day's shopping, but the weather forecast is bad and it's too risky.'

'Perhaps in a few days—it would do Claudia a lot of good. How are the three men?'

'In good shape; two of them will be coming back in a few days, the boy will have to stay for a bit, but he's got relatives in Tromso, so it won't be too bad for him.' He was staring at her steadily. 'Everyone here is proud of you, do you know that?'

She looked down at her empty plate and could think of nothing to say. Presently she broke a silence which had gone on for too long. 'Mr Savage…'

'And that's another thing—why am I always Mr Savage? We have Lars and Arne and Knut and Mr Savage, as though I were some mid-Victorian ogre. My name is Simon.'

She poured herself more coffee which she didn't want, but it gave her something to do. She said very quietly: 'But you were an ogre,' and heard his sigh, and the next moment he had got to his feet.

'Well, I've some work to do,' he was icily bland. 'Goodnight.'

She didn't see him again until the following evening and by then she was tired and a little cross. Claudia had been very trying, although there were signs that she was pulling herself together again. After all, Lars had promised to come up for the following weekend. Louisa reminded her of this at frequent intervals and talked herself hoarse about the new clothes Claudia insisted she must have. 'I shall want a great deal of money, heaps of it,' she declared. 'Simon will just have to foot the bills. I'm not getting married without a rag to my back!' An inaccurate statement Louisa ignored, only too happy to get Claudia in a more cheerful frame of mind. She wasn't quite as happy when Claudia brought the matter up at the supper table. The conversation between the three of them had been a little forced and Simon looked tired and bad-tempered too. But to her surprise he agreed placidly that Claudia should have enough money to buy what she needed. He even suggested that she might like to fly to Oslo and shop there.

'Does that mean that we can get away from here soon?' Claudia demanded.

'Very soon now—it's up to you, Claudia.'

'I'm on the waggon,' she promised him. 'I swore to Lars that I'll not drink another drop, and I won't—you see, I don't need to. What about Louisa?'

His glance flickered over her before he answered his stepsister.

'I think we might dispose with Louisa's services very shortly,' he said casually. Just as though I'm not sitting here, thought Louisa indignantly, and quelled the temptation to ask when she was to go. Let him tell her, she couldn't care less. She just stopped herself in time from tossing her head.

She didn't have long to wait. 'How about the end of the week?' he asked smoothly. 'Lars is coming up for the weekend, isn't he? I shall be finished here in four or five days. I don't see why you and Lars shouldn't go back together, and we can put Louisa on a flight the day before that.'

'To London?' asked Claudia without much interest.

'Where else?' Again that quick glance.

She conjured up a smile and said brightly: 'Oh, how lovely, home for Christmas!'

The very thought appalled her. She would have to find another job before that—go to an agency and take anything, preferably something that kept her so busy she wouldn't have a moment to remember Norway and Claudia or, for that matter, Simon Savage.

Now that plans were made and Claudia felt secure in a happy future, she shed her bad habits like some old outworn skin. For the next two days she got up for breakfast, insisted on taking Louisa on to the slope to teach her more about skiing, made her own bed and spent barely an hour on her face and hair. Louisa could hardly believe that this was the same woman who had engaged her in London, the change was so great. Of course, Claudia still took little interest in anyone else but herself and Lars. Beyond supposing that Louisa would get herself another job quickly she didn't mention her going and even remarked that it would be delightful to be on her own—at least until she married, she added quickly. 'You're not a bad kid,' she told Louisa, 'but it's like having a ball and chain attached to me, but I suppose you have to put up with that if you're a nurse—a necessary evil, aren't you?' She had laughed and Louisa had laughed with her. No one had ever called her that before, it gave her a nasty cold feeling in her insides, but she would have died rather than let Claudia see how shattered she felt.

And Simon made it much worse that evening, talking at great length and with remarkable fluency for him about the delights of the Norwegian Christmas. 'Everything shuts down at midday on Christmas Eve,' he informed her, 'and there's a traditional dish of dried lamb served in the evening and afterwards everyone gathers round the Christmas tree and sings carols before the presents. Christmas Day is much the same and on the next day—our Boxing Day—they give enormous parties with skiing and sleigh rides and masses of food.' He fixed Louisa with his dark eyes. 'You would have enjoyed it, Louisa.'

She gave him a cross look. Of course she would have enjoyed it, the idea of going back to England didn't appeal to her at all, but what else could she do? They had made it plain enough that she was no longer needed—they would probably be relieved to see her go. She toyed with the idea of staying in Bergen. Christmas wasn't so far off and if she was careful, she would have enough money. There had been little or no chance to spend much, but if she did Claudia might think that she was staying deliberately in order to spy on her. Besides, she had made it plain that she would be glad to see her go. She said woodenly: 'I'm sure I should, it sounds delightful.' And as she said it she was struck by the sudden knowledge that that was what she wanted more than anything in the world—to stay in Norway for Christmas, for ever, if necessary, just as long as she could be with Simon Savage. Falling in love with him had been the last thing she had expected to do. He was ill-tempered, brusque, impatient and intolerant. He was also, she now perceived, the only man she wanted to marry.

'How utterly silly!' she muttered, and earned a surprised look from him. She said the first thing which entered her head: 'Do I fly direct to England or must I change planes?'

'Tromso to Bergen and Bergen to Heathrow.'

'How nice,' she observed idiotically, and waffled on about the journey, the delights of Christmas at home, seeing her friends again, so intent on painting a carefree picture of her future that she quite missed Simon's puzzled look which presently turned to speculation.

And if she had hoped, during her wakeful night, for some small sign that he might want to meet her again at some time, she was disappointed. He was more austere than usual over the breakfast table, telling Claudia in a forthright manner that on no account were they to go skiing that day. 'There's bad weather coming,' he assured her, 'probably there'll be no flights to Tromso...'

'Then Lars won't be able to come?'

'Probably not.'

She shot him a furious look. 'Then I shall go to him.'

'No, if you get to Tromso and the planes are grounded there, you might not be able to get back here. I suggest that you ring him during the morning.' He had gone before she could answer and Louisa was forced to listen to recriminations for the next ten minutes or so; not that she listened very hard, for her head was full of her own problems.

Lars telephoned during the morning. There were violent snowstorms in the south of the country and all flights had been cancelled and he would come just as soon as he could—a statement which met with an outburst of tears on Claudia's part and an hysterical request to be taken to Bergen at once. Even Lars's promise that if the weather delayed him for too long he would travel by the coastal steamer did little to cheer her up. He rang off finally and Claudia went up to her room and locked the door.

It was getting on for midday when she came downstairs again, and daylight, which would last a mere two hours or so, had come. The sky was blue and there wasn't a cloud to be seen from the window and she pointed this out to Louisa. 'They've slipped up,' she said hopefully. 'There's not a sign of snow.'

Louisa glanced out at the sky. 'We can't see a great deal from here,' she pointed out. 'Would you like me to start your packing?'

Claudia sprawled in a chair and picked up a book. 'After lunch—would you go to the shop for me? There are several things I simply must have—I'll make a list while you get your jacket.'

It was quite a long list and Louisa read it with surprise. 'But you can get most of these in Bergen. I mean, none of them are urgent...'

Claudia barely glanced up from her reading. 'Don't argue. I want them now—unless you're too lazy to go and get them?'

Louisa bit back an angry retort and went out of the house without a word. What did it matter, she asked herself tiredly; what did anything matter?

It took her fifteen minutes to do the shopping by the time she had waited her turn, waited while the various odds and ends were found and then had a short chat with Arne's sister. As she started back again, she could

see that the fjord's waters were dark and heaving slug-
gishly and that the blue sky had become less vivid. Perhaps there was bad weather coming after all. She went
into the house and straight into the sitting room. Claudia wasn't there, so she picked up her basket and went
along to the kitchen. Elsa was standing by the table,
getting the lunch and looking put out.

'I am glad you are here,' she began. 'Miss Savage
has gone out and there is bad weather coming fast. She
would not listen to me. She has taken her skis too. I
think that Mr Savage should be told, for she will be lost
once the snow comes.'

Louisa dumped her basket on the table. 'Did she say
where she was going?' and when Elsa shook her head:
'How long ago?'

'Ten minutes, perhaps.'

'Then I'll try and catch her up and get her to come
back. Make me some coffee, Elsa, and put it in a thermos, and I want a torch, and then telephone Mr Savage.' Louisa was searching around for the rucksack
which hung in the kitchen and when she had it, rammed
in some slices of bread Elsa had just cut and a slab of
chocolate and a ball of string she saw on the dresser.
She hadn't a very good idea of what one took on such a
trip and probably there would be no need to use any of
them, all the same she added the coffee and the torch.
It had all taken a few precious minutes and Claudia
might be miles away by now. She put on the rucksack,
urged Elsa to telephone without delay, collected her
skis from the back door and hurried through the snow,
past the last of the houses, where she put on her skis

and started cautiously up the slope where they usually went. Claudia had gone that way; she could see the ski marks very plainly. Once she got to the top she would be able to see in all directions.

It was an interminable time before she got there and in her haste she fell down twice and getting on to her feet again took all her patience and strength, but once there, she stood, fetching her breath, scanning the scene before her. The mountains stretched for miles, snow-covered, terrifying in their grandeur, but far more terrifying was the great bank of cloud, yellow at the edges, devouring the blue sky, and the first hint of the bitter wind hurrying it along at a furious pace. But it wouldn't help to study the sky. She lifted her goggles and surveyed the slopes ahead of her. It took her a minute to spot Claudia, who had skied down the reverse side of the slope and was just beginning to work her way up on the farther side. She was following the route she and Lars had taken together, Louisa guessed. There was a narrow valley which would take her back towards the fjord. Louisa trembled at the thought of the journey ahead of her; she had never ventured farther than the spot she was on at that moment and she was frankly scared. But the longer she stood there, the more terrified she would be. She let out a ringing shout in the hope that Claudia would hear her and for a moment the distant figure paused, but then went on again. Louisa put her goggles back on, took one despairing look at the clouds racing towards her, and set off.

Surprisingly it wasn't as bad as she had expected. The slope was longer than the one she had practised on but no steeper. She reached the bottom, still scared to death but rather pleased with herself, too, and started the laborious climb up the other side. Claudia had disappeared over the ridge and heaven knew what nightmares waited on the other side. A few paper-dry snowflakes began to fall and Louisa, by a great effort, kept her pace deliberate. Hurrying would mean another spill and she hadn't the time to waste. By the time she reached the top the snow was falling in earnest and it was getting ominously dark. She stood at the top, gasping for breath, and looked around her. There wasn't much to see now, for there was a thick curtain of snow and the wind had gathered a ferocious strength. She gazed around helplessly. Claudia's ski tracks had already been covered by the snow, and there was no way of knowing which way she had gone. She wiped her goggles, turned her back to the wind and shouted with all her might.

There was an answering shout, very faint; impossible to tell from where it came. She couldn't see the lower slopes ahead of her. Suppose she skied to the bottom, passed Claudia and had to come back? She would lose her way and make matters worse. She said out loud: 'Oh, God, please give a hand,' and just for a few seconds the wind dropped and the snow thinned, and away to her left, half way down, she saw a small dark object.

'Oh, thanks very much,' said Louisa fervently, and plunged downwards at an angle, going very carefully. She hadn't learned to turn on skis yet and she hoped she had got the direction right.

She had, she was on top of Claudia before she could stop herself, and they both fell in a mêlée of arms and legs and skis. Claudia was up first and pulled Louisa to her feet. She said bitterly: 'I've been all kinds of a fool—I'm sorry, Louisa,' which was the first time she had ever apologised to her. And probably the last, thought Louisa, busy brushing snow off herself.

'We'll have to make some sort of shelter,' she shouted above the wind. 'I asked Elsa to ring Simon, they'll be out looking for us by now, but we'll freeze if we stay here.'

Claudia clutched at her arm. 'There's a hut somewhere close—we passed it when we came this way, Lars and I. It's somewhere to the left, on an outcrop of rock, it's got a turf roof.'

Louisa remembered the string in her rucksack. 'Let's find it,' she shouted back, 'but we'd better tie ourselves together.' She turned her back. 'In the rucksack.'

It was a botched-up job, what with thick mitts they dared not take off and granny knots which didn't stay done up, but in the end they achieved a double line of string fastening them together. It would certainly snap if one of them fell, but it was better than nothing at all. The snow was falling so thickly now that they couldn't see more than a few feet in front of them; but through the gloom it was still possible to make out the outline of the mountains whenever the wind dropped and the snow stopped swirling around them. Claudia remembered that the hut was on the lower slope of a mountain with a peak which towered above the rest. They had to wait a little while before she could locate it and even when they did they weren't sure that they weren't skiing in circles. When they at last saw the hut in front of their noses after several false starts they were ready to cry with fright and relief and tiredness—indeed, Claudia did burst into tears, and Louisa, on the verge of snivelling herself, told her sharply to stop at once. 'Unless you want to die of cold,' she said. 'Get inside, do—I've got coffee with me and some bread and chocolate and we'll do exercises to keep warm.'

'No one will ever find us,' wailed Claudia.

'Simon will,' declared Louisa stoutly. 'I'm going to shine my torch presently.' She had pushed Claudia into the tiny place and turned to look round at their surroundings. It was a very small hut but stoutly built, with no windows and an open small door, but at least it was shelter. She took off her rucksack, opened the coffee and gave some to Claudia, had some herself and then shared the food, and when they had devoured the last crumb she made Claudia jump up and down and wave her arms. It was difficult, the two of them in the tiny place, floundering about, bumping into each other, but she kept Claudia at it until they were both exhausted even though they were less frozen. Claudia sat down on the rucksack and declared that she had to rest even if she froze solid, and Louisa let her, for the time being at least.

'Why did you do it?' she asked.

'Oh, I don't know—I suppose I was disappointed and upset, and I don't take kindly to not getting my own way, and I've always made a point of doing the opposite of whatever Simon has told me to do.' Claudia gave a choked laugh. 'If we ever get out of this I'll be a reformed character!' She glanced at Louisa. 'Why did you come after me?'

'I'm still in Simon's employ.' The thought of him made her want to cry. She said matter-of-factly: 'I'm going to have a try with the torch. What's the time?'

'Just after two o'clock.'

It seemed a lot longer than the two hours since she had started out from the house. Surely a search party would be out looking for them by now? She put her head cautiously round the edge of the door and saw that for the moment the snow had lessened, although the wind was still blowing hard. The thought of the journey back, if ever they were lucky enough to make it, made her feel sick.

It was a pity that she never could remember SOS in Morse, but surely any kind of light in such a desolate spot would attract attention—if only it could be seen. And she had lost her sense of direction, too, which meant sending a beam to all points of the compass. Nothing happened; she repeated her flashes several times and then went to crouch inside again. Claudia had gone to sleep and Louisa wasn't sure if this was a good thing or not. She decided not to wake her for half an hour and got down beside her on the iron hard floor, holding her close so that they might share each other's warmth.

The half hour went slowly. At the end of it she got up again, wakened an unwilling Claudia and after five minutes waving their arms and stamping their feet, she poked her head out once more. It seemed to her that the appalling weather wasn't quite so appalling

as it had been. She had no idea how long such storms
lasted and as the daylight hours had already passed, it
was too dark to see any possible landmarks, but she
was sure that the snow was lessening. She flashed her
torch and peered hopefully for a reply, and when there
wasn't one, flashed it again. Nothing happened. She
would wait ten minutes and then try again. She took
one last look and turned round to scan the gloom behind her—and saw a light.

The torch was still in her hand; excitement made
her drop it. She searched for it frantically, quite forgetting to shout. She had to have the torch; whoever it
was might miss them and they would die of cold and
hunger. She was still grovelling round, sniffing and
sobbing under her breath, when someone swished to
a halt within inches of her, plucked her off the ground
and wrapped her so close that she had no breath.

'So there you are,' said Simon, and kissed her cold
face hard and still with one arm round her, turned the
torch slung round his neck so that it shone behind him.
'The others will be here in a minute. Where's Claudia?'

'Inside.'

He pushed her back into the hut and followed. He
spoke gently to Claudia, who was in floods of tears,
and only grunted when she paused long enough to say:
'You took long enough—I could have died, and I won't
go back until the snow stops.'

Simon had coffee with him. He shared it between
them and they had barely finished it when men began
crowding into the small place, cheerful men who declared that the weather was improving, offering more

coffee, handing out sandwiches, making much of them. Arne, who had crouched beside Louisa, said kindly: 'You see that now you are a good skier—you will no longer be afraid.'

She smiled back at him. 'Oh, but I shall! I'm a complete coward, and I'm so sorry that we—we got lost; that you all had to come and look for us, and in this appalling weather.'

She didn't know that Simon was behind her. She spilt her coffee when he said quietly: 'You have no need to apologise, Louisa, it was very brave of you to follow Claudia, who should have known better. My God, what trouble that woman has been to me, and how glad I am that Lars is fool enough to take her on for the rest of his life.'

'They'll be very happy,' Louisa mumbled.

They had two sledges with them. Claudia was wrapped up and strapped into one of them, but Louisa absolutely refused to travel on the other. 'I'll manage very well,' she declared firmly. 'It's the last chance I'll have of skiing before I leave and I don't want to miss it.'

They travelled in two files and Simon stayed with her the whole way, and when she fell over, which she did several times, he picked her up, dusted her down, and urged her on again, almost without speaking. She had never been so happy in her life before. The snow and wind were suddenly wonderful, the mountains not terrifying at all; she could ski and Mr Savage had turned into Simon at last. She closed her eyes, remembering his kiss, and fell over once more. They were almost home by then. Heaven, she felt sure, was just round the corner.

CHAPTER NINE

BUT HEAVEN WAS rather further away than Louisa had thought. There was a good deal of bustle and confusion once they were back at home. Claudia demanded a great deal of attention, declaring that she felt faint, that she must have a hot bath at once, that she needed food, that she must telephone Lars immediately. She had thanked the men perfunctorily before she had gone upstairs, and it was left to Louisa and Elsa to hand round coffee and pastries and thank them more warmly. And Simon, when she looked for him, had disappeared. She shook hands with their rescuers and when the last of them had gone, went slowly upstairs to Claudia, who was calling for her.

'Where have you been?' she asked impatiently. 'I want you to rub in that cream for me—my skin will be ruined. Lord, I'm tired!'

'And so am I,' observed Louisa shortly, making quick work of the creaming and bustling Claudia into bed without giving her a chance to think of anything else she wanted done. 'Elsa's staying late, she'll bring you up your supper presently. I'm going to have a bath.'

She was still in it daydreaming about Simon when he came back into the house. He didn't stay long; Elsa told him that his stepsister was in bed and she thought Louisa was going to bed too. He thanked her quietly and went to the hotel and had a meal there—which was a pity, because presently Louisa went downstairs, looking a little wan, but nicely made up and wearing one of her Norwegian sweaters and a thick skirt, all ready to have her supper with Simon. But the table, she saw at once, was laid for one and when she asked, Elsa told her that Mr Savage had only called in for a moment to see if they were all right before going to the hotel.

And although she was tired and remarkably sleepy by now, Louisa waited patiently until Elsa had gone home and the clock struck the hour of ten. But Simon didn't come. If he had wanted to he would have been back by now—and what a good thing, she told herself, for she would have made a fool of herself if he had. It was time she learnt that kisses could mean nothing. She had no doubt that when they met in the morning he would be Mr Savage once more.

She was right. She went down to breakfast alone, because Claudia was certain that she was going to have a cold, and found him already at table eating the heavenly porridge Elsa made so beautifully. He wished her good morning, barely glancing at her and enquiring after Claudia.

'She thinks she's caught a cold,' said Louisa.

'Impossible. The one thing you can't get in these parts is the common cold.' He spoke coldly, very sure of himself, and she gave his bowed head a loving look, suddenly conscious of the fact that tomorrow she would be having breakfast with him for the last time. She put down her spoon, quite unable to eat, and he said at once: 'What's the matter? Aren't you well?'

He sounded so impatient that she picked up her spoon again and made herself finish the bowlful. 'I've never felt better,' she told him. 'I'm getting excited about going home.'

He put down the paper he was studying. 'I find that hard to believe,' he observed evenly. 'You don't like your home—besides, you kissed me very thoroughly yesterday.'

She went very red but met his eyes frankly. 'I was very glad to see you—I thought we were going to die. I—I got carried away.'

'Ah, you kissed me in fact under great provocation.'

'I—well, yes, that's about it. I'm sorry, I expect people do silly things when they're a bit upset.'

Simon lowered his eyes to the paper. 'And not only when they're upset,' he observed.

And that was the sum total of their conversation. Louisa did have a try just once. She began: 'I do want to thank you...'

His laconic 'Don't' stopped her more effectively than anything else could have done.

The storm had blown itself out. There was a great deal more snow, and the waters of the fjord carried small chunks of ice on its steely grey surface, but the sky was clear. There would be more storms, of course, but planes and helicopters were flying again, Lars would be coming to fetch his Claudia back to Bergen and Louisa would leave as had been arranged. No one had given her a ticket yet, although Simon had mentioned casually that he had it. She took Claudia's breakfast upstairs, finished the last of her packing, and put on her outdoor things. There was nothing more for her to do until she left in the morning and her room, shorn of her small possessions, looked uninviting. The sky was clear and the brief day wasn't far off. The little huddle of houses, painted in their cheerful blues and pinks and greens, gleamed in the street lamps' bright beams and the snow reflected them, so that one hardly noticed the darkness. The shop was full and she went inside to say goodbye and then on to the quay to speak to Arne and several of the other men who had become her friends.

She stayed talking for a few minutes and then struggled through the snow to the curve of the fjord to get a last look at the bridge. It was finished, they had told her, and was to be opened very shortly. Men were busy there now, packing up the scaffolding and piling it tidily at either end. When spring came, it would be taken away and the little wooden huts where they had worked during the winter months would go too. It was a beautiful bridge, curving gracefully across the grey water. Louisa turned away wanting to cry, then made her way back to the hotel, where she had coffee and a long talk with the owner.

The afternoon dragged. There was no sign of Simon and Claudia had elected to stay in bed, exclaiming crossly that of course she had a cold and what did Simon know about it anyway. Louisa sat by the stove and tried to make up her mind what she would do. She had plenty of friends, but she had no intention of wishing herself upon them at no notice at all. And she couldn't face her stepmother—she didn't give Frank a thought. Somehow he had slid away into a past which wasn't important any more.

She had a solitary tea and went on sitting there, sad and forlorn and quite unable to be anything else. Elsa went presently and she took Claudia up the supper she had asked for and then laid the table for two.

Simon didn't come. Louisa ate her meal with a book propped up before her, staring at the same page without reading it, and presently went to bed. She hadn't expected to sleep, but she did, to wake heavy-eyed when her alarm went at seven o'clock. She was almost glad that she would be going within an hour or so; to get it over quickly was all she wanted. She showered and dressed and packed her overnight bag, then went downstairs.

Simon was at the kitchen table eating his breakfast and she sat down opposite him and began on the porridge Elsa put before her. He had said nothing beyond 'Good morning', but there was an envelope beside her plate. She looked at it and then at him and he said shortly: 'Your salary, Louisa,' and added after a tiny pause: 'Thank you for all the care and attention you've given Claudia. It must have been tiresome for you. I hope you'll find something—someone more congenial for your next patient.'

She glanced at him, her eyes very large and soft. She would have liked to have said something suitable in reply, but her throat had closed over. To her horror she felt tears pricking her eyelids and she pushed back her chair and got up. 'Simon,' she whispered without realising that she had said it. 'Simon…' She swallowed the lump in her throat and said in a breathy little voice: 'I'm not hungry. I must finish my packing.'

She went to her room and sat on her bed, and presently Elsa appeared without a word and put a tray of coffee down on the dressing table and went away again. Louisa drank all the coffee, tidied up her face, put on her outdoor things and went to say goodbye to Claudia.

'Going?' Claudia was only half awake and not best pleased at being disturbed. 'Oh, well, goodbye—we're not likely to see each other again, are we?' She added grudgingly: 'Of course if you should ever come to Bergen you must come and see us.' She rolled over and closed her eyes, and Louisa went and fetched her bag and went downstairs. The launch was leaving at eight o'clock and there was only five minutes left.

Elsa was in her outdoor clothes too and when Louisa started to say goodbye she said: 'I'm coming to see you off, Louisa,' and they walked down to the quay together with never a sight of Simon. Louisa gave Elsa a hug, shook hands once again with the little crowd who had come to see her off, and was helped into the launch—and there was Simon, longer and leaner than ever, standing on the deck talking to Arne. He nodded when he saw her and the people on the quay shouted and waved as the launch slowly crept away from them, out into the fjord. She stood waving until they were distant spots under the bright lights of the little quay and then went into the cabin. She hadn't expected Simon to be there—indeed, she hadn't been thinking rationally at all, for she still had no ticket. She hadn't opened the envelope either. Presently she would do so, and ask about her ticket too, but just for a moment she wanted to sit still and pull herself together. It would never do to let him see that her heart was breaking. He came into the cabin presently, taking up most of the space, and she asked him in a composed voice if she might have her ticket.

'All in good time,' he told her. 'Are you warm enough?'

'Yes, thank you.' Then she asked, 'Are you going to Tromso, too?' and blushed at the silliness of the question, but she was answered without a flicker of amusement:

'Well, yes, I am.' And then: 'Don't come on deck, it's very cold.' He went again as silently as he had come.

The journey seemed so short, but only because she wanted it to last for ever. She could see the lights of Tromso as they sped round the last bend; in another five minutes they would be there. She had no idea where the airport was and she didn't much care. She supposed there would be a taxi for her. She wouldn't want to wait around, saying goodbye would be bad enough however quick it was.

Simon came back into the cabin, bringing a gust of icy air with him. 'Ready?' he asked, and picked up her bag.

They had berthed when she went outside and there was a Land Rover parked on the quay. She shook hands with Arne and the boy with him and stepped on to the hard-packed snow, to be joined almost at once by Simon.

'We're going in the Land Rover,' he told her, and when she stared up at him questioningly: 'I'm flying to Bergen—in fact I'm flying to Heathrow with you.' He put her bag down and pulled her close. 'I didn't dare tell you,' and at her look of astonishment: 'You see, when we met I thought, "There's a brown mouse of a girl with a sharp tongue," and then before I knew what was happening I was in love with you. Oh, I did my best to ignore it, and I thought that if I ignored you too I'd be safely back in my bachelor state in no time— only it didn't work out like that. You were under my skin, in my bones, my very heartbeat. And I'd gone out of my way to make you dislike me so that it would be easier for me to get over you. Only I haven't done that, my darling.' He stared down at her, unsmiling, even a little grim. 'I've discovered that I can't face life without you, indeed I doubt if I could build another bridge. You had a wretched life with Claudia—if only you could bear to take me on instead...' A snowflake fell on to her nose and he paused and brushed it off very gently. 'My dearest little Louisa, if only you'd marry me!'

It was bitingly cold and a few snowflakes followed the first one, but Louisa hadn't noticed. She wasn't aware of the men on the launch watching them, or the driver of the Land Rover, for that matter. She had never felt so happy or so warm in her life before.

'Oh, dear Simon, of course I will! I love you, too; I never want to leave you.'

He kissed her then, long and hard and with so much

warmth that she wondered in a dreamlike way how she could ever have considered him austere and cold. He was most satisfyingly not either of those things. She kissed him back and then leaned back a little in his arms. 'It's a funny place to have a proposal,' she added shakily.

He smiled at her. 'I suppose it is.' He looked round and caught Arne's interested eye and shouted something to him which sent him and the boy as well as the driver hurrying over to them to pump their arms and utter congratulations before they finally got into the Land Rover.

Louisa sat with her hand in Simon's and at the airport she went through reception and Customs and boarded the plane without taking any note at all of her surroundings. She tucked her hand in his again as they were airborne, drank the coffee that was brought round, ate the sandwich she was given like an obedient child, and then went to sleep, her head on his shoulder. And at Bergen there was only a brief wait before they were on the flight to Heathrow. She ate lunch this time, far too excited and happy to have much appetite. They didn't talk much, only as they started the descent to the airport she asked: 'Where are we going?'

'Home,' said Simon, 'to Wiltshire. Shall we be married there and go back to Norway for our honeymoon?'

'Oh, yes, please!' She was still too excited to bother about the details—besides, Simon was there to see to everything. She heaved a sigh of pure happiness and went to sleep again.

There was a car waiting for them when they left

Heathrow—a Daimler Sovereign. As Louisa settled into the seat beside Simon she asked: 'How did it get here—this car? Is it yours?'

He nodded. 'When I go abroad I garage it close by and they bring it here for me—it's convenient.' He dropped a kiss on her cheek. 'Not long now, love. About two hours' drive.'

They drove down the M3, through a rain-sodden landscape, strangely green after the snow and the mountains, and then took the road to Warminster, but before they reached it Simon turned off the road, down a country lane which wandered up and down the gentle hills until it reached a very small village. It had a church in its centre and a cluster of houses and cottages round it and standing well back, taking up all of one side of the square, a splendid Queen Anne house with large square windows and a beautiful front door with a fanlight over it and a white-painted porch. Simon drove through the open gate at the side of the narrow front garden and stopped the car.

'Home,' he said, undid her safety belt and leaned across to open the door for her and then got out himself. By the time they had reached the door it was open with a plump smiling woman on the porch, beaming a welcome at them.

'Mrs Turner, my housekeeper.' He corrected himself: '*Our* housekeeper. Mrs Turner, this is my future wife, Miss Louisa Evans.' He waited while they shook hands and then swept Louisa across the hall and into a small room, lined with bookshelves, its great desk covered with maps and papers. He took Louisa in his arms and pulled the cap off her head.

'This is where I start my bridges,' he said very quietly, 'and this is where our heaven starts, my darling.'

Louisa put up her face to be kissed. 'I thought it would be just round the corner, and it was,' she told him. She would have explained further, but there seemed no point. To be kissed was far more satisfactory.

* * * * *

CAROLINE'S WATERLOO

CHAPTER ONE

THE NARROW BRICK road wound itself along narrow canals, through wide stretches of water meadows and small clumps of trees and, here and there, a larger copse. Standing well away from the road there were big farmhouses, each backed by a great barn, their mellow red brick glistening in the last rays of the October sun. Save for the cows, already in their winter coats, and one or two great horses, there was little to be seen and the only other movement was made by the four girls cycling briskly along the road. They had come quite a distance that day and now they were flagging a little; the camping equipment each carried made it heavy going, and besides, they had lost their way.

It had been easy enough leaving Alkmaar that morning, going over the Afsluitdijk and into Friesland, pedalling cheerfully towards the camping ground they had decided upon, but now, with no village in sight and the dusk beginning to creep over the wide Friesian sky, they were getting uneasy.

Presently they came to a halt, to look at the map and wonder where they had gone wrong. 'This doesn't go anywhere,' grumbled the obvious leader, a tall, very pretty girl. 'What shall we do? Go back—and that's miles—or press on?'

They all peered at the map again, one fair head, two dark ones and an unspectacular mouse-brown. The owner of the mouse-brown hair spoke:

'Well, the road must go somewhere, they wouldn't have built it just for fun, and we've been on it now for quite a while—I daresay we're nearer the end than the beginning.' She had a pretty voice, soft and slightly hesitant, perhaps as compensation for her very ordinary face.

Her three companions peered at the map again. 'You're right, Caro—let's go on before it's quite dark.' The speaker, one of the dark-haired girls, glanced around her at the empty landscape. 'It's lonely, isn't it? I mean, after all the towns and villages we've been through just lately.'

'Friesland and Groningen are sparsely populated,' said Caro, 'they're mostly agricultural.'

The three of them gave her a tolerant look. Caro was small and quiet and unassuming, but she was a fount of information about a great many things, because she read a lot, they imagined with a trace of pity; unlike the other nurses at Oliver's, she was seldom invited to go out by any of the young doctors and she lived alone in a small bedsitter in a horrid shabby little street convenient to the hospital. She had any number of friends, because she could be relied upon to change off-duty at a moment's notice, lend anything needed without fuss, and fill in last-minute gaps. As she was doing now; the nurse who should have been in her place had developed an appendix and because four was a much better number with which to go camping and biking, she had been roped in at the last minute. She hadn't particularly wanted to go; she had planned to spend her two weeks' holiday redecorating her room and visiting art galleries. She knew almost nothing about art, but she had discovered long ago that art galleries were restful and pleasant and there were always other people strolling around for company, even though no one ever spoke to her. Not that she minded being alone; she had grown up in a lonely way. An orphan from childhood, the aunt she had lived with had married while Caro was still at school and her new uncle had never taken to her; indeed, over the years, he had let it be known that she must find a home for herself; her aunt's was too small to house all three of them. If she had been pretty he might have thought differently, and if she had tried to conciliate him he might have had second thoughts. As it was, Caroline hadn't seen her aunt for two years or more.

'Well, let's get on,' suggested Stacey. She tossed her blonde hair back over her shoulders and got on to her bike once more, followed by Clare and Miriam with Caro bringing up the rear.

The sun seemed to set very rapidly and once it had disappeared behind them, the sky darkened even more rapidly. But the road appeared to run ahead of them, clearly to be seen until it disappeared into a large clump of trees on the horizon. There were distant lights from the farmhouse now, a long way off, but they dispelled the loneliness so that they all became cheerful again, calling to and fro to each other, discussing what they would eat for their supper and whose turn it was to cook. They reached the trees a few minutes later, and Stacey, still in front, called out excitedly: 'I say, look there, on the left—those lights—there must be a house!' She braked to take a better look and Clare and Miriam, who hadn't braked fast enough, went into her, joined seconds later by Caro, quite unable to stop herself in time. She ploughed into the struggling heap in front of her, felt a sharp pain in her leg and then nothing more, because she had hit her head on an old-fashioned milestone beside the cycle path.

She came to with a simply shocking headache, a strange feeling that she was in a nightmare, and the pain in her leg rather worse. What was more, she was being carried, very awkwardly too, with someone supporting her legs and her head cradled against what felt like an alpaca jacket—but men didn't wear alpaca jackets any more. She tried to say so, but the words didn't come out right and she was further mystified by a man's cockney voice close to her ear, warning someone to go easy. She wanted to say, 'My leg hurts,' but talking had become difficult and when she made her eyes open, she could see nothing much; a small strip of sky between tall trees and somewhere ahead lights shining. She gave up and passed out again, unaware that the awkward little party had reached the house, that Stacey, obedient to the cockney voice, had opened the door and held it wide while the others carried her inside. She was unaware too of the size and magnificence of the hall or of its many doors, one of which was flung open with some force by a large man with a sheaf of papers in his hand and a scowl on his handsome features. But she was brought back to consciousness by his commanding voice, demanding harshly why he was forced to suffer such a commotion in his own house.

It seemed to Caro that someone should speak up and explain, but her head was still in a muddle although she knew what she wanted to say; it was just a question of getting the words out. She embarked on an explanation, only to be abruptly halted by the harsh voice, very close to her now. 'This girl's concussed and that leg needs attention. Noakes, carry her into the surgery.' She heard his sigh. 'I suppose I must attend to it.'

Just for a moment her addled brain cleared. She said quite clearly: 'You have no need to be quite so unfeeling. Give me a needle and thread and I'll do it myself.'

She heard his crack of laughter before she went back into limbo again.

She drifted in and out of sleep several times during the night and each time she opened her eyes it was to see, rather hazily, someone sitting by her bed. He took no notice of her at all, but wrote and read and wrote again, and something about his austere look convinced her that it was the owner of the voice who had declared that she was concussed.

'I'm not concussed,' she said aloud, and was surprised that her voice sounded so wobbly.

He had got to his feet without answering her, given her a drink and said in a voice which wasn't going to take no for an answer: 'Go to sleep.'

It seemed a good idea; she closed her eyes.

The next time she woke, although the room was dim she knew that it was day, for the reading lamp by the chair was out. The man had gone and Stacey sat there, reading a book.

'Hullo,' said Caro in a much stronger voice; her head still ached and so did her leg, but she had stopped feeling dreamlike.

Stacey got up and came over to the bed. 'Caro, do you feel better? You gave us all a fright, I can tell you!'

Caro looked carefully round the room, trying not to move her head because of the pain. It was a splendid apartment, its walls hung with pale silk, its rosewood furniture shining with age and polishing. The bed she was in had a draped canopy and a silken bedspread, its beauty rather marred by the cradle beneath it, guarding her injured leg.

'What happened' she asked. 'There was a very cross man, wasn't there?'

Stacey giggled. 'Oh, ducky, you should have heard yourself! It's an enormous house and he's so good-looking you blink…'

Caroline closed her eyes. 'What happened?'

'We all fell over, and you cut your leg open on Clare's pedal—it whizzed round and gashed it badly, and you fell on to one of those milestones and knocked yourself out.'

'Are you all right? You and Clare and Miriam?'

'Absolutely, hardly a scratch between us—only you, Caro—we're ever so sorry.' She patted Caro's arm. 'I've got to tell Professor Thoe van Erckelens you're awake.'

Caro still had her eyes shut. 'What an extraordinary name…'

Her hand was picked up and her pulse taken and she opened her eyes. Stacey had gone, the man—presumably the Professor—was there, towering over her.

He grunted to himself and then asked: 'What is your name, young lady?'

'Caroline Tripp.' She watched his stern mouth twitch at the corners; possibly her name sounded as strange to him as his did to her. 'I feel better, thank you.' She added, 'It was kind of you to sit with me last night.'

He had produced an ophthalmoscope from somewhere and was fitting it together. 'I am a doctor, Miss Tripp—a doctor's duty is to his patient.'

Unanswerable, especially with her head in such a muddled state. He examined her eyes with care and silently and then spoke to someone she couldn't see. 'I should like to examine the leg, please.'

It was Stacey who turned back the coverlet and removed the cradle before unwinding the bandage which covered Caro's leg from knee to ankle.

'Did you stitch it?' asked Caro, craning her neck to see.

A firm hand restrained her. 'You would be foolish to move your head too much,' she was told. 'Yes, I have cleaned and stitched the wound in your leg. It is a deep, jagged cut and you will have to rest it for some days.'

'Oh, I can't do that,' said Caro, still not quite in control of her woolly wits, 'I'm on duty in four days' time.'

'An impossibility—you will remain here until I consider you fit to return.'

'There must be a hospital…' Her head was beginning to throb.

'As a nurse you should be aware of the importance of resting both your brain and your leg. Kindly don't argue.'

She was feeling very peculiar again, rather as though she were lying in a mist, listening to people's voices but quite unable to focus them with her tired eyes. 'You can't possibly be married,' she mumbled, 'and you sound as though you hate me—you must be a mi—mi…'

'Misogynist.'

She had her eyes shut again so that she wouldn't cry. He was being very gentle, but her leg hurt dreadfully; she was going to tell him so, but she dropped off again.

Next time she woke up it was Clare by the bed and she grinned weakly and said: 'I feel better.'

'Good. Would you like a cup of tea?—it's real strong tea, like we make at Oliver's.'

It tasted lovely; drinking it, Caroline began to feel that everything was normal again. 'There's some very thin bread and butter,' suggested Clare. Caro devoured that too; she had barely swallowed the last morsel before she was asleep again.

It was late afternoon when she woke again. The lamp was already lighted and the Professor was sitting beside it, writing. 'Don't you have any patients?' asked Caroline.

He glanced up from his writing. 'Yes. Would you like a drink?'

She had seen the tray with a glass and jug on it, on

the table by her bed. 'Yes, please—I can help myself; I'm feeling fine.'

He took no notice at all but got up, put an arm behind her shoulders, lifted her very gently and held the glass for her. When she had finished he laid her down again and said: 'You may have your friends in for ten minutes,' and stalked quietly out of the room.

They crept in very silently and stood in a row at the foot of the bed, looking at her. 'You're better,' said Miriam, 'the Professor says so.' And then: 'We're going back tomorrow morning.'

Caro tried to sit up and was instantly thrust gently back on to her pillow. 'You can't—you can't leave me here! He doesn't like me—why can't I go to hospital if I've got to stay? How are you going?'

'Noakes—that's the sort of butler who was at the gate when we fell over—he's to drive us to the Hoek. The bikes are to be sent back later.'

'He's quite nice,' said Clare, 'the Professor, I mean—he's a bit terse but he's been a perfect host. I don't think he likes us much but then of course, he's quite old, quite forty, I should think; he's always reading or writing and he's away a lot—Noakes says he's a very important man in his profession.' She giggled, 'You can hardly hear that he's Dutch, his English is so good, and isn't it funny that Noakes comes from Paddington? but he's been here for years and years—he's married to the cook. There's a housekeeper too, very tall and looks severe but she's not.'

'And three maids besides a gardener,' chimed in Miriam. 'He must be awfully rich.'

'You'll be OK,' Stacey assured her, 'you'll be back in no time. Do you want us to do anything for you?'

Caro's head was aching again. 'Would you ask Mrs Hodge to go on feeding Waterloo until I get back? There's some money in my purse—will you take some so that she can get his food?'

'OK—we'll go round to your place and make sure he's all right. Do you have to pay Mrs Hodge any rent?'

'No, I pay in advance each month. Is there enough money for me to get back by boat?'

Stacey counted. 'Yes—it's only a single fare and I expect Noakes will take you to the boat.' She came a bit nearer. 'Well, 'bye for now, Caro. We hate leaving you, but there's nothing we can do about it.'

Caro managed a smile. 'I'll be fine—I'll let you know when I'm coming.'

They all shook hands with her rather solemnly. 'We're going quite early and the Professor said we weren't to disturb you in the morning.'

Caroline lay quietly after they had gone, too tired to feel much. Indeed, when the Professor came in later and gave her a sedative she made no demur but drank it down meekly and closed her eyes at once. It must have been quite strong because she was asleep at once, although he stayed for some time, sitting in his chair watching her, for once neither reading nor writing.

She didn't wake until quite late in the morning, to find Noakes's wife—Marta—standing by the bed with a small tray. There was tea again and paper-thin bread and butter and scrambled egg which she fed Caro with just as though she were a baby. She spoke a little English too, and Caro made out that her friends had gone.

When Marta had gone away, she lay and thought about it; she felt much more clear-headed now, almost herself, but not quite, otherwise she would never have conceived the idea of getting up, getting dressed, and leaving the house. She couldn't stay where she wasn't welcome—it was like her uncle all over again. Perhaps, she thought miserably, there was something about her that made her unacceptable as a guest. She was on the plain side, that she already knew, and perhaps because of that she was self-effacing and inclined to be shy. She had quickly learned not to draw attention to herself, but on the other hand she had plenty of spirit and a natural friendliness which had made her a great number of friends. But the Professor, she felt, was not one of their number.

The more she thought of her scheme, the more she liked it; the fact that she had a considerable fever made it seem both feasible and sensible, although it was neither. She began, very cautiously, to sit up. Her head ached worse than ever, but she ignored that and concentrated on moving her injured leg. It hurt a good deal more than she had expected, but she persevered until she was sitting untidily on the edge of the bed, her sound foot on the ground, its stricken fellow on its edge. It had hurt before; now, when she started to dangle it over the side of the bed, the pain brought great waves of nausea sweeping over her.

'Oh, God!' said Caro despairingly, and meant it.

'Perhaps I will do?' The Professor had come softly into the room, taking great strides to reach her.

'I'm going to be sick,' moaned Caro, and was, making a mess of his beautifully polished shoes. If she hadn't felt so ill she would have died of shame, as it was she burst into tears, sobbing and sniffing and gulping.

The Professor said nothing at all but picked her up and laid her back in bed again, pulling the covers over her and arranging the cradle just so over her injured leg before getting a sponge and towel from the adjoining bathroom and wiping her face for her. She looked at him round the sponge and mumbled: 'Your shoes—your lovely shoes, I'm so s-sorry.' She gave a great gulp. 'I should have gone with the others.'

'Why were you getting out of bed?' He didn't sound angry, only interested.

'Well, I thought I could manage to dress and I've enough money, I think—I was going back to England.'

He went to the fireplace opposite the bed and pressed the brass wall bell beside it. When Noakes answered it he requested a clean pair of shoes and a tray of tea for two and waited patiently until these had been brought and Noakes, accompanied by a maid, had swiftly cleared up the mess. Only then did he say: 'And now suppose we have a little talk over our tea?'

He pulled a chair nearer the bed, handed her a cup of tea and poured one for himself. 'Let us understand each other, young lady.'

Caroline studied him over the rim of her cup. He talked like a professor, but he didn't look like one; he was enormous and she had always thought of profes-

sors as small bent gentlemen with bald heads and untidy moustaches, but Professor Thoe van Erckelens had
plenty of hair, light brown, going grey, and cut short,
and he had no need to hide his good looks behind a
moustache. Caro thought wistfully that he was exactly
the kind of man every girl hoped to meet one day and
marry; which was a pity, because he obviously wasn't
the marrying kind…

'If I might have your full attention?' enquired the
Professor. 'You are sufficiently recovered to listen to
me?'

Her head and her leg ached, but they were bearable.
She nodded.

'If you could reconcile yourself to remaining here
for another ten days, perhaps a fortnight, Miss Tripp?
I can assure you that you are in no fit condition to do
much at the moment. I shall remove the stitches from
your leg in another four days and you may then walk
a little with a stick, as from tomorrow, and provided
your headache is lessening, you may sit up for a period of time. Feel free to ask for anything you want, my
home is at your disposal. There is a library from which
Noakes will fetch a selection of books, although I advise you not to read for a few days yet, and there is
no reason why you should not sit in the garden, well
wrapped up. You will drink no alcohol, nor will you
smoke, and kindly refrain from watching television
for a further day or so; it will merely aggravate your
headache. I must ask you to excuse me from keeping
you company at any time—I am a busy man and I have
my work and my own interests. I shall of course treat

you as I would any other patient of mine and when I
consider you fit to travel, I will see that you get back
safely to your home.'

Caro had listened to this precise speech with astonishment; she hadn't met anyone who talked like that before—it was like reading the instructions on the front
of a medicine bottle. She loved the bit about no drinking or smoking; she did neither, but she wondered if
she looked the kind of girl who did. But one thing was
very clear. The Professor was offering her hospitality
but she was to keep out of his way; he didn't want his
ordered life disrupted—which was amusing really; now
if it had been Clare or Stacey or Miriam, all pretty girls
who had never lacked for men friends, that would have
been a different matter, but Caroline's own appearance
was hardly likely to cause even the smallest ripple on
the calm surface of his life.

'I'll do exactly as you say,' she told him, 'and I'll
keep out of your way—you won't know I'm here. And
thank you for being so kind.' She added: 'I'm truly
sorry about me being sick and your shoes…'

He stood up. 'Sickness is to be expected in cases
of concussion,' he told her. 'I am surprised that you, a
nurse, should not have thought of that. We must make
allowances for your cerebral condition.'

She looked at him helplessly. Underneath all that pe-
dantic talk there was a quite ordinary man; for some
reason, the professor was concealing him. After he had
gone she lay back on her pillows, suddenly sleepy, but
before she closed her eyes she decided that she would

discover what had happened to make him like that. She must make friends with Noakes...

She made splendid progress. The Professor dressed her leg the next morning and when Marta had draped her in a dressing gown several sizes too large for her, he returned to lift her into a chair by the open window, for the weather was glorious and the view from it delightful. The gardens and the house were large and full of autumn colours, and just to lie back with Marta tucking a rug over her and settling her elevenses beside her was bliss. She had been careful to say very little to the Professor while he attended to her leg; he had made one or two routine remarks about the weather and how she felt and she had answered him with polite brevity, but now he had gone and despite his silence, she felt lonely. She sipped the warm milk Marta had left for her and looked at the view. The road was just visible beyond the grounds and part of the drive which led to it from the house; presently she heard a car leaving the house and caught a glimpse of it as it flashed down the drive: an Aston Martin—a Lagonda. The Professor must have a friend who liked fast driving. Caro thought that it might be rather fun to know someone who drove an Aston Martin, and even more fun to actually ride in one.

She was to achieve both of these ambitions. The Professor came as usual the following morning after breakfast to dress her leg, but instead of going away immediately as he usually did he spoke to Juffrouw Kropp who had accompanied him and then addressed himself to Caro.

'I am taking you to the hospital in Leeuwarden this

morning. You are to have your head X-rayed. I am certain that no harm has come from your concussion, but I wish my opinion to be confirmed.'

Caro eyed him from the vast folds of her dressing gown. 'Like this?' she asked.

He raised thick arched brows. 'Why not? Juffrouw Kropp will assist you.' He had gone before she could answer him.

Juffrouw Kropp's severe face broke into a smile as the door closed. She fetched brush and comb and make-up and produced a length of ribbon from a pocket. She brushed Caro's hair despite her protests, plaited it carefully and fastened it with the ribbon, fetched a hand mirror and held it while Caro did things to her face, then fastened the dressing gown and tied it securely round Caro's small waist. Like a well-schooled actor, the Professor knocked on the door, just as though he had been given his cue, plucked Caro from the bed and carried her downstairs where Noakes stood, holding the front door wide. The Professor marched through with a muttered word and Noakes slid round him to open the door of the Aston Martin, and with no discomfort at all Caro found herself reclining on the back seat with Noakes covering her with a light rug and the Professor, to her astonishment, getting behind the wheel.

'This is your car?' she asked, too surprised to be polite.

He turned his head and gave her an unfriendly look. 'Is there any reason why it shouldn't be?' he wanted to know, coldly.

She said kindly: 'You don't need to get annoyed. It's

only that you don't look the kind of man to drive a fast car.' She added vaguely: 'A professor...'

'And no longer young,' he snapped. 'I have no interest in your opinions, Miss Tripp. May I suggest that you close your eyes and compose yourself—the journey will take fifteen minutes.'

Caroline did as she was bid, reflecting that until that very moment she hadn't realised what compelling eyes he had; slate blue and very bright. When she judged it safe, she opened her eyes again; she wasn't going to miss a second of the ride; it would be something to tell her friends when she got back. She couldn't see much of the road because the Professor took up so much of the front seat, but the telegraph poles were going past at a terrific rate; he drove fast all right and very well, and he didn't slow at all until she saw buildings on either side of them and presently he was turning off the road and stopping smoothly.

He got out without speaking and a moment later the door was opened and she was lifted out and set in a wheelchair while the Professor spoke to a youngish man in a white coat. He turned on his heel without even glancing at her and walked away, into the hospital, leaving her with the man in the white coat and a porter.

How rude he is, thought Caro, and then: poor man, he must be very unhappy.

She was wheeled briskly down a number of corridors to the X-ray department. It was a modern hospital and she admired it as they went, and after a minute or so, when the white-coated man spoke rather diffidently to her in English, showered him with a host of questions. He hadn't answered half of them by the time they reached their destination and she interrupted him to ask: 'Who are you?'

He apologised. 'I'm sorry, I have not introduced myself. Jan van Spaark—I am attached to Professor Thoe van Erckelens's team. I am to look after you while you are here.'

'A doctor?'

He nodded. 'Yes, I think you would call me a medical registrar in your country.'

The X-ray only took a short while, and in no time at all she was being wheeled back to the entrance hall, but here, to her surprise, her new friend wished her goodbye and handed her over to a nurse, who offered a hand, saying: 'Mies Hoeversma—that is my name.'

Caro shook it. 'Caroline Tripp. What happens next?'

'You are to have coffee because Professor Thoe van Erckelens is not quite ready to leave.'

She was wheeled to a small room, rather gloomy and austerely furnished used, Mies told her, as a meeting place for visiting doctors, but the coffee was hot and delicious and Mies, although her English was sketchy, was a nice girl. Caro, who had been lonely even though she hadn't admitted it to herself, enjoyed herself. She could have spent the morning there, listening to Mies describing life in a Dutch hospital and giving her a lighthearted account of her own life in London, but the door opened, just as they had gone off into whoops of mirth over something or other, and the porter reappeared, spoke to Mies and wheeled Caro rapidly away, giving her barely a moment in which to say goodbye.

'Why the hurry?' asked Caro, hurriedly shaking hands again.

'The Professor—he must not be kept waiting.' Mies was quite serious; evidently he had the same effect on the hospital staff as he had on his staff at home. Instant, quiet obedience—and yet they liked him...

Caroline puzzled over that as she was whisked carefully to the car, to be lifted in by the Professor before he got behind the wheel and drove away. Jan van Spaark had been there, with two other younger men and a Sister, the Professor had lifted his hand in grave salute as he drove away.

He seemed intent on getting home as quickly as possible, driving very fast again, and it was a few minutes before Caroline ventured in a small polite voice: 'Was it all right—my head?'

'There is no injury to the skull,' she was assured with detached politeness. 'Tomorrow I shall remove the stitches from your leg and you may walk for brief periods—with a stick, of course. You will rest each afternoon and read for no more than an hour each day.'

'Very well, Professor, I'll do as you say.' She sounded so meek that he glanced at her through his driving mirror. When she smiled at him he looked away at once.

He carried her back to her room when they reached the house and set her down in the chair made ready for her by the window. 'After lunch I will carry you downstairs to one of the sitting rooms. Are you lonely?'

His question took her by surprise. She had her mouth open to say yes and remembered just in time that he wanted none of her company.

'Not in the least, thank you,' she told him. 'I live alone in London, you know—I have a flat, close to Oliver's.'

He nodded, wished her goodbye and went away—she heard the car roar away minutes later. Not a very successful morning, she considered, although he had wanted to know if she were lonely. And she had told a fib—not only was she lonely, but the flat she had mentioned so casually was in reality a bedsitter, a poky first floor room in a dingy street... She was reminded forcibly of it now and of dear old Waterloo, stoically waiting for her to come back. She longed for the sight of his round whiskered face and the comfort of his plump furry body curled on her knee. 'I'm a real old maid,' she said out loud, and then called, 'Come in,' in a bright, cheerful voice because there was someone at the door.

It was Noakes with more coffee. 'And the Professor says if yer've got an 'eadache, miss, yer ter take one of them pills in the red box.'

'I haven't got a headache, thank you, Noakes, not so's you'd notice. Has the Professor gone again?'

'Yes, miss—Groningen this time. In great demand, 'e is.'

'Yes. It's quiet here, isn't it? Doesn't he ever have guests or family?' Noakes hesitated and she said at once: 'I'm sorry, I had no right to ask you questions about the Professor. I wasn't being nosey, though.'

'I know that, miss, and I ain't one ter gossip, specially about the Professor—'e's a good man, make no mistake, but 'e ain't a 'appy one, neither.' Caro poured a cup of coffee and waited. 'It used ter be an 'ouse full when I first come 'ere. Eighteen years ago, it were—come over on 'oliday, I did, and took a fancy ter living 'ere after I met Marta. She was already working 'ere, kitchenmaid then, that was when the Professor's ma and pa were alive. Died in a car accident, they did, and he ups and marries a couple of years after that. Gay times they were, when the young Baroness was 'ere…'

'Baroness?'

Noakes scratched his head. 'Well, miss, the Professor's a baron as well as a professor, if yer take my meaning.'

'How long ago did he marry, Noakes?' Caroline was so afraid that he would stop telling her the rest, and she did want to know.

'It was in 1966, miss, two years after his folk died. Pretty lady she was, too, very gay, 'ated 'im being a doctor, always working, she used ter say, and when 'e was 'ome, looking after the estate. She liked a gay life, I can tell you! She left 'im, miss, two years after they were married—ran away with some man or other and they both got killed in a plane crash a few months later.'

Caro had let her coffee get cold. So that was why the Professor shunned her company—he must have loved his wife very dearly. She said quietly: 'Thank you for telling me, Noakes. I'm glad he's got you and Mrs Noakes and Juffrouw Kropp to look after him.'

'That we do, miss. Shall I warm up that coffee? It must be cold.'

'It's lovely, thank you. I think I'll have a nap before lunch.'

But she didn't go to sleep, she didn't even doze. She sat thinking of the Professor; he had asked her if she were lonely, but it was he who was the truly lonely one.

CHAPTER TWO

THE PROFESSOR TOOK the stitches out of Caro's leg the
next morning and his manner towards her was such
as to discourage her from showing any of the sympathy she felt for him. He had wished her a chilly good
morning, assured her that she would feel no pain, and
proceeded about his business without more ado. Then
he had stood back and surveyed the limb, pronounced
it healing nicely, applied a pad and bandage and suggested that she might like to go downstairs.

'Well, yes, I should, very much,' said Caro, and
smiled at him, to receive an icy stare in return which
sent the colour to her cheeks. But she wasn't easily put
off. 'May I wear my clothes?' she asked him. 'This
dressing gown's borrowed from someone and I expect
they'd like it back. Besides, I'm sick of it.'

His eyebrows rose. 'It was lent in kindness,' he
pointed out.

She stammered a little. 'I didn't mean that—you
must think I'm ungrateful, but I'm not—what I meant
was it's a bit big for me and I'd like…'

He had turned away. 'You have no need to explain

yourself, Miss Tripp. I advise you not to do too much today. The wound on your leg was deep and is not yet soundly healed.' He had left her, feeling that she had made a mess of things again. And she had no sympathy for him at all, she assured herself; let him moulder into middle age with his books and his papers and his lectures!

With Marta's help she dressed in a sweater and pleated skirt and was just wondering if she was to walk downstairs on her own when Noakes arrived. He held a stout stick in one hand and offered her his arm.

'The Professor says you're to go very slowly and lean on me,' he advised her, 'and take the stairs one at a time.' He smiled at her. 'Like an old lady,' he added.

It took quite a time, but she didn't mind because it gave her time to look around her as they passed from one stair to the next. The hall was even bigger than she had remembered and the room into which she was led quite took her breath away. It was lofty and square and furnished with large comfortable chairs and sofas, its walls lined with cabinets displaying silver and china and in between these, portraits in heavy frames. There was a fire in the enormous hearth and a chair drawn up to it with a small table beside it upon which was a pile of magazines and newspapers.

'The Professor told me ter get something for yer to read, miss,' said Noakes, 'and I done me best. After lunch, if yer feels like it, I'll show yer the library.'

'Oh, Noakes, you're all so kind, and I've given you all such a lot of extra work.'

He looked astonished. 'Lor' luv yer, miss—we enjoy 'aving yer—it's quiet, like yer said.'

'Yes. Noakes, I've heard a dog barking…'

'That'll be Rex, miss. 'E's a quiet beast mostly, but 'e barks when the Professor comes in. Marta's got a little cat too.'

'Oh, has she? So have I—his name's Waterloo, and my landlady's looking after him while I'm away. It'll be nice to see him again.'

'Yes, miss. Juffrouw Kropp'll bring coffee for you.'

It was indeed quiet, sitting there by herself. Caroline leafed through the newspapers and tried to get interested in the news and then turned to the magazines. It was almost lunchtime when she heard the Professor's voice in the hall and she sat up, put a hand to her hair and then put on a cheerful face, just as though she were having the time of her life. But he didn't come into the room. She heard his voice receding and a door shutting and presently Juffrouw Kropp brought in her lunch tray, set it on the table beside her and smilingly went away again. Caro had almost finished the delicious little meal when she heard the Professor's voice again, speaking to Noakes as he crossed the hall and left the house.

She was taken to the library by a careful Noakes after lunch and settled into a chair by one of the circular tables in that vast apartment, but no sooner had he gone than she picked up her stick, eased herself out of her chair and began a tour of the bookshelves which lined the entire room. The books were in several languages and most of them learned ones, but there were a number of novels in English and a great many medical books in that language. But she rejected them all for a Dutch-English dictionary; it had occurred to her that since she was to spend several more days as the Professor's guest, she might employ her time in learning a word or two of his language. She was deep in this task, muttering away to herself when Noakes brought a tea tray, arranged it by her, and asked her if she was quite comfortable.

'Yes, Noakes, thank you—I'm teaching myself some Dutch words. But I don't think I'm pronouncing them properly.'

'I daresay not, miss. Tell yer what, when Juffrouw Kropp comes later, get 'er ter 'elp yer. She's a dab hand at it. Nasty awkward language it is—took me years ter learn.'

'But you always speak English with the Professor?'

'That's right, miss—comes as easy to 'im as his own language!'

Caroline ate her tea, feeling much happier now that she had something to do, and when Juffrouw Kropp came to light the lamps presently, she asked that lady to sit down for a minute and help her.

Caro had made a list of words, and now she tried them out on the housekeeper, mispronouncing them dreadfully, and then, because she was really interested, correcting them under her companion's guidance. It whiled away the early evening until the housekeeper had to go, leaving her with the assurance that Noakes would be along presently to help her back to her room.

But it wasn't Noakes who came in, it was the Professor, walking so quietly that she didn't look up from her work, only said: 'Noakes, Juffrouw Kropp has been such a help, only there's a word here and I can't remember...'

She looked round and stopped, because the Professor was standing quite close by, looking at her. She answered his quiet good evening cheerfully and added: 'So sorry, I expected Noakes, he's coming to help me up to my room. I'd have gone sooner if I'd known you were home.'

She fished the stick up from the floor beside her and stood up, gathering the dictionary and her pen and paper into an awkward bundle under one arm, only to have them removed immediately by the Professor.

He said stiffly: 'Will you dine with me this evening? Since you are already downstairs...'

Caroline was so surprised that she didn't answer at once, and when she did her soft voice was so hesitant that it sounded like a stammer.

'Thank you for asking me, but I won't, thank you.' She put out a hand for the dictionary and he transferred it to the other hand, out of her reach.

'Why not?' He looked annoyed and his voice was cold.

'You don't really want me,' she said frankly. 'You said that I wasn't to—to interfere with your life in any way and I said I wouldn't.' She added kindly: 'I'm very happy, thank you, I've never been so spoiled in all my life.' She held out her hand; this time he gave her the dictionary.

'Just as you wish,' he said with a politeness she found

more daunting than coldness. He took the stick from her, then took her arm and helped her out of the room and across the hall. At the bottom of the staircase he picked her up and carried her to the wide gallery above and across it to her room. At the door, he set her down and opened it for her. His 'Goodnight, Miss Tripp' was quite without expression. Caroline had no way of knowing if he was relieved that she had refused his invitation or if he was angry about it. She gave him a quiet goodnight and went through the door, to undress slowly and get ready for bed; she would have a bath and have her supper in her dressing gown by the fire.

Marta came presently to help her into the bath, turn down the bed and fuss nicely round the room, and after her came one of the maids with her supper; soup and a cheese souffle with a salad on the side and a Bavarian creme to follow. Caroline didn't think the Professor would be eating that, nor would he be drinking the home-made lemonade she was offered.

The house was very quiet when she woke the next morning and when Marta brought her her breakfast tray, she told her that Noakes had gone with the Professor to the airfield just south of the city and would bring the car back later.

'Has the Professor gone away?' asked Caroline, feeling unaccountably upset.

'To England and then to Paris—he has, how do you say? the lecture.'

'How long for?' asked Caro.

Marta shrugged her shoulders. 'I do not know—five, six days, perhaps longer.'

Which meant that when he came home again she would go almost at once—perhaps he wanted that. She ate her breakfast listlessly and then got herself up and dressed. Her leg was better, it hardly ached at all and neither did her head. She trundled downstairs slowly and went into the library again where she spent a busy morning conning more Dutch words. There didn't seem much point in it, but it was something to do.

After lunch she went into the garden. It was a chilly day with the first bite of autumn in the air and Juffrouw Kropp had fastened her into a thick woollen cape which dropped around her ankles and felt rather heavy. But she was glad of it presently when she had walked a little way through the formal gardens at the side of the house and found a seat under an arch of beech. It afforded a good view of her surroundings and she looked slowly around her. The gardens stretched away on either side of her and she supposed the meadows beyond belonged to the house too, for there was a high hedge beyond them. The house stood, of red brick, mellowed with age, its many windows gleaming in the thin sunshine; it was large with an important entrance at the top of a double flight of steps, but it was very pleasant too. She could imagine it echoing to the shouts of small children and in the winter evenings its windows would glow with light and guests would stream in to spend the evening… not, of course, in reality, she thought sadly; the Professor had turned himself into a kind of hermit, excluding everyone and everything from his life except work and books. 'I must try and make him smile,' she said out loud, and fell to wondering how she might do that.

It was the following morning, while she was talking to Noakes as he arranged the coffee tray beside her in the library, that they fell to discussing Christmas.

'Doesn't the Professor have family or friends to stay?' asked Caro.

'No, miss. Leastways, 'e 'olds an evening party—very grand affair it is too—but 'e ain't got no family, not in this country. Very quiet time it is.'

'No carols?'

Noakes shook his head. 'More's the pity—I like a nice carol, meself.'

Caro poured out her coffee. 'Noakes, why shouldn't you have them this year? There are—how many? six of you altogether, aren't there? Couldn't you teach everyone the words? I mean, they don't have to know what they mean—aren't there any Dutch carols?'

'Plenty, miss, only it ain't easy with no one ter play the piano. We'd sound a bit silly like.'

'I can play. Noakes, would it be a nice idea to learn one or two carols and sing them for the Professor at Christmas—I mean, take him by surprise?'

Noakes looked dubious. Caroline put her cup down. 'Look, Noakes, everyone loves Christmas—if you could just take him by surprise, it might make it seem more fun. Then perhaps he'd have friends to stay—or something.'

It suddenly seemed very important to her that the Professor should enjoy his Christmas, and Noakes, looking at her earnest face, found himself agreeing. 'We could 'ave a bash, miss. There's a piano in the drawing room and there's one in the servants' sitting-room.'

'Would you mind if I played it? I wouldn't want to intrude…'

'Lor' luv yer, miss, we'd be honoured.'

She went with him later that day, through the baize door at the back of the hall, down a flagstoned passage and through another door into a vast kitchen, lined with old-fashioned dressers and deep cupboards. Marta was at the kitchen table and Juffrouw Kropp was sitting in a chair by the Aga, and they looked up and smiled as she went in. Noakes guided her to a door at the end and opened it on to a very comfortably furnished room with a large table at one end, easy chairs, a TV in a corner and a piano against one wall. There was a stove half-way along the further wall and warm curtains at the windows. The Professor certainly saw to it that those who worked for him were comfortable. Caroline went over to the piano and opened it, sat down and began to play. She was by no means an accomplished pianist, but she played with feeling and real pleasure. She forgot Noakes for the moment, tinkling her way through a medley of Schubert, Mozart and Brahms until she was startled to hear him clapping and turned to see them all standing by the door watching her.

'Cor, yer play a treat, miss,' said Noakes. 'I suppose yer don't 'appen to know *Annie Get Yer Gun?*'

She knew some of it; before she had got to the end they were clapping their hands in time to the music and Noakes was singing. When she came to a stop finally, he said: 'Never mind the carols, miss, if yer'd just play now and then—something we could all sing?'

He sounded wistful, and looking round at their faces

she saw how eager they were to go on with the im-
promptu singsong. 'Of course I'll play,' she said at once.
'You can tell me what you want and I'll do my best.'
She smiled round at them all; Noakes and Marta and
Juffrouw Kropp, the three young maids and someone
she hadn't seen before, a quite old man—the gardener,
she supposed. 'Shall I play something else?' she asked.

She sat there for an hour and when she went she had
promised that she would go back the following evening.
And on the way upstairs she asked Noakes if she might
look at the piano in the drawing-room.

She stood in the doorway, staring around her. The
piano occupied a low platform built under the window
at one end, it was a grand and she longed to play upon
it; she longed to explore the room too, its panelled walls
hung with portraits, its windows draped with heavy
brocade curtains. The hearth had a vast hood above
it with what she supposed was a coat of arms carved
upon it. All very grand, but it would be like trespassing to go into the room without the Professor inviting
her to do so, and she didn't think he would be likely
to do that. She thanked a rather mystified Noakes and
went on up to her room.

Lying in bed later, she thought how nice it would be
to explore the house. She had had glimpses of it, but
there were any number of closed doors she could never
hope to have opened for her. Still, she reminded herself bracingly, she was being given the opportunity of
staying in a lovely old house and being waited on hand
and foot. Much later she heard Noakes locking up and
Rex barking. She hadn't met him yet; Noakes had told

her that he was to be kept out of her way until she was quite secure on her feet. 'Mild as milk,' he had said, 'but a bit on the big side.' Caroline had forgotten to ask what kind of dog he was. Tomorrow she would contrive to meet him; her leg was rapidly improving, indeed it hardly hurt at all, only when she was tired.

Her thoughts wandered on the verge of sleep. Would the Professor expect to be reimbursed for his trouble and his professional services, she wondered, and if so how would one set about it? Perhaps the hospital would settle with him if and when he sent a bill. He wouldn't be bothered to do that himself, she decided hazily; she had seen a serious middle-aged woman only that morning as she crossed the hall on her way to the library and Noakes had told her that it was the secretary, Mevrouw Slikker, who came daily to attend to the Professor's correspondence. Undoubtedly she would be businesslike about it. Caro nodded her sleepy head at this satisfactory solution and went to sleep.

She walked a little further the next day, following the paths around the gardens and sitting down now and again to admire her surroundings. She wondered if the Professor ever had the time to admire his own grounds and thought probably not, he was certainly never long enough in his own house to enjoy its comforts and magnificence. She wandered round to the back of the house and found a pleasing group of old buildings grouped round a courtyard, barns and stables and a garage and a shed which smelled deliciously of apples and corn. It was coming out of this interesting place that she came face to face with an Old English sheepdog. He stood almost to her waist and peered at her with a heavily eyebrowed whiskered face. 'Rex!' she cried. 'Oh, aren't you a darling!' She extended a closed fist and he sniffed at it and then put an enormous paw on each of her shoulders and reared up to peer down at her. He must have liked what he saw, for he licked her face gently, got down on to his four feet again and offered a head for scratching. They finished their walk together and wandered in through a little side door to find Noakes looking anxious.

'There you are, miss—I 'opes yer 'aven't been too far.' His elderly eyes fell upon Rex. ''E didn't frighten yer? 'E's always in the kitchen with Marta in the mornings. I'll take 'im back...'

'Oh, Noakes, please could he stay with me? He's company and ever so gentle. Is he allowed in the house?'

'Lor' yes, miss. Follows the Professor round like a shadow, 'e does. Well, I don't see no 'arm.' He beamed at her. 'There's a nice lunch for yer in the library and Juffrouw Kropp says if yer wants 'er this afternoon she's at yer disposal.'

So the day passed pleasantly enough, and the following two days were just as pleasant. Caro did a little more each day now; the Professor would be back in two days' time, Noakes had told her, and she had to be ready to leave then. She had no intention of trespassing on his kindness for an hour longer than she needed to. Of course she would have to get tickets for the journey home, but that shouldn't take long, and Noakes would help her and perhaps the Professor would allow him to drive her to the station in Leeuwarden; she had already discovered that the train went all the way to the Hoek—all she would need to do was to get from it to the boat. She had mentioned it carefully to Noakes when he had been clearing away her supper dishes, but he had shaken his head and said dubiously that it would be better to consult the Professor. "'E may not want yer to go straight away, miss,' he suggested.

'Well, I should think he would,' she told him matter-of-factly, 'for I'm quite well now and after all, he didn't invite me as a guest. He's been more than kind to let me get well here and I mustn't stay longer than absolutely necessary.'

Noakes had shaken his head and muttered to himself and then begged her to go down to the sitting-room and play for them all again—something she had done with great pleasure, for it passed the evenings very nicely. When she was on her own she found that she had an increasing tendency to think about the Professor—a pointless pastime, she told herself, and went on doing it nonetheless.

It rained the next day, so that she spent a great deal of it in the library, with Rex beside her, poring over her dictionary. She was making progress, or so she thought, with an ever-lengthening list of words which she tried out on members of the staff. All rather a waste of time, she knew that, but it passed the days and in some obscure way made the Professor a little less of a stranger. She went earlier than usual to play the piano that day, perhaps because the afternoon was unnaturally dark and perhaps because she was lonely despite Rex's company. And Noakes and his staff seemed pleased to see her, requesting this, that and the other tune, beating time and tra-la-ing away to each other. Presently, with everyone satisfied, Caroline began to play to please herself; half forgotten melodies she had enjoyed before her aunt had married again and then on to Sibelius and Grieg, not noticing how quiet everyone had become; she was halfway through a wistful little French tune when she stopped and turned round. 'Sorry, I got carried away,' she began, and saw the Professor standing in the doorway, his hands in his pockets, leaning against the door frame.

He didn't smile, indeed, he was looking coldly furious, although his icily polite: 'Pray don't stop on my account, Miss Tripp,' was uttered in a quiet voice.

Caroline stood up rather too hard on the bad leg so that she winced. 'You're angry,' she said quickly, 'and I'm sorry—I have no right to be here, but you're not to blame Noakes or anyone else—I invited myself.'

She wanted to say a great deal more, but the look of annoyance on his face stopped her. She wished everyone goodnight in her newly acquired Dutch and went past him through the door and along the passage. He caught up with her quite easily before she could reach the staircase, and she sighed soundlessly. He was going to lecture her and she might as well have it now as later; perhaps she might even get him to see that no harm had been done, indeed he might even be glad that his staff had enjoyed a pleasant hour.

She turned to face him. 'It's a pity you frown so,' she said kindly.

He looked down his splendid nose at her. 'I have very

good reason to frown, Miss Tripp, and well you know it. I return home unexpectedly and what do I find? My butler, my housekeeper, my cook, the maidservants and the gardener being entertained by you in the servants' sitting-room. Probably if I had come home even earlier I should have found you all playing gin rummy in the cellars.'

She made haste to reassure him. 'Not gin rummy—it was canasta, and we played round the kitchen table— just for half an hour,' she added helpfully. 'You see, I'm learning Dutch.'

His fine mouth curved into a sneer. 'Indeed? I cannot think why.'

Caroline said in her quiet hesitant voice: 'Well, it's something to do, you know. I'm quite well, you see.'

His voice was silky and his voice cold. 'Miss Tripp, you have disrupted my household—when one considers that I have done my best to help you and I find your behaviour intolerable.'

She stared back at him, her lip caught between her teeth, because it was beginning to tremble. After a long moment she said: 'I'm sorry, Professor.'

He turned on his heel. 'I'm glad to hear it—I hope you will mend your ways.'

He went into his study without another word and she went to her room, where she sat on her bed to review the situation. The Professor was going out to dinner that evening, she had heard Noakes say so—to one of his grand friends, she supposed, where the girls knew better than to play the piano in the servants' room and said things to make him smile instead of frown. Oh well…

she got up and went across to the tallboy where her
few possessions were housed and laid them on the bed,
fetched her duffle bag from the cupboard and began
to pack. She did it neatly and unhurriedly. There was
plenty of time; she would eat her supper alone presently,
as she always did, and when everyone had gone to the
kitchen for their own meal, she would slip away. She
would have to leave a letter. She frowned a long while
over its composition, but at length it was done, neatly
written and sealed into an envelope. She would have
to leave it somewhere where Noakes wouldn't find it at
once. The Professor's study would be the best place, he
always went straight there when he came home, shutting himself away in his own learned lonely world—for
he was lonely, Caroline was sure of that.

She finished her packing and went down to her
supper which this evening had been set in the dining
room, a richly sombre place. She felt quite lost sitting
at the great oval table surrounded by all the massive
furniture, but she made a good meal, partly to please
Noakes and partly because she wasn't sure when she
would have the next one. And Noakes was uneasy, although the Professor, he assured her, hadn't been in
the least angry—indeed, he had hardly mentioned the
matter. Noakes hoped—they all hoped—that tomorrow she would play for them again, but first he would
ascertain if the Professor objected to her visiting the
servants' sitting-room.

Caroline made some cheerful reply, finished her
meal, mentioned that she would go to bed early and
went upstairs. When she crept down half an hour later

there was no sound. Everyone was in the kitchens by now and she wouldn't be missed, probably not until the morning, or at least until the Professor came home, and that would be late. She had put on her anorak, counted her money carefully and carried her bag downstairs before going to the study and putting the letter on the Professor's desk. She paused in the doorway for a last look; his desk was an orderly clutter of papers and books and his chair was pushed to one side as though he had got up in a hurry. She sighed deeply, closed the door gently, picked up the duffle bag and went to the door. Her leg was aching a little and she had bandaged it firmly because as far as she knew she would have to walk quite a distance before she could get a bus—the nearest village wasn't too far away, she had found that out from Juffrouw Kropp. If there wasn't a bus she would have to thumb a lift.

She put out a reluctant hand and opened the door. It was heavy, but it swung back on well-oiled hinges, revealing the Professor, key in hand, about to open it from outside. Caro, taken completely by surprise, stood with her mouth open, gaping at him. He, on the other hand, evinced no surprise, nor did he speak, merely took her duffle bag from her, put a large hand on her chest and pushed her very gently back into the house, and then just as gently shut the door behind him. Only then did he ask: 'And where were you going, Caroline?'

'Home—well, the hospital, actually.' He had never called her Caroline before—no one called her that, but it sounded rather nice.

'Why?' He stood blocking her path, the duffle bag on the floor beside him.

It seemed silly to have to explain something to him which he already knew all about. 'I've upset your household: I can quite see that I've been a perfect nuisance to you. I'm very grateful for all you've done for me—and your kindness—but I'm quite able to go back now and... Well, thank you again.'

His harsh laugh made her jump. Quite forgetting to be meek, she said severely: 'And there's no need to laugh when someone thanks you!'

'It strikes me as ironic that you should express gratitude for something you haven't had. I cannot remember being kind to you—I merely did what any other person would have done in similar circumstances, and with the minimum of trouble to myself. If I had been a poor man with a wife and children to care for and had offered you help and shelter at the cost of my and their comfort, that would have been quite a different kettle of fish. As it is, I must confess that I have frequently forgotten that you were in the house.'

Caro didn't speak. A kind of despair had rendered her dumb; her head was full of a mixed bag of thoughts, most of them miserable.

He put out a hand and touched her cheek awkwardly. 'Have you been lonely?'

Living in a bedsitter had taught her not to be lonely. She shook her head, still feeling the touch of his finger.

'And you will be glad to get back—to your flat and your friends. I doubt if you will be allowed to work for a little while.'

She had found her voice at last. It came out in a defiant mutter: 'I shall be awfully glad to get back.'

The gentleness had gone out of his voice; it sounded cold and distant again, just as though he didn't care what she did. 'Yes—I see. But be good enough to wait until the morning. I will arrange a passage for you on the night ferry tomorrow and Noakes shall drive you to the Hoek and see you on board.'

Caroline said stiffly: 'Thank you.'

'You have sufficient money?'

She nodded dumbly.

'Then go to bed.' His eye had caught her bandaged leg. 'Your leg is worse?'

'No. I—I put a crepe bandage on it because I thought I might have to walk for a bit.'

He stared at her without expression, then: 'Come to the study and I will take a look and if necessary re-bandage it.'

He prodded and poked with gentle fingers, dressed it lightly and said: 'That should see you safely to Oliver's—get it looked at as soon as you can. It will do better without a dressing.' He held the study door open and offered a hand. 'Goodbye, Caroline.'

His hand was cool and firm and she didn't want to let it go.

'Goodbye, Professor. I shall always be grateful to you—and I'm sorry that I—I disturbed your peace and quiet.'

Just for a moment she thought he was going to say something, but he didn't.

CHAPTER THREE

CARO ARRIVED BACK at Meadow Road during the morning and the moment she opened the door of number twenty-six, Mrs Hodge bounced out of her basement flat, avid for a good gossip.

'Your friends came,' she said without preamble, 'said you had a bad cut leg and concussion; nasty thing concussion; you could 'ave died.' She eyed Caro's leg with relish and then looked disappointed, and Caro said almost apologetically:

'I don't need a bandage any more. Thank you for looking after Waterloo, Mrs Hodge.'

'No trouble.' Mrs Hodge, a woman who throve on other people's troubles, felt her sympathy had been wasted. 'Your rent's due on Monday.'

Caro edged past her with the duffle bag. 'Yes, I know, Mrs Hodge. I'll just see to Waterloo and unpack and then go back to the hospital and see when I'm to go back.'

She went up the stairs and unlocked the door at the back of the landing. Not one of Mrs Hodge's best rooms, but it was quieter because it overlooked back yards and there was a tiny balcony which was nice for Waterloo.

He came to meet her now and she picked him up and laid him on her shoulder while he purred in her ear, delighted to have her back. Caroline sat down on the divan which did duty as a bed at night and looked around her.

The room was small and rather dark and seemed even more so after the Professor's spacious home; she had done the best she could with pretty curtains and cushions and a patchwork cover for the divan, but nothing could quite disguise the cheap furniture or the sink in one corner with the tiny gas cooker beside it. Caro, not given to being sorry for herself, felt a lump in her throat; it was all such a cruel contrast... She missed them all, the Professor, even though he didn't like her, Noakes and Marta, Juffrouw Kropp... She had been utterly spoilt, waited on hand and foot, and she, who had never been spoilt, had loved it. Right up until the moment she had gone on board, too, with Noakes seeing to her bag and getting her magazines to read and having a word with someone or other so that she had a super cabin to herself and a delicious meal before she had gone to bed. She had tried to pay him, but he had said very firmly that the Professor would deal with that later. Caroline had hoped that although he had said goodbye to her, she would have seen the Professor again before she left, but he had left the house after breakfast and wasn't back when she went away, with the entire staff gathered at the door to see her off.

She roused herself, gave Waterloo a saucer of milk and put on the kettle; a cup of tea would cheer her up and when she had drunk it she would unpack, dust and tidy her room and go round to Oliver's, and on the way back she would buy a few flowers to brighten up the place.

In the office at Oliver's, standing in front of Miss Veron's desk, she was astonished to hear from that lady that the Professor had written a letter about her, suggesting in the politest manner possible that she should have a few days' sick leave before she resumed work on the wards.

'A good idea, Staff Nurse,' said Miss Veron kindly. 'I expect you would like to go home or visit friends— suppose you report for duty in five days' time? You'll go back to Women's Surgical, of course. I'm sure Sister will be glad to see you.'

Caro thanked her and walked slowly back through the busy streets to Meadow Road, stopping on the way to do some shopping and indulge in the extravagance of a bunch of flowers. She would have been glad to have gone straight back to work, for she had no family and although she had a number of friends, to invite herself to go and stay with them was something she had never even dreamed of. So she spent the next four days giving her room an extra clean, reading the books she fetched from the library and talking to Waterloo. She hadn't let anyone at the hospital know that she was back; they would have been round like a flash with offers to go to the cinema, invitations to go out to a meal—morning coffee. But most of them had boyfriends or family and she shrank from being pitied; only a few of her closest friends knew that she had no family and that she hated to talk about it. Actually she need not have worried about being pitied, for she turned a bright face to the world; those who didn't know her well considered her a self-sufficient girl bent on a career, and her close friends took care never to mention it.

She went back on duty on the fifth morning, but she didn't see her friends until the coffee break when they all met in the canteen. The precious fifteen minutes was spent in answering questions; Clare, Stacey and Miriam were all there, wanting to know how she had got on, whether her leg was quite better, whether she had enjoyed herself, whether the Professor had entertained her...

'Well, not to say entertain,' observed Caro. 'He was very kind to me and saw to my leg and took me to be X-rayed at the hospital in Leeuwarden. I—I kept out of his way as much as I could—I mean, he is an important man, Noakes says, and had very little leisure.'

'I could go for him,' said Stacey. 'A bit old, perhaps, but very elegant and a man of the world, if you know what I mean, if only he'd come out from his books and lectures. He must have been crossed in love!'

Caro didn't say anything. She wasn't going to tell them about his wife; it was all a long time ago and besides, it had been a confidence on Noakes's part. She shuddered, imagining the Professor's cold rage if he ever discovered that she knew about his past unhappiness, and Miriam, noticing it, asked: 'What's worrying you, Caro? Is the ward busy?'

Caro was glad to change the subject and talked about

something which lasted them until it was time to return to their wards.

Women's Surgical was busy all right; what with Sir Eustace Jenkins's round, a twice-weekly event which was stage-managed as carefully as any royal procession; yesterday's operations cases still attached to drips and tubes and underwater pumps and needing constant care and attention, and over and above these, the normal ward routine of dressings and escorting to X-Ray, Physiotherapy and the usual thundering round looking for notes and Path. Lab. forms which somehow always got mislaid on round days. Caro, hovering at Sister's elbow, ready to interpret that lady's raised eyebrow, shake of the head, or lifted finger and smooth her path to the best of her ability, was quite glad when it was dinner time. She left Sister to serve the puddings and went down to the first meal, queuing for her portion of steamed cod, mashed potato, and butter beans, and devouring it with the rest of her friends at speed so that there would be time to go over to the home and make a pot of tea.

She had more tea presently in Sister's office, having been bidden there to be told that Sister would be going on holiday in a week's time and Caro would be taking over the ward. 'Just for two weeks,' Sister Pringle smiled a little. 'Good practice for you, Caro—you're in the running for my job. I'm leaving to get married in a few months' time and they're keen to get someone who's likely to stay for a few years. After all, I've been here for eight years—they wanted me to stay on, but I've had enough of being a career girl. I'll make way for you.'

Caro, not sure if this was a compliment or an admission that she was unlikely to get married, thanked her superior nicely and hoped that she would be adequate while left in charge.

'Well, I can't see why not—Sir Eustace likes you and you have a nice way with the student nurses. There are some heavy cases coming in, though, and it'll be take-in week...'

Caro bowed her head obediently over the notes Sister had before her. She wouldn't mind being busy, if she kept her thoughts occupied sufficiently she didn't have time to think about the Professor—a bad habit she had got into, and one which she must conquer even if only for her own peace of mind.

But she continued to think about him a great deal, picturing him alone in that great house, leading a hermit's life. It was a pity, she told Waterloo that evening as she cooked their supper, that he couldn't find some beautiful girl, exactly suited to him, and fall in love with her and get married. No sooner had she thought that than she left the sausages in the pan to fry themselves to a crisp because following hard on its heels was the second thought—that there was nothing in the world she would like more than to be that girl. Only she wasn't beautiful and she certainly wasn't suited to him; she had annoyed him excessively and he must have been delighted to see the back of her.

She sat down on the divan with Waterloo tucked under one arm. On the other hand, if she were given the chance, she would make him happy because that, she knew all at once, was what she wanted to do more than anything else in the world. She gave a watery chuckle. A more ill-suited pair than herself and the Professor would be hard to find, and why, oh, why had she fallen in love with him? Why couldn't it have been someone she might have stood a faint chance of attracting: someone insignificant and uninteresting and used to living on not much money, just sufficiently ambitious to wish to buy his own semi-detached in a suburb and keep his job, recognising in her a kindred spirit.

Only she wasn't a kindred spirit. She hated her narrow life, she wanted to be free; she wasn't sure what she wanted to do, but certainly it wasn't to be tied to a man who didn't look higher than a safe job.

She went on sitting there, oblivious of the sausages and Waterloo's voice reminding her about his supper, lost in a happy daydream where she was beautiful, well dressed and the apple of the Professor's eye. A changed Professor, of course, enjoying the pleasure of life as well as his work, discussing his day with her, planning it so that he could see as much of her as possible— wanting to be with her every minute of his leisure. She would play to him on that beautiful piano in his grand drawing-room, in a pink organza dress, and when he came into his house each evening she would meet him in the hall with their beautiful children around her. It was all absurd and impossible and very real in her mind's eye: if it hadn't been for the smell of burning sausages it might have gone on for hours. As it was, she came back to reality, removed the charred bits from the pan, opened a can of beans, fed Waterloo and made tea before going round to the local library to change her books. She came back with Fodor's Guide to the Netherlands and then spent the evening reading about Friesland, with the Professor's handsome severe features superimposed on every page.

Sister departed a week later, thankfully handing over the ward keys to Caroline with the heartfelt wish that she would be able to manage. 'Not that you're not capable,' said Sister, 'but it's take-in tomorrow.' She added happily: 'We shall be on Majorca—and in swimsuits— can you imagine it? In November, too.'

But there was no time to be envious of Sister Pringle. Take-in weeks were always busy, and this particular one was worse than usual. Several young women were admitted with black eyes, broken noses, cracked bones and severe contusions after taking part in a demonstration march about something or other and falling foul of a rival faction on the way. These had been followed by two victims of a gas explosion in one of the small terraced houses close to the hospital, and no sooner were they settled in their beds than an old lady who had fallen over in the street and cut her head was admitted for observation. Caro found her hands full and they remained like that for most of the week. She sighed with relief when she went off duty on the seventh day. After midnight they would have comparative peace on the ward; she would catch up with the paperwork, see to the off-duty and have time to chat to each of the patients as she took round the post—and the nurses should be able to catch up on their off-duty.

She rose from her bed at the beginning of the second week of Sister's absence in the pleasant expectation of an uneventful week.

And so it was for the first few hours. The nurses, happy in the knowledge that there would be no urgent call to ready a bed for yet another emergency, began on the morning's routine with a good will and Caro, having fulfilled her ambition to have a nice long chat with each patient in turn, organised the day's tasks, made a sortie to the X-ray department with the firm determination to discover the whereabouts of a number of missing films, and answered the telephone at least a dozen times, before she settled herself in the office to puzzle out the off-duty for the following two weeks. She was halfway through this tedious task when there was a knock on the door and before she could say anything, it was opened and Professor Thoe van Erckelens stalked in.

Caroline didn't speak, she was too surprised—and besides, after the first second or two, her heart raced so violently that she had no breath. She just sat where she was and stared at him with huge hazel eyes.

'Ha,' observed the Professor, 'you are surprised to see me.'

He looked ill-tempered, tired too. It was an awful waste of one's life to love a man who didn't care a row of pins for one. She took a steadying breath and said in her quiet voice: 'Yes, Professor, I am. I expect you have a consultation here? Shall I…?'

He came right into the office and shut the door. 'No, I came to see you.'

She opened her eyes and her mouth too. 'Whatever for?' She went on earnestly: 'I can't really spare the time unless you wanted to see a patient—there's Mrs Possett's dressing and two patients to go for X-ray.'

He dismissed Mrs Possett with a wave of his hand. 'What I have to say will take five minutes—less.'

Caroline folded her small, nicely cared for hands in her lap and gave him her full attention. He didn't move from the door. 'Will you marry me, Caroline?'

She stayed very still. After a moment she asked: 'Me? Is this a joke or something, Professor?'

'No, and if you will be good enough to give me your full attention and not interrupt I will explain.'

She glanced around her just to make sure that she wasn't dreaming. The office was much as usual, its desk an orderly muddle of forms and charts and papers, chilly, foggy air coming in through the open window, the radiator as usual gurgling gently into tepid warmth. The only difference was the Professor, taking up most of the available space and apparently suffering from a brainstorm. She said in a tranquil voice which quite masked her bewilderment: 'I'm listening,' and made herself look at him. She was rewarded by a forbidding stare.

'I'm forty,' he told her almost angrily. 'I have been married before—thirteen years ago, to be precise. My wife left me for another man within two years of our marriage and she—both of them—were killed in an accident a year later. I have had no wish to marry again.'

He shrugged huge shoulders, 'Why should I? I have my work, enough money, a well run home and there are always girls—pretty girls if I should wish for female company.'

He paused to study her and she flinched because no doubt he was comparing her homely face with the young ladies in question. 'However, after you had left my house I missed you—my household miss you. They have worn gloomy faces ever since you left—quite ridiculous, of course—even Rex and the cats...' He paused again, searching her quiet face as though he were trying to discover what there was about her that could disrupt his organised life. Presently he went on. 'You are an extraordinary girl,' he declared irritably, 'you have no looks, no witty conversation, quite deplorable clothes—and yet I find that I am able to talk to you—indeed, I find myself wishing to discuss the various happenings of my day with you. I am not in love with you and I have no wish to be; I need a calm quiet companion, someone sensible who isn't for ever wanting to be taken out to dinner or the theatre, nor demand to know where I am going each time I leave the house. I need... I need...'

'A sheet anchor,' supplied Caro in a sensible voice. 'No demands, no curiosity, just a—someone to talk to when you feel inclined.'

He looked surprised. 'You understand then; I have no need to explain myself further. And above all, no romantic nonsense!' He gave her a bleak look which wrung her soft heart. 'You will have a pleasant life; the servants are already devoted to you and you will have my friends and sufficient money. And in return I ask for companionship when I need it, someone to sit at my table and play hostess to my guests and run my home as I like it. Well?'

Caro studied his face. He meant every preposterous word of it and he expected her to say yes then and there. I must change him just a little, she thought lovingly, he must be got out of his lonely arrogant world and learn to enjoy himself again—he must have been happy once. Aloud she said in a tranquil voice: 'I must have time to think about it.'

'Time? Why should you need time? You have no family.' He looked deliberately round the little room. 'And nothing but a hard-working future.'

Here was another one who took it for granted that no one wanted to marry her. 'You make it sound like a bribe,' she told him.

His mouth was a straight bad-tempered line. 'Nothing of the sort. I have offered you marriage. I hope that I am not such a hypocrite that I pretend affection for you—liking, yes; you annoy me excessively at times and yet I must admit that I like you. Well?'

She smiled a little. 'I'll tell you tomorrow. I must sleep on it.'

'Oh, very well, if you want it that way. I thought you were a sensible girl.'

'I am, that's why I have to think about it.'

There was a knock on the door and he opened it, glaring at the student nurse standing outside so that she sidled past him uneasily.

'It's all right, Nurse,' said Caro soothingly. 'What's the matter?'

'Mrs Skipton's dressing's down ready for you to see, Staff.'

'I'm coming now,' she smiled reassuringly, and the nurse retreated, casting an interested eye upon the Professor as she went—a remarkably handsome man even though he looked as black as a thundercloud.

He closed the door with a snap behind her and then stood in front of it so that although Caro had got to her feet she was forced to a halt before him. 'I do have to go,' she told him mildly.

He opened the door. 'I'll see you tomorrow, Caroline.'

She walked past him into the ward, looking as serene as she always did while her insides turned somersaults. The nurse who had been to the office rolled her eyes upwards and shrugged her shoulders for the benefit of the junior nurse with her. 'Poor old Staff,' she murmured, 'as prim as a maiden aunt even with that gorgeous man actually talking to her!'

'I'll have the forceps, Nurse,' said Caro briskly. She had seen the look and rightly guessed at the murmur. It would be fun, she mused as she deftly removed the rubber drain from Mrs Skipton's shrinking person, to see the girl's face when she announced her engagement to the Professor.

Because she was going to marry him, she had no doubts about that, and not for any of the reasons he had given her, either. He hadn't even thought of the only reason which mattered—that she loved him.

It was typical of the Professor not to mention when and where he would see her on the following day. Caroline spent the whole of it in a state of pleasurable excitement, one ear cocked for the telephone, and her eyes sliding to the ward door every time it opened. In the end she went off duty after tea, telling herself that he had forgotten all about her, thought better of it, or what seemed more likely, she had dreamed the whole thing. She explained this to Waterloo at some length as she gave him his supper and then went to peer into the cupboard and see what she could cook for her own meal. A tin of soup, she decided, and then a poached egg on toast with a pot of tea. And while she had it she would finish that interesting bit in Fodor's Guide about Friesland having its own national anthem. She knelt to light the gas fire, but before she could strike a match there was a knock on the door. Her heart shot into her mouth, but she ignored it; the Professor had no idea where she lived and she hoped and prayed that he never would. It would be her landlady, she supposed, and went to open the door.

She had supposed wrong. It was the Professor, looming large on the narrow landing. The sheer size of him forced her to retreat a few steps so that he was inside before she could say a word. He stood looking around him unhurriedly and asked: 'This is your flat?'

'Good evening,' said Caro, and didn't answer him.

He turned his eyes on to her then. 'I've annoyed you—probably you didn't wish me to know that you lived in a bedsitter in this truly deplorable neighbourhood.'

'It's convenient for Oliver's.' She added indignantly: 'It's my home.'

His eyes lighted on Waterloo, waiting impatiently for the fire to be lighted. 'Your cat?'

'Yes—Waterloo. I found him there when he was a kitten.'

'He will of course return with us to Huis Thoe.'

She had scrambled to her feet. 'But I haven't said I'd…marry you.'

'Perhaps we might go somewhere and have dinner and discuss it.'

She stared at him, wondering if there was another girl in the world who had had such a dry-as-dust proposal. Her first inclination was to refuse, but she was hungry and soup and an egg weren't exactly gastronomic excitements. 'I'll have to change,' she said.

'I will wait on the landing.' He opened the door and a strong aroma of frying onions caused his winged nostrils to flare. He didn't speak, only gave her an eloquent look as he closed it quietly.

There wasn't much choice in the rickety wardrobe, but the few clothes she had were presentable although the Professor had called them deplorable. How would he know anyway, leading the life he did? Caroline put on a plain wool dress of dark green, combed her hair, did things to her face, found her good wool coat, her best shoes, her only decent handbag, gave Waterloo a saucer of food and assured him that she wouldn't be long, and left the room. The Professor was standing quietly, but giving the impression of an impatient man holding his impatience in check with a great effort, and she could hardly blame him; the smell of onions had got considerably worse.

They went down the narrow stairs and out into the street where he took her by the arm and hurried her on to the opposite pavement. 'The car is at Oliver's,' and at her quick questioning glance, 'and if you are wondering why I didn't go and fetch it while you were changing I will admit to a fear that if I did so you might have changed your mind and disappeared by the time I had got back.'

Caroline paused to stare up at him in the dusk. 'Well, really—is that your opinion of me? I would never dream of…'

'I am aware of that; it was merely a remarkably silly notion which entered my head.'

He wasn't going to say any more than that. They walked the short distance in silence and he opened the door of the Aston Martin for her. Settling himself beside her, he remarked: 'I've booked a table at the Savoy Grill Room.'

'Oh, no!' exclaimed Caro involuntarily. 'I'm not dressed…'

'The Grill Room,' he reminded her, and glanced sideways at her. 'You look all right to me.'

She had the idea that he hadn't the vaguest notion of what she was wearing; probably he never would have, for he never really looked at her for more than a few seconds at a time. If it came to that, very few did.

The Grill Room was full and she felt shy of her surroundings as they went in, but they were shown at once to their table and although she would have preferred one in a quiet corner where she could have been quite unnoticed, nothing could have bettered the attention they received.

She sipped at the sherry she had been given and studied the menu, mouthwateringly lengthy; she settled for salmon mousse, tournedos, sautéed straw potatoes and braised celery, and when it came ate it with appetite, replying politely to her companion's desultory conversation as he demolished a grilled steak. She enjoyed the Beaujolais he offered her too, but prudently refused a second glass, which was just as well, for the sherry trifle was deliciously rich. It was when the waiter had cleared the table and set coffee before them that the Professor abandoned his dinner table conversation and asked abruptly: 'Well, you've slept on it, Caroline, and now I should like your answer. Is it yes or no?'

She handed him his coffee cup without haste. He had asked a plain question, he was going to get a plain answer. 'Yes.'

She watched his face as she spoke and found it rather daunting to see his calm expression quite unchanged. 'Very well, we can now make plans for our marriage. As soon as possible, don't you think?'

'Very well, but I have to give in my resignation at Oliver's, Prof… What am I to call you?'

He smiled a little. 'Radinck. If you have no objection, I can arrange that you leave very shortly. We can be married here by special licence. Do you wish to invite anyone? Family? Friends?'

'I have an aunt—no one else—she's married now and I don't think she will want to come to the wedding.

I expect some of my friends from the hospital would like to come to the church.'

'I'll see about it and let you know. Have you sufficient money to buy yourself some clothes?'

Caroline thought of her little nest egg, hoarded against a rainy day. 'Yes, thank you.'

He nodded. 'You can of course buy anything you want when we return, but I presume you will want something for the wedding.' His voice held a faint sneer.

'I won't disgrace you,' she told him quietly, and was pleased to see him look a little taken aback. If she hadn't loved him so much she would have been furious.

He begged her pardon stiffly and she said kindly: 'Oh, that's all right—it'll be super to have some decent clothes.' She wrinkled her forehead in thought. 'Something I can travel in and wear afterwards...'

He passed his cup for more coffee. 'Perhaps I should point out to you that you can buy all the clothes you want when you are my wife. I—we shall live comfortably enough.' He sat back in his chair. 'Now as to the actual wedding...'

He had thought of everything; the arrangements for her to leave, the obtaining of the marriage licence, giving up her bedsitter, a basket for Waterloo's comfortable transport to Holland. There would be no honeymoon, he told her, and that didn't surprise her at all, honeymoons were for two people in love, but she was surprised when he said: 'We will go tomorrow and buy the wedding rings and I will give you your engagement ring—I brought it over with me but forgot to bring it with me this evening.'

She didn't know whether to laugh or cry at that.

Radinck took her back to Meadow Road presently, waiting at her front door while she climbed the stairs and unlocked her own door. His goodnight had been casual and, to her ear, faintly impatient. Probably he found her boring company, but in that case why did he want to marry her? Probably he was tired. She got ready for bed, made a pot of tea because she was too excited to sleep and sat in front of the gas fire with Waterloo beside her, politely listening while she recounted the evening's happenings to him.

She was off in the evening again the next day and she supposed Radinck would meet her then; certainly there was no time to go buying wedding rings during the day—but apparently he thought differently.

Caroline had got well into the morning's routine when he came on to the ward with Sir Eustace, and Caro, hastily pulling down her sleeves, went down the ward to meet them, wondering which patient they wanted to see.

They wished her good morning and Sir Eustace said jovially: 'Well, Staff Nurse, I am delighted at the news that you are to marry. I haven't come to do a round, only to beg the pleasure of giving you away.'

Caro pinkened. 'Oh, would you? Would you really? I did wonder… I haven't got any relations…'

'I shall be delighted—Radinck will let me know the day when you've decided it.' He beamed at her. 'And now I must go to theatre—I'm already late.'

She escorted him to the door and went back to the Professor, who hadn't said a word after his good morning and in answer to her look of enquiry he observed: 'It is rather public here, perhaps we might go to the office for a minute.'

She led the way, offered him a seat which he declined and sat down at the desk. 'I will be outside at twelve o'clock,' he told her. 'You will go to your dinner then, I believe? We can go along to Apsleys and get the rings and have a quick lunch somewhere.'

'But I'll be in uniform—there's only an hour, you know—there'll never be time... I don't mind missing lunch.'

'Put a coat over your uniform. I'll see that you get back on duty on time.' He took a small box out of a pocket. 'This was my mother's—she had small hands, like yours, and I hope it will fit.'

He opened the box and took out a great sapphire ring set in a circle of rose diamonds and when she held out her hand, slipped it on to her finger. It fitted exactly. Caro, who was inclined to be superstitious, thought it was a good omen.

She thanked him for it and longed to throw her arms round him and kiss him, but instead she said: 'It's very beautiful: I'll take great care of it.'

He nodded carelessly. 'You will wish to get on with your work—I'll meet you at noon.'

He had gone before she could do more than nod.

It wasn't entirely satisfactory going out in her winter coat which was brown and didn't match her black duty shoes and stockings. She had made her hair tidy and powdered her nose, but rushing down to the front door of the hospital she thought crossly that all the girls she knew would have refused flatly to go out looking so ridiculous; but there again, she reminded herself, Radinck considered she dressed deplorably anyway; he wouldn't notice.

If he did he said nothing, merely stowed her in the car and drove smoothly to Apsleys where they must have expected him, for they were attended to immediately by a quiet-voiced elderly man, who said very little as he displayed rings of every variety before them.

The Professor gave them a cursory glance. 'Choose which you prefer, Caroline,' he suggested. He sounded bored, and just for a moment resentment at his lack of interest at what should be an important event to them both almost choked her, but her common sense came to her rescue; why should he be interested? Buying the ring was to him only a necessary part of getting married. She picked a perfectly plain gold one and the man measured her finger and found her one to fit it before doing the same for the Professor. While he was away wrapping them up, Radinck said quietly: 'You aren't wearing your ring.'

'It's in the box in my pocket. I haven't had a chance—I mean, I can't wear it on duty and I forgot to wear it now—I'm not used to it yet.'

'Will you put it on?'

She did so, and when the man came back he saw it and smiled nicely at her. It made her feel much better and almost happy.

It hadn't taken much time: there was more than half an hour before she had to return to the ward, but when the Professor turned the car back in the direction of Oliver's she supposed that he had decided that there wasn't time for even a snack lunch and in all fairness she had said that she wouldn't mind missing her lunch. But in Cheapside he slowed the car, parked it and walked her into Le Poulbot where it seemed they were expected.

'I took the liberty of ordering for you since we have only a short time,' observed Radinck, 'filets de sole Leonora and a glass of white wine to go with it, and perhaps a sorbet.'

She was surprised at his thoughtfulness and stammered her thanks. 'But it means you have to rush over lunch too,' she pointed out.

'I'm not in the habit of sitting over my meals,' he observed. 'When one is by oneself it is a waste of time— one gets into bad habits...'

Caroline resolved silently to get him out of them even if it took her a lifetime and took care not to chat while they ate. Actually she longed to talk; there was so much she wanted to know, but she would have to wait: when he had made all the arrangements he would doubtless tell her. She was surprised when he asked: 'Which day do you wish to choose for the wedding?'

She said with some asperity: 'Well, how can I choose until I know when I'm to leave and when you want to go back to Holland?'

He waved aside the waiter and sat back to watch her eating her sorbet.

'Ah, yes—I saw your Senior Nursing Officer this morning. You may leave in five days' time—by then I shall have the licence, would any day after that suit you?'

She felt a surge of excitement at the very idea.

'That's…' she counted on her fingers, 'Sunday. Would Tuesday suit you? That would give me time to pack my things. Will you be here until then?'

He shook his head. 'I'm going back tomorrow—there are several patients I have to see. I'll come back on Sunday and see you then. Would you like to go to an hotel until the Tuesday?'

She was surprised again. 'That's very kind of you, but I'll stay in Meadow Road if you don't mind—Waterloo, you know.'

'Ah, yes, I had forgotten.' He glanced at his watch. 'We had better go.'

His leavetaking was casual. No one looking at the two of them, thought Caro, would have guessed that they were going to be married within a week. She watched him get into his car and drive away, her eyes filled with tears. She knew nothing about him; where he was staying, what he was doing in London, if he had friends…the only thing she was sure of was that she loved him enough to bear with his ways.

CHAPTER FOUR

FIVE DAYS, CARO DISCOVERED, could last for ever, especially when one didn't know what was going to happen at the end of them. The Professor had said he was going to see her on Sunday, but once again he had forgotten to mention time or place. True, she had enjoyed several hours of shopping which had left her very satisfied and reduced her nest egg to a few paltry pounds, all the same she wished very much that Sunday would come.

And finally come it did and Caro, burdened with a variety of presents from her friends and fellow nurses, left Oliver's early in the afternoon. She had several hours of overtime due to her and Sister Pringle, generous after her holiday, had told her to go early rather than wait until six o'clock. She had been surprised to find her staff nurse engaged and on the point of leaving, but she had been pleased too; Caro got on well with everyone in her quiet way and she would be missed. She would miss her life at Oliver's too, she thought, as she crossed the busy street in front of the forbidding exterior and made her way to Meadow Road, but she wasn't daunted at the idea of living in another country; she would have lived wherever Radinck was and not complained.

She fed Waterloo, made herself a pot of tea and spread her packages on the bed—an early morning tea-set from Stacey, Miriam and Clare, a tea-cosy from the nurses on the ward, a bright pink bath towel from the ward maid and the orderlies and some handker-chiefs from Sister Pringle, and over and above these, a cut glass vase from all her friends. She admired them at length, for with no family of her own, presents had been few and far between. After she had had her tea she went to the wardrobe and looked at the new clothes hanging there. Her wedding outfit, covered in a plastic wrapper, took up most of the room; it was a rather plain fine wool dress in a warm amber colour which, if the weather should prove cold, would go very well under her winter coat. She had bought a small velvet hat to go with it, rather expensive shoes and gloves and a leather handbag. Not even the Professor would be able to find fault with them, she considered. She had bought a suit too, a multi-coloured tweed with a Marks and Spencer sweater to go with it, and more shoes, a sensible pair for walking in, and new undies and slacks. She would have liked some new luggage to pack them in, but her case, although shabby, was quite adequate and she wanted a few pounds in her purse; Radinck had talked about an allowance in a cool voice which had made her de-termined not to make use of it until she was forced to.

He arrived just as she was making toast for her tea. The afternoon had turned wet and chilly and Caroline had drawn the curtains and got out the Fodor's Guide once more. She was sitting on the wool rug she had made for herself, the bread toasting on a fork, Waterloo sitting beside her, when Radinck thumped on the door. No one else thumped like that. She knew who it was and called to him to come in. She didn't get up but went on with her toast-making, saying merely: 'Hello, Radinck, would you like some tea? I'm just going to make it.'

'Thank you, that would be nice.' He took off his car coat and sat down in the shabby chair beside the fire.

'Have you just arrived?' she asked.

'Yes, they told me at Oliver's that you had left.' His eyes lighted on the presents still laid out on the divan and he looked a question.

'Wedding presents,' said Caro cheerfully, turning her toast. 'I've never had so many things all at once in my life.'

He said, 'Very nice,' and dismissed them. 'You are ready for Tuesday?'

'Yes, I think so.' She buttered the toast and got up to put the kettle on.

Radinck looked tired and even more severe than usual and so aloof that Caroline didn't dare to utter the words of sympathy crowding into her head. Instead she made the tea, poured him a cup and put it, with the toast, on a stool by his chair, and then set about making more toast.

Presently when he had drunk his tea and she had given him a second cup she asked in her soft voice: 'You haven't changed your mind? You really want me to marry you, Radinck? One often gets ideas that don't work out…'

'I still want to marry you, Caroline.' He had relaxed, leaning back eating his toast, stroking Waterloo who had got on to his knee. 'I thought that we might go out for dinner.'

'Thank you, that would be nice.'

'And tomorrow? I have to be at the hospital in the morning, but perhaps we might go out in the afternoon. You have finished your shopping?'

'Yes, thank you—I have only to pack.'

He nodded. 'They are all delighted at Huis Thoe. You realise that we have to return by the night boat on Tuesday?'

'Yes.' She bit into her toast, trying to think of something to add and couldn't. She was astonished when he asked:

'What is the colour of your dress?'

'The one I've bought for the wedding? I suppose you'd call it dark amber.' She took a sip of tea and went on: 'I know you aren't interested in what I wear, it's a very plain dress—quite nice, you know, but no one's likely to take a second look at me, if you see what I mean.'

He raised his thick eyebrows. 'And is that your ambition? I have always understood that women—especially young ones—like to be noticed.'

'Not with a face like mine, they wouldn't,' Caro assured him.

He eyed her gravely. 'Your figure is not displeasing,' he observed, and sounded almost as surprised at his words as she was.

He didn't have to wait on the landing this time. She

had adopted the old-fashioned idea of wearing her best clothes on Sundays even if she wasn't going anywhere; it made the day seem a little different from all the others, so she was ready when Radinck suggested that they should go.

This time he took her to the Connaught Hotel Restaurant and because it was Sunday evening her green wool dress didn't seem too out of place, and she really wouldn't have minded; she had the sapphire on her finger, proclaiming that she had some sort of claim on her companion—although judging by the looks she received from some of the younger women sitting near them, it wasn't at all justified—besides, she was hungry. She did full justice to the cheese soufflé—as light as air, followed by filets de sole princesse and rounded off by millefeuille from the sweet trolley, all nicely helped down by the champagne the Professor had ordered. Caro wasn't very used to champagne; she wasn't sure if she liked it, but with the second glass she assured her companion that it was a drink which grew on one, and although she hadn't intended to make him laugh, he actually did.

She spent the next morning packing her clothes and putting her small treasures and ornaments, carefully wrapped, into a large cardboard box.

She was quite ready when Radinck called for her, dressed in the new suit, her face carefully made up. It was most gratifying when he remarked casually: 'You look nice—is that new?'

She told him yes, reflecting that it had been worth

the scandalous price she had paid for it at Jaegers; a lukewarm compliment but still a compliment.

They went to the Connaught again and when she observed how very nice it was, the Professor agreed pleasantly enough. 'I stay here if I'm in England for a few days,' he told her, and she fell to wondering where he went if his stay was protracted. Her thoughts must have been mirrored on her face, for after a pause he said:

'I have a small house in Essex, but it is hardly worth going there unless I'm over for a week or more.'

'What exactly do you do?' she asked carefully. 'That's if you don't mind telling me.'

He didn't answer her at once but remarked testily: 'Why is it that so many remarks you make appear to put me in the wrong, Caroline?' and before she could deny this: 'I am a physician, specialising in heart conditions, and the various diseases consequent to them.'

'But you lecture?'

'Yes.'

'And of course you're a consultant as well. Do you travel a great deal?'

He frowned a little. 'What a great many questions, Caroline!'

She agreed cheerfully. 'But you see, Radinck, if I ask them now, you'll never have to answer them again, will you?'

'That is true. I hope you don't expect to travel with me? I'm used to being alone—I concentrate better.'

She eyed him with pity wringing her heart, but all she said was: 'Of course I don't—I haven't forgotten that I'm to be a sheet anchor.'

He gave her a hard suspicious look which she met with a clear friendly gaze.

She hadn't asked what they were doing with the rest of the afternoon. She expected to be taken to Meadow Road, but it seemed that Radinck had other plans, for after lunch he left the car at the hotel and hailed a taxi. It cost Caro a great effort not to ask him where they were going, but she guessed that he was waiting for her to do just that. In the taxi he said: 'I have a wedding gift for you, but I wish you to see it first—it may not please you.'

She would have been a moron not to have been pleased, she thought presently, standing in front of the triple mirror in an exclusive furrier's shop. Mink, no less—ranch mink, he had carefully explained, because he thought that a coat made from trapped animals might distress her. It was a perfect fit, and when she remarked upon this he had told her casually that Clare had very kindly supplied her measurements.

She thanked him quietly and sincerely, careful to do it while the sales lady wasn't there. 'I can wear it tomorrow,' she told him. 'I was going to wear my winter coat...'

She understood then that for his wife to return to Huis Thoe in anything less than a mink coat would have upset everyone's idea of the fitness of things. She reflected with some excitement that she would be expected to dress very well, go to the hairdressers too and use the kind of make-up advertised so glossily in *Harpers* and *Vogue*. It struck her then that she was going to be a baroness—ridiculous but true. Just for a moment she quailed at the thought, but then her sensible head told her that it didn't matter what either of them were if they could love each other—and she already did that; it was just a question of getting Radinck to fall in love with her. She wasn't quite sure how she was going to do it, but it would be done.

Leaving the shop Radinck observed: 'I hope you will be pleased. I thought it would be pleasant if we gave a small dinner party for your friends and Sir Eustace and my best man this evening. At the hotel in my rooms; we shall have to leave directly after we have been married tomorrow, so there is no question of giving a lunch party then.'

'How nice,' said Caro faintly. 'C-can I wear this dress?'

'Certainly not. It will be black ties—your three friends are wearing long dresses. Have you no evening gown?'

She shook her head. 'Well, no—you see I don't go out a great deal.' Not at all, she added silently, but pride stopped her from saying so aloud.

'In that case tell me where you would like to buy a dress and we'll go there now.'

'Oh, I couldn't...'

He said coolly: 'Don't be so old-fashioned, Caroline—it is perfectly permissible for a man to buy his future wife a dress should he wish to do so. We will go to Fortnum and Mason.'

Caro goggled at him. 'But I've never been there in my life—not to buy anything.'

'Then it's time you did.'

He was there and she was getting out of the car before she could think of any argument against this and was led unresisting to the Dress Department where the Professor, looking more severe than ever, was instantly attended to by the head sales lady.

Having made his wishes clear he took himself off to a comfortable chair and left Caro to be led away by the sales lady to go through a selection of dresses which were all so stunning that she had no idea what she wanted.

It was the sales lady who pointed out that green was a good colour for hazel eyes and furthermore she had just the thing to suit, and if that wasn't to madam's taste, there was a charming honey-coloured crêpe or a grey crêpe de Chine…

Caro, almost delirious with excitement, tried them all on in turn and settled for the green; organza over silk with full sleeves gathered into tight buttoned cuffs and a low ruffled neckline. And when the sales lady suggested that she might like some rather pretty sandals to go with it, she agreed recklessly. She told Radinck about the sandals as they left the shop. 'I had no evening shoes,' she explained gravely, 'so I hope you don't mind. They were rather expensive.'

She hadn't been able to discover the price of the dress; the sales lady had been vague and she had watched Radinck sign a cheque without showing any signs of shock. She hoped that it hadn't been too expensive, but it wasn't until later that evening while she was dressing that she saw its label; a couture garment, and her mind boggled at the cost.

They had tea presently in a tiny shop all gilt and white paint, with the most heavenly cakes Caro had ever eaten, and on the way back she thanked him fervently and then went scarlet when he said coldly: 'You have no need to be quite so fulsome in your thanks. I have hardly lavished a fortune upon you, Caroline.'

She turned her head and looked out of the car window, wanting to burst into tears; the last thing she must ever do before him. She said brightly, proud of her steady voice, 'How dark it grows in the afternoons—but I like winter, don't you?'

She didn't see his quick glance at her averted face. 'You will be able to skate on the canal near Huis Thoe if it freezes enough.' His voice was casual and quite different from the biting tones he had just used. Caroline supposed she would learn in time—not to mind when he snubbed her, not to mind when he was cold and distant; there would surely be times when they could talk together, get to know each other. It would take time, but after all, he had said that he liked her.

He had to go back to the hospital that evening. He left her at Meadow Road, said that he would call for her at half past seven and drove away, leaving her to tell Waterloo all about it, wash her hair, do her face and put on the new dress. She had been ready and waiting half an hour or more before he returned, pleased with her appearance and hoping that he would be pleased too.

His cool 'very nice!' when he arrived was rather less than she had hoped for and his further: 'The dress is pretty,' although truthful, hardly flattered her, but she thanked him politely, tucked Waterloo up in his box and picked up the new fur coat. It was almost frightening how the touch of his cool hands on her shoulders as he held it for her sent her insides seesawing.

The evening was a great success; Clare, Miriam and Stacey had been fetched by the best man whose name Caro, in her excitement, didn't catch, although she remembered afterwards that he had said that he had an English wife who had just had a baby, and Sir Eustace and his wife arrived a few minutes after them. They all looked very elegant, Caro considered, drinking champagne cocktails in the elegant room Radinck had taken her to; her friends did credit to the occasion and sadly seemed on better terms with their host than she did. Just as he did with them. It was strange, she mused a little cloudily because of the champagne, that he should want to marry her when she never amused him, but there again, she couldn't imagine any of them allowing him to lead the quiet, studious life he seemed to enjoy. But her low spirits didn't last for long; the ring was admired, as was the coat, and her friends' pleasure at her change of fortune was genuine enough. And Lady Jenkins, under the impression that it was a love match and knowing that Caro had no parents, became quite motherly.

They dined late and at leisure at the round table set up in the Professor's sitting room at the hotel. Iced melon was followed by lobster thermidor and rounded off with ices, trifle and charlotte russe. They drank champagne and over coffee the Professor observed that it hardly seemed right to have a wedding cake before the wedding, but he had done his best to substitute that with petits fours, covered in white icing and decorated with silver leaves and flowers.

It was almost midnight when the party broke up and everyone went home, cracking jokes about seeing them at the church in the morning. When they had all gone, Caro put on her coat once more and was driven back to Meadow Road, making polite conversation all the way. She only stopped when Radinck remarked: 'You're very chatty—it must be the champagne.'

He didn't sound annoyed, though, only a little bored, so she said, 'Yes, I expect it is,' and lapsed into silence until they reached the house. He got out first, opened her door and went with her up the stairs, to take the key from her hand and open the door. The contrast after the spacious elegance of the hotel room was cruel, but he didn't say anything, only gave her back her key, cautioned her to be ready when he came for her in the morning and wished her goodnight.

'Goodnight,' said Caro hurriedly, because she hadn't thanked him yet and he seemed in a hurry to be gone. 'It was a delightful dinner party, thank you, Radinck.' And when he muttered something she added: 'I'll be ready when you come.'

She smiled at him and shut the door quite briskly, leaving him on the landing. She loved him so very much, but she mustn't let that weaken her resolve to alter his stern outlook on life. She suspected that he was a man who had always had his own way, even to shutting a door when he wanted to and not a moment before. A small beginning, but she had to start somewhere.

She slept dreamlessly with Waterloo curled up in a

tight ball on her feet and was up much earlier than she
needed to be, and true to her word, she was dressed
and ready when Radinck came for her. Waterloo and
her luggage were to be collected after the ceremony.
Caroline cast a look round the little room and followed
Radinck down the stairs to the car. The drive to the
church was a short one and they hardly spoke. At the
door she was handed over to Sir Eustace waiting in
the porch and given a small bouquet of rich yellow roses
which the Professor took from the back of the car. He
nodded briefly at her and just for a moment she panicked, staring up at him with eyes full of doubt, and
he must have seen that, for he smiled suddenly and
she glimpsed the man under the calm mask and all her
doubts went. If he could smile like that once, he could
do it again, and she would make sure that he did. She
took Sir Eustace's arm and walked firmly down the
aisle to where Radinck, towering over everything in
sight, waited for her.

She had no clear recollection of the ceremony. The
best man had given her an encouraging smile as she
reached Radinck's side, but the Professor didn't look
at her at all. Indeed, he looked rather grim during the
short service. Only as he put the ring on her finger he
smiled slightly. She wanted to smile too, but she didn't;
she would have to remember to remain friendly and undemanding quite without romantic feelings; he didn't
hold with romance. That was something else which
she had to alter.

There was to be no wedding breakfast. Everyone
said goodbye in the church porch and Caro got into

the car beside Radinck, not feeling in the least married and resolved to change his life for him. Indeed when Clare put her head through the window and exclaimed: 'Good lord, you're a baroness now!' she started to deny it and then declared: 'I'd forgotten that— Oh, dear!' She looked so woebegone at the idea that Clare laughed at her.

The Professor didn't intend to waste time; Caro's luggage was put in the boot, Waterloo, in a travelling basket, was arranged on the back seat, and with a hurried word to Mrs Hodge, who looked aggrieved because it hadn't been a proper wedding at all, Caro settled herself tidily beside the Professor. Afterwards, she had no very clear recollection of the journey either. They travelled by Hovercraft from Dover and although they stopped for lunch and again for tea, she had no idea what they had talked about or what she had eaten. The Professor had laid himself out to be pleasant and she had been careful not to chat, answering him when he made some observation but refraining from discussing the morning's ceremony. It was he who asked her if she had been pleased with her wedding, in much the same manner as someone asking if she had enjoyed her lunch, and she told him yes, it had been very nice— a colourless statement, but she could think of nothing better to say. She did enquire the name of the best man and was told he was Tiele Raukema van den Eck, not long married to an English girl. 'You must meet her,' suggested the Professor casually. 'She's rather a nice little thing—they've just had a son.'

It seemed there was no more to be said on the subject. Caro sat quietly as they sped northward and wondered if Noakes and the other servants would be glad to see her. Radinck had said that they had missed her, but going back as the lady of the house was quite a different kettle of fish.

She need not have worried. They were greeted with wide smiles and a great deal of handshaking and when that was done, Noakes led them into the drawing room where, on a small circular table in the centre of the room, was a wedding cake. Caro stopped short and gave a delighted laugh. 'Radinck, how kind of you to think of...'

She looked at him, still laughing, and saw at once that she had been mistaken. He was as surprised as she was—it must have been Noakes.

He was standing in the doorway with Juffrouw Kropp and Marta and the others grouped around him, waiting to be praised like eager children. Caro hoped that they hadn't heard her speak to Radinck; she turned to them now. 'Noakes, all of you—what a wonderful surprise! We're both thrilled; it is the most beautiful cake. Thank you—all of you.' She went on recklessly: 'I'm going to cut it now and we'll all have a piece with some champagne. We were going to have the champagne anyway, weren't we, Radinck?'

She turned a smiling face towards him, her eyes beseeching him to act the part of a happy bridegroom. After all, it was only for once; every other night he could go to his study and spend the evenings with his books.

He met her look with a mocking smile she hoped no

one else saw. 'But certainly we will drink champagne,' he agreed. 'Noakes, fetch up half a dozen bottles and get someone to set out the glasses. And thank you all for this magnificent cake.' He repeated it all in Dutch and there was handclapping and smiling and a good deal of bustling to and fro until the champagne had been brought and they went to cut the cake. Caroline, handed the knife by Noakes and alone with the Professor at the table for a moment, said softly; 'I'm afraid it's the custom for us both to hold the knife...'

His hand felt cool and quite impersonal and touched her only briefly. He was disliking the happy little ceremony very much, she knew that; perhaps it reminded him of his first wedding. He'd been in love then...

They ate the cake and drank the champagne and presently Juffrouw Kropp took Caroline upstairs to her room to tidy herself for dinner. It was a different bedroom this time; a vast apartment in the front of the house with an equally vast bed with a brocade coverlet to match the blue curtains and beautiful Hepplewhite furniture. A bathroom led from it and on the other side a dressing room, another bathroom and another bedroom, all leading one to another. Juffrouw Kropp beamed and smiled before she went away, and left alone, Caro explored more thoroughly; it was all very splendid but comfortable too. She tidied herself, did her hair and went downstairs again to join Radinck in the drawing-room, where they made conversation over their drinks before going in to dinner.

Marta had excelled herself with little spinach tarts, roast duckling with black cherries and a bombe surprise. Caro, desperately maintaining a conversation about nothing much, ate some of everything although she had no appetite, because Marta would be upset to see her lovely dishes returned to the kitchen half eaten, and she drank the hock Noakes poured for them, a little too much of it, which was a good thing because it made her feel falsely cheerful.

They had their coffee in the drawing-room and Noakes went away with a benign smile which drew down the corners of the Professor's mouth so that Caro, now valiant with too much drink, said cheerfully: 'You've hated every minute of it, haven't you, Radinck? But I'm going to my room in a few minutes, only before I go I'd like to thank you for giving me such a nice wedding.' She added kindly: 'It's only this one evening, you know, you won't have to do it ever again. You asked me not to disturb your life, and I won't, only they all expected...' She pinkened faintly. 'Well, they expected us to look—like...'

'Exactly, Caroline.' He had got to his feet. 'I'm only sorry that I didn't think of the wedding cake.' He smiled at her: it was a kind, gentle sort of smile and it held a touch of impatience. She said goodnight without fuss and didn't linger. She thought about that smile later, as she got ready for bed. It had been a glimpse of Radinck again, only next time, she promised herself, he would smile without impatience. It might take a long time, but that was something she had.

She woke early while it was still almost dark. She had opened the door to the verandah outside her room before she got into her enormous bed, and Waterloo,

after a long sound sleep on her feet after his lengthy
journey and hearty supper, was prowling up and down
it, talking to her. She got up, put on her new quilted
dressing gown and slippers and went to join him.

The sky was getting paler every minute, turning
pink along the horizon; it was going to be a lovely
November day, bright and frosty. Somewhere Caroline could hear Rex barking and the sound of horses'
hooves and then Radinck's whistle to the dog. So that
was what he did before breakfast. She vowed then and
there to learn to ride.

One of the maids, Ilke, brought her her early morning tea presently, and told her smilingly that breakfast
would be at half past eight, or would she rather have
it in bed?

Caro elected to go downstairs. She had never had
her breakfast in bed, for there had been no one to bring
it to her, and the idea didn't appeal to her very much.
She bathed and put on her suit and one of the Marks
and Spencer sweaters and went down to the hall. It was
absurd, but she wasn't sure where she was to breakfast. When she had been staying in the house she had
seen only the library, the drawing-room and the dining-
room, but there were several more doors and passages
leading from the hall and she had no idea where they
led. She need not have fussed; Noakes was waiting to
conduct her to a small, cosy room leading off the hall,
where there was a bright fire burning and a table laid
ready for her. Of the Professor there was no sign and
she thought it might sound silly if she asked Noakes
where he was, so she bade him a smiling good morn-

ing, and while she made a good breakfast, listened to his carefully put advice.

'There's Juffrouw Kropp waiting ter show yer the 'ouse, ma'am, and then Marta 'opes yer'll go to the kitchens and take a look at the menu, and anything yer wants ter know yer just ask me. We're all that 'appy that yer're 'ere, ma'am.'

'Noakes, you're very kind to say so, and I'm happy too. When I've found my feet we must have some more singing—I still think we should do something about Christmas, don't you?' She remembered something. 'And, Noakes, I want your help. Is there someone who can teach me to ride? I—I want to surprise the Professor.'

His cheerful face spread into a vast smile. 'Now ain't that just the ticket—the Professor, 'e rides a treat, great big 'orse 'e's got, too, but there's a pony as is 'ardly used. Old Jan'll know—I'll get 'im to come and see yer and I'll come wiv 'im.'

'Thank you, Noakes—it must be a secret, though.' Caroline finished her coffee and got up from the table. 'I'm going to fetch Waterloo and take him round the house with Juffrouw Kropp, then he'll feel at home. Where's Rex?'

'Gone with the Professor. Most days 'e does, ma'am.'

It took all of two hours to go over the house. She hadn't realised quite how big it was, with a great many little passages leading to small rooms, and funny twisted stairs from one floor to the next as well as the massive front staircase. She would have got lost if it hadn't been for Juffrouw Kropp, leading her from one room to the next, waiting patiently while she examined its contents, and then explaining them in basic Dutch so that Caro had at least some idea of them. They were all beautifully furnished and well-kept, but as far as she could make out, never used. A house full of guests, she dreamed to herself, all laughing and talking and dancing in the evening in that lovely drawing-room and riding out in the mornings, with her riding even better than the best there. She sighed and Juffrouw Kropp asked her if she were tired, and when she shook her head in vigorous denial, preceded her downstairs to visit the glories on the ground floor.

The drawing-room she knew, also the library and the morning-room. Now she was conducted round a second sitting-room, furnished with deep armchairs, a work table from the Regency period, several lamp tables and two bow-fronted display cabinets. A lovely room, but not used, she felt sure. Well, she would use it. There was a billiard room too, a garden room and a small room furnished with a desk and chair and several filing cabinets—used by the secretary, Caroline supposed. There was a luxurious cloakroom too and a great many large cupboards as well as several rooms lined with shelves and a pantry or two.

She hoped she would remember where each of them was if ever she needed it, although she couldn't think why she should. The first floor had been easy enough; her own room and the adjoining ones took up half the front corridor and most of one side, and the half a dozen bedrooms and their bathrooms on that floor took up the rest of its space; the smaller rooms and passages she would have to explore later.

She drank her coffee presently, concentrating on what she had seen, reminding herself that it was hers now as well as Radinck's and he would expect her to be responsible for his home. She had no intention of usurping Juffrouw Kropp's position, but it was obvious that even that experienced lady expected her to give orders from time to time.

The kitchens she already knew, but now it was a question of poking her mousy head into all the cupboards and lobbies and dressers while it was explained to her what was in all of them and then, finally, she was given a seat at the kitchen table and offered the day's menu. Noakes translated it for her while Marta waited anxiously to see if she would approve, and when that had been done to everyone's satisfaction, Noakes led her back to the smaller sitting-room, where she had decided to spend her leisure and where after a few minutes Jan was admitted.

Noakes had to act as go-between, of course, but Jan agreed readily enough to teaching her. The pony, he agreed with Noakes, was just right since the Baroness was small and light. Caro, who had forgotten that she was a baroness, felt a little glow of pleasure at his words. They decided that she should begin the very next morning, and well pleased with herself, she got her coat and took herself off for a walk.

She lunched alone, since the Professor didn't come home, and in the afternoon she curled up in the library and had another go at her Dutch. She would have to have lessons, for she was determined to learn to speak it as quickly as possible, but in the meantime she could at least look up as many words as she could. She and Juffrouw Kropp were to go through the linen cupboard on the following morning. She would make her companion say everything in her own language and she would repeat it after her; she would learn a lot that way. And tomorrow she would get Noakes to drive her into Leeuwarden so that she could buy some wool and fill her time with knitting. More flowers about the house too, she decided, and an hour's practice at the piano each day. There was more than enough to keep her busy.

She went upstairs to change after her solitary tea; she put on her wedding dress again and then went to the drawing-room to wait for Radinck, taking a book with her so that it wouldn't look as though she had been there ages, expecting him.

When he did get home, only a short time before dinner, she wished him a cheerful good evening, volunteered no information as to her day, hoped that he had had a good one himself and took up her book again. He had stressed that she wasn't to interfere with his way of living and she would abide by it. She accepted a drink from him and when he excused himself on the plea of work to do before dinner, assured him that she didn't mind in the least.

They met at the dinner table presently and over an unhurried meal talked comfortably enough about this and that, and as they got up to go into the drawing-room for their coffee Caro said diffidently: 'Don't come into the drawing-room unless you want to, Radinck. I'll get Noakes to bring coffee to your study.'

He followed her into the room and closed the door. He said irritably: 'I'll take my coffee where I wish to, Caroline. I'm sure you mean well, but kindly don't interfere.' He glared down at her. 'I shall be going out very shortly.'

Her voice was quite serene. 'Yes, Radinck. Do you like your coffee black?' She poured it with a steady hand and went to sit down, telling herself she wasn't defeated, only discouraged.

CHAPTER FIVE

THE DAYS PASSED, piling themselves into a week. Caro, awake early as usual by reason of Waterloo's soliloquy as he paced the balcony, sat herself up against her lace-trimmed pillows and began to assess the progress she had made in that time. Nothing startling, she conceded, ticking off her small successes first: her riding lessons had proved well worth the effort. She had got on to Jemmy, the pony, each morning under Jan's eagle eye and done her best while her tutor muttered and tutted at her and occasionally took her to task in a respectful manner, while the faithful Noakes translated every word. And she had learned the geography of the house, having gone over it several times by herself and once or twice with Juffrouw Kropp, learning the names of the various pieces of furniture from that good lady.

She had applied herself to her Dutch too; even though she had little idea how to converse in that language she had worried her way through a host of useful words. Besides all this, she had got Noakes to drive her to Leeuwarden, where she had bought wool and a pattern and started on a sweater for Radinck's Christmas present; probably he would never wear it, but she was getting a lot of pleasure from knitting it, although as the instructions were in Dutch she had had to guess at a good deal of the pattern and enlist Juffrouw Kropp's help over the more difficult bits.

Her eyes fell on Waterloo, who having finished his early morning exercise, was sitting in the doorway washing his elderly face; he at least was happy with the whole house to roam and a safe outdoors with no traffic threatening his safety, and she shared his opinion. The grounds round the house were large and beyond the red-brick wall which encompassed them were water meadows and quiet lanes and bridle paths. Caroline had roamed at will during the week, finding her way around, going to the village where she was surprised to be greeted by its inhabitants. She still found it strange to be addressed as Baroness and she had had a struggle to answer civilly in Dutch, but smiling and nodding went a long way towards establishing a sort of rapport.

But with Radinck she had made no progress at all. He was polite, remote and continued to live his own life, just as though she wasn't there. True, once or twice he had discussed some interesting point regarding his work with her, asked her casually if she had been to the village and informed her that now their marriage had been put in the *Haagsche Post* and *Elseviers* they might expect visitors and some invitations, and had gone on to suggest that she might like to go to Leeuwarden or Groningen and buy herself some clothes, and the following morning his secretary had given her a cheque book with a slip of paper inside it on which the Professor had scrawled: Your allowance will be paid into the bank quarterly. The sum he had written had left Caroline dumbfounded.

But it was early days yet, she reminded herself cheerfully. He would be surprised and, she hoped, delighted to discover that she could ride. The last thing she wanted to happen was for him to feel ashamed of her because of her social shortcomings, even if he didn't want her as a wife she would manage his home just as he wanted it, entertain his friends and learn to live his way of life. She owed him that, and never mind how impatient and irritable he became.

She drank her morning tea and presently went downstairs to her breakfast, to stop in the doorway of the breakfast room. Radinck was sitting at the table, a cup of coffee in one hand, a letter he was reading in the other.

He got up when he saw her, pulled out a chair and said politely: 'Do sit down; I forgot to tell you yesterday that I have given myself a day off. I thought we might go down to den Haag so that you can do some shopping. My mother always got her things from Le Bonneterie there—it's rather like a small Harrods, and you might possibly like it—if not, we can try somewhere else.'

Caroline didn't like to mention that she had never bought anything in Harrods. She agreed happily; a whole day in his company, even if he had nothing much to say to her, would be heaven, but here she was to be disappointed, for in the car, racing across the Afsluitdijk, he mentioned casually that he had a consultation at the Red Cross Hospital in den Haag and after leaving her at Le Bonneterie he would rejoin her there an hour or so later. 'I daresay it will take you that time to buy your clothes. I suggest that you get a sheepskin jacket and some boots—it can be cold once the winter comes.'

Caroline started doing sums in her head; her allowance was a generous one but she had no idea how much good clothes cost in Holland. She would need several dresses, she supposed, and more separates and some evening clothes.

'You're very silent,' remarked Radinck presently.

'Well, I was just thinking what I needed to buy. Would two evening dresses do?'

'Certainly not—there will be a hospital ball in Leeuwarden in a few weeks' time, and another one in Groningen and any number of private parties. At Christmas I invite a number of guests to the house, but before then we will have an evening reception so that you meet my friends.'

She had to get this straight. 'But you like to lead a quiet life; you told me so—you like to work and read in the evenings. You'll only be inviting them because of me.'

'That is so.' They were flying down the E-10 and there was plenty to capture her interest, only she had too much on her mind.

'Yes, but don't you see?' she persisted in her quiet voice, 'you're having to do something you don't want to do.' She went on quickly, looking straight ahead of her, 'You don't have to do it for me, you know. I'm—

I'm very happy—besides, I'd feel scared at meeting so many strange people.'

'Once you have met them they won't be strange.' The calm logic of his voice made her want to stamp her feet with temper. 'And to revert to our discussion, I suggest that you buy several dresses of a similar sort to the one you wore at our wedding.' He glanced sideways at her. 'The suit you are wearing is nice, why not get another one like it? And some casual clothes, of course.'

Caroline said tartly: 'Do you want me to change my hairstyle too? It could be tinted and cut and permed and...'

'You will leave your hair exactly as it is.' He added stiffly, 'I like it the way you wear it.'

She was so surprised that she asked quite meekly: 'How much money am I to spend? I could get a great deal with about half of my allowance.' She frowned. 'And will they take my cheque? They don't know me from Adam.'

'I shall go with you. You will have no difficulty in writing cheques for anything you want, Caroline, but this time you will leave me to pay the bill when I come to fetch you.'

'Oh—all right, and I'll pay you back afterwards.'

'I do not wish to be repaid. Caroline, did I not tell you that I was a rich man?'

'No—at least I can't remember that you did. You did say that there was plenty of money, but I don't suppose that's the same as being rich, is it?'

A muscle twitched at the corner of the Professor's

firm mouth. 'No,' he agreed quietly, 'it's not quite the same.'

They were in the heavily populated area of the country now, for he had turned away from Amsterdam and was working his way round the city to pick up the motorway to den Haag on its southern side. As they took the road past Leiden which would lead them to the heart of den Haag, Caro said: 'It's very pretty here and there are some beautiful houses, only I like yours much better.'

'Ours,' Radinck reminded her.

The city was full of traffic and people and a bewildering number of narrow streets. The Professor wove his way into the heart of the shopping centre and turned away down a side street to stop after a moment or two before a large shop with elegantly dressed windows. It was quiet there, the houses all round it were old and there were few people about, and Caro took a deep breath of pure pleasure at the thought of spending the next hour or two in the dignified building, spending money without having to count every penny before she did so.

The Professor was known there. An elderly woman with a kind face listened carefully to what he had to say, smiled and nodded and without giving Caro time to do more than say, 'Goodbye,' led her away.

The next hour or so was blissful: Caro, guided discreetly by the elderly lady, became the possessor of a sheepskin jacket because Radinck had told her to buy one, a suit—dogtooth check with a short jacket and a swinging pleated skirt—three Italian print dresses and a finely pleated georgette jersey two-piece because although she didn't think she needed it she couldn't bear not to have it, a dashing bolero and skirt with a silk blouse to go with them and four evening dresses: she would probably never wear more than one of them despite what Radinck had said, but it was hard to call a halt, especially with the elderly lady egging her on in her more than adequate English. And then there was the question of suitable shoes, stockings to go with them, gloves, a little mink hat to go with her coat, and since it seemed a shame not to buy them while she had the opportunity, undies. She was wandering back from that department and had stopped to examine the baby clothes in the children's department when Radinck joined her. She flushed under his mocking eyes and said defensively: 'I was on my way back. They're adding it up—the bill, I mean—I had a few minutes...'

She put down the muslin garment she had been admiring and walked past him. 'It's a lovely shop,' she told him chattily to cover her awkwardness. 'I've bought an awful lot. Did you have a successful consultation?'

He gave some non-committal answer, made some remark to the sales lady and then studied the bill. Caro, watching his face, was unable to discover his feelings about it. His expression gave nothing away, although the total was such that if it had been handed to her she would have screamed at the amount.

But he didn't mention it. The packages and boxes loaded into the boot, Caroline was invited to get into the car, and within ten minutes she found herself in a small, very smart restaurant, drinking a sherry and eyeing a menu with an appetite sharpened by its contents. And not only did Radinck not mention it, but he talked. He told her about the hospital where he had been that morning and the patients he had seen, he even discussed the conditions he had been asked to examine. Just for a while the bland mask slipped a little and Caro, always a good listener, became a perfect one, listening intelligently, asking the right question at the right moment and never once venturing an opinion of her own, and she got her reward, for presently he observed: 'You must forgive me, I am so used to being alone—I have been uttering my thoughts and you must have been bored.'

'No, I wasn't,' said Caro forthrightly. 'I'm interested—you forget that I'm a nurse, but there are bits I don't quite understand. You were telling me about Fröhlich's syndrome—I can't quite see how hypophosphatisia can't be medically treated—if it's just a question of calcium...'

The Professor put down his coffee cup. 'Well, it's like this...'

For a bridegroom of rather more than a week, his conversation was hardly flattering: she might have been sitting there, wearing a sack and a false nose, but to Caro, it was the thin—very thin   edge of the wedge.

Back home again she went straight to her room with one of the maids bearing her various parcels. Radinck was going out again and she hoped he might tell her where, but in this she was disappointed. He was leaving the house without a word before she had reached the top of the staircase. She consoled herself by trying on every single thing she had bought, and it was only

as she took off the last of the evening dresses that she
remembered her daydream—playing to Radinck in a
lovely pink dress, and none of the dresses were pink;
she would have to go to den Haag again and buy one.
Meanwhile she might do a little practising while she
waited for him to come back.

He wasn't coming. Noakes met her in the hall with
the news that the Professor had just telephoned to say
that he wouldn't be back for dinner, and Caroline, anxious to keep her end up, said airily: 'Oh, yes, Noakes,
he did say he might have to stay. I'll have mine on a
tray, please, and if none of you have anything better to
do, shall we get together over those carols presently?'

She was so disappointed that she could eat hardly
any of the delicious food Noakes brought presently, and
even though she told herself she was a fool to have expected Radinck to have changed his ways all at once,
she was hard put to it to preserve a cheerful face. It
helped, of course, discussing the carols with Noakes
and Marta and Juffrouw Kropp and the others. She sat
at the piano, trying out the various tunes to find those
they knew—and when they had, she was thrilled to discover that they sang rather well. With the aid of Noakes
and her dictionary, she prevailed upon some of them to
sing in harmony—it was a bit ragged, but there were
several weeks to go to Christmas and if Radinck was
going to be away most evenings, there was ample time
to rehearse.

She made herself think about her new wardrobe and
the carols as she got ready for bed, banishing Radinck

from her mind. Easier said than done: he kept popping up all over the place.

It was after breakfast the following morning that he telephoned her to say that he was going to Brussels and wouldn't be back until the next day, late in the evening. 'So don't wait up for me,' his voice sounded cool over the wire. 'I haven't got Rex with me, so would you mind walking him—once a day will do, he is very adaptable.'

Caroline made her voice equally cool; rather like an efficient secretary's. 'Of course.' She wanted to tell him to take care of himself, to ask what he was going to do in Brussels, but she didn't; she said goodbye in a cheerful voice and rang off.

The day went by on leaden feet. Not even her riding lesson raised her spirits, although she was doing quite well now, trotting sedately round and round the field nearest the stables, with Rex keeping pace with Jemmy. He did the same thing again on the following morning, taking upon himself the role of companion and pacemaker, and because the weather was changing with thunderous skies swallowing the chilly blue, Caroline spent the afternoon in the library, conning her Dutch and knitting away at the sweater, with Waterloo and Rex for company, and because she had to keep up appearances, she changed into one of her new dresses that evening and dined alone at the big table, feeling lost but not allowing that to show, and after an hour working away at the carols again she went up to her room, meeting Noakes's enquiry as to whether she knew at what time the Professor would be back with a serene: 'He said late, Noakes, and I wasn't to wait up. I should lock up if he's not back by eleven o'clock—ask Marta to leave a thermos jug of coffee out, would you?'

It was long after midnight when the Professor returned. Caro, lying wide awake in her bed, heard the gentle growl of the car and saw its lights flash past her windows and presently her husband's firm tread coming up the stairs and going past her door. Only then did she curl up into a ball with Waterloo as close as he could get and sleep.

It was raining when she awoke, and cold and dark as well. None of these mattered, though. Radinck was home again and she might even see him before he left the house—perhaps he would be at breakfast. She got dressed in the new suit and the wildly expensive brogue shoes she had bought to go with it, and went downstairs.

He wasn't there, and Noakes, remarking on her early appearance, observed, 'Back late, wasn't 'e, ma'am? I 'eard him come in—ever so quiet.'

'Yes, I know, though I was still awake, Noakes.'

'Pity 'e 'ad ter go again so early—no proper rest. 'E works too 'ard.'

'Yes, Noakes, I know he does.' She gave the elderly face a sweet smile. 'Noakes, it's too wet for me to go riding, I suppose?'

'Lor', yes, ma'am—best stay indoors. Juffrouw Kropp wanted to ask about some curtains that want renewing.'

'I'll see her after breakfast and then go to the kitchens.'

It was still only ten o'clock by the time she had fulfilled her household duties and the rain had lessened a

little. 'I'm going for a walk,' she told Noakes. 'I won't
take Rex with me and I won't go far—I just feel like
some exercise.'

She put her new hooded raincoat on over the new
suit, found her gloves and let herself out of a side door.
The rain was falling steadily and there was a snarling
wind, but they suited her mood. She walked briskly
across the gardens, into the fields behind the wall, and
joined the country lane, leading away to a village in
the distance. She had walked barely half a mile when
she saw a slow-moving group coming towards her—a
cart drawn by a stout pony and surrounded by a family of tinkers. They were laughing and shouting to each
other, not minding the weather, carefree and happy.
Except for a small donkey tied to the back of the cart;
it wasn't only wet, it was in a shocking condition, its
ribs starting through its dirty matted coat, and it was
heavily in foal. It was being ruthlessly beaten with a
switch wielded by a shambling youth, and Caro, now
abreast of the whole party, cried 'Stop!' so furiously
that they did. She took the switch from the youth and
flung it into the canal by the side of the lane, then she
mustered her Dutch. '*Hoeveel?*' she asked imperiously,
pointing at the deplorable beast, and then with a flash
of inspiration, she pointed to herself and added: 'Baroness Thoe van Erckelens.'

She was pleased to see that the name meant something
to them. The leader of the party, a scruffy middle-aged
man, gave her a respectful look, even if a bit doubtful.
Caroline had to dispel the doubt; she turned and pointed
again, this time towards Huis Thoe, just visible behind

its high wall. While they were all staring at it she went over to the dejected little beast and began to untie the rope round its neck, and when they would have stopped her, held up a firm little hand. '*Ik koop*,' she told them, and waved towards the house, the rope in her hand, hoping that 'how much' and 'I'll buy' would be sufficient to make them agree, for the life of her she couldn't think of anything else to say to the point. Yes, one more word. She ordered briskly '*Kom*' and had the satisfaction of seeing them bunch together round the cart once more, obviously waiting for her to lead the way.

She didn't know anything about donkeys, and she prayed that this one would answer to the gentle tug she gave its worn bridle. It did, and she made her way to the front, not hurrying because the donkey's hooves were in a frightful state. It took longer to go back too, because she thought the tinkers might be more impressed if she went in through the main gates, and every yard of the way she was hiding panic that they might come to their senses and make off with the donkey before she could reach home. But the gates were reached at last and she singled out the scruffy man, beckoning him to follow her, leaving the rest of them grouped in the drive staring at them. The man began to mutter to himself before they reached the sweep before the house, but Caroline didn't listen. She was planning what she would do; open the door and shout for Noakes to mind the donkey and keep an eye on the man while she fetched some money—and that was another problem; how much did one pay for a worn out starving animal? Perhaps Noakes would know.

The Professor, home early for his lunch and thus

breaking a rule he had adhered to for years without knowing quite why, was standing at the drawing-room windows, staring out over the grounds, aware of disappointment because Caro wasn't home. He frowned at the dripping landscape before him and then frowned again, staring even harder. Unless his splendid eyesight deceived him, his wife, a most disreputable man and a very battered donkey were coming up his drive, and what was more, there were people clustered round the gates, peering in. Something about the small resolute figure marching up to the front door sent him striding to open it and down the steps to meet her.

Caro, almost at the door and seeing her husband's vast form coming down the steps with deliberate speed, felt a wave of relief so strong that she could have burst into tears. She swallowed them back and cried: 'Oh, Radinck, I'm so glad you're home!' She had to raise her voice because he was barely within earshot. 'I've bought this poor little donkey, but I don't know how much to pay the man—I got him to come with me while I fetched the money. I thought Noakes would know, but now you're here you can tell me.' She looked up at him with complete confidence and added, just in case he didn't realise the urgency of the occasion: 'She's a jenny and she's going to foal soon; they were beating her, and just look at her hooves!'

The Professor looked, running a gentle hand over the bruised back, bending to examine each wretched neglected hoof, then he straightened up to tower over the tinker.

Caro couldn't understand a word he was saying. His

voice was quiet and unhurried, but the tinker looked at first cowed and then downright scared. Finally, the Professor produced his notecase, selected what he wanted from its contents and handed them to the man, who grabbed them and, looking considerably shaken, made off as fast as his legs would carry him.

Caro watched him join his family at the gates and disappear. 'That was splendid of you, Radinck,' she said in deep satisfaction. 'I couldn't understand what you said, of course, but you scared him, didn't you? Oh, I'm so very glad you were here... I'll pay you back in a minute, but I ought to see to this poor thing first. What did you say to that horrid man?'

Her husband looked down at her, a half smile twitching his mouth. 'Enough to make him very careful how he treats any more animals he may own in future, and allow me to give her to you as a gift.' The half smile became a real one and she smiled back at him in delight. 'Tell me, how did you get him to come here?'

She told him and he laughed, a bellow of genuine amusement which set her hopeful heart racing, although all she said was, 'We ought to get in out of this rain. Where shall I take her?' And before he could answer: 'There's that barn next to the stables where the hay's kept...'

He gave her a questioning look. 'I didn't know you were interested in the stables—yes, the barn would do very well.'

Caroline began to lead the animal towards the back of the house. 'I'm not sure what donkeys eat. I'll ask Jan—he'll get me some carrots, though.'

Radinck gave her an amused glance. 'Jan too?' he asked, and then: 'She can go into the south field with the horses once she's rested.'

They were halfway there when Caro asked: 'What did you mean—"Jan too"?'

He answered her carelessly: 'Oh, you seem to have a way with people, don't you? The servants fall over themselves to please you and now Jan, who never does anything for anyone unless he wants to.'

'He's a dear old man,' declared Caro warmly, remembering Jan's deep elderly voice rumbling out the carols of an evening. 'He had a frightful cold, you know—I told him what to do for it.' She glanced sideways at him. 'I hope you don't mind?'

He sounded irritable. 'I don't suppose it would make any difference whether I minded or not. Give me that rope, and be good enough to go up to the house and ask Noakes to get Jan and young Willem, then telephone the vet and tell him to come out as soon as he can to examine an ill-treated donkey in foal.'

'Yes, of course.' Caroline smiled happily at his rather irritable face. 'I'll go at once. Radinck, what shall we call her?'

He was staring at her with hard eyes as though he couldn't bear the sight of her. 'What could be more appropriate than Caro?' he wanted to know mockingly.

She hadn't taken a dozen steps before he was beside her, his hands on her shoulders so that she had to stop.

'I'm sorry, that was a rotten thing to say.'

She had gone a little white and the tears were thick in her throat, but she managed a smile. 'As a matter of fact it's a very good name for her.' She added earnestly: 'It doesn't matter, really it doesn't.'

'It does—you didn't deserve it, Caroline.' His voice was gentle. 'What shall we call her? We have a Waterloo and a Rex and the kitchen cat is called Anja—how about Queenie, and if the foal is a boy we can call him Prince.'

Caro had no doubt that he was trying to placate her hurt feelings, and although it wasn't much the tiny flame of hope she kept flickering deep down inside her brightened a little; at least he had realised that he had hurt her. She smiled at him a bit crookedly. 'That's a splendid name,' she agreed. 'I'll get Noakes.'

She slipped away before he could say anything else and took care not to return until she saw Jan and Willem going towards the stables.

Radinck had fetched a bucket of water and some oats while she had been gone and now the three men stood watching the donkey making a meal. She was still happily munching when Mijnheer Stagsma arrived. Radinck explained briefly what had happened, introduced Caro and waited patiently while the vet wished her happiness in her marriage, congratulated her on her rescue of the donkey, hoped that his wife would have the pleasure of calling on her soon and enquired how she liked her new home.

He was a youngish man with a friendly face. Caro would have enjoyed talking to him, but out of the corner of her eye she saw her husband's bland face watching them. He was growing impatient, so she brought their cheerful little talk to a friendly end and indicated the patient.

Mijnheer Stagsma took a long time, muttering to himself and occasionally saying something to the Professor. At length he came upright again.

'Nothing serious, I think—starved, of course, but that can be dealt with, and I'll deal with those hooves as soon as she's stronger. I should think she'll have the foal in a week or so—it's hard to tell in her present state. I'll give her a couple of injections and some ointment for those sores on her back. Who'll be looking after her?'

Caro, striving to understand what he said, looked at Radinck. He answered the vet, spoke to Willem who grinned and nodded and then turned to Caro, telling her what the vet had said.

'Oh, good—Willem doesn't mind feeding her? I don't...'

'No, not you, Caroline. You may visit her, of course, and take her out when she is better, but Willem will tend her and clean out the barn.'

She supposed that being a baroness barred her from such chores. 'If you say so,' she said happily, 'but I simply must learn Dutch as quickly as possible.'

The glimmer of a smile touched her husband's face. 'You seem to manage very well—but I'll arrange for you to have lessons.'

They wished the vet goodbye, standing together on the sweep as he drove down the drive and out of sight.

'Oh, dear—should I have asked him in for a drink?' asked Caro.

'I already did so, but he couldn't stop—he's a very busy man.'

'And nice—so friendly.' She didn't see the look her husband shot at her. 'May I go back and look at Queenie?'

He turned away to go into the house. 'There is no need to ask my permission, Caroline. I am not your gaoler—you are free to do exactly what you like as long as you don't interfere with my work.'

'Not your work,' said Caro, suddenly passionate, 'your life—and never fear, Radinck, I'll take care never to do that.'

She marched away, her chin in the air, in one of her rare tempers.

But her tempers didn't last long. Within half an hour they were lunching together and although she didn't apologise for her outburst she tried to be friendly. She supposed that it was for Noakes's benefit that Radinck met her conversational efforts more than halfway. It was a disappointment when he told her that he wouldn't be home for dinner. She spent her afternoon wrestling with an ever-lengthening list of Dutch words and the evening coaching her choir once again, and before she went to bed she went down to the stables to take a look at Queenie. The little donkey looked better already, she thought. She pulled the ragged ears gently, offered a carrot and went back to the house, where she mooned around for another hour or so before going to bed much later than usual, hoping that Radinck would come back before she did. But there was no sign of him. She fell

asleep at last and didn't hear him return in the small
hours of the morning.

She was up early and with Waterloo in attendance
went down to see how Queenie had fared. Willem was
already there, cleaning out the barn and feeding her, and
Caro, trying out some of her carefully acquired Dutch,
made out that the donkey had improved considerably,
but Willem was busy and she didn't like to hinder him,
so she wandered off again into the crisp morning—just
right for a ride, she decided, and with Waterloo trotting
beside her, hurried back for breakfast.

Jan was waiting for her when she got to the stables and Jemmy greeted her with a toss of the head
and a playful nip. Caroline mounted his plump back
and walked him out of the yard and into the field beyond. Walk round once, Jan had told her, then trot round
once. She did so, watched by the old man, and then because she was feeling confident and enjoying herself
she poked Jemmy's fat sides with her heels and started
off again. Jemmy was enjoying himself too; his trot
broke into a canter and Caro, her hair flying, let out
a whoopee of delight. They were three quarters of the
way round the field when she saw Radinck standing
beside Jan.

CHAPTER SIX

THERE WAS ONLY one thing to do and that was to go on. Caroline finished circling the field and pulled up untidily in front of Radinck. Jan was standing beside him, but she couldn't tell from the craggy old face if anything had been said. To be on the safe side she leaned down from her saddle. 'Don't you dare be angry with Jan!' she hissed fiercely. 'I made him teach me—he thought I was doing it as a lovely surprise for you.'

'And were you?' It was impossible to tell if Radinck was angry or not.

'Well, yes—but not just for you. I thought that as you're a baron and have a lot of posh friends you might be ashamed of me if I couldn't do all the things they do...'

The gleam in Radinck's eyes became very pronounced, but he answered gravely: 'That was very thoughtful of you, Caroline. Were you going to use it as an argument in favour of inviting my—er—posh friends here?'

He was impossible! She looked away from him at the gentle countryside around them. 'No,' she said evenly, 'I promised that I wouldn't interfere with your life, didn't I? You seem to have forgotten that. It was only that I didn't want to let you down.'

'I beg your pardon, you are...' He stopped and started again. 'I should enjoy your company each morning before breakfast.'

'Would you really?' Her eyes searched his face. 'I saw you the first morning we were here, you know, that's when I made up my mind to learn to ride. But I'm not very good, it was lucky I didn't fall off just now.'

'Jan has taught you very well.' Radinck turned and spoke to the old man, who grinned at him and answered at some length, and then turned back to her. 'Jan says that all you need now is practice. It is a pity that I have an appointment this morning, otherwise I would have ridden with you.' His gaze swept over her. 'But I think you must have the right clothes. I'm free after lunch until the early evening. I'll take you into Leeuwarden and get you kitted up.'

Caro stammered a little. 'Oh, that would be s-super, but isn't it taking up your time? If you tell me where to go, I c-could go on my own.'

'We'll go together, Caroline,' and just as she was relishing this he added briskly: 'You would have no idea what to get, in the first place, and the shop is extremely hard to find.'

He was right about the shop; it was tucked away in a narrow street lined with old gabled houses, squeezed between a shirtmakers and a gentleman's hatters. Following Radinck inside, Caro wondered where on earth the customers went, and then discovered that the narrow little shop went back and back, one room opening into the next. The owner of the shop knew Radinck; he was ushered into a small room at the back, its walls lined with shelves stacked with cloth and boxes of riding boots and beautifully folded jodhpurs. Here he was given a chair while Caro was whisked into a still smaller room where, with an elderly lady to observe the conventions, she was fitted with boots, several white sweaters and shirts, a riding hat, a crop and a pair of jodhpurs, and finally the jacket. Looking at herself in the mirror she hardly recognised her image. 'Oh, very elegant,' she said out loud, and, obedient to the old tailor's beckoning finger, went rather shyly to show herself to Radinck. She stood quietly while he looked her over.

'Very nice, Caroline,' and then, to her surprise: 'What size are you?'

'In England I'm a size ten, I don't know what I am in Holland.' She was on the point of asking him why he wanted to know and then thought better of it; instead she said, 'Thank you very much, Radinck.'

He gave her a half smile. 'What else can you do, Caroline?'

She gave him a surprised look. 'Me? Well, nothing really—I can swim, but only just, if you know what I mean, and I can play the piano a bit and dance a bit...'

'You drive a car?'

She shook her head. 'No—I've never needed to, you see.'

'You shall have lessons and later on a car of your own. Tennis?'

'Well, yes.' She added waspishly: 'I hope I've passed.'

He turned away from her. 'You would have done that even if you could do none of these things. If you're quite satisfied with the things we'll get them packed up and I'll drive you back.'

She had deserved the snub, she supposed. She wondered for the hundredth time why Radinck had married her; she hadn't been a very good bargain.

Fairmindedness made her stop there; he had wanted a sheet anchor and she had said that she would be one. She belonged in the background of his life, always there when he wanted her, and it would be a good thing if she remembered that more often.

On the way back she did her best. 'I expect,' she said carefully, 'that now you've had time to think about it, you'd rather I didn't ride with you in the mornings— it's something you hadn't reckoned on, isn't it? And that wasn't why I wanted to learn to ride,' she finished with a rush.

He had turned off the motorway and had slowed the pace a little, because the road was narrow. 'I didn't think it was; shall we try it out for a day or two and see what happens?'

Caroline agreed quietly and just as quietly wished him goodbye presently. He had already told her that he had an appointment and she forbore from asking him if he would be home for dinner. She was surprised when he told her that he would see her about seven o'clock.

She wore one of the new dresses, a silk jersey in old rose with a demure stand-up collar and long sleeves, and when he got back she was sitting by the fire in the drawing-room engrossed in some tapestry work she had bought as an alternative to the sweater. She wished him a demure good evening and set a group of stitches with care. There was a pleasantly excited glow under the new dress, for Radinck had paused in the doorway and was looking at her in a way he had never looked at her before. The stitches went all wrong, but this was no time to look anything but serene and casual. She went on stitching, the needle going in and out, just as though she knew what she was doing; there would be a lot of unpicking to do later. Radinck advanced into the room, offered her a drink and went to fetch it from the sofa table under the window. As he handed it to her he observed, with the air of a man trying out words he had almost forgotten: 'You look pretty, Caroline.'

The glow rushed to her cheeks, but she answered composedly: 'Thank you—this is one of my new dresses, it is charming, isn't it?'

'I was referring to you, Caroline.'

'Oh, how kind.' That sounded silly, so she added: 'The right clothes make such a difference, you know.'

She bent to scratch Rex's woolly ear and then offered the same service to Waterloo, sitting beside the dog. 'I went to see Queenie this evening,' she told him. 'It's a wonder how she's picked up, and Willem's done wonders with her coat already.'

'I've just come from there—she's reacting very nicely to the antibiotic.' Radinck sat down in the great winged chair opposite her, his long legs stretched out, his glass in his hand, and when she looked up briefly it was to find him staring at her again, his eyes very bright. It seemed a good idea to apply herself to her tapestry and by the time Noakes came to announce dinner was ready she had made a fine mess of it.

And to her surprised delight, after dinner, instead of going to his study or out again, Radinck followed her into the drawing-room and sat drinking his coffee, giving no sign of wanting to go anywhere else. Her fingers shook as she fell upon the tapestry once again, but her face was quiet enough as she gave him a quick peep. He had stretched himself out comfortably and was reading a newspaper—perhaps he had forgotten that she was there.

But he hadn't, and presently he began to talk; observations on the news, describing an interesting case he had had at the hospital that day and going on to ask her if she would like to start Dutch lessons straight away as he had found someone suitable to teach her.

She replied suitably to everything he said and presently, loath to do so, for she could have sat there for ever with him, she declared her intention of going to bed; it would never do for him to discover that she was eager for his company. She gave him a quiet good-night and went to the door, aware as she went through it that he was looking at her again. She was halfway along the gallery above the hall when he called to her, and she stopped and leaned over the balustrade to ask 'Yes, Radinck?'

'You have forgotten that we are to ride together in the morning?'

'No, Radinck. Shall I meet you at the stables?'

'No, I shall be here at half past seven.' He said good-night again as she turned away.

Contrary to her expectations Caroline slept dream-lessly until she was wakened by Ilke with her morning tea. She drank it while she dressed, afraid of being late. Actually she raced downstairs with a couple of minutes to spare, to find Radinck waiting for her. She thought he looked splendid in his riding kit and longed to tell him so. He wished her good morning and without wasting time they went to the stables. It was almost light with a clear sky and a cold wind and the grass was touched with frost. 'If it gets much colder you will have to stop riding—once the ground gets too hard there's more chance of a toss.'

She said, 'Yes, Radinck,' meekly. Frost or no frost, she would go on riding as long as he did.

The stables were lighted and Willem was there, busy with Jemmy and Rufus, Radinck's great bay horse. Caro, her fingers crossed, contrived to mount neatly and watched while Radinck swung himself into the sad-dle, whistled to Rex, and led the way out of the yard. He hadn't fussed over her at all, merely wanted to know if she were ready and carelessly told her to straighten her back. 'We'll go over the fields as far as the lane and go round the outside of the wall,' he told her. 'Don't trot Jemmy in the fields, but you may do so in the lane.'

Caro, completely overshadowed by man and horse, craned her neck to answer him. 'Yes, very well, but I expect you like a gallop, don't you?'

'Yes, I do—but not this morning. I must find a quiet little mare for you and then we can gallop together—it hardly seems fair to expect Jemmy to do more than trot.'

She patted the pony's neck. 'He's a darling—wouldn't he mind if I rode another horse?'

Radinck laughed. 'He's been here for years—he's quite elderly now, he'll be good company for Queenie and her foal.'

They reached the first field and once out of it started to trot, and presently when they reached the gate to the lane beyond Radinck said: 'Now try a canter, Caroline.'

She acquitted herself very well, although by the time they got back she was shaking with nerves, terrified that she would fall off or do something stupid, but she didn't, and had the pleasure of hearing her husband say as they went indoors: 'That went very well—do you care to ride each morning while the weather's fine?'

She tried not to sound eager. 'Oh, please, if you'd like to.'

He turned to give her a suddenly cool look. 'I should hardly have asked you if I hadn't wanted to, Caroline. Shall we have breakfast in fifteen minutes?'

'Yes, I'll tell Juffrouw Kropp.' She went along the passage to the kitchen, gave her message and went upstairs to shower and change, her feelings mixed. Radinck had seemed so friendly, then suddenly he had drawn back and looked at her as though he didn't like her after all. She was in two minds not to go down to breakfast, but if she didn't he might think that she minded being snubbed... She changed into a tweed skirt and sweater, tied her hair back and went to join him.

He was already at the table when she got downstairs, but he got up to draw out her chair, handed her her letters, and went back to reading his own. It was to be a silent meal, she guessed; for the time being she wasn't a sheet anchor at all, only a nuisance. She murmured a cheerful good morning to Noakes when he came with fresh coffee, and immersed herself in her post—a letter from Clare, excitedly telling her the news that she was engaged, one from her aunt, asking vaguely if she were happy and regretting that she hadn't been able to attend the wedding, and a card from Sister Pringle inviting her to her wedding in the New Year. Caroline was wondering what to do about it when Radinck leaned across and handed her a pile of opened letters. 'Invitations,' he told her. 'Will you answer them?'

She glanced through them and counted six and looked up in surprise. 'But Radinck, how strange! I mean, we've been here for almost two weeks and no one has even telephoned, and now all these on the same day.'

His smile mocked her. 'My dear girl, have you forgotten that we are supposed to be newlyweds? It would hardly have been decent to have called on us or invited us anywhere for at least a fortnight.' He tossed a letter across the table to her. 'Here's a letter from Rebecca—Tiele's wife. She wants us to go over for drinks soon—she will ring you some time today.'

'Am I to accept?'

He looked faintly surprised. 'Of course. Tiele is a close friend, and I hope you and Rebecca will be friends too. As for the others, if I tell Anna to type out the correct answer in Dutch perhaps you would copy it and get them sent off.'

Caroline glanced through them; three invitations to drinks, one to the burgermeester's reception in Leeuwarden and two for evening parties.

'But, Radinck—' she began, and stopped so he looked up rather impatiently.

'Well?'

'You don't like going out,' she observed, not mincing her words. 'You said so—you like peace and quiet and time to read and...'

'You do not need to remind me, my dear Caroline, I am aware of what I like. However, there are certain conventions which must be observed. We will accept the invitations we receive, and at Christmas I will—I beg your pardon—we will give a large party. By then you will have met everyone who is acquainted with me and we can revert to a normal life here. You will have had the opportunity of making any friends you wish and doubtless you will find life sufficiently entertaining.'

Words bubbled and boiled on Caro's tongue, and she went quite red in the face choking them back. The awful thought that she was fighting a losing battle assailed her, but not for long; she had had a glimpse just once or twice of Radinck's other self hidden away behind all that ill humour. She told herself that it needed patience and all the love she had for him, and she had plenty of both.

Rebecca telephoned later that morning and Caro liked her voice immediately. 'We're not far from you,' said Rebecca, 'and I've been dying to come and see you, but Tiele said you were entitled to a couple of weeks' peace and quiet together. Will you come over for drinks? Could Radinck manage tomorrow evening, do you think—I'm going to invite you to dinner too, but if he's got something on, ring me back, will you, and we'll be content with drinks. Have you settled down?'

'Yes, thank you, though I wish I could speak Dutch, but everyone's so kind.'

'Radinck told Tiele that you were managing very well—have you started lessons yet?'

'No, but Radinck said he'd found someone to teach me.'

Rebecca giggled. 'Well, you've not had much time to bother about lessons, have you?'

She rang off presently and Caro went to her room and looked through her wardrobe, wondering what she should wear. She came to the perfectly normal female conclusion that she hadn't anything, and then changed her mind. The rose pink jersey would do; it had had a good effect the other evening, and after all, it was Radinck she wanted to notice her, not Tiele and Rebecca.

She broached the subject of going to dinner when Radinck came home for lunch and managed not to show her disappointment when he said that it was quite impossible. He had a hospital governors' meeting to attend at eight o'clock; he would drive her back from the Raukema van den Ecks and go straight on to the hospital where he would get a meal later. He looked at her sharply as he said it, but she met the look calmly, remarking that it would be nice to meet another English girl. 'She sounded sweet,' she declared. 'Would you like your coffee here or in the drawing-room?'

'I'm due back in ten minutes—I won't wait. Don't wait dinner for me either, Caroline; I'll have some sand-wiches when I get back.' He was at the door when he paused and asked: 'Will you come riding tomorrow morning?'

'Well, yes, I should like to. The same time?'

He nodded as he went out of the room.

Caroline didn't see him for the rest of that day, but he was waiting for her when she went downstairs the next morning. The weather was being kind, cold and windy but dry, and the skies were clear. She acquitted herself very well, although Radinck had very little to say as they rode across the fields and after a few re-marks about Queenie and a request that she should be ready that evening by half past six he fell silent. It was when they had returned to the house and were crossing the hall that he observed that he would be unable to get home for lunch. He spoke in his usual austere way, but she thought that she detected regret and her spirits rose.

They stayed that way too. The morning filled with her visit to see Marta, a solemn consultation with Juf-frouw Kropp about the renewal of some kitchen equip-ment, a visit to Queenie, now looking almost plump, and an hour at the piano. And the afternoon went quickly too. By half past five Caroline was upstairs in her room trying out different hairstyles and making up her face. In the end she toned down the make-up and decided to keep to her usual hairstyle, partly because she was afraid that if she attempted anything else it would disintegrate halfway through the evening. The pink jersey dress was entirely satisfactory, though. She gave a final long look in the pier glass, and went down to the sitting-room.

It wasn't quite half past six and she hadn't expected Radinck to be waiting for her, but he was, in an elegant dark suit, looking as though he hadn't just done a day's work at the hospital, only sat about in idleness. Caroline wondered how he did it. He allowed himself very little recreation. One day, she thought with real terror, he would have a coronary...

He got up as she went in, took her coat from her and held it while she got into it and they went out together. Beyond greeting her he had said nothing and nor had she, but once on the sweep she was surprised into exclaiming: 'But where's the Aston Martin?'

There was another car standing there and she went closer to see what it was. A Panther de Ville; she had only seen one or two before. Now she admired the elegance and choked over its price. She hadn't quite believed Radinck when he had said that he was rich, now she decided that she had been mistaken. Only someone with a great deal of money could afford to buy, let alone run such a motor car. 'What a lovely car,' she said faintly. 'Is it yours?'

'Yes.' He opened the door and she got in, cudgelling her brains to find some way of making him say more than yes or no. She was still worrying about it as he drove off and since he had very little to say during the brief journey, she had time to worry some more. Perhaps it was a good thing when they arrived and she had to empty her head of worries and respond to the friendly welcome from Tiele and his wife.

Rebecca, Caro was relieved to see, wasn't pretty; beautifully made up, exquisitely dressed, but not pretty, although it was apparent at once that her husband considered her the most beautiful woman in the world.

They took to each other at once and Caro was borne away to see the new baby before they had drinks. 'A darling,' declared Caro, and meant it.

'Yes, he is,' agreed his doting mother, 'but he keeps us busy, I can tell you, although we've got a marvellous nanny.' She giggled enchantingly. 'The poor dear doesn't get a look in!' She tucked an arm into Caro's as they went down the stairs. 'Tiele's a splendid father— he's a nice husband too. Radinck's a dear, isn't he? And that's a silly question!' They had reached the drawing-room and she laughingly repeated her remark to the men. 'As though Caro's going to admit anything!' she declared. Caro was glad to see that Radinck laughed too, although he didn't look at her, which was a good thing because she had got rather pink in the face.

There seemed to be a great deal to talk about and she found herself listening to Radinck's voice, warm and friendly, teasing Becky, exchanging views with Tiele, including her punctiliously in the talk so that they gave what she hoped was a splendid impression of a happily married couple. She was sorry to leave, but since they were to see each other again at the burgermeester's reception, she was able to echo her husband's '*Tot ziens*' cheerfully enough. But he showed no inclination to discuss their evening, indeed he didn't speak until they were almost halfway home.

'You enjoyed your evening?' he asked her. 'You liked Becky?'

'Very much; she's sweet, and such a darling little baby.'

Her husband grunted and she wished she hadn't said that; she hurried on to cover the little silence: 'It's nice that we shall see each other at the reception.'

'Yes. You will also meet a number of my friends there. You answered the invitations?'

'Yes, and three more came with the afternoon post.'

'Will you leave them on the hall table? I'll make sure they're friends and not just acquaintances.'

'You're not coming in before you go—wherever you're going?'

'I have no time.' She couldn't help but notice how cold his voice had become. She sighed very softly and didn't speak again until they reached the house, when she said hurriedly: 'No, don't get out, Radinck, I'm sure you're pressed for time.'

She jumped out of the car and ran up the steps where the watchful Noakes was already standing by the open door. 'We'll ride in the morning?' Radinck called after her. Caroline had been afraid he wasn't going to say that, so, careful not to sound eager, she said over her shoulder: 'I'll see you then,' and ran indoors.

She saw him much sooner than that, though. Left alone, she had whipped down to the stables to see how Queenie was, gone round the outside of the house with Rex, who was feeling hurt because Radinck had gone

without him, had her dinner, conducted her choir and
then gone upstairs to bed. She had been there two hours
or more sitting up against her pillows reviewing her
evening when she heard Queenie's voice—not loud,
not nearly loud enough to rouse everyone else in the
house, with their rooms right on the other side. Nor
would Willem hear her, living as he did in a small cottage on the estate boundary with his mother. The noise
came again and Caro got out of bed, put on her quilted
dressing gown, whipped a pair of boots from the closet,
and crept through the house. Radinck wasn't in and
she had no idea when he would return. She could take
a look at Queenie and if things weren't going right,
she could get a message to Willem or old Jan, who
would know what to do, and if necessary she could get
Mijnheer Stagsma.

She let herself out of the side door nearest the stables,
into the very cold, clear night, and, glad of her boots
but wishing she had put on something thicker than a
dressing gown, made her way to the yard. There was
a light in the barn. She switched it on and went to peer
at the donkey. Queenie looked back at her with gentle
eyes. She was lying down on her bed of straw and even
to Caro, who didn't know much about it, it was obvious that she was about to produce her foal. But whether
she was in need of help was another thing. She might
have been calling for company; after all, it was a lonely
business, giving birth.

Caro knelt down by Queenie's head and rubbed the
long furry ears; for the moment she wasn't sure what to
do. 'I'll wait just for a few minutes,' she told Queenie,

'and if something doesn't start to happen by then I'll go and get help. It's a pity that Radinck isn't here, but even if he were, I wouldn't like to bother him. You see, Queenie, he doesn't...' Her soft voice spiralled into a small shriek as her husband spoke from the dimness of the door.

'I saw the light—it's Queenie, isn't it?' He came and stood beside the pair of them, and it was difficult to see his face clearly. Caroline nodded, her heart still thumping with fright, and he took off his car coat and his jacket, rolled up his shirt sleeves and knelt down to take a closer look at the donkey. 'Any minute now,' he pronounced. 'Everything looks fine. How long have you been here?'

'Ten minutes, perhaps a little longer.'

'Did she wake you up?'

She answered without much thought. 'No—I hadn't been to sleep.'

He had his head bent. 'It's almost two o'clock.' He turned to look at her then, a slow look taking in her tousled hair and the dressing gown. 'My dear good girl, it's winter! You should have put on something warmer than that.'

'I am wearing my boots,' Caro declared as though that was a sufficient answer, and added: 'I didn't want to waste time in case Queenie was ill.'

'And what did you intend to do?' he wanted to know.

'Well, I said I'd wait just a few minutes and then if she went on groaning and looking distressed I thought I'd go and get Jan up—only he's old, I didn't want to bother him.'

He put a gentle hand on the beast's heaving flanks. 'You didn't want to bother me either, Caroline.' His voice was quiet.

'No.' For something to do she ran her fingers through her untidy hair.

'Leave your hair.' He still spoke quietly and she dropped her hands in astonishment. After a moment he said: 'Look!'

The foal was enchanting. 'We shall be able to call him Prince,' observed Radinck as they watched him get to his wobbly legs and nuzzle his mother. 'Caroline, do you think you could make some hot mash? Willem should have it ready for the morning over in the far corner. There's a Primus—just warm it up, Queenie could do with it now. I'll stay here for a minute or two just to make sure everything's as it should be.'

Caroline went obediently, found the mash and the stove and waited while it heated, and presently went back with it to find that Radinck had fetched a bucket of water which Queenie was drinking thirstily. She gobbled down the mash too, standing between the pair of them. She was still far from being in the pink of condition, but she was clean and combed and content. Caro, sitting back on her heels so that she could see more of the foal, observed: 'Oh, isn't it lovely? She's so happy.' She caught her breath. 'What would have happened to her if we hadn't taken her in?'

'Oh, she would have been left in a field to fend for herself.' Radinck didn't add to that because Caro's eyes were filled with tears.

'In a couple of days she shall go out into the fields

with the horses. She's almost strong enough—they like company, you know, and horses like them.'

Queenie finished her meal, arranged herself comfortably on the straw with the foal beside her and wagged her ears. 'She's telling us we can go,' said Radinck. 'She'll do very well until Willem comes.' He pulled Caro to her feet, draped his jacket round her and walked her back through the moonlight night to the side door. Inside she would have gone to bed, but he kept an arm round her shoulders. 'I have a fancy for a cup of tea,' he declared. 'Let's go to the kitchen and make one—it will warm you, too.'

He seemed to know where everything was. Caro, her arms in the sleeves of his jacket to make things a little easier, got mugs, sugar and milk while he fetched a teapot and a tea canister, found a loaf and some butter and put them on the table. 'Didn't you have any dinner?' asked Caro.

'Yes—only it was a very dainty one. I have been famished for the last hour.'

'Oh, that's a terrible feeling,' agreed Caro, 'and one always thinks of all the nicest things to eat. I've often...' She stopped herself just in time. He wouldn't want to know that she had sometimes been rather hungry; hospital meals cost money and although one could eat adequately enough if one were careful, there was never anything left over for chocolate eclairs and steak and sole bonne femme.

'Well?' asked Radinck.

'Nothing.' She busied herself pouring the tea

while he sliced bread and spread it lavishly with butter.

Caroline hadn't enjoyed a meal as much for a long time. It was as though Radinck was a different person. She wasn't just having a glimpse of him as he really was, he was letting her get to know him. She found herself talking to him as though she had known him all her life. She had forgotten to worry that he might, at any moment, revert to his normal severe manner. Everything was wonderful. She sat there, eating slices of bread and butter, oblivious of her tatty appearance, talking about Queenie, and her riding and how she was going to learn to speak Dutch and what fun it was to have found a friend in Becky. And Radinck did nothing to stop her—indeed, he encouraged her with cleverly put questions which she answered with all the spontaneous simplicity of a small girl. It was the old-fashioned wall clock striking a ponderous three which brought her up short. She began to collect up the mugs and plates, stammering a little. 'I'm sorry—I've kept you out of bed, I don't know what came over me.'

He took the things from her and put them back on the table. 'Leave those. Will you be too tired to ride in the morning?'

'Tired? Heavens, no, I wouldn't miss...' She stopped herself again. 'The mornings are lovely at this time of year,' she observed rather woodenly.

Radinck was staring down at her. 'I must agree with you, Caroline—the mornings are lovely.' He turned away abruptly and went over to the sink with the teapot and she watched him, idly sticking her hands into

the pockets of his jacket which she still wore draped
round her. There was something in one of them. She
just had time to pull it almost out to look at it before
he turned round; she only had a glimpse, but it was
enough. It was a handkerchief—a woman's handkerchief, new but crumpled.

They walked out of the kitchen together and up the
stairs, and all the way Caroline told herself that she had
no reason to mind so much. She had taken her hands out
of the pockets as though they were full of hot coals and
handed him his jacket with a murmur of thanks, aware
of a pain almost physical. If she was going to feel like
this every time she encountered some small sign that
she wasn't the only woman in his life, then she might
just as well give up at once. Of course, the handkerchief could belong to an aunt or a cousin or…he had no
relations living close by. It could belong, said a nasty
little voice at the back of her head, to whoever it was
he went to see almost every evening in the week. Then
why had he married her? Couldn't the handkerchief's
owner have been a sheet anchor too? She thought of herself as a shabby, reliable coat, always at hand hanging
on the back door, necessary but never worn anywhere
but in the back yard in bad weather, whereas a really
smart coat would be taken from the closet with care
and pride and displayed to one's friends.

At the top of the stairs she wished him goodnight
and was quite unprepared for his sudden swoop and
his hard, quick kiss. She turned without a word and

fled into her room, aware that any other girl with her
wits about her would have known how to deal with
the situation.

CHAPTER SEVEN

IF CARO HADN'T been so sleepy she might have lain awake and pondered Radinck's behaviour, but beyond a fleeting sense of elation mixed with a good deal of puzzlement, there was no time to think at all; she was asleep as her head touched the pillow. And in the morning there was no time for anything but getting dressed by half past seven. As she went downstairs she did wonder if she would feel awkward when she saw him, but that need not have worried her. He offered her a cool good morning, led her down to the stables, watched her mount, had a word with Willem about Queenie, and led the way into the fields. They rode in almost complete silence and on their return, even the sight of Queenie and her foal called forth no more than a further businesslike discussion with Willem as to their welfare. They were back to square one, thought Caro. Last night had been an episode to be forgotten or at least ignored. She remembered the hanky with a pang of sheer envy, subdued it with difficulty and loitered to add her own remarks to Willem, who, with the rest of the staff at Huis Thoe, made a point of understanding her peculiar Dutch.

By the time she got down to breakfast, Radinck was almost ready to leave. Caroline wasn't in the least surprised when he mentioned that he wouldn't be home for lunch. She was glad that there was so much to keep her occupied. It wasn't until after lunch that the wicked little thought that she might take another look at the handkerchief in Radinck's jacket pocket entered her head. The suit was to be sent to the cleaners, along with her dressing gown; they would be in one of the small rooms leading from the passage which led to the kitchen.

They were there all right. Feeling guilty, she searched every pocket and found the handkerchief gone. It must be something very precious to Radinck and it served her right for snooping. Feeling ashamed of herself, she put on her sheepskin jacket, pulled a woollen cap over her head and went to find Rex, prowling in discontent from room to room. He had been left behind again. They went a long way, indeed they were still only half-way home in the gathering dusk when Radinck opened his house door. He had a large box under one arm and went at once to the sitting-room where Caro liked to spend her leisure.

The room was empty of course, and in answer to his summons, Noakes informed him that the Baroness had gone out with Rex. 'Been gorn a long time, too,' observed Noakes. 'Great walker, she is too.' He turned to go, adding with a trusted old friend's freedom: 'Walking away from somethin', if yer ask me.'

His employer turned cold blue eyes on him. 'And what exactly does that mean?'

Noakes threw him a quick shrewd look. 'Just me opinion, Professor, take it or leave it, as you might say.'

'She's unhappy? The Baroness is unhappy?'

'Not ter say unhappy—always busy, she is, with this and that—flowers in the rooms and ordering stores and learning Dutch all by 'erself. 'Omesick, I've no doubt, Professor.' He added defiantly: 'She's on 'er own a lot.'

The master of the house looked coldly furious. 'I have my work, Noakes.'

'And now, beggin' yer pardon, Professor, you've got 'er as well.'

The Professor looked like a thundercloud. 'It is a good thing that we are old friends, Noakes...'

His faithful butler had a prudent hand on the door. 'Yes, Professor—I'd not 'ave said any of that if we 'adn't been.'

The austere lines of the Professor's face broke into a smile. 'I know that, Noakes, and I value your friendship.'

Caro walked in half an hour later, her cheeks glowing, her hair regrettably untidy. As she came into the hall from the garden door, Rex beside her, she saw Noakes on his stately way to the kitchen.

'Noakes!' she cried. 'We've had a lovely walk, I'm as warm as toast. And don't frown at me, I've wiped Rex's feet. I went to see Queenie too and she's fine.' She had thrown off her jacket and was pulling the cap off her head when the sitting-room door opened and she saw Radinck.

Her breath left her, as it always did when she saw him. After a little silence she said: 'Hullo, Radinck, I didn't know you'd be home early. I hope you've had tea—we went further than we meant to.'

He leaned against the wall, his bland face giving nothing away. 'I waited for you, Caroline.' He nodded at Noakes who hurried kitchenwards and held the door wide for her to go in. The room looked very welcoming; the fire burned brightly in the grate and Waterloo had made himself comfortable before it, joined, after he had made much of his master, by Rex. Caro sat down on the little armchair by the work table she had made her own, smoothed her hair without bothering much about it, and picked up her tapestry work. She had painstakingly unpicked it and now had the miserable task of working it again. She smiled across at her husband. 'I hope it's scones, I've been showing Marta how to make them.'

He said gravely: 'I look forward to them. Caroline, are you lonely?'

The question was so unexpected that she pricked her finger. She said rather loudly: 'Lonely? Why, of course not—there's so much to do, and now I'm going to start Dutch lessons, tomorrow, and Juffrouw Kropp is teaching me how to be a good housekeeper, and there are the animals...' She paused, seeking something to add to her meagre list of activities. 'Oh, and now there's Becky...'

Noakes brought in the tea tray then and she busied herself pouring it from the George the Second silver bullet teapot into the delicate cups. It wasn't being rich that mattered, she mused, it was possessing beauti-

ful things, lovingly made and treasured and yet used
each day...

'Queenie and Prince are doing very well,' remarked
Radinck.

She passed him his cup and saucer. 'Yes, aren't they?
I went to see them this morning—twice, in fact... Oh,
and I asked Juffrouw Kropp to see that your suit went
to the cleaners.'

'I imagined you might; I emptied the pockets.' He
stared at her so hard that she began to pinken, and to
cover her guilty feelings about looking for that hanky,
bent to lift the lid of the dish holding the scones.

'Will you have a scone?' she asked. 'Marta's such a
wonderful cook...'

'And your dressing gown? That was ruined, I imagine.'

'Well, yes, but I think it'll clean—it may need several...'

'I don't think I should bother, Caroline.' He bent
down and took the box from the floor beside his chair.
'I hope this will do instead.'

Caroline gave him a surprised look, undid the berib-
boned box slowly and gently lifted aside the layers of
tissue paper, to lift out a pale pink quilted satin robe,
its high neck and long sleeves edged with chiffon frills;
the kind of extravagant garment she had so often stared
at through shop windows and never hoped to possess.

'It's absolutely gorgeous!' she exclaimed. 'I shall
love wearing it. Thank you very much, Radinck, it was
most kind of you.' She smiled at him and just for once
he smiled back at her.

They had a pleasant tea after that, not talking about anything much until Caro reminded him that they were to go to the burgermeester's reception the following evening.

'You have a dress?' Radinck enquired idly, 'or do you want to go to den Haag shopping—Noakes can easily drive you there.'

'Oh, I have a dress, thank you. It's—it's rather grand.'

'Too grand for my wife?' He spoke mockingly, but she didn't notice for once.

'Oh, oh, no, but it's rather—there's not a great deal of top to it.' She eyed him anxiously.

The corners of Radinck's stern mouth twitched. 'It was my impression that—er—not a great deal of top for the evening was all the fashion this season.'

'Well, it is. The sales lady said it was quite suitable, but I—I haven't been to an evening party for some time and I'm not sure...'

'The sales lady looked very knowledgeable,' said Radinck kindly, and forbore from adding that she would know better than to sell the Baroness Thoe van Erckelens anything unsuitable. 'Supposing you put it on and I'll take a look at it before we leave tomorrow—just to reassure you.'

'Oh, would you? I wouldn't like people to stare.' Caroline added reluctantly: 'I don't think I'm much good at parties.'

'Neither am I, Caroline, but you don't need to worry. Everyone is eager to meet a bride, you know.' His voice held a faint sneer and she winced and was only partly comforted by his: 'I'm sure the dress will be most suitable.'

Caro repeated this comforting observation to herself while she examined herself in the long mirror in her bedroom, dressed ready for the reception. There was no doubt about it, it was a beautiful dress; a pale smoky grey chiffon over satin with a finely pleated frill round its hem and the bodice which was causing her so much doubt, finely pleated too.

She turned away from her reflection, caught up the mink and went quickly down the staircase before she lost her nerve.

The drawing-room door was half open and Noakes, appearing from nowhere opened it wide for her to go through. Radinck was standing with his back to the hearth with Rex and Waterloo sitting at his feet enjoying the warmth. Caro nipped across the stretch of carpet and came to a breathless halt. 'Well?' she asked.

Radinck studied her leisurely. 'A charming dress,' he pronounced finally, 'exactly right for the occasion.'

She waited for him to say more, even a half-hearted compliment about herself would have been better than nothing at all, but he remained silent. And she had taken such pains with her face and hair and hands...

She said in a quiet little voice: 'I'm ready, Radinck,' and picked up her coat which Noakes had draped over a chair.

He didn't answer her but moved away from the fire to fetch something lying on one of the sofa tables. She thought how magnificent he looked in his tails and white tie, but if she told him so, he might think that she was wishing for a compliment in her turn.

He crossed the room to her, opened the case in his hand and took out its contents. 'This was my mother's,' he told her. 'I think it will go very well with this dress. Turn round while I fasten it for you.'

The touch of his fingers made her tremble although she stood obediently still, and then went to look in the great gilded mirror on one wall. The necklace was exquisite; sapphires linked by an intricate chain of diamonds, a dainty, costly trifle which went very well with her dress. She touched it lightly with a pretty hand, acknowledging its beauty and magnificence, while at the same time aware that if it had been a bead necklace from Woolworths given with all his love she would have worn it for ever and loved every bead.

She turned away from the mirror and got into the coat he was holding, picked up the grey satin purse which exactly matched her slippers and went with him to the car. On the way to Leeuwarden she asked: 'Is there anything special I should know about this evening?'

'I think not. I shall remain with you and see that you meet my friends, and once you have found your feet, I daresay you will like to talk to as many people as possible. It will be like any other party you have been to, Caroline.'

It was on the tip of her tongue to tell him that she had been to very few parties and certainly never to a grand reception, but pride curbed her tongue. She got out of the car presently, her determined little chin well up, and went up the steps to the burgermeester's front door, her skirts held daintily and with Radinck's hand under her elbow. She had a moment of panic in the enormous entrance hall as she was led away by a severe maid to remove her coat, and cast a longing look at the door—it was very close; she had only to turn and run…

'I shall be here waiting for you, Caroline,' said her husband quietly.

The reception rooms were on the first floor. Caroline went up the wide staircase, Radinck beside her, her heart beating fit to choke her. There were people all around them, murmuring and smiling, but Radinck didn't stop until they reached the big double doors opening on to the vast apartment where the burger-meester and his wife were receiving their guests. She had imagined that their host would be a large impressive man with a terrifying wife. He was nothing of the sort; of middle height and very stout, he had a fringe of grey hair and a round smiling face which beamed a welcome at her. She murmured politely in her carefully learned Dutch and was relieved when he addressed her in English.

'So, now I meet you, Baroness,' he chuckled, 'and how happy I am to do so. We will talk presently; I look forward to it.' He passed her on to his wife with a laughing remark to Radinck, who introduced her to a tall thin lady with a beaky nose and a sweet expression. Her English was fragmental and Caro, having repeated her few phrases, was relieved when Radinck took the conversation smoothly into his own hands before taking her arm and leading her into the room.

He seemed to know everyone there, and she shook hands and murmured, forgetting most of the names immediately until finally Radinck whisked her on to the floor to dance.

He danced well, but then so did she; not that she had had much chance to show her skill, but she had always loved dancing and it came naturally to her. She floated round in his arms, just for a little while a happy girl, although a peep at his face decided her not to talk. It was bland and faintly smiling, but the smile wasn't for her; she had the horrid feeling that he was doing his social duty without much pleasure. On the whole she was glad when the music stopped and Tiele and Becky joined them, and when the music started again it was Tiele who asked her to dance.

Unlike Radinck he chatted in an easy casual way, telling her how pretty she looked, how well she danced and wanting to know if she and Radinck would be at the hospital ball.

'Well, you know, I'm not sure about that—there were so many invitations...' And when her partner looked surprised: 'Does Radinck always go?'

Tiele studied her earnest face carefully. 'Oh, yes, though it's always been a bit of a duty for him—not much fun for a man on his own, you know. But you're sure to be there this year. We must join forces for the evening.'

He was rewarded by her smile. 'I'd like that—it's all rather strange, you know, and my Dutch isn't up to much.'

'Never mind that,' he told her kindly. 'You dance

like a dream and everyone's saying that you're just right for Radinck.'

She blushed brightly. 'Oh, thank you—I hope you're right; I don't mind what people say really, only I do want Radinck to be proud of me.'

Tiele's eyes were thoughtful, but he said easily: 'He's that all right!'

And after that Caroline went from partner to partner. There seemed to be no end to them, and although she caught glimpses of Radinck from time to time he made no attempt to approach her. It wasn't until they all went down to supper that he appeared suddenly beside her, took her arm and found her a seat at a table for four, before going in search of food at the buffet. Becky and Tiele, following them in, hesitated about joining them until Becky said softly: 'Look, darling, he's only danced with her once this evening. If it had been you I'd have boxed your ears! Look at her sitting there—she's lonely.'

'I'd rather look at you, my darling, and I don't think Radinck would like his ears boxed.'

'Well, of course he wouldn't, and Caro's clever enough to know that.' Becky added darkly: 'He's been leading a bachelor life too long—she's such a dear, too.'

'Which allows us to hope that he will become a happily married man, my love.'

Caro had seen them. Becky gave her husband's arm a wifely nip and obedient to this signal, they went to join her. Tiele said easily: 'Do you mind if we join you?' He settled his wife in a chair beside Caro. 'I suppose Radinck is battling his way towards the sandwiches—

I'll join him.' He touched his wife lightly on her arm. 'Anything you fancy, darling?'

Becky thought briefly. 'Well, I like vol-au-vents, but only if they've got salmon in them, and those dear little cream puffs. What are you having, Caro?'

'I don't know.' Caro smiled brightly, wishing with all her heart that Radinck would call her darling in that kind of a voice and ask her what she would like, as though he really minded. Tiele, she felt sure, would bring back salmon vol-au-vents and cream puffs even if he had to go out and bake them himself.

But it seemed that these delicacies were readily obtainable, for he was back in no time at all with a tray of food and Radinck with him. Caro accepted the chicken patties he had brought for her, had her glass filled with champagne and declared herself delighted with everything. And Radinck seemed to be enjoying himself, laughing and talking with Tiele and teasing Becky and treating herself with charming politeness. Only she wondered how much of it was social good manners, hiding his impatience of the whole evening. It wasn't until Becky remarked: 'We shall all see each other at the hospital ball, shan't we? Can't we go together?' that Caro saw the bland look on his face again and heard the sudden coolness in his voice.

'I'm not certain if we shall be going—I've that seminar in Vienna.'

'Isn't that on the following day?' asked Tiele.

'Yes, but I've one or two committees—I thought I'd go a day earlier and settle them first.' He glanced at

Caro. 'I don't think Caroline will mind—we have so many parties during the next few weeks.'

Becky opened her mouth, caught her husband's quelling eye and closed it again, and Caro, anxious to do the right thing, observed with a cheerfulness she didn't feel that of course Radinck was quite right and she wouldn't mind missing the ball in the least.

'You could come with us,' suggested Becky, but was answered by Radinck's politely chilling:

'Might that not seem a little strange? We have been married for such a short time.'

'Oh, you mean that people might think you'd quarrelled or separated or something,' observed Becky forthrightly. 'Caro, let's go and tidy up for the second half,' and on their way: 'Caro, why don't you go to Vienna with Radinck?'

Caro tried to be nonchalant and failed utterly. 'Oh, he wouldn't want me around.' She went on quickly in case her companion got the wrong idea, 'He works so hard.' Which didn't quite seem adequate but was all she could think of.

Back on the dance floor, she almost gasped with relief when Radinck swept her into a waltz. She had been in a panic that he would introduce her to some dry-as-dust dignitary and leave her with him, or worse still, just leave her. They danced in silence for a few minutes before he asked her if she was enjoying herself.

'Yes, thank you,' said Caro. 'You have a great many friends, haven't you, and they are all very kind.'

'They have no reason to be otherwise.' He spoke so austerely that her champagne-induced pleasure dwindled away to nothing at all. She danced as she always did, gracefully and without fault, but her heart wasn't in it. Radinck was doing his duty again and not enjoying it, although she had to admit that nothing of his feelings showed on his face. The dance finished and he relinquished her to another partner and she didn't see him again until the last dance, when he swept her on to the floor again—but only, she thought sadly, because it was customary for the last dance to be enjoyed by married couples and sweethearts together.

They left quickly, giving Caro barely time to say goodbye to Becky. 'I'll telephone,' cried Becky, 'and anyway we'll see each other at the Hakelsmas' drinks party, won't we?'

Radinck maintained a steady flow of casual talk as they drove home. Caro listened when it seemed necessary and, once in the house, bade him a quiet goodnight and started up the staircase. She was halted halfway up by his query as to whether she wouldn't like a cup of coffee with him, but she paused only long enough to shake her head, glad that he was too far away to see the tears in her eyes. The evening, despite the dress, had been a failure. He had evinced no pleasure in her company and she had no doubt at all that the moment she was out of sight he would turn away with a sigh of thankfulness and go to his study, to immerse himself in his books and papers. She undressed very quickly and took off the necklace; tomorrow she would return it to him.

Ilke, not having been told otherwise, woke her early so that she might go riding, but she drank her tea slowly and then lay, listening for the sound of Rufus's hooves on the cobblestones. Presently, after they had died away, she got up, bathed and dressed in her new suit, did her face and hair and went down to her breakfast. Radinck was back by then, already halfway through his own meal, and she said at once as she went in: 'Good morning—no, don't get up, I'm sure you have no time.'

She slipped into her chair and sipped the coffee Noakes had poured for her and took a slice of toast.

'You were too tired to ride,' stated Radinck.

'Me, tired? Not in the least.' She gave him a sunny smile and buttered her toast, and after a moment or two he picked up his letters again, tossing several over to her as he did so.

'Will you answer these? Drinks mostly, I think.'

'You want me to refuse them?'

He looked impatient. 'Certainly not. Why should you think that?'

Caroline didn't answer. After all, she had told him once; she wasn't going to keep on. Instead she got on with her breakfast and when Noakes went out of the room, she got up and put the necklace carefully beside her husband's plate.

'Thank you for letting me wear it,' she said.

He put down the letter he had been reading to stare at her down his handsome nose. 'My dear Caroline, I gave it to you.'

She opened her hazel eyes wide. 'Oh, did you? I thought you'd lent it to me just for the evening. How kind—but I can't accept it, you know.'

'Why not?' Radinck's brows were drawn together in an ominous frown.

She did her best to explain. 'Well, it's not like a present, is it? I mean, one gives a present because one wants to, but you gave me the necklace to wear because your wife would be expected to have the family jewels.'

Radinck crumpled up the letter in his hand and hurled it at the wastepaper basket.

'What an abominable girl you are, Caroline! As I said some time ago, you have this gift of putting me in the wrong.'

'I'm sorry if you're annoyed, but I can't possibly accept it, though I'll wear any jewellery you like when we go out together.'

He said silkily: 'Don't count on going out too often, Caroline, I'm a busy man.'

'Well, I wasn't going to.' She gave him a thoughtful look, and added kindly: 'You're very cross—I daresay you're tired. We should have left earlier last night.'

The silkiness was still there, tinged with ice now. 'When I wish you to organise my life, Caroline, I will say so. I am not yet so elderly that I cannot decide things for myself.'

'Oh, you're not elderly at all,' said Caro soothingly. 'You're not even middle-aged. How silly of you to think that; you must know that you're…' She stopped abruptly and he urged her blandly:

'Do go on.'

'No, I won't, you'll only bite my head off if I do.' She took a roll and spread it with butter and cheese. 'What time do you want to go to Mevrouw Hakelsma's party? Only so that I'll be ready on time,' she added hastily.

'It is for half past seven, isn't it? I should be home by six o'clock. Will you see that dinner is later?'

'Would half past eight suit you? I'll tell Juffrouw Kropp.'

He nodded. 'I should like to leave the Hakelsmas' place within an hour; I've a good deal of work waiting.'

Caro kept her face cheerful. 'Of course. Just nod and wink at me when you're ready to leave.'

Radinck got up from the table. 'I shall neither nod nor wink,' he told her cuttingly. 'You are my wife, not the dog.' He stalked to the door. 'I'll see you this evening.'

She said, 'Yes, Radinck,' so meekly that he shot her a suspicious look and paused to say:

'It will be short dresses this evening.'

She said 'Yes, Radinck,' again, still so meek that he exclaimed forcefully:

'I wish you would refrain from this continuous "Yes, Radinck", as though I were a tyrant!'

'Oh, but you're not,' Caro assured him warmly. 'That's the last thing you are; it's just that you've lived so long alone that you've forgotten how to talk. Never mind, you'll soon get into the habit again now that I'm here.' She gave him a limpid smile and he said something in a subdued roar, something nasty in his own language, she judged, as she watched him go.

She finished her breakfast, inspected more cupboards under Juffrouw Kropp's guidance, discussed the evening's dinner with Marta and then arranged the flowers, a task she enjoyed even though it took a long time, and then went down to see how Queenie was getting on. Willem was there and they stood admiring the little donkey and her son, carrying on a conversation, which, while completely ungrammatical on Caro's part, Willem understood very well. She had sugar for the horses too, and Jemmy whinnied when he saw her, looking at her so reproachfully that she changed after lunch and, with Jan keeping a watchful eye on her, rode round the fields. Which didn't leave her much time for anything else. She was ready, wearing one of her new dresses, pink silk jersey with a demure neck and long sleeves, well before six o'clock, and went to sit in the smaller of the sitting-rooms, industriously knitting. It was half past six when Noakes came to tell her that Radinck was on the telephone.

He sounded austere. 'I'm sorry, Caroline, but I shall be home later than I expected. Perhaps you could ring Mevrouw Hakelsma and say all the right things. I don't expect we can get there much before eight o'clock.'

She said, 'Yes, Radinck,' before she could stop herself, but what else was there to say? 'OK, darling,' wouldn't have pleased him at all. She went along to the kitchen and prudently arranged for dinner to be delayed, then went back to her knitting.

Radinck got home at half past seven, looking tired, which somehow made him more approachable.

Caro wished him a pleasant good evening. 'Would you like a sandwich before you go upstairs?' she asked.

He had gone to the sofa table where the tray of drinks

was. 'Thank you, I should—I missed lunch. What will you drink?'

'Sherry, thank you.' She pressed the old-fashioned brass bell beside the hearth and when Noakes came asked for a plate of sandwiches.

Radinck was famished. He devoured the lot with his whisky, looking like a tired, very handsome wolf who hadn't had a square meal for days. Caro watching him, bursting with love, sighed soundlessly; he needed someone to look after him so badly.

He went away presently, to rejoin her in a little while looking immaculate in one of his beautifully cut dark suits. She got up at once, laid her knitting on the work table and went with him into the hall where Noakes was waiting with their coats. Radinck helped her into hers and shrugged on his own coat, and Caro, with a quick whisper to Noakes to be sure and have dinner ready to put on the table the moment they got back, followed Radinck out to the car.

The Hakelsmas lived on the outskirts of Leeuwarden, in a large red-brick villa full of heavy, comfortable furniture. Caro had already met them at the burgermeester's reception and liked them both—in their forties, jolly, plump and kind. They had a large family, and three of them were there helping to entertain the guests, of whom there seemed to be a great many.

Caro murmured her set piece to her host and hostess, accepted a glass of sherry and something called a *bitterbal* which she didn't like at all, and was swept away to go from one group to the other, careful never to lose sight of Radinck. He seemed very popular, laughing and talking as though he liked nothing better than standing about drinking sherry and making small talk, and some of the girls there were very pretty and he appeared to be on very good terms with them. Caro, swept by a wave of jealousy, tried not to look at him too much. She had never thought of him as being likely to fall in love with anyone else, but there was no earthly reason why he shouldn't. One couldn't help these things. Of course she had every intention of trying to make him fall in love with her, but she began to wonder if the competition was too keen. Her not very pleasant thoughts were interrupted by Becky's voice.

'Hullo—you're looking wistful. Why?' She beamed at Caro. 'You're late. Did Radinck get held up?'

'Yes. There are a lot of people here, aren't there? I expect I met most of them at the burgermeester's.'

'Don't worry, it took me months to remember everyone's name, but they're all very sweet about it, and we'll all be seeing each other quite a lot during the next few weeks. Radinck gave an enormous party last year—are you having one this year too?'

'I think so.'

'Well, I expect now he's got you, he'll go out more. He's always been a bit of a recluse—well, ever since…'

'His first wife died? That's understandable, isn't it?' Caro smiled at Becky and let her see that she knew all about the first wife and it didn't matter at all.

On their way home presently, she said carefully: 'Radinck, I don't a bit mind not going to all these parties if you don't want to. After all, everyone knows you're a very busy man—mind you,' she observed thoughtfully, 'I daresay you don't need to do as much work as you do, if you see what I mean. Becky said you didn't go out much before—before we got married, and I did promise you that I'd not interfere with your life…'

She couldn't see his face, but she could tell from his voice that he was frowning. 'I thought that I had made myself clear; we will attend as many of these parties as possible, give an evening party ourselves, and then I shall be able to return to what you call my life. For most of the year there is very little social life on a big scale, only just before Christmas and at the New Year. Once that is over…' He slowed the car a little and Caro, thankful for the chance to talk to him even if only for a brief while, said unhappily: 'You hate it, don't you? I'm glad it's only for a few weeks. What a pity I can't get 'flu or something, then we couldn't go…'

'That is a singularly foolish remark, Caroline. Of course you won't get anything of the sort.'

But just for once he, who was so often right, was wrong. Caro woke up in the morning feeling faintly peculiar. She hadn't got a headache, but her head felt heavy, and moreover, when she got out of bed her feet didn't seem to touch the ground. She had no appetite for her breakfast either, but as Radinck was reading his letters and scanning the morning's papers, she didn't think that mattered. He was never chatty over the meal; she took some toast and crumbled it at intervals just in case he should look up, and drank several cups of coffee which revived her sufficiently to bid him goodbye in a perfectly normal way. They weren't going anywhere that evening and she would be able to go to bed early, as he so often went straight to his study after dinner. She went through her morning routine, visited Queenie and Prince, took Waterloo for a brief walk in the gardens and retired to the library to struggle with her Dutch. But she didn't seem able to concentrate, not even with the help of several more cups of coffee. She toyed with her lunch, which upset Noakes very much, and then went back to the sitting-room, got out her knitting and curled up in Radinck's chair with Waterloo on her lap. He was warm and comforting and after a very short time she gave up trying to knit and closed her eyes and dozed off into a troubled sleep, to be wakened by a worried Noakes with the tea tray.

'Yer not yerself, ma'am,' he declared. 'Yer ought to go ter bed.'

She eyed him hazily. 'Yes, I think I will when I've had tea, Noakes. It's just a cold.'

She drank the teapot dry and went off to sleep again, her cheeks flushed and her head heavy. She didn't wake when Radinck, met at the door by an anxious Noakes, came into the room.

Caro looked small and lonely and lost in his great chair and he muttered something as he bent over her, a cool hand on her hot forehead. She woke up then, staring into the blue eyes so close to hers. 'I feel very grotty,' she mumbled. 'I meant to go to bed... I'll go now.'

She began to scramble out of the chair and he picked her up with Waterloo still in her arms. 'You should have gone hours ago,' he said almost angrily. 'You weren't well at breakfast—why didn't you say so then?'

He was mounting the staircase and she muttered: 'I can walk,' and then: 'I thought I'd feel better. Besides, I didn't think you noticed.'

Noakes had gone ahead to open the door and Radinck laid her on the bed, asked Noakes to fetch Juffrouw Kropp and then pulled the coverlet over Caro, who was beginning to shiver. 'So sorry,' she told him, 'such a nuisance for you. I'll be quite all right now.'

He didn't answer but waited until Juffrouw Kropp came into the room, spoke to her quietly and went away, while that lady undressed Caro as though she had been a baby, tucked her up in her bed and went to fetch Radinck, walking up and down the gallery outside. Caro, feeling so wretched by now that she didn't care about anything at all, put out her tongue, muttered and mumbled ninety-nine and then swallowed the pills she was given. She was asleep in five minutes.

She woke a couple of hours later, feeling very peculiar in the head, and found Radinck bending over her again. He looked large and solid and very dependable, and she sighed with relief because he was there.

'Now you won't have to go to the party tomorrow,' she told him, still half asleep, 'and there's a dinner party...when? Quite soon; we needn't go to that either.' She closed her eyes and then opened them wide again. 'I'm so glad, you can have peace and quiet again.'

She dropped off again, so that she didn't hear the words wrung so reluctantly from Radinck's lips. Which was a pity.

She felt a little better in the morning, but her recollection of the night was hazy; she had wakened several times and there had been a lamp by the bed, but the rest of the room had been in shadow. And once or twice someone had given her a drink, but she had been too tired to open her eyes and see who it was. Radinck came to see her at breakfast time, pronounced himself satisfied as to her progress and went away again, leaving her with Waterloo for company. Presently Juffrouw Kropp came and washed her face and hands, brushed her hair and then brought her a tray of tea—nice strong tea with a lot of milk, and paper-thin bread and butter.

Caro dozed through the day. Lovingly tended by Juffrouw Kropp, Marta and the maids, it seemed to her that each time she opened her eyes there was someone in the room looking anxiously at her. Towards teatime Noakes came in with a vase of autumn flowers and a message from Becky and Tiele, and that was followed by a succession of notes and several more flower arrangements.

'But I've only got 'flu,' said Caro. 'I mean, there's really no need…'

'Very well liked, yer are, ma'am,' said Noakes with deep satisfaction. 'The phone's bin going on and off all afternoon with messages.'

'But how did they all know?'

'The Professor will 'ave cancelled your engagements, ma'am.'

Caro nodded. She wasn't enjoying having 'flu, but at least it was making Radinck happy. She drank her tea and after a struggle to keep awake, slept again.

She woke to find Radinck at the foot of the bed, looking at her, and she assured him before he could ask her that she was feeling a great deal better. She sat up against the pillows, happily unaware of her wan face and tousled hair. 'And look at all these flowers,' she begged him, 'and I'm not even ill. I feel a fraud!'

He said seriously: 'You have no need to—you have a quite violent virus infection of the respiratory system.'

It was silly to get upset, but somehow he had made her feel like a patient in a hospital bed; someone to be cured of an ailment with a completely impersonal care. Her eyes filled with tears until they dripped down her cheeks and although she put up an impatient hand to rub them away, there seemed no end to them. Radinck bent over her, a handkerchief in his hand, but she pushed it away. 'I'm perfectly all right,' she told him crossly. 'It's just that I don't feel quite the thing.' She added peevishly: 'I think I'd like to go to sleep.'

She closed her eyes so that he would see that she really meant that, and although the tears were still pouring from under her lids, she kept them shut. And after a minute or so she really did feel sleepy in a dreamy kind of way, so that the kiss on her cheek seemed part of the dream too. She woke much later and remembered it—it had been very pleasant; dreams could be delightful. She dismissed the idea that Radinck had kissed her as ridiculous and wept a little before she slept again.

CHAPTER EIGHT

TWO DAYS LATER Caro was on her feet again. She had been coddled and mothered by Juffrouw and Marta, ably backed by the maids and old Jan who sent in flowers each day from his cherished hothouses, the whole team masterminded by Noakes. No one could have been kinder. Even Radinck, visiting her twice a day, had been meticulous in his attentions. Although that hadn't stopped him telling her that he would be going to Vienna that evening. 'You wouldn't wish to go to the hospital ball,' he pointed out with unescapable logic, 'and much though I regret having to leave you while you are feeling under the weather, my presence is hardly necessary to your recovery. My entire—I beg your pardon—our entire staff are falling over themselves to lavish attention upon you.' He gave her a mocking little smile. 'I leave you in the best of hands.'

Caro had agreed with him in a quiet little voice. Normally she wouldn't have allowed herself to feel crushed by his high-handedness, but she wasn't quite herself. Her chances of making him fall in love with her seemed so low they hardly bore contemplation. She wished him goodbye and hoped he would have a good trip and that the seminar would be interesting, and then, unable to think of anything else to say, sat up in bed just looking at him.

'Goodbye, Caroline,' said Radinck in a quite different voice, and bent and kissed her cheek. She didn't move for quite a while after he had gone, but presently when Waterloo jumped on to the bed and gave her an enquiring butt with his head, she scratched the top of it in an absent manner. 'I didn't dream it, then,' she told him. 'He kissed me then as well. Now, I wonder...'

It was probably a false hope, but at least she could work on it. She got bathed and dressed and went downstairs, to be fussed over by everyone in the house, and all of them remarked how much better she looked.

She felt better. Somewhere or other there was a chink in her husband's armour of cool aloofness; she would have to work on it. Much cheered by the thought, she spent her day catching up on her Dutch, knitting like a fury and entertaining Rex, who with his master gone, was feeling miserable.

'Well, I feel the same,' Caro told him, 'and at least he's glad to see you when he comes home.' She insisted on going to the servants' sitting-room to rehearse the carols after dinner too, although Noakes shook his head and said she ought to be in bed.

'Well, yes, I'm sure you're right,' Caro agreed, 'but Christmas is getting close and we do want to put on a perfect performance. I think that tomorrow evening we'd better get together in the drawing-room so that you'll all know where to stand and so on. The moment the Professor comes home on Christmas Eve, you can all file in and take up your places and the minute he comes into the room you can start. It should be a lovely surprise.'

She went to bed quite happy presently with Waterloo to keep her company and Juffrouw Kropp coming in with hot milk to sip so that she would sleep and strict instructions to ring if she wanted anything during the night.

They were all such dears, thought Caro, curled up cosily in the centre of the vast bed. Life could have been wonderful if only Radinck had loved her even a little. But that was no way to think, she scolded herself. 'Faint heart never won Radinck,' she told Waterloo, on the edge of sleep.

The weather was becoming very wintry. She woke in the morning to grey, woolly clouds, heavy with snow and the sound of the wind racing through the bare trees near the house. But the great house was warm and very comfortable and she spent her morning doing the flowers once again, with Jan bringing her armsful of them from his hothouses. There was Marta to talk to about the meals too; something special for dinner on the following day when Radinck would return. The day passed quickly. Caroline ate her dinner with appetite with Noakes brooding over her in a fatherly way, then repaired to the drawing-room.

They were all a little shy at first. The room was grand and they felt stiff and awkward and out of place until Caro said in her sparse, excruciating Dutch: 'Sing as though you were in your own sitting-room—remem-

ber it's to give the Professor pleasure and it's only because this is the best place for him to hear you.'

They loosened up after that. They were well embarked on *Silent Night* with all the harmonies just right,
when the Professor unlocked his own front door. No one
heard him. Even Rex, dozing by the fire, was deafened
by the choir. He stood for a moment in the centre of the
hall and then walked very quietly to the drawing-room
door, not quite closed. The room was in shadow with
only a lamp by the piano and the sconces on either side
of the fireplace alight. He pushed the door cautiously a
few inches so that he could look in and no one saw him.
They were grouped round Caro at the piano, her mousy
head lighted by the lamp beside her, one hand beating
time while the other thumped out the tune. Radinck
closed the door gently again and retreated to where he
had cast down his coat and bag and let himself out of
the house again. The car's engine made no noise above
the sighing and whistling of the wind. He drove back
the way he had come, all the way to the airport on the
outskirts of Leeuwarden where he parked the car, telephoned his home that he had returned earlier than he
had expected, then got back into the car and, for the
second time, drove himself home.

Caro had received the news of Radinck's unexpected
return with outward calm. 'We'll find time to rehearse
again tomorrow,' she told them all. 'Now I think if
Marta would warm up some of that delicious soup just
in case the Professor's cold and hungry...'

She closed the piano and went to sit in the sitting-
room by the fire, her tapestry in her hands. She even

had time to do a row or two before she heard Radinck open the door, speak to Noakes, on the watch for him, and cross the hall to open the sitting-room door.

'What a nice surprise!' she smiled as he came into the room. 'Would you like dinner or just soup and sandwiches?'

'Coffee will do, thank you, Caroline.' He sat down opposite her. 'You are feeling better, I can see that, and being sensible, sitting quietly here.'

'Oh, I've been very sensible,' she assured him. 'Would you like coffee in your study?'

He looked annoyed. 'My dear girl, I have just this minute returned home and here you are, banishing me to my study!'

Caro went red. 'I'm sorry, I didn't mean it like that, only you so often do go there—I thought you might rather be alone.'

'Very considerate of you; I prefer to remain here. What have you been doing with yourself?'

'Oh, almost nothing—the flowers and catching up with my Dutch, and showing Marta how to make mince pies...'

'I surprised you playing the piano before we married,' he said. 'Do you remember? Don't you play any more?'

Caro's red face went pale. 'Yes—well, sometimes I do.'

He sat back in his chair, relaxed and at ease, and watched while Noakes placed the coffee tray at Caro's elbow. 'Have you any plans for Christmas?' he asked idly.

She stammered a little. 'I understand from Noakes that you don't—that is, you prefer a quiet time.'

'I am afraid that over the years I have got into the habit of doing very little about entertaining—I did mention the party which I give, did I not? Is there anything special you would enjoy? A little music perhaps?'

'Music?' Caro's needle was working overtime, regardless of wrong stitches. She took a deep breath. 'Oh, you mean going to concerts and that sort of thing; Becky was telling me…but you really don't have to bother. We did agree when we married that your life wasn't to be changed at all, but you've already had to go to these parties with me and you must have disliked them very much. I'm very happy, you know, I don't mind if I don't go out socially.'

'I thought girls liked dressing up and going out to parties.'

'Well, yes, of course, but you see I don't enjoy them if you don't.' She hadn't meant to say that. She stitched a whole row, her head bowed over her work, and wished fruitlessly that the floor would open and swallow her up.

'And what precisely do you mean by that?' asked Radinck blandly.

'Nothing, nothing at all.' And then, knowing that she wouldn't get away with that, she added: 'What I meant was that I feel guilty because you have to give up your evenings doing something you don't enjoy when you might be in your study reading…and writing.'

'Put like that I seem to be a very selfish man. I must endeavour to make amends.'

Caro gave him a surprised glance. He wasn't being sarcastic and his voice held a warm note she hadn't heard before.

'You're not selfish,' she told him in a motherly voice. 'No one would expect you to change your whole way of life, certainly I wouldn't. You've devoted yourself to your work and the staff adore you—so do the animals.'

'And what about you, Caroline?'

She took her time answering. 'You must know that I have a great regard for you, Radinck.' She looked across at him, her loving heart in her eyes and unaware of it. 'You have no need to reproach yourself; you made it very clear before we married that you didn't want to change your life, and I agreed to that. I'm very content.'

His eyes were searching. 'Are you? Perhaps I have done wrong in marrying you, Caroline—you might have found some younger man…'

'I wish you wouldn't keep harping on your great age!' declared Caro hotly. Suddenly she could stand no more of it. She threw down her embroidery carelessly, so that the wools flew in all directions, and hurried out of the room and up to her bedroom, where she burst into tears, making Waterloo's fur very damp while she hugged him. 'What am I going to do?' she asked him. 'One minute I think he likes me a little and then he says he regrets marrying me…' Which wasn't quite true, although that was how it seemed to her.

She went to bed because there was nothing else to do, but she didn't go to sleep; she lay listening to the now familiar sounds in the old house—the very faint clatter from the kitchens, Rex's occasional bark, the tread of Noakes's rather heavy feet crossing the hall, the subdued clang as he closed the gate leading to the garden from the side door, even faint horsey noises from the stables. It was a clear, cold night, and sounds carried. Presently she heard Noakes and Marta and the rest of them going up the back stairs at the end of the gallery on their way to bed, and after that the house was quiet save for the various clocks striking the hour, each in its own good time.

It was almost one o'clock and she was still awake when she heard cars travelling fast along the road at the end of the drive, and the next moment there was a kind of slow-motion crashing and banging and the sound of glass splintering and then distant faint cries. She was out of bed and pulling back the curtains within seconds and saw lights shine out as the front door was opened and Radinck went running down the drive, his bag in his hand. Caroline didn't stop to take off her nightie but pulled on a pair of slacks, bundled a sweater on top of them, and rushed downstairs in her bare feet. Her wellingtons were in one of the hall cupboards; she got into them just as Noakes came down the stairs with a dressing gown over his pyjamas.

'You'll need a coat, Noakes,' said Caro, 'and thick shoes, it's cold outside, then will you come to the gate and see if the Professor wants you to telephone.' She didn't wait for him to reply but opened the door and started down the drive. Something was on fire now, she could smell it and see the flickering of flames somewhere on the road to the left of the gates. But there were no cries any more, although she thought she could hear voices.

There were two cars, hopelessly entangled, and one was blazing with thick black smoke pouring from it. Well away from it there were people on the grass verge of the road, some sitting and two lying, and she could see Radinck bending over them. She fetched up beside him, took the torch he was holding from him and shone it on the man lying on the ground. 'Noakes is coming as soon as he's got his coat on,' she said quietly.

'Good girl!' He was on his knees now, opening the man's jacket. 'Shine the light here, will you? There are scissors in my bag, can you reach them?'

Noakes arrived then, out of breath but calmly dignified. He listened to what Radinck had to say and with a brisk: 'OK, Professor,' turned and went back again. 'And bring some blankets and towels with you!' shouted Radinck after him.

The man was unconscious with head injuries and a fractured pelvis. They made him as comfortable as they could and moved on to the other silent figure close by. Head injuries again, and Radinck grunted as he bent to examine him, but beyond telling Caro to wrap one of the towels Noakes had brought back round the man's head and covering him with a blanket he did nothing. There were three people sitting on the frosty grass— an elderly man, a woman of the same age and a girl. Radinck looked at the older woman first, questioning her quietly as he did so. 'Shock,' he said to Caro, 'and a fractured clavicle—fix it with a towel, will you?' He moved on to the man, examined him briefly, said,

'Shock and no injuries apparent,' and then bent over the girl.

The loveliest girl Caro had ever set eyes on; small and fair with great blue eyes, and even with her hair all over the place and a dirty face she was breathtaking. 'Were you driving?' asked Radinck.

It was a pity that Caro's Dutch didn't stretch to understanding what the girl answered, nor, for that matter, what Radinck said after that. She held the torch, handed him what he wanted from his bag and wished with all her heart that she was even half as lovely as the girl sitting between them. She had looked at Radinck's face just once and although it wore the bland mask of his profession, she knew that he found the girl just as beautiful as she did; he would have been a strange man if he hadn't. The girl said something to him in a low voice and he answered her gently, putting an arm round her slim shoulders, smiling at her and then, to Caro's eyes at least, getting to his feet with reluctance.

'Stay with them, will you, Caroline?—this poor girl's had a bad shock, the others aren't too bad. I'll take a look at the other two, though there's nothing much to be done until we get them to hospital.' He stood listening for a moment. 'There are the ambulances now.'

He went away then and presently as the two ambulances slowed to a halt, Caro saw him directing the loading of the two unconscious men. The first ambulance went away and he came over to where she was waiting with the other three casualties. 'Go back to the house,' he told her. 'There's nothing more you can do. Get a warm drink and go to bed. I'll follow these people in to the hospital, there may be something I can do.' She hesitated, suddenly feeling unwanted and longing for a reassuring word. He had spoken briskly, as he might have spoken to a casual stranger who had stopped to give a hand, only she felt sure that he would have added his thanks.

'Do as I say, Caroline!' and this time he sounded urgent and coldly angry. She turned without a word and went down the drive, her feet and hands numb with cold, and climbed the steps slowly to where Juffrouw Kropp was waiting, wrapped in a dressing gown, and any neglect she had suffered at her husband's hands was instantly made up for by the care and attention she now received. Hardly knowing what was happening, she was bustled upstairs and into bed where Juffrouw Kropp tucked her in as though she had been a small girl and Marta waited with a tray of hot drinks. Both ladies stood one each side of the bed, while she sipped hot milk and brandy, reassured themselves that she had come to no harm and then told her firmly to go to sleep and not to get up in the morning until one or both of them had been to see her.

'But I'm not ill,' protested Caro weakly.

'You have had the grippe,' Juffrouw Kropp pointed out. 'The Professor will never forgive us if you are ill again.'

Caro searched her muddled head for the right words. 'He's gone to the hospital—he'll be late and cold...'

'Do not worry, Baroness, he will be cared for when he returns. Now you will sleep.'

'I ought to be there.' Caro spoke in English, not caring whether she was understood or not.

'No, no, he would not like that.'

She gave up and closed her eyes, not knowing that while Marta crept out with the tray, Juffrouw Kropp perched herself on the edge of a chair and waited until she was quite sure that Caro slept.

She wakened to find that lady standing at the foot of the bed, looking at her anxiously, but the anxious look went as Caroline sat up in bed and said good morning and then gave a small shriek when she saw the time.

'Ten o'clock?' she exclaimed, horrified. 'Why didn't someone call me? Is the Professor back?'

Juffrouw Kropp shook her head. 'He telephoned, Baroness. He will be back perhaps this afternoon, perhaps later.'

Caro plastered a cheerful smile on her face. 'Oh, yes, of course, he'll be busy. I'll get up.'

'Marta brings your breakfast at once—there is no need for you to get up, *mevrouw*, it will snow before long and it is very cold outside.'

Under Juffrouw Kropp's eagle eye Caro put her foot back in bed. 'Well, it would be nice,' she conceded. The housekeeper smiled in a satisfied way and shook up the pillows.

'There has been a telephone call for you—Baroness Raukema van den Eck—she heard about the accident. I asked her to telephone later, Baroness. She hopes that you are all right.'

It was nice to have a friend, reflected Caro, sitting up in bed eating a splendid breakfast, someone who wanted to know how you were and really minded. Not like Radinck. She choked on a piece of toast and pushed the tray away and got up.

It wasn't until the afternoon that Radinck telephoned, and by then any number of people had rung up. Becky, of course, wanting to know exactly what had happened, asking if Caroline were quite better, did she need anything, would she like to go over and see them soon. 'Tiele saw Radinck for a few minutes this morning,' went on Becky. 'He was getting ready to drive one of the crash people home—the girl who was driving. You'll know that, of course. I must say it's pretty good of him to go all the way to Dordrecht with her—let's hope the snow doesn't get any worse.'

Caro had made some suitable reply and put down the phone very thoughtfully. Of course, there might be some very good reason why Radinck should take the girl back home—something urgent—but there were trains, and cars to hire and buses, and most people had friends or family who rallied round at such a time. She did her best to forget about it, answered suitably when a number of other people she had met at the burgermeester's reception telephoned, took Rex for a quick walk in the garden, despite Juffrouw Kropp's protests that she would catch her death of cold, and settled down by the fire to con her Dutch lessons.

The weather worsened as the day wore on; it was snowing hard by the time Radinck telephoned. He sounded cool and rather casual and Caroline did her best to be the same. 'I'm in Dordrecht,' he told her. 'I took Juffrouw van Doorn back to her home; she had no way of reaching it otherwise and her parents must stay in hospital for a few days. I shall do my best to get back this evening, but the weather isn't too good.'

'It's snowing hard here,' said Caro, anxious not to sound anxious. 'If you'd rather not drive back—I expect you can find a hotel or something.'

'Juffrouw van Doorn has offered me a bed for the night—probably I shall accept it. You're all right?'

'Perfectly, thank you.' And even if I weren't, she added silently, I wouldn't tell you. 'Do you want me to tell anyone? Have you any appointments for the morning?'

His low laugh came very clearly over the wire. 'Really, Caroline, you are becoming the perfect wife! No, there's no one you need telephone. I can do it all from here.'

'Very well—we'll expect you when we see you.'

'Caroline—about last night—'

She interrupted him ruthlessly. 'I'm sorry, I must go. Goodbye, Radinck.'

The rest of the day was a dead loss.

They were to go to a party the following evening. Becky had telephoned to know if they were going and Caro had improvised hurriedly and said that they expected to be there but Radinck would let her know the moment he could leave Dordrecht. 'The weather's awful there,' she invented, 'and I told him not to come home until the roads were clear.'

And Becky had said how wise she was and she hoped they'd see each other the next day.

There was no word from Radinck the next day. Caro

ordered the meals as though he were expected home, took Rex for a snowy walk, rehearsed her choir and then telephoned the people whose party they were to attend and made their excuses. She was on the rug before the fire in the sitting-room when Radinck walked in, with Waterloo purring beside her and Rex leaning heavily against her. He bounded to the door as Radinck came in and Caro looked round and then got slowly to her feet. 'You didn't telephone,' she observed, quite forgetting to say hullo.

'No, I'm sorry I couldn't get back sooner—the roads are bad.' He fended Rex off with a gentle hand and sat down. 'How quiet and peaceful you look, Caroline.'

Appearances can be deceptive, she thought. She wasn't either, inside her she boiled with rage and misery and jealousy and all the other things which were supposed to be so bad for one. 'I hope the trip wasn't too bad,' she remarked. 'Would you like some coffee?'

'Yes, thanks. Aren't we supposed to be going to the Laggemaats' this evening?'

'Yes, but I telephoned them about an hour ago and told them that as you weren't back we would probably not be able to go. I hope I did right.'

'Quite right. Did you not wonder where I was?'

She said evenly: 'When we married you particularly stressed the fact that that was something I was never to do.'

She poured the coffee Noakes had brought and handed Radinck a cup.

He said testily: 'You seem to have remembered every word I said and moreover, are determined to keep to it.'

Caroline didn't answer that but asked in her quiet little voice: 'How are the people who were hurt in the accident?'

'The first man is in intensive care, the second man died on the way to hospital—I think you may have guessed that; the two older people who were in the second car are to remain under observation for another day or so. Their daughter—Ilena—I drove home.'

Caro busied herself pouring a cup of coffee she didn't want. 'Oh, yes, Becky told me when she telephoned yesterday.' She was careful to keep all traces of reproach from her voice. 'I'm so glad she wasn't hurt; she was the loveliest girl I've ever seen.'

'Extraordinarily beautiful,' agreed Radinck blandly, 'and so young, too. She asked me to stay the night and I did.'

'Very sensible of you,' declared Caro calmly. 'Travelling back in all that snow would never have done.'

'What would you say if I told you that I've never allowed bad weather to interfere with my driving?'

She could say a great many things, thought Caro, and all of them very much to the point. She didn't utter any of them but said prudently: 'I think it was very wise of you to make an exception to your rule.'

She put down her coffee cup and picked up her work again, glad to be able to busy herself with something.

Radinck stretched out his legs and wedged his great shoulders deeply into his chair. 'Don't you want to know why I took Ilena home?'

'You must have had a good reason for doing so—I

daresay she was badly shaken and not fit to travel on her own.'

'She was perfectly able to go on her own. I drove her because I wanted to prove something to myself.' He frowned. 'I seem to be in some confusion of mind—about you, Caroline.'

She looked up from her work, her eyes thoughtful as she studied his handsome and, at the moment, ill-tempered face. Her heart was thundering against her ribs. That he was about to say something important was evident, but what, exactly? She had promised herself that she would make him love her, but it seemed probable that she had failed and he was going to tell her so. She said steadily: 'If you want to talk about it I'm listening, Radinck.'

It was a pity that just at that moment the telephone on the table beside him should ring. He lifted the receiver and listened, frowning, and then embarked on what Caro took to be a list of instructions about a patient. The interruption gave her time to collect her thoughts, which were, however, instantly scattered by the entry of Noakes, announcing Tiele and Becky.

'We were on our way to the Laggemaats',' explained Becky, 'and Tiele thought it would be an idea to pop in and see how you were.'

She kissed Caro, offered a cheek to Radinck and perched herself on a chair close to Caro, spreading the skirts of her dress as she did so.

'That's pretty,' observed Caro. 'It's new, isn't it? I love the colour. I was going to wear a rather nice green...'

Tiele had bent to kiss her cheek and said laughingly: 'Oh, lord—clothes again! Radinck, take me to your study and show me that agenda for the seminar at Brussels. Are you going? We could go together—we need only be away for a couple of days.'

The two men went away and Becky, declining coffee, remarked: 'We weren't sure if Radinck would be back. The roads are very bad further south. He telephoned Tiele about some patient or other quite late last night—said he'd gone to a hotel in Dordrecht and planned to leave early this morning, but he got held up—you know all that, of course.' She ate one of the small biscuits on the coffee tray. 'He must have been glad to have handed that girl over to her aunt—a bit of a responsibility—supposing he'd got landed in a snowdrift!' She giggled engagingly.

Caro had listened to this artless information in surprise and a mounting excitement. If what Becky had told her was true, why had Radinck let her think that he'd stayed at the girl's house? Had he wanted to make her jealous? On the other hand, did he want her to believe that he had thought better of their dry-as-dust marriage and wanted to put an end to it? More likely the latter, she considered, although that was something she would have to find out. She wasn't sure how and she had a nasty feeling that whatever it was Radinck had been going to say wouldn't be said—at least not for the moment.

In this she was perfectly right. The van den Ecks went presently and Radinck went almost at once to his study with the observation that he had a good deal of paperwork to do. Which left Caro with nothing better to do than go to bed.

CHAPTER NINE

THE SNOW LAY thick on the ground when Caro looked out of her windows in the morning. It was barely light and she could see Radinck, huge in a sheepskin jacket, striding down to the stables with Rex at his heels. He would be going to see how Queenie fared before walking Rex in the fields beyond. It would have been lovely to be with him, she thought, walking in the early morning cold, talking about his work and planning a pleasant evening together. Which reminded her that there was another party that evening and presumably they would be going: a doctor from the hospital and his wife—she searched her memory and came up with their name—ter Brink, youngish if she remembered aright and rather nice. She would have to ring Becky and ask what she should wear. She bathed and dressed and went downstairs and found Radinck already at the table.

It was hardly the time or place to expect him to disclose what he had intended to say to her, but she sat down hopefully and began her breakfast. But beyond a polite good morning, the hope that she had slept well, and could he pass her the toast, he had nothing to say, but became immersed in his letters once again. Caroline was glad that she had a modest pile of post beside her plate for once. It seemed to keep her occupied and by reading each letter two or three times, she spun out her interest in them until Radinck put his own mail down and got to his feet.

'You feel well enough to go to the ter Brinks' this evening?' he asked her pleasantly.

'Oh yes, thank you. Where do they live?'

'Groningen—not far. I should be home about tea-time and we shall need to leave here about half past six.' He paused on his way to the door. 'Be careful if you go out—it's very cold and treacherous underfoot.'

'Yes, Radinck.' She smiled at him as she spoke and he came back across the room and kissed her hard and quick. Caroline sat a long while after he had gone trying to decide whether he had meant it or whether he was feeling guilty; she remembered all the books she had read where the husband had tried to make amends to his wife when he had neglected her by being kind to her, only in books they sent flowers as well.

They arrived a few hours later—a great bouquet of fragrant spring flowers; lilac, and hyacinths, tulips and daffodils, exquisitely arranged in a paper-thin porcelain bowl. The card said merely: Flowers for Caroline, and he had written it himself and scrawled Radinck at the end. Caroline eyed them at first with delight and then with suspicion. Was he, like the guilty husbands in all the best novels, feeling guilty too? She was consumed with a desire to find out more about the beautiful girl

in Dordrecht. She was a satisfyingly long way away, but
absence made the heart grow fonder, didn't it?

Caro spent the whole day vacillating between hope
and despair, so that by the time Radinck came home
she was in a thoroughly muddled state of mind—made
even more muddled by his unexpected friendly attitude
towards her. He had always—well, almost always—
treated her with punctilious politeness, but seldom with
warmth. Now he launched into an account of his day,
lounging back in his great chair, looking to be the epit-
ome of a contented man and even addressing her as
Caro, which seemed to her to be a great step forward in
their relationship. She went up to change her dress presently; it was to be a long dress occasion and she chose
one of the dresses she had bought in den Haag. A rose
pink crêpe-de-Chine, patterned with deeper pink roses,
it had a high neck and long tight sleeves and the bodice
was finely tucked between lace insertions. She swept
downstairs presently, her mink coat over her arm, and
then stopped so suddenly that she very nearly tripped
up. She had never thanked Radinck for his flowers.

A deep chuckle from the end of the hall made her
look round. Radinck was sitting on a marble-topped
side table, swinging his long legs, the picture of elegance. 'Such a magnificent entry!' he observed. 'Just
like Cinderella at the ball—and then you stopped as
though you'd been shot. What happened?'

'Oh, Radinck, I remembered—I'm so sorry, I never
thanked you for the flowers, and they're so lovely. I
hope you don't mind—I put them in my room, but I'll
bring them downstairs tomorrow...'

'I'm glad they pleased you.' He swung himself off the table and came towards her. 'That is a charming dress, and you look charming in it, Caro. I have something for you; I hope you will wear it.'

He took a box from a pocket and opened it and took out a brooch, a true lovers' knot of diamonds. 'May I put it on for you?'

He held the lovely thing in the palm of his hand and she put out a finger to touch it. 'It's magnificent!' she breathed. 'Was it your mother's?'

His hand had closed gently over the brooch and her fingers. 'No—I chose it yesterday as I came through den Haag on my way home. I want to give it to you, Caro, and I want you to wear it.'

She looked up into his face; his eyes were bright and searching and his brows were raised in a questioning arc.

'Why?' asked Caro, her head full of the girl in Dordrecht. Flowers, and now this heavenly brooch—it was even worse than she had thought, although Radinck didn't look in the least like a guilty husband.

'I'm afraid to answer that,' said Radinck surprisingly, and pinned the brooch into the lace at her neck with cool steady fingers.

And when he had done it: 'It's my turn to ask a question,' he smiled down at her. 'Why did you ask why, Caroline?'

Oh dear! thought Caro, now I'm Caroline again, and said carefully: 'Well, first you sent me those heavenly flowers and now you've given me this fabulous brooch, and you see, in books the husband is always extra nice to his wife when he's been neglecting her or—or falling in love with someone else—then he buys his wife presents because he feels guilty...'

He looked utterly bewildered. 'Guilty?' he considered it for a moment. 'Well, yes, I suppose you're right.'

Caro's heart dropped like a stone into her high-heeled, very expensive satin sandals. 'So there's no need to say any more, is there?' she asked unhappily.

Strangely, Radinck was smiling. 'Not just now, perhaps—I don't really think that we have the time—we are already a little late.'

She said yes, of course, in her quiet hesitant voice and got into her coat, then sat, for the most part silent, as he drove the Panther de Ville to Groningen, almost sixty kilometres away. The roads were icy under a bright moon, but Radinck drove with relaxed ease, carrying on a desultory conversation, not seeming to notice Caroline's quiet. He certainly didn't present the appearance of a guilty husband who had just been found out by his wife. Caro stirred in her seat, frowning. She could be wrong...

There wasn't much chance to find out anything more at the party. The ter Brinks were a youngish, rather serious-minded couple living in a large modern house on the outskirts of Groningen, and Caro found herself moving round their drawing-room, getting caught up in the highbrow conversations among their guests. She had met most of them already and almost all of them spoke excellent English, but—typical of her, she thought—she got pinned into a corner by an elderly gentleman, who insisted on speaking Dutch despite her denial of all knowledge of that language, so that all she could do was to look interested, say '*neen*' and '*ja*' every now and then and pray for someone to rescue her.

Which Radinck did, tucking a hand under her arm and engaging the elderly man in a pleasant conversation for a few minutes before drifting her away to the other end of the room.

'My goodness,' said Caro, when they were safely out of earshot, 'I only understood one word in a hundred—thank you for rescuing me, Radinck. What was he talking about?'

Her husband's firm mouth twitched. 'Nuclear warfare and the possibility of invasion from outer space,' he told her blandly.

'Oh, my goodness—and all I said was yes and no—Oh, and once I said *Niet waar* in a surprised sort of way.'

Radinck's shoulders shook, but he said seriously: 'A quite suitable remark, especially if you sounded astonished. "You don't say" is an encouraging remark to make—it sounds admiring as well as astonished, which after all was what Professor Vinke expected to hear.'

'Oh, good—I'd hate to let you down.'

He had guided her to another corner, standing in front of her so that she was shut off from the room. 'I believe you, Caroline. It is a pity that you cannot return my opinion.' He took her hand briefly. 'Caro, perhaps I'm going away for a day or two. Are you going to ask me where and why?'

She stared down at his fingers clasping hers. 'No, I don't break promises.'

He sighed. 'Perhaps the incentive isn't enough for you to do that…'

And after that there was no further chance to talk. They were joined by friends, and presently Tiele and Becky came across to talk to them and although they left soon afterwards they only discussed the party on their way home. They didn't talk about anything much at dinner either, and afterwards Radinck wished her a cool goodnight and went away to his study. And yet, thought Caro, left alone to drink her coffee by the fire in the drawing-room, he had looked at her very intently once or twice during the meal, just as though he was wanting to say something and didn't know how to start.

She went to bed presently and made a point of being down in time to share breakfast with Radinck the following morning. It was hardly the best time of the day to talk to him, but she didn't feel she could bear to go on much longer without asking more questions. When he had read his post she said abruptly: 'I'm going to break my promise after all. Are you going to Dordrecht?'

Radinck put his coffee cup down very slowly. 'Why should I wish to go to Dordrecht?' His eyes narrowed. 'Ah, now I see—the flowers and brooch were to cover my neglect, were they?' His voice held a sneer. 'You really believe that I would go tearing off after a girl young enough to be my daughter, just like your precious novels?' He got to his feet, looking to her nervous gaze to be twice his normal size and in a very bad temper indeed. 'Well, Caroline, you may think what you wish.'

'When are you going?' she asked, for there seemed no point in retreating now. 'And you needn't be so very bad-tempered; you wanted to know if I was going to ask you where you were going, and now I have you're quite peevish…'

He stopped on his way to the door. 'Peevish? Peevish? I am angry, Caroline.' He came back to tower over her, still sitting at the table.

'And why do you keep on calling me Caroline?' asked Caro. She had cooked her goose and it really didn't matter what she said now. 'And sometimes you say Caro.'

He said silkily: 'Because when I call you Caroline I can try and believe that you are someone vague who has little to do with my life, only I find that I no longer can do that…'

'And what am I when I'm Caro?' she asked with interest.

'Soft and gentle and loving.' He bent and kissed her soundly. 'You have brought chaos to my life,' he told her austerely, and turned on his heel and went.

Caro sat very still after he had gone. Things, she told herself, had come to a head. It was time she did something about it. And he hadn't told her when he was going to Dordrecht, or even if he was going there. She poured herself more coffee and applied her wits to the problem.

She got up presently and went to the telephone. Radinck's secretary at his rooms was quite sure that he wasn't going anywhere, certainly not to Dordrecht, and at the hospital, in answer to her carefully worded enquiries, she was told that the Professor had a full day ahead of him. So he had been making it up…to

annoy her? To get her interested in what he did? She
wasn't sure, but his kiss had been, even in her inexperienced view, a very genuine one. Caroline nodded her
mousy head and smiled a little, then went to the little
davenport in the sitting-room and after a great deal of
thought and several false starts, composed a letter. It
was a nicely worded document, telling Radinck that
since they didn't agree very well, perhaps it would be
as well if she went away. She read it through, put it in
its envelope and went in search of Willem, who, always
willing, got out the Mini used by the staff for errands
and rattled off to Leeuwarden, the letter in his pocket.

It was unfortunate that Radinck happened to be
doing a round when Willem handed in his letter with
the request that it should be delivered as soon as possible; the round took ages and it was well after lunch
before a porter, tracking him down in the consultants'
room, making a meal off sandwiches and beer, handed
it to him. He read it quickly and then read it again, before reaching for the telephone. He had been a fool, he
told himself savagely; Caro had believed that he had
gone to Dordrecht because he had been attracted to that
girl—and he shouldn't have let her believe that he had
stayed there, either. He was too old to fall in love, he
reminded himself sourly, but he had, and nothing would
alter the fact that little Caro had become his world.

Noakes answered the phone and listened carefully
to the Professor's instructions. The house was to be
searched very thoroughly; he had reason to believe that
the Baroness, who wasn't feeling quite herself, could
be in one of its many rooms. Radinck himself would

call at the most likely places where she might be and then come home.

He spent the rest of the afternoon going patiently from one friend's house to the next, calling at the shops he thought Caro might have visited and then finally, holding back his fear with an iron hand, going home.

Caro had been sitting working quite feverishly at her knitting for quite some time before she heard the car coming up the drive, the front door bang shut and Radinck's footsteps in the hall. It was a great pity that the speech she had prepared and rehearsed over and over again should now fly from her head, leaving it empty—not that it mattered. The door was flung open and her husband strode in, closing it quietly behind him and then leaning against it to stare across at her. Meeting his eyes, she realised that she had no need to say anything, a certainty confirmed by his: 'Caro, you baggage—how long have you been here?'

'Since—well, since Willem took my note.'

'The house was searched—where did you hide?'

'Behind the door.' She made her voice matter-of-fact, although her hands were shaking so much that stitches were being dropped right left and centre. She wished she could look away from him, but she seemed power-less to do so. Any minute now he would explode with rage, for he must be in a fine temper. His face was white and drawn and his eyes were glittering.

Caroline was completely disarmed when he said gently: 'I have been out of my mind with worry, my darling. I thought that you had left me and that I would never see you again. I wanted to kill myself for being

such a fool. I had begun to think that you were beginning to love me a little and that if I had patience I
could make you forget how badly I had treated you.' He
smiled bleakly. 'I have just spent the worst two hours
of my life…'

Caro's soft heart was wrung, but she went on ruin-
ing her knitting in what she hoped was a cool manner.
'I didn't mean you to be upset,' she explained gruffly.
'You see, I had to know…well, I thought that if you m-
minded about me at all, you would look for me, but if
you didn't then I'd know I had to go away.' She dropped
three stitches one after the other and added mournfully:
'I haven't put it very clearly.' Not that it mattered now.
He hadn't said that he loved her and everybody called
everyone else darling these days.

Radinck crossed the room very fast indeed. 'Put
that damned knitting down,' he commanded, 'you're
hiding behind it.' She had it taken from her in a ruth-
less manner which completed the havoc she had already wrought, but it really didn't matter, for Radinck
had wrapped her in his arms. 'To think that I had to
wait half a lifetime to meet you and even then I fought
against loving you, my darling Caro!' He put a finger
under her chin and turned her face up to his. 'I think
I fell in love with you when you told me to give you a
needle and thread and you'd do it yourself…only I'd
spent so many years alone and I didn't believe there
was a girl like you left in the world.' He smiled a little.
'I carry one of your handkerchiefs, like a lovesick boy.'

He kissed her gently and then very hard so that she
had no breath. 'My beautiful girl,' he told her, 'when

I came in just now and saw you sitting there it was as though you'd been here all my life, waiting for me to come home.'

'Well, dear Radinck, that's just what I was doing.' Caroline's voice shook a little although she tried hard to sound normal. 'Only I didn't know if you would.'

He kissed her again. 'But I did, dear heart, and I shall always come home to you.'

She had a delightful picture of herself, with her delightful children, waiting in the hall for Radinck to come home…and now she would be able to wear the pink organza dress. She smiled enchantingly at the idea and Radinck smoothed the mousy hair back from her face and asked: 'Why do you smile, my love?'

She leaned up to kiss him. 'Because I'm happy and because I love you so much.'

A remark which could have only one answer.

* * * * *

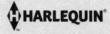

#4459 HER BROODING ITALIAN BOSS
by Susan Meier
Pregnant and broke, Laura Beth takes a job with brooding yet brilliant artist Antonio Bartulocci. But this fiery Italian proves to be a difficult boss! Can she remind him of all that's good in this life?

#4460 THE HEIRESS'S SECRET BABY
by Jessica Gilmore
When heiress and CEO Polly Rafferty discovers her no-strings summer fling had *very* unexpected consequences, her gorgeous new vice CEO, Gabe Beaufils, is the only person she can trust with her baby secret...

#4461 A PREGNANCY, A PARTY & A PROPOSAL
by Teresa Carpenter
Falling pregnant after a fling with infamous Ray Donovan was not part of event coordinator Lauren Randall's plan! But can she stop herself from falling for her baby's father?

#4462 BEST FRIEND TO WIFE AND MOTHER?
by Caroline Anderson
After a near-miss down the aisle, Amy Driver is rescued by TV chef and best friend Leo Zaccharelli. But after spending time with him and his adorable daughter, Ella, could their friendship lead to forever?

RESOLUTELY POLLY HELD the glass up over the man's face
and tipped it. For one long moment she held it still so that the
water was perfectly balanced right at the rim, clear drops so
very close to spilling over the thin edge.

And then she allowed her hand to move the glass over the
tipping point, a perfect stream of cold water falling like rain
onto the peacefully slumbering face below.

Polly didn't quite know what to expect; anger, shock,
contrition or even no reaction at all. He was so very deeply
asleep after all. But what she didn't expect was for one red-
rimmed eye to lazily open, for a smile to play around the
disturbingly well-cut mouth or for a hand to shoot out and
grab her wrist.

Caught by surprise, she stumbled forward, falling against
the chaise as the hand snuck around her waist, pulling her
down, pulling her close.

"*Bonjour, chérie.*" His voice was low, gravelly with
sleep and deeply, unmistakably French. "If you wanted me
to wake up you only had to ask."

It was the shock, that was all. Otherwise she would have
moved, called for help, disentangled herself from the strong
arm anchoring her firmly against the bare chest. And she
would never, *ever* have allowed his other hand to slip around

her neck in an oddly sweet caress while he angled his mouth toward hers—she would have moved away long before the hard mouth claimed hers in a distinctly unsleepy way.

It was definitely the shock keeping her paralyzed under his touch—and she was definitely *not* leaning into the kiss, opening herself up to the pressure of his mouth on hers, the touch of his hand moving up her back, slipping round her rib cage, brushing against the swell of her breast.

Hang on, his hand was where?

Polly pulled away, jumping up off the chaise, resisting the urge to scrub the kiss off her tingling mouth.

Or to lean back down and let him claim her again.

"What do you think you're doing?"

"Saying *au revoir* of course." He had shifted position and was leaning against the back of the chaise, his eyes skimming every inch of her until she wanted to wrap her arms around her torso, shielding herself from his insolent gaze.

"Au revoir?" Was she going mad? Where were the panicked apologies and the scuttling out of her office?

"Of course." He raised an eyebrow. "As you are dressed to leave I thought you were saying goodbye. But if it was more of a good morning—" the smile widened "—even better."

"I am not saying *au revoir* or good morning or anything but *what on earth are you doing in my office and where are your clothes?*"

Don't miss this sparkling new romance by Jessica Gilmore, THE HEIRESS'S SECRET BABY!

Available February 2015 wherever Harlequin® Romance books and ebooks are sold!

www.Harlequin.com

HREXP0115

HARLEQUIN®

A *Romance* FOR EVERY MOOD™

Stay up-to-date on all your
romance-reading news with the
Harlequin Shopping Guide,
featuring bestselling authors, exciting new
miniseries, books to watch and more!

The newest issue will be delivered right to you
with our compliments! There are 4 each year.

Signing up is easy.

EMAIL

ShoppingGuide@Harlequin.ca

WRITE TO US

HARLEQUIN BOOKS
Attention: Customer Service Department
P.O. Box 9057, Buffalo, NY 14269-9057

OR PHONE

1-800-873-8635 in the United States
1-888-343-9777 in Canada

Please allow 4-6 weeks for delivery of the first issue by mail.

JUST CAN'T GET ENOUGH?

Join our social communities
and talk to us online.

You will have access to the latest
news on upcoming titles and special
promotions, but most importantly,
you can talk to other fans about your
favorite Harlequin reads.

Harlequin.com/Community

Facebook.com/HarlequinBooks

Twitter.com/HarlequinBooks

Pinterest.com/HarlequinBooks

HARLEQUIN®

A Romance FOR EVERY MOOD™

Love the Harlequin book you just read?

Your opinion matters.

Review this book on your favorite book site, review site, blog or your own social media properties and share your opinion with other readers!